Economic and Financial Evaluation

ECONOMIC AND FINANCIAL EVALUATION
Measurement, Meaning and Management

Edited by Michael Mulreany

INSTITUTE OF PUBLIC □
ADMINISTRATION

First published 1999
Institute of Public Administration
57–61 Lansdowne Road
Dublin 4
Ireland
Reprinted 2005
Reprinted 2008
Reprinted 2013
Reprinted 2015

ISBN 978-1-902448-21-3

British Library Cataloguing-in-Publication Data
A catalogue record for this book is available from the British Library.

Typeset in 10/12.5 Times Roman by Computertype Ltd., Dublin
Printed in Ireland by Gemini International Ltd.

To Mark

Contents

Acknowledgements

This book underwent a long gestation and prolonged drafting. It represents the work of researchers, practitioners and lecturers from diverse backgrounds but with a common interest in evaluation. The contributors have been extremely generous in devoting time to the book and profoundly patient in dealing with the many queries along the way. I am grateful for their co-operation and forbearance.

At the outset of the work I received valuable advice from Niall O'Donnellan of Enterprise Ireland. Students at the Institute of Public Administration were an important sounding board for some of the material and the Institute's library was an incomparable resource. Patricia Ryan of the IPA was of great assistance at different times during the design and drafting stages and Pat Hall, Kathleen Harte, Tony McNamara and Eleanor Ashe were most helpful at the final stages. Thérèse, other family members, and friends were supportive and encouraging throughout.

My particular thanks is due to Laura Foley for her assistance in collating material, arranging text and solving technical problems.

Contributors

Richard Boyle is Senior Research Officer, Institute of Public Administration

Philip Byrne is Finance Specialist, Institute of Public Administration

Patrick Clavin is a member of the Garda Síochána

J. Peter Clinch is Director of Graduate Studies, Department of Environmental Studies, University College Dublin

Frank J. Convery is Heritage Trust Professor of Environmental Studies, Department of Environmental Studies, University College Dublin

Sylvia Dempsey is Lecturer in Accounting, Dún Laoghaire Institute of Art, Design and Technology

Aidan Horan is Senior Finance Specialist, Institute of Public Administration

Owen Keegan is Director of Traffic, Dublin Corporation

Fergal Lynch is a civil servant in the Department of Health and Children

Francis McGeough is Project Director, Conference of Heads of Irish Universities

Martina Maloney is Assistant Town Clerk, Galway Corporation

Michael Mulreany is Senior Lecturer in Economics, Institute of Public Administration

Fergal Somerville is a civil servant in the Department of Health and Children

Evaluation and Value for Money

MICHAEL MULREANY

Introduction

Evaluation in the sense used in this book is the process of assessing the extent to which project, programme or policy objectives have been achieved and how economically and efficiently. Evaluations are conducted either 'ex post' or while the projects, programmes or policies are underway. Appraisals, by contrast, though they use similar techniques, are generally conducted 'ex ante'. Monitoring is the process of checking progress against a plan and, though related, is different from evaluation.

An understanding of evaluation naturally requires a knowledge of economy, efficiency and effectiveness and of the conceptual and technical issues arising in measurement.

Considerations of economy, efficiency and effectiveness may appear cold, calculating and relentlessly functional. Yet they are at the heart of controversies over matters such as the relative merits of market and state resource allocation, the impact of public policies and, even, the performance of national economies. Considerations of economy, efficiency and effectiveness are central to decisions about privatisation, the liberalisation of trade and factor movements, the reform of agricultural and industrial policies, the reform of taxation, and the level, quality and pricing of government services. This is a formidable list but not an exhaustive one. The pursuit of efficiency and effectiveness has intensified the need for economic and financial evaluation with which subsequent chapters are concerned.

This chapter aims to explore major issues that arise in the literature on economy, efficiency and effectiveness. Broadly, we will consider issues of definition, of measurement and of management reform in pursuit of value for money. What emerges will provide both an overview of a complex area and a backdrop for subsequent chapters.

Because of the complex and wideranging nature of economy, efficiency and effectiveness the treatment in this chapter will necessarily be selective. Every effort is made in what follows to minimise complexities and, where possible, technical matters are confined to end-notes. A glossary of terms used in this, and subsequent, chapters is presented in Appendix 1.

Clarifying concepts

The words economy, efficiency and effectiveness are sometimes used imprecisely. We will proceed by clarifying the meaning of efficiency and then identifying the interrelationship between efficiency, effectiveness and economy.

Efficiency

A central concern for any society is the efficiency with which it produces and distributes goods and services.

Efficiency in production

Efficiency in production is labelled variously as productive efficiency, technical efficiency, x-efficiency, managerial efficiency and internal efficiency but here we will generally use the term productive efficiency.[1] Whatever the label, the emphasis is squarely on the supply-side of the economy. Production is efficient if there is no waste, in other words if it is impossible to increase the output of one good without reducing the output of another. Conversely, production is inefficient if by simply reallocating inputs it would be possible to increase the output of one commodity without reducing the output of another. The input-mix is therefore important in productive efficiency. The happy condition of productive efficiency is achieved when firms and industries produce at the lowest possible cost.

In essence, the idea of productive efficiency is relatively straightforward. It focuses on the internal processes of firms and industries and exists when a given output uses the minimum amount of inputs. Viewed in a slightly more positive light, productive efficiency leads to the maximum output that could possibly be produced from given inputs.

What causes an enterprise to produce inefficiently, i.e. above minimum cost? The reason is waste in any of its forms – overmanning, carrying excess stocks, overgenerous expense accounts, low productivity and so forth. Waste exists in the private as well as the public sector. The Commission of the European Communities (1988) has indicated that the elimination of waste in private sector enterprises is an important benefit deriving from the increased competitive pressures in the single European market. Particularly in large firms and especially those beyond the early entrepreneurial stage of development, there may be a divorce of ownership from control. The owners (or 'principals') may seek maximum profits and minimum costs but the hired managers (or 'agents') who are in control may pursue other goals, e.g. an 'easy life', which involve production at higher than minimum costs. In order to impose their wills, the owners will need to monitor, at a cost, the behaviour of managers. Because information about particular circumstances and about managerial behaviour is skewed in favour of managers, then owners may have to offer incentives in order to change managerial behaviour. This is a variation on the 'principal-agent' problem, other aspects of which we will encounter in due course.

Of course, waste also exists in the public sector and the question naturally arises whether one sector is likely to be more inefficient in production than the other. In the public sector there is no easily identifiable equivalent to the private sector shareholder to appropriate the savings from reduced waste. For this reason and because of the absence of threats of take-over and bankruptcy the public sector might be expected to be more prone to inefficiency. However, much depends on the degree to which competition exists. If, for example, we were to compare a monopolistic private sector firm with a public sector equivalent then it may not be clear-cut which has the most 'organisational slack'. This is a matter to which we will return, in slightly greater depth, below.

Leaving aside, for the present, the question of comparative public-private sector efficiency, some of the methods for improving productive efficiency in the public service are worthy of note. Particularly in the past decade, market disciplines have been introduced to the public sector. For example, contracting-out of government services has been instituted in many OECD countries and savings have ensued (Oxley et al, 1990). Competition such as exists between suppliers where there is a choice between healthcare schemes or between schools (or where vouchers allow consumers of public services to make direct choices) will also tend to improve efficiency. Another method aimed at improving productive efficiency in the public sector is the process of efficiency 'scrutinies' or audits designed to uncover wasteful practices. The movement in developed economies toward increased accountability, based on decentralised authority combined with clear objectives and priorities, can be expected to lead to improvements in productive efficiency. More immediate and crude methods exist. For example 'budgetary stress' and consequent pressure for efficiency could be induced by setting reduced expenditure targets or by restricting the income of government agencies or of local government. Such was the case in the UK when, at various times, central government reduced grants to local authorities, penalised authorities which exceeded expenditure targets and placed a limit or 'cap' on incomes from local rates.

Before concluding this section it is well to emphasise that inefficiency in production is not exclusively associated with problems of the 'time-and-motion' type. Inefficiencies may be brought about due to the form, content or mode of implementation of government intervention. For example, regulation by placing a ceiling on a firm's profits may in certain circumstances reduce rather than increase the incentive to seek economies in production. This sort of inefficiency assumes greater importance as the role of government increasingly evolves as 'steering not rowing', i.e. toward rule-setting, regulating and enforcing.

Unquestionably, unemployment is the greatest waste of resources inasmuch as the resources are left unused. There is no scope in this text to develop on this, other than to note that in the desired eventuality of fully employed resources there would still be need to pursue productive efficiency, i.e. production at the lowest possible cost.

Efficiency in distribution

Even if goods and services are produced at lowest cost, resources can still be used inefficiently if the output-mix contains too much of one product and too little of another. Efficiency in distribution, or allocative efficiency, takes account of consumer preferences. The emphasis accordingly shifts from the supply-side to considerations of demand. At the extreme, if goods and services are being produced which no one wants to buy, then clearly there is an inefficient use of resources. Such was the case in centrally planned economies where there were examples of production of extremely thick glass and very heavy nails which technically met plan requirements but were unusable.

Allocative efficiency exists where it is impossible, by redistributing products among individuals, to make one person better off without making someone else worse off. The condition which guarantees such efficiency is that the cost of an extra unit of output should be equal to the consumer's willingness-to-pay.[2] If, for example, consumers are willing to pay more for an extra unit of output than it costs, then the product is underproduced and there is allocative inefficiency. We cannot here go deeper into the technical properties of allocative efficiency. Rigorous treatments can be found in introductory and intermediate economics textbooks (e.g. Begg et al 1997, Koutsoyiannis 1984, Stiglitz 1988). However, our limited treatment does bring out essential features of allocative efficiency by emphasising the concern about whether too little or too much is being produced. By taking account of consumer preferences, allocative efficiency is concerned with markets, in contrast with productive efficiency which is concerned with the internal processes of enterprises. Allocative efficiency prompts questions such as: do the goods or services produced actually meet the public's demands? A different type of question is asked about productive efficiency; a typical question might be whether too many people are employed in the production process.

Allocative efficiency is hampered in public and private sectors where there is no consumer choice whether due to monopoly supply or lack of choice within programmes. Greater consumer choice, a better informed public and a more participatory democracy – an election every four-to-five years is a poor gauge of public desires – will all tend to improve allocative efficiency in the public sector.

It is, unfortunately, much more difficult to answer questions about allocative efficiency in the public than the private sector. It may be hard for consumers to specify, for example, what level and quality of defence they require, the type of land-use planning system best suited to their area or what amount and quality of graduates they expect from universities. Quantification and specification is easier in the case of productive efficiency where questions about the least cost combination of inputs arise.

The difficulty in quantification associated with questions of allocative efficiency helps explain why management reforms, such as efficiency scrutinies, in the public sector have been largely confined to matters of productive efficiency. This is not to deny that greater attention is being paid to consumers of public services; we have already alluded to the movement toward greater consumer choice between schools and healthcare schemes. The efficiency gains from improved consumer choice complement the productive efficiency gains as suppliers compete for consumers free to exercise a measure of choice. Moreover, greater account is taken of the consumer of public services by means of consumer surveys and analyses of complaints by the public. Yet it is wise not to be over-optimistic due to the difficulties, already noted, in quantifying consumer preferences in the public sector. We will return to this matter later in the chapter.

Productive and allocative efficiency: privatisation

The distinction between productive and allocative efficiency is useful in a number of ways. We have just seen that it can explain why some efforts at public sector reform may be more effective than others: it is easier to quantify inputs than outputs in the public sector.

The distinction between productive and allocative efficiency also informs the debate about privatisation, one of the key aspects of economic policy-making in recent decades. Vickers and Yarrow (1988) examined the case of privatising a public sector monopoly. They show that in the private sector the monopolist in pursuit of monopoly profit will increase price and reduce output below the level of allocative efficiency. However, privatisation will also affect the pattern of management incentives and thence the tendency to monitor costs; hence managers in the privatised enterprise may achieve greater productive efficiencies than when the enterprise was under public control. A privatised monopoly, therefore, may bring improved productive efficiency but reduced allocative efficiency and the overall effect on efficiency will depend on the relative size of these countervailing effects. Of course, in this example we are examining the case of a monopoly transferred from public to unregulated private ownership. Indeed Vickers and Yarrow show that the degree of competition and the effectiveness of regulation may have more important effects on performance than does the form of ownership, i.e. public or private.

Competition is particularly beneficial inasmuch as it leads to improvements in both allocative and productive efficiency. Vickers and Yarrow (1991) draw particular attention to potential for improved productive efficiency under competition due to the possibility of performance comparison. Contracting-out is especially interesting because it combines privatisation with competition. We have already noted that savings from contracting-out have been identified in several OECD countries. However, contracting-out is not without its hazards including the possibilities of collusion at the tendering stage and the running down of quality during the execution of contracts. An important question that arises with contracting-out, and indeed with any form of privatisation is, how sustainable are any initial gains?

Modern theories of competition have an important bearing on efficiency. The theory of contestable markets argues that even in a market with a few relatively large firms there can be a threat of competition if new firms can enter and, if they wish, exit the market without losing the money they invested. By extension, the theory of contestable markets would imply the imposition of competitive disciplines on privatised monopolistic firms where liberalisation measures allow potential rivals freedom of entry. If this were so then we might hope for efficiency gains when measures to improve liberalisation accompany the privatisation of monopolistic firms. It is, however, difficult to be enthusiastic about these prospects when one considers the likelihood that existing dominant firms may seek to protect themselves against new entrants.

Leaving considerations of competition aside we can turn briefly to an examination of the argument, already encountered, that privatisation leads to greater monitoring of costs and hence greater productive efficiency. This argument rests on a key assumption, namely that the monitoring of public sector managers by politicians is weaker than the monitoring of private sector managers by shareholders. Politicians may indeed have other priorities than monitoring state-owned enterprises, though some degree of monitoring will always be present, particularly if tackling perceived inefficiency either seems to be necessary for meeting budget targets or appears politically popular. However, the seemingly severe monitoring of managers in private enterprises may be deceptive. Effective monitoring by shareholders would necessitate 'efficient markets' in which information about performance is easily acquired. However, acquiring information is costly and this alone can engender shareholder inertia. In such a case the managers may pursue matters not likely to be approved by shareholders. Nonetheless there does exist a potentially powerful check on private managers through the buying and selling of shares, particularly in cases where shareholders specialise in holding certain types of shares and hence are likely to react against any perceived poor decisions by managers. The prospect of profit is a powerful incentive to monitor performance and it is natural to expect some gains in efficiency as a result. One should guard however against simplistic expectations of inevitable substantial gains.

From this brief review of efficiency issues arising out of privatisation some of the complexities of comparing public and private enterprises emerge. It is not surprising therefore that empirical work on the relative performance of public and private enterprise is less than fully conclusive. Dunsire et al (1991) analysed ten organisations in the UK which had undergone major changes in capital market status including, in several cases, privatisation. They found that fewer than half the organisations studied provided convincing support for the hypothesis that improvement in enterprise performance is associated with a change in status away from public toward private ownership. Similarly, Martin and Parker (1997) conducted a detailed empirical study of eleven privatised UK companies and found no systematic evidence that public enterprises are less technically efficient than private enterprises. Surveys of comparative studies can be found in Millward and Parker (1983), Levitt and Joyce (1987) and Vickers and Yarrow (1988, 1991). Millward and Parker found no systematic evidence that public enterprises are less cost effective than private enterprises. Levitt and Joyce found evidence of faster productivity growth among some public sector workers than among comparable private sector workers. In general, they found that among the organisations studied, the performance of government departments was not inferior to that of comparable private sector organisations. Vickers and Yarrow found that private enterprises were superior in terms of internal efficiency but that where enterprises had market power neither public nor private enterprises had a clear edge in efficiency. However, private firms tended to show an efficiency advantage in conditions of competition but this was not a consistent finding in all studies. The evidence, it seems, is as conclusive as that.

Productive and allocative efficiency: bureaucracy

The distinction between productive and allocative efficiency is again useful in understanding the analysis of bureaucracy. This analysis is based on the proposition that it is difficult for the legislature to control the permanent administrative machinery of the state. This echoes modern analyses of the private sector firm which stress the separation of ownership from control and the possibility of managers pursuing objectives other than those of the owners. The modern analysis of bureaucracy dissents from the idea that policy implementation follows on slavishly from policy formulation. Instead, those who implement policy are assumed to possess considerable discretion and to act out of self-interest. Bureaucrats, rather than being neutral, are seen as forming with politicians a bilateral monopoly.

What emerges from this conception of public sector resource allocation is that fabled economic mogul, the 'budget-maximising bureaucrat'. Niskanen (1971) saw the factors motivating bureaucratic behaviour as 'salary, perquisites of office, public reputation, power, patronage, output of the bureau, ease of making changes, and ease of managing the bureau'. He argued that all but the last two of these were positively related to the total budget of the bureau and that accordingly each bureau would seek to maximise its budget.

It is easy to see elements of reality in this view. Certainly the superior information possessed by bureaucrats could provide scope for the pursuit of self interest. However, there are also defects in the Niskanen approach. Cromien (1986) pointed to the countervailing forces of internal departmental controls and concern for the national interest. It could be further argued that under some of the public sector management reforms, which we discuss in a later section, success in cutting costs would be, for some public servants, an indicator of achievement and an avenue for promotion.

The Niskanen model, though flawed, has clear implications for efficiency. A bureau which maximises its budget will produce more output than the public would knowingly wish to finance: the services provided are not what consumers prefer. The Niskanen model, therefore, points out a potential source of allocative inefficiency.

A related problem arises with instances of 'supplier-induced demand'. Examples can be drawn from either the public or the private sectors. In essence the argument is that professional 'agents', such as doctors, lawyers and financial consultants, often make decisions on behalf of their clients or 'principals'. This is, therefore, a variant of the principal-agent problem. If the professional provides more than the client needs then allocative inefficiency results. Brown and Jackson (1990) extend this type of reasoning to encompass the relationship between voters and politicians and argue that where the latter do not implement the preferences of the former there is allocative inefficiency.

The Niskanen critique of bureaucracy emphasises allocative inefficiency but there is also the possibility of productive inefficiency. Costs may rise above their minimum because in a non-profit-making organisation which cannot go bankrupt and in which salary may be restricted, there may be little incentive to minimise cost. Indeed, as is the case in private enterprises, there may be difficulties in monitoring performance to ensure that costs are reduced to a feasible minimum.

Bureaucracy therefore is a potential source of productive and allocative inefficiency in the supply of public sector goods and services. But considerations of supply alone provide too narrow a perspective. Government (representing the public) provide the demand for public services and the analysis of the demand process is underdeveloped. Among the unanswered questions on the demand-side are whether local government will respond better than central government to the public, and whether voter pressure on politicians to tackle inefficiencies is a significant countervailing force to the inefficiencies arising on the supply-side. Furthermore, according to the Niskanen critique it would appear that public sector budgets are too big. There is some support for this conclusion on the demand-side. For example, Buchanan and Tullock (1962) argued that politically active interest groups cause upward pressure on expenditures and that this is not counteracted by pressure from taxpayers who are less likely to form groupings. This view stands in opposition to Downs (1960) who argued that taxpayers feel the impact of taxes but that the benefits of expenditures are widely spread and that accordingly budgets would be too small. Quantification in this area presents major difficulties but where the Downs' type argument prevails there will be pressures offsetting inefficiencies on the supply-side. Where the Buchanan and Tullock type argument prevails in conjunction with the Niskanen scenario then budgets would seem to be on an upward trajectory that could be described as 'expansio ad absurdum'.

Some reassurance that pressures for growth are more temperate is available by looking at the process of decision-making underlying budgets. This process tends to build fresh allocations on top of each previous year's budget outcome and is commonly known as 'incrementalism' (Wildavsky, 1964). Under this process each bureau applies for more than it expects to get; after negotiations to trim the excess, each bureau hopes to emerge with more than the previous year's allocation. Attempts to alter the process, so as to impose greater rationality of choice, have been unsuccessful. For example, zero-based-budgeting, which required fresh justification of each expenditure item each year, foundered for a variety of reasons including the difficulties of acquiring and processing information. The incrementalist process is certainly less demanding, and less expensive, in the use of available resources but is inefficient where an original misallocation of resources is carried forward annually. Jackson (1982) provides a detailed treatment of incrementalism not possible within the confines of this chapter. It will not further detain us except to add that re-evaluations of base-line expenditures at intervals longer than one year, i.e. a less ambitious type of zero-based budgeting, or, alternatively, multi-year budgeting might help address the source of inefficiency of compounding original misallocations over time.

Economy, efficiency and effectiveness – the '3Es'

Thus far we have concentrated on efficiency; we now widen the discussion to include effectiveness and economy. In order to distinguish between the three concepts it is useful to think in terms of the familiar economic model of an enterprise based on inputs, throughputs (sometimes called intermediate outputs), outputs and effects (or outcomes). Economy is exclusively concerned with inputs, efficiency relates inputs to outputs, and effectiveness relates outputs to effects or desired outcomes. Each concept is more fully described in what follows.

- *Economy* is the purchase of inputs at the lowest cost. There is an improvement in economy if actual input is less than planned input. A shift to cheaper inputs, for example of staff, premises or energy will promote economy.

- *Efficiency* can be viewed either as obtaining the maximum output from given inputs or as achieving the minimum level of inputs for a given level of output. This is a fuller concept than economy inasmuch as it relates inputs to outputs. Efficiency may for example be measured by utilisation rates such as the utilisation of hospital beds, or of recreational facilities.

- *Effectiveness* is the extent to which outputs achieve objectives or policy aims. The actual output may differ from the planned output or outcome. For example, if mortality rates are higher than expected or if examination pass rates are lower than planned, then certain health and education outputs may be said to be ineffective.[3]

This formulation of economy, efficiency and effectiveness covers familiar ground. Economy and efficiency are broadly equivalent to productive efficiency; effectiveness, and its corollary of the appropriate output mix, is broadly equivalent to allocative efficiency. There is a change of terminology rather than of substance. In what follows it may help to think of economy and efficiency as indicators of productive efficiency and of effectiveness as an indicator of allocative efficiency. All three concepts – economy, efficiency and effectiveness – are commonly collectively termed value for money.[4]

A graphical representation of efficiency and effectiveness based on the input–activity–output–effect chain is given in Figure 1.1.

Figure 1.1: Efficiency and effectiveness

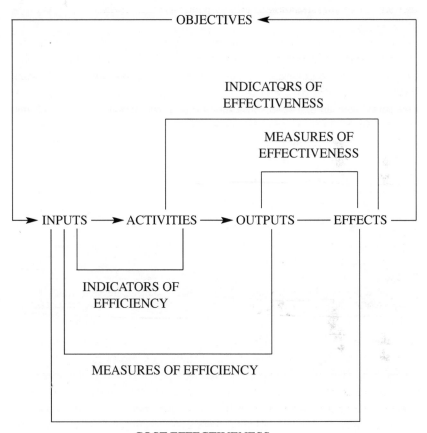

In the public sector, interest in value for money is not new but it has acquired a new lease of life in recent years in line with attempts both to control public expenditure and to allocate this expenditure among ever increasing demands for services. Progress in achieving value for money has, however, been uneven. It is relatively straightforward to acquire information on economy and efficiency but measurement of effectiveness has proved elusive. Data on inputs and on the relation between inputs and outputs are internal to an organisation and hence readily available. By contrast, data on effectiveness is external to the organisation and accordingly difficult and expensive to acquire. Moreover, difficulties may arise if, in order to establish the effectiveness of a service, consumers are consulted about their preferences: we have already noted the example that many people may not easily be able to formulate preferences about the level and quality of services such as defence. Consumer preferences are, by contrast, much easier to establish in a market system.[5]

Fundamental problems in assessing effectiveness centre around the specification of objectives. It is notoriously difficult to specify the objectives of public sector organisations – objectives such as promoting the public interest are difficult to pin down. By contrast, in private sector enterprises objectives such as improving profitability, gaining market share or creating shareholder wealth seem unambiguously clear.

Even when, at first sight, the objectives of public sector organisations seem obvious there may be problems in store. We may think it obvious that the objective of hospitals is to improve health. Roberts (1990), however, points out that there is no simple definition of health: health may be defined negatively as 'absence of disease' or positively as 'optimal physical, mental and social well-being'. Similarly, we might ask whether the objective of education is to prepare students for the jobs-market, to improve students in a cultural and social sense or to, somehow, combine the economic and cultural purposes.

If there are combined or multiple objectives then a question arises about the relative importance of each aim. Failure to establish this will confound attempts to gauge effectiveness. To some extent the problem of multiple objectives may be shared with private sector organisations but there the underlying pursuit of profit provides a benchmark of effectiveness.

One can easily conjure up other potential hazards posed by the specification of objectives in public sector organisations. An organisation which specifies easily attainable objectives will appear effective and indeed more effective than an organisation which sets more difficult objectives. It may be that some objectives conflict, as in the case where a state-owned enterprise combines economic objectives with social objectives such as providing services to remote areas. Difficulties may also arise if objectives change over the period of time in which effectiveness is being assessed. Alternatively, it may be the case, if objectives are not clearly stated, that a sponsoring state department may have a different conception of objectives than a state agency which delivers a service. Indeed an underlying problem besetting the assessment of effectiveness is, as noted by Tomkins (1987), that there are several 'stakeholders', such as managers, consumers and service professionals, with an interest in any given service whose views may need to be consulted before policy-makers set strategic goals.

Looking beyond the specification of objectives, other important questions arise in dealing with effectiveness. Concentration on whether outputs meet objectives should not displace due attention to strategic questions such as whether the objectives are appropriate or worthy.

Moreover, the problems don't just apply to the objectives side of the effectiveness ratio: there are also problems with outputs. It is not always easy to specify the output of public service much less what is a unit of public service output. For example, part of the output of the police service is crime prevention. It is obviously difficult to quantify and assign a relative importance to this facet of police work compared to, say, crime detection.

Much public sector output takes the form of policy formulation which is difficult to measure in quantity or quality terms. One could scarcely do so by counting pages per day or the production of green and white papers. However, it is possible to evaluate the quality of policy in certain instances (see for example HM Treasury 1988).

There is also the difficulty often found in, but not unique to, the public sector that output may not be obvious for several years as, for example, in the case of medium-term policy.

There may even be difficulties in distinguishing outputs from effects. Roberts (1990) makes the rather macabre observation that death may be both an 'output' and an outcome of hospitalisation. In a similar fashion one might ask if patient satisfaction is a throughput or an outcome of healthcare.

Effectiveness relates actual output to planned output or effects. However, there may be unplanned effects. Jackson (1988) notes that the measurement of performance can change behaviour which yields unintended effects. For illustration, he notes that a police force whose success is judged by the number of arrests may have a high incidence of wrongful arrest; similarly schools whose success is judged by the number of high level grades attained may emphasise cramming by students rather than personal development.

The pursuit of economy and efficiency may also have unintended consequences. If, for instance, hospitals are required to be cost effective in terms of bed use, they may either release patients prematurely or perform certain types of surgery designed to speed up the rate of bed use. High rates of readmission or instances of patients succumbing to the risks of surgery, would be unintended consequences of the pursuit of efficiency. This example also serves to illustrate possible conflicts between efficiency and effectiveness. Short-term efficiency gains, in terms of improved rates of bed use, which lead to long-term consequences of a high readmission rate, is hardly the effect intended by policymakers. We will return to issues surrounding unplanned effects and unintended consequences in the section which follows.

It possible to use resources efficiently to produce services that the public does not particularly want, in the wrong place or at the wrong time. And it is possible that slavish pursuit of cost minimisation may be counterproductive. Levy and Salvadori (1987) in their book *Why Buildings Fall Down* put the point well when they contrast the long-standing structures of the Parthenon in Athens and St Peters in Rome with some modern structures such as the Hyatt Regency Hotel in Kansas City built in 1980 which collapsed in 1981. They concluded that a major reason for the collapse of modern structures was the economic factor of cost minimisation. However, these are extreme cases.

In modern democratic societies there is continuing pressure to provide more efficient and effective public services or to reform the services which exist. The methods used to improve economy and efficiency include reducing the input of people, energy and consumables, reallocating these inputs, changing processes, increasing competition, contracting-out, performance review and improving the quality of information used by managers. Improvements in economy and efficiency should also ensue from the devolution of managerial responsibility and the use of devolved budgeting which makes local managers accountable at the point of service. Where there is 'year-end-waste' in the form of unnecessary using up of budgets to ensure continuation of the level of budget allocation in the subsequent year this can be dealt with by the use of multi-year budgets. In the final analysis once the source of inefficiency is identified and assessed it is possible to put in place suitable remedies.

The methods used to improve effectiveness include clearer specification of objectives, the inclusion of stakeholders in the setting of objectives, increased competition, customers' questionnaires, the analysis of customer feedback and complaints and so forth.

To successfully pursue improvements in efficiency and effectiveness it is necessary to be able to measure in some way the extent of the problem in the input–output–effect chain and the degree to which remedial action has been, or is being, successful. We will consider issues which arise in measurement in the section which follows.

Measurement and measurement problems

Basic questions underlying the approach to evaluation are as follows: Are objectives clear? Can progress toward them be measured? Is there more than one output? Can outputs change? Do outputs conflict? Are outcomes the exclusive or direct result of inputs? Is there joint input to an output (such as the joint inputs of healthcare, housing standards and nutrition to the output of health)? and, Should unplanned outcomes be included in analysis?

The evaluator attempts to produce work which is both valid and reliable. The process is valid when an evaluation matches what is being evaluated. For example, a driving test is a valid test of driving ability whereas a written test is not. External validity refers to the likelihood that the outcome of an evaluation would be the same if the evaluation was repeated in a different setting. An evaluation is reliable when the outcome is the same if carried out more than once by the same or different assessors having access to the same data or evidence.

Of course, the evaluator needs access to sufficient data. For example, if customer complaints are being assessed as part of an evaluation of effectiveness then the evaluator will need data on the frequency, complexity and nature of the complaints.

Output and performance measurement enable the monitoring of value for money in the public sector and therefore perform a roughly similar task to measures of profitability in the private sector. Economists have traditionally used variables such as productivity or unit costs as indicators of efficiency.[6] This tradition is carried on in the public sector by measurements such as the total factor productivity index which in mathematical form relates inputs such as wages, rents and capital costs to outputs such as planning applications processed and library loans (Daffern and Walshe 1990).

In certain areas of the public sector, efficiency can be gauged in a roughly similar way to the private sector. For example, the Revenue Commissioners may measure efficiency by expressing the cost of collecting tax revenue as a percentage of tax receipts and a library service by comparing over time the number of books accessioned, catalogued and issued. Health authorities have been using diagnosis related groups, i.e. groups of health interventions with similar costs, in order to improve measured efficiency.

For reasons already given in the previous section, measurement of economy and efficiency are more advanced than measurements of effectiveness. There has, however, been some progress in analysing effectiveness, with the development of measures of some outcomes or (proxies) for outcomes. In education, for instance, there are measures of income differentials enjoyed by graduates as well as monitoring of their employment record and in health there are measures such as immunisation take-up rates. In policing, the final objective might be to reduce burglaries but a measurable intermediate objective might be to sensitise the public to the risk and to persuade them to use more alarms and locks.

Returning to considerations of efficiency, a similar use of proxy may be appropriate if there are difficulties in measuring outputs. In such cases intermediate outputs, such as the grades achieved by students or the number of patients seen by doctors, might be used. However, the use of intermediate outputs or objectives are less than fully satisfactory substitutes for final outputs and objectives.

Public sector output has been measured over a long period in national accounts. Beeton (1988) provides a brief summary of developments in measurements of public sector output. Of particular interest is the convention adopted in the national accounts to value public services by the cost of the input (predominantly wages and salaries).[7] This convention can be justified on the basis that there are difficulties in pricing public sector output where it does not pass through the market. This convention is, however, an abstraction from reality. If the value of a service is identical to the value of the manpower employed in its delivery then any improvement in the productivity of that manpower will not be reflected in the value of output. In other words, there is an implicit assumption of zero productivity growth and hence any improvements in productivity, such as those associated with management reforms in the public sector, will not register in the national accounts. Oddly, measured output will increase if a public servant gets promoted onto a higher pay scale and then works less hard. This assumption of zero productivity growth also has the unfortunate effect of distorting comparisons between the public and private sectors. Productivity increases in the private sector will reduce unit costs but similar increases in the public sector would leave unit costs unchanged. This distortion is sometimes referred to as 'the relative price effect'.

Next we will move on to consider some of the difficulties encountered with output measurement, performance measurement (i.e. precise measures of performance), and performance indicators (i.e. less precise or indicative measures of performance). A knowledge of these difficulties is important inasmuch as it helps prevent falling into traps in measurement.

Measurement difficulties and 'diseases'

Double counting is a common problem encountered in economic measurement. In education, for example, research income might be seen as an indicator of performance because such income implicitly attests to a good research record. If research income is also seen as an indicator of input then there will be double counting with the same income registering twice as a positive indicator (see Cave and Hanney, 1990).

A further pitfall to beware in economic measurement is the assumption that in the absence of a policy intervention there would be no improvement. To avoid this pitfall analysts ask what would most likely have happened without the policy intervention. In the case of an industrial grant the analyst would attempt to anticipate what development would otherwise occur. A 'with-without' test of this nature will give an estimate of the net benefit of the grant. Similarly in assessing the benefits of industrial training we might ask what level of skills might be acquired by other means in the absence of an industrial training service.

A recurrent difficulty which arises in the literature on output and performance measurement is that of allowing for changes in quality. If, for example, the interval at which refuse is collected were to be extended, with the consequence that the same volume of refuse was collected but less regularly, or if refuse were collected at less convenient times for householders and businesses, then the output measurement for the service might not change but the quality of the service would deteriorate. Sometimes output and performance measures are adjusted by a quality factor, such as class-size in the case of education, but such adjustments are inevitably imprecise. Apart from quality there may be other immeasurables. It would be difficult to measure an intangible output like disease prevention. How could one measure the output or performance of a public art gallery or museum? A proxy such as number of visits or charge per visit is a poor indicator. Moreover, as we have seen above, some public sector output such as policy formulation is intrinsically difficult to measure.

Another family of problems arises out of the probability that the existence of output and performance measures may change the behaviour of those being assessed.[8] There may be an understandable inclination to skew effort toward those activities being measured. If, for example, a university department is being judged by the amount of published research produced or the number of citations of published work by staff, then a possible reaction could be that research work would displace preparation for, and number of, lectures. Alternatively, staff may be tempted to publish incomplete or trivial work or may engage in excessive self-citation of their previous work. Moreover, a large volume of published work or a high rate of citation is not *ipso facto* an infallible indicator of the value of the research (Cave and Hanney, 1990). Other forms of 'gaming' may include the performance of the more easily achieved tasks at first, perhaps in the hope of moving elsewhere before the harder tasks become inevitable. Yet another form of gaming is illustrated by Jackson (1987) who notes that, in the absence of proper scrutiny, measured results such as reductions in maintenance costs per square metre might be achieved by deferring spending into the future. This may lead to the unintended consequence of a more pronounced deterioration of the capital stock.

Among the other unintended consequences of measuring output and performance may be to encourage short-term thinking in an effort to satisfy measures taken on an annual basis. This in turn may, for instance, lead to a reduction in initiative or innovation. Yet a further unintended consequence would be if the existence of measures led both assessors and assessed to assign lower priority to the less easily measured activities. Alternatively, the existence of measures might lead to a defensive attitude among those assessed, resulting in wasteful efforts to sabotage the measures. The reactions of employees and service professionals has, therefore, significant implications for the process of management.

Unintended consequences generally impose costs to which can be added the costs of the input of time and personnel to setting, inspecting and auditing standards. There is also the cost of compliance, i.e. the time and money spent by those assessed in meeting the requirements of assessment. Of course, these costs are justified if they lead to greater benefits in terms of efficiency and effectiveness.

Another set of problems arises out of the need to disaggregate. If there are a number of people working together on a project it may be difficult to disaggregate the efforts and productivity of individuals. If, for example, there is joint research it may be that one person had a disproportionately large input. Other problems of the same nature arise if there is joint output such as crime prevention and crime detection: or where there are joint objectives such as, in education, to promote personal development, to provide cultural enrichment and to prepare students for the job market.

Evaluations need to compare like with like. Clearly if output and performance measures are to be used to compare organisations at a given point in time or to compare a given organisation or service over a period of time then it is necessary to compare organisations or services of the same scale, producing similar outputs in similar areas. A surgeon in an urban area may see more patients and perform more operations than his peer in a rural area but *prima facie* this cannot be construed as greater efficiency due to the greater ease of travel and higher population densities in some urban areas compared to some rural areas.

It is also important to allow for the possible influence of other factors. In assessing healthcare, for example, life expectancy may increase for a particular age-group over a period of time but the improvement may in part be due to factors external to healthcare such as improvements in public sanitation and public housing, or improvements in food and in attitudes towards exercise. In general, it is important to distinguish between joint causation and exclusive causation and between correlation and causation. A case of the latter is where a public awareness programme on crime is associated with an increase in the crime-rate; it clearly would be wrong to infer a causative relationship between public awareness and crime. We will return to external influences later in this article.

Bouckaert (1995) argued that in certain cases measurement of performance may be dysfunctional and create difficulties for organisations in achieving their goals. Performance measurement unlike, say, a thermometer may not be neutral.

Bouckaert describes a number of measurement diseases which formalise some of the difficulties just discussed. One such is where measured output differs from real output. This can occur, for example, where citation circles of academics quoting each other lead to an inflated measure of importance. Another instance is where measurement itself stimulates output. For example, output might be deliberately increased to enable cost per unit of output to fall – a clearly wasteful way to meet a unit cost target. Yet another measurement disease occurs where the pursuit of efficiency causes employees to focus on measurable objectives thereby losing sight of client needs and leading to a deterioration in service quality.

A further possible source of difficulty is where the greater the number of points of measurement the greater the perceived output. For example, more police officers may perceive more crime and, therefore, the crime rate may rise along with the deployment of more police. In a similar vein, better medical records may reveal a higher suicide rate.

Boukaert also refers to a familiar measurement disease (similar to the 'gaming' which we have already noted) which occurs when measurement causes a shifting of activity away from intended actions and outputs. For example where the employees of a public agency are appraised by the number of interviews they conduct there will be a motivation toward conducting as many interviews as possible at the expense of spending adequate time with clients. Alternatively, if caseload is used as a measure there will be an incentive to keep files, even for easy cases, open as long as possible. The 'shifting disease' can be seen particularly clearly where schools are assessed by their success and failure rates at examinations, thereby creating an incentive among certain schools to select the more intelligent candidates from among their applicants.

Such is the volume of potential hazards in measurement that it may seem disabling. However, a clear view of the hazards is useful in designing and conducting evaluations. Properly constructed and conducted evaluations can bring many advantages such as allowing comparison with best practice and over time, diagnosing problems, facilitating learning within organisations about performance and promoting accountability.

In the light of these difficulties and the problems with assessing effectiveness discussed earlier in this article, it is not surprising to learn that continual efforts are being made to improve measurement of value for money.[9] Barrow and Wagstaff (1989 p. 78) argue that performance indicators are 'singularly inadequate' in gauging inefficiency. They criticise not only the weakness of performance indicators in dealing with outcomes but also the 'ad hoc' nature of indicators chosen with little basis in economic rationale. They demonstrate the potential of efficiency measurement using statistical and quantitative techniques. Measurement of inefficiency based on economic theory, which clearly specifies the type of efficiency being analysed, would appear to have decided advantages over the more scattergun approach associated with performance indicators.

The most developed and soundly based economic evaluation of efficiency is to be found in investment appraisal. Techniques such as cost benefit analysis are employed in investment appraisal to assess the efficiency of alternative projects and policies. The rational weighing-up of costs against expected benefits is an important aspect of the process of public and private management. Detailed treatment of investment appraisal and cost-benefit analysis is provided in chapters five and eight of this volume. Even allowing for the sophistication of investment appraisal techniques there is still a need for careful design of evaluations in order to avoid common pitfalls and to make effective choices. In the case of industrial grants, for example, it is proper to ask questions such as whether a project would proceed anyhow in the absence of grant aid, whether a project is likely to fail prematurely, and whether a grant-aided project contributes to national output and national efficiency. Addressing this type of question raises evaluation above the mechanical application of techniques.

Evaluation techniques

Though the application of techniques is not sufficient it certainly is a necessary aspect of evaluation. Different methodologies have been applied to the measurement of efficiency. These include regression models, data envelopment analysis and free disposal hull methodology. Regression models are parametric, i.e. they use functional forms to relate outputs to inputs, and are treated in standard statistical and econometric texts. Data envelopment analysis and the free disposal hull methodology are non-parametric, i.e. they use no functional form to relate outputs to inputs. These methods are not always covered in standard texts and will be briefly reviewed here. More complete accounts of these methods can be found in Barrow and Wagstaff (1989) and Bouckaert (1993).

Data envelopment analysis can be used to identify the most efficient method of undertaking an activity or to show how close an organisation is to efficiency. By contrast, cost-benefit analysis which is discussed in chapter eight of this volume can establish whether or not an activity should be undertaken.

Figure 1.2 provides an illustration of data envelopment analysis. In this figure the output of five authorities is shown, each of which produces a single output Y with two inputs X1 and X2.

Figure 1.2: Data envelopment analysis

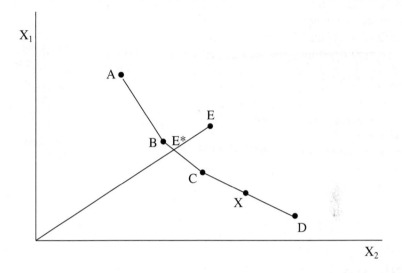

In the absence of detailed information there is no reason to suppose authorities A,B,C or D to be inefficient. For example, B uses more of X2 than A but less of X1. Similarly, B uses more of X1 than C but less of X2.

Authority E, however, is technically inefficient because it uses more of both inputs than B but produces no more output.

The line segments linking the efficient authorities A, B, C and D provide an efficiency frontier which envelops inefficient authorities such as E. Points along the line segments AB, BC and CD represent hypothetical authorities formed by taking weighted averages of the input combinations of authorities A, B, C and D. Point X, for example, is obtained by taking half of C's and half of D's input combinations.

The efficiency of an authority such as E is measured as OE*/OE where OE* marks the intersection of the efficiency frontier and a ray from the origin. Put simply, E is being compared to a weighted average of B and C.

The free disposals hull method has many similarities to data envelopment analysis. What follows draws heavily on Bouckaert (1993) who attempted to measure efficiency in civil registry offices in Flanders in Belgium. The number of employees expressed as full time equivalents represented input and the number of inhabitants was taken as a proxy for and indicator of output.

Table 1.1 shows the data for the eleven cities in the study and Figure 1.3 illustrates the data.

Table 1.1: Civil Registration: input (full time equivalent), and output (number of inhabitants)

City	Input	Output in inhabitants
A	15.9	37,588
B	18.7	52,310
C	25.1	67,923
D	27.2	68,366
E	29.0	76,273
F	34.8	61,499
G	38.5	65,798
H	43.1	75,515
I	45.0	76,384
J	55.2	85,015
K	64.3	115,982

Figure 1.3: Civil Registration: input (full time equivalents) and output (inhabitants of the city)

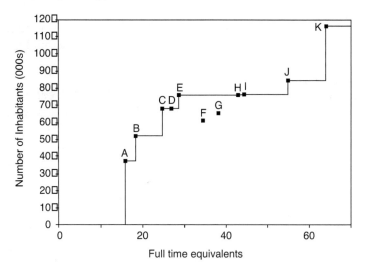

The free disposal hull technique is based on best practice observations, in this case cities which 'dominate' in the sense of producing relatively more output with less input. In Figure 1.3 input inefficiencies can be read horizontally and output inefficiencies vertically. The cities C, D and E dominate the less efficient cities F and G and city E dominates city H.

Inefficiency can be measured using the data in Table 1.1. For example, city E is more efficient than H because E needs 29 full time equivalents to serve a population of 76,273 whereas H needs 43.1 to serve 75,515. Input inefficiency therefore can be expressed as 29/43.1 or 0.67 and output inefficiency as 75,515/76,273 or 0.99. Total inefficiency is the average of input and output inefficiency, in this case 0.83.

The foregoing methods of evaluation adopt an economic perspective. The most advanced economic methods are cost effectiveness and cost benefit analysis and these are treated in detail elsewhere in this volume.

Experimental evaluations

The experimental approach to evaluation is so named because the evaluator intervenes to create a change and analyses it using methods similar to those of a scientist in a laboratory.

In order to assess the effect of a policy or service (e.g. healthcare) intervention an experimental evaluation may make use of a control group, i.e. a group to whom the intervention does not apply. Such a group is used as a baseline against which to assess the effects on the group to which the intervention does apply. The two groups should be similar: properly chosen groups allow the separation of the direct effects of the intervention from alternative or external factors.

The classic experimental evaluation design is the randomised controlled trial. In such a trial two similar groups, an experimental and control group respectively, are created with people allocated randomly to each group. The experimental group receives an intervention and the control group a placebo.

Generally the experiment tests a hypothesis that the experimental group will significantly differ from the control group on some measurable characteristic.

Experimental evaluations need to be conducted with great care in order to ensure the validity of results. The results will not be valid of there is non-equivalence between experimental and control groups or if there is a disproportionate drop-out rate in one of the groups. If an experiment is conducted over a significant period of time there is a danger that people may change behaviour during the test. Alternatively, there may be an 'instrument bias' if separate parts of an experiment are conducted by different people with different abilities.

One of the great pitfalls in experimental research is caused by the influence of external events. For example, an evaluation of the effectiveness of a car-safety inspection programme may set out to examine the effect of safety improvements on traffic fatalities. An external event in this case might be a contemporaneous anti-drink-driving campaign. Hence any reduction in traffic fatalities may be due to a combination of both the safety and anti-drink-driving programmes and the effects of the safety programme alone will be difficult to isolate.

The experimental evaluation perspective confronts issues which arise generally in evaluation. These are issues of recognition and controlling for bias, the collection and use of data, the specification of the hypothesis or objective, clarity in linking causes to effects and vigilance for validity and reliability. There is no further scope to discuss experimental methods of evaluation here; a detailed treatment can be found in Rossi and Freeman (1993).

Our discussion at this juncture of evaluation techniques has necessarily been brief and confined to those techniques not treated in detail in subsequent chapters. The application of techniques is indisputably important in evaluation. We should bear in mind, however, that errors in the evaluation process are as likely, and possibly more likely, to occur at a conceptual level as in the application of techniques.

Management reforms in the public sector

Public sector management reforms have gathered pace over the past decade and the pursuit of value for money has been central to these reforms.

Notable developments have occurred across OECD countries in the fields of information, incentives, devolution of responsibility, and accountability (Oxley et al, 1990). There have been improvements in the costing of activities and in the dissemination of information to management. Efficiency incentives, such as performance related pay and promotion, have developed, though not dramatically. Devolution to spending departments and agencies of responsibility for budgets has relieved central budget departments from detailed control and freed them to set targets and to order priorities. Spending departments have acquired greater control over the allocating and timing of expenditure. Accompanying the devolution of responsibility has been the heightened emphasis on managerial accountability which in turn has spawned independent audits and efficiency review units. Value for money audits (dealt with in detail in chapter seven of this volume) requiring assessment of economy, efficiency and effectiveness have taken root alongside the more traditional audit which emphasised the accuracy of financial statements and compliance with legal requirements. Public servants are seen not just as administrators but increasingly as managers of resources. Of course, the emphasis of reform has not just been on internal processes; there has also been a sharper focus on the customer of public services.

The efforts to introduce market forces underscore an important point, namely that competition has a prominent role in engendering efficiency. Contracting-out is just one of a number of attempts to promote the ways of the market in the public sector. For example, market disciplines are represented by increasing resort to user-charges in various OECD countries and by the movement in the UK to enable health authorities to buy healthcare from a number of competing providers.

Greater emphasis is placed on management by results or performance than on management by expenditure or activity. Consequently, performance budgeting, performance control and evaluation of results are growing in importance.

In commenting on the range of reforms, just outlined, it is appropriate to recall that improvements are more likely to result in productive efficiency than in allocative efficiency. It is easier to specify and pursue improvements in economy and efficiency than in effectiveness. It is important also to take serious account of the culture of the public service. Crude and insensitive implementation of economic mechanisms or cost accounting techniques can evoke defensive reactions. We have already noted some of the problems associated with reactions by service professionals to performance measurement. If management reforms are perceived as mere devices for cost cutting there may be resistance. Moreover, there may be difficulties in the relationship between central and decentralised control. Previous initiatives such as Planning, Programming Budgetary Systems (PPBS) and Zero Based Budgeting (ZBB) encountered difficulties with internal organisation 'politics' and inter-departmental 'politics' (Tomkins, 1987).

Allowance must also be made for the diversity of the public sector. The public sector is a large collection of authorities, agencies, and businesses with one thing in common: partial or total funding by the public purse. The service delivered by the police force is quite different to the more administrative type service provided by a social welfare department. It is much more difficult to assess productive efficiency for crime detection or prevention than it is for claims processing by a social welfare department. Some departments have closer relations than others with their clients: the relationship between a Department of Agriculture and farmers is unlikely to be the same as the relationship between tax authorities and taxpayers. These diversities in type and complexity of service, and in relationships, may have implications for economy, efficiency and effectiveness and consequently for the choice of method to promote value for money.

Transplanting private sector management practices and market processes to the public sector requires long-term commitment and political will. In the absence of either or both, the transplant might be rejected. Alternatively, subtle and adverse dynamics may arise in the process. If private sector methods are applied without, as some might see it, commensurate private sector rewards then there may be a loss of able public sector staff to the private sector.

On balance, management reforms in the public sector are positive. Performance measurement enables the identification of good and poor performances and helps indicate operational improvements. Devolved spending authority, improved incentives, better information, greater accountability and the use of cheaper private sector suppliers all contribute to economy, efficiency and effectiveness.

Equity – 'the fourth E'

The scope of this chapter does not extend to encompass a detailed coverage of equity but some comment is possible.

Where economists confine themselves to analysing changes which make at least one person better off without making anyone else worse off, they are attempting to exclude from analysis any subjective comparison which would arise if one person's gain was contrasted to another's loss. Economists must however enter the area of interpersonal comparison when dealing with many economic policies but in so doing must somewhat relinquish the comfort of objectivity.

Efficiency is not an exclusive criterion to be applied in policy formation; considerations of income distribution are also important. Policies which improve efficiency may increase inequalities in income distribution. Conversely, attempts to increase equity, for example by progressive taxes and redistribution by social welfare transfers, may detract from efficiency if those who pay taxes reduce work effort or investment and if the level of social welfare transfers deters some from seeking work.

There is often a trade-off between efficiency and considerations of equity and equality (see Okun, 1975). At the level of the enterprise this may be manifested in multiple objectives, for example where a state agency is expected to pursue commercial objectives including efficient operation as well as non-commercial objectives such as widespread provision of services or low-price provision of services. Political decision-making on the role of public enterprises in economic and social development may have significant implications for efficiency. Also in the political domain, Flynn et al (1988) note that account must be taken of yet another 'E' namely electability and that considerations of efficiency may have to pass the 'electability indicators' test.

The concern for equity is one of the factors which differentiates the public from the private sector. It is also one of the reasons why private sector management techniques may not automatically transfer to all areas of the public sector.

Applying measurement techniques in the areas of inequality, inequity and the, different but related, area of poverty gives rise to lively debate. A flavour of this can be got from a consideration of some of the issues that arise in measuring poverty.

Poverty is often defined by use of a poverty line and the extent of poverty may be measured by a head-count or an income gap. An absolute definition of poverty classifies as poor, householders with an income below the official poverty line. A relative definition classifies as poor, those with an income less that a set percentage of median, or mean, income.

Geary (1989) provides a succinct treatment of the weaknesses of poverty measures as follows:

> A policy directed at the very poor which brought their incomes to just below the poverty line would have no effect on the head-count measure of poverty; likewise, if the incomes of those below the poverty line fell; *ceteris paribus*, the head-count measure would not increase. Not only does the measure not respond to changes in the incomes of those who remain below the poverty line, but it will fall if transfers among those in poverty lead to anyone crossing the poverty line. Similarly, a transfer from someone above the poverty line to someone below it will increase measured poverty if the donor is brought below the poverty line as a result.
>
> When the poverty line is defined in relative terms, the anomalies increase. If 50 per cent of the median income is chosen as the poverty line, a 10 per cent rise or fall in everyone's income, *ceteris paribus*, has no effect on measured poverty; neither has an across the board increase in income. If the poverty line is defined as 50 per cent of mean income … an increase in the incomes of, say, those in the top 5 per cent income distribution, *ceteris paribus*, would actually *increase* measured poverty because mean income would increase. In other words, if the rich got richer, *by definition* there would be more people counted as poor. Correspondingly, if the incomes of the top 5 per cent fell, mean income would fall, the poverty line would fall and fewer people would be counted as poor. In fact, an increase in the incomes of the poorest could increase poverty measured in this way, by raising mean income and the poverty line.

Once again we see the difficulties that arise in applying measures. These difficulties should not deter measurement. Instead they should inform the process of measurement and lead to improvements which increase the validity and reliability of evaluation.

Conclusion

This chapter has distinguished between different types of efficiency, examined various aspects of measurement and highlighted some major developments in the reform of public sector management designed to promote value for money.

The chapter has emphasised evaluation primarily against the background of the public sector. This is appropriate at a time when a wide variety of methods is being used to improve the delivery of public goods and services.

In broad terms the methods to improve delivery are: privatisation, the use of market-type mechanisms, decentralisation, the creation of autonomous executive agencies and greater output and customer-orientation. The process of privatisation tends to define the extent of the public sector. The other methods tend to improve the productivity of the public sector both internally and in dealing with the public.

In pursuing improvements in delivery, public administration places increasing reliance on clarity of purpose, contracting-out, better quality information both for internal management and for the public, greater openness to the public and improved financial management and control.

The objective of these developments is to improve the efficiency, effectiveness and quality of public services. For example, there is an expectation of getting more out of public resources by delegating them to managers, allowing them the freedom to use the resources but also holding them accountable for the outcome. Improvement in the delivery of public services can be seen in such indicators as rates of turnaround, reduction in error and speed of response.

Gothic excursions into the precise meaning of efficiency or the design problems of performance measures are of little use in their own right. It is important to understand these matters in order to assess where progress has been made and where it remains to be made. We have repeatedly seen that allocative efficiency, or considerations of effectiveness, have been virtual orphans in the movement toward value for money. The 'evaluative state' is likely to remain a major economic and political preoccupation but adequate weighting of allocative efficiency is necessary in future developments. Furthermore, existing public sector reforms have achieved relatively modest improvements in efficiency (Oxley et al, 1990). The design of public service reforms may have an important bearing on future improvements.

This chapter has also emphasised that public sector management reforms such as decentralised budgets, performance measurement and value for money auditing, run just part of the efficiency and effectiveness gamut. Competition, whether in the form of contracting-out or increased choice of public services, is also important.

We have also noted that matters of operational efficiency should not detract from strategic thinking. The analysis and measurement of efficiency and effectiveness must form part of a sustained and coherent management strategy. Economic integration in Europe, increasing environmental consciousness, the ageing of populations in developed countries, along with many other developments, place burdens of adjustment on both public and private sectors. Increased public sector efficiency is a necessary part of the adjustment process but is not in itself sufficient.

In subsequent chapters of this volume we will examine different aspects of evaluation. Broadly speaking the early chapters deal with the process of evaluation. Then we look at aspects of financial and economic evaluation. Finally we look at aspects of evaluation in specific cases namely transport, the environment, healthcare, local government and policing.

NOTES

1. There are nuances of difference between some of these terms. Technical efficiency relates input combinations to output. There may be a number of technically efficient combinations which lead to maximum output. Full productive efficiency will require choosing from a number of technically efficient combinations that which involves least cost.

   Inefficiency in producing output can occur either by output being less than the maximum level attainable from the level of available inputs (i.e. technical inefficiency) or by the use of the wrong input proportions to produce the output (this is known as price inefficiency or as a variant of allocative inefficiency which we encounter later in the chapter).

   In the former case greater productivity is required from all inputs but the input-mix can remain unchanged. In the latter case inputs are being used efficiently but the input mix is wrong so the remedy lies in altering input proportions such as the ratio of nurses to doctors in a hospital.

   Cost effectiveness, or economic efficiency, may be different from technical efficiency: gold may be a technically efficient component in electronic circuitry but is not the most cost effective.

   Cost effectiveness depends firstly on physical productivity, i.e. the ratio of the quantity of output to the quantity of input as shown for example by physical output per man hour. Secondly cost effectiveness depends on the prices of inputs. Putting physical productivity and price together we get a measure of unit cost which in turn is the measure of cost effectiveness. Unit cost can be expressed either as the total cost of input divided by the quantity of output produced or as the price of input divided by the productivity of the input.

2. The strict condition for allocative efficiency is that price equals marginal cost. Price indicates the value to the consumer of the last unit consumed and marginal cost indicates the value that inputs to the extra unit would have in their best alternative use. Therefore (using 'A' and 'B' as designations of alternative uses) if the price of good 'A' is (i) greater than or (ii) less than marginal cost of good 'A' then resources should be either (i) moved from good 'B' into good 'A' or (ii) moved from good 'A' to good 'B'. Price is equal to marginal cost and allocative efficiency is ensured under conditions of perfect competition.

3. Definitions of economy, efficiency and effectiveness can be more firmly established by looking at a more formal presentation of value for money (see Daffern & Walshe 1990).

   Value for money =

   $$\underset{(1)}{\frac{\text{Actual Input}}{\text{Value of Input}}} \times \underset{(2)}{\frac{\text{Planned Input}}{\text{Actual Input}}} \times$$

   $$\underset{(3)}{\frac{\text{Planned Output}}{\text{Planned Input}}} \times \underset{(4)}{\frac{\text{Actual Output}}{\text{Planned Output}}} \times \underset{(5)}{\frac{\text{Value of Output}}{\text{Actual Output}}}$$

   Economy is represented by (2) Planned Input/Actual Input
   Effectiveness is represented by (4) Actual Output/Planned Output
   Planned Efficiency is represented by (3) Planned Output/Planned Input.

4. Two further concepts namely service level and take-up are sometimes encountered. Service level relates resources to the target population, for example by relating the number of leisure facilities to the population in a catchment area. The take-up of services relates the target population to outputs, for example by estimating the proportion of the population in a catchment area who use a leisure facility.

5. In establishing consumer preferences it is necessary to bear in mind that direct consumers of public services are not synonymous with the taxpayers who fund the services. There is therefore an important question to address: Are there different types of 'consumer' of public services? Another problem will arise where surveys are used to establish consumer preferences if such surveys are seen as a form of complaints procedure.

6. Productivity is not the same thing as efficiency. Productivity will take the form of a ratio such as the annual output per person employed. This differs from productive efficiency which imposes a condition that for a given output the least cost combination of inputs be used. It is also worthy of note that high productivity is not synonymous with profitability. A firm with high levels of productivity may be unprofitable if consumers are unwilling to buy the product. Productivity and profitability though not the same thing are related and can both be used along with unit costs as indicators of efficiency.

7. Recently there have been attempts to directly measure for national income purposes the output of parts of the public sector. For example, in education there have been attempts to measure output by 'quality adjusted pupil numbers' rather than the number of teachers.

8. A general example of the change in behaviour is the greater compliance with regulations by people when they think they are being evaluated than when they think they are not. This is known as the 'police car effect.'

9. A further difficulty arises if the information provided by performance indicators is wrongly used in allocating resources. Cave and Hanney (1990) note that there will be a misallocation of resources if data on average returns are used in allocating marginal resources.

REFERENCES

Barrow, M. and A. Wagstaff (1989). 'Efficiency Measurement in the Public Sector: An Appraisal', *Fiscal Studies,* Vol 10, No 1, pp 72-97

Beeton, D. (1988). 'Performance Measurement: The State of the Art', *Public Money and Management*, pp 99-103

Begg D., S. Fischer and R. Dornbusch (1997). *Economics,* Third Edition, Maidenhead: McGraw Hill

Bouckaert, G. (1993). 'Efficiency Measurement from a Management Perspective: A Case of the Civil Registry Office in Flanders', *International Review of Administrative Sciences*, Vol 59, No1, pp 11-27

Bouckaert, G. (1995). 'Improving Performance Measurement', in A. Halachmi and G. Bouckaert (eds), *The Enduring Challenges in Public Management: Surviving and Excelling in a Changing World*, San Francisco: Jossey-Bass

Brown, C.V. and P.M. Jackson (1990). *Public Sector Economics,* Fourth Edition, Oxford: Basil Blackwell

Buchanan, J.M. and G. Tullock (1982). *The Calculus of Consent,* Ann Arbour: University of Michigan Press

Cave, M. and S. Hanney (1990). 'Performance Indicators for Higher Education and Research', in M. Cave, M. Kogan and R. Smith (eds), *Output and Performance Measurement in Government: The State of the Art*, London: Jessica Kingsley, pp 60-85

Commission of the European Communities, Research on 'The Cost of Non-Europe' Project, Luxembourg: Office for Official Publications of the EC, 1988

Cromien, S. (1986). Comment, in J. Bristow and D. McDonagh, *Public Expenditure: the Key Issues*, Dublin: IPA

Daffern, P. and G. Walshe (1990). 'Evaluating Performance in the Department of the Environment', in M. Cave, M. Kogan and R. Smith (eds), *Output and Performance Measurement in Government: The State of the Art*, London: Jessica Kingsley, pp 143-64

Downs, A. (1960). 'Why the Government Budget is too small in a Democracy', *World Politics*, Vol 12, pp 541-63

Dunsire, A., K. Hartley and D. Parker (1991). 'Organisational Status and Performance: Summary of the Findings', *Public Administration* Vol 69, No 1, pp 21-40

Flynn, A., A. Gray, W. Jenkins and B. Rutherford (1988). 'Making Indicators Perform', *Public Money and Management*, pp 35-41

Geary, P.T. (1989). 'The Measurement and Alleviation of Poverty: A review of some issues', *The Economic and Social Review*, Vol 20, No 4, pp 293-307

HM Treasury (1988). *Policy Evaluation: A Guide for Managers*, London: Stationery Office

Jackson, P.M. (1987). 'Performance Measurement and Value for Money in the Public Sector: The Issues', in *Performance Measurement in the Public and Private Sectors*, London/Edinburgh: ICAS/CIPFA, pp 9-17

Jackson, P.M. (1988). 'The Management of Performance in the Public Sector', *Public Money and Management*, pp 11-16

Jackson, P.M. (1982). *The Political Economy of Bureaucracy*, Oxford: Philip Allan.

Koutsoyiannis, A. (1979). *Modern Microeconomics*, Second Edition, London: Macmillan

Levitt, M.S. and M.A.S. Joyce (1987). *The Growth and Efficiency of Public Spending*, Cambridge: Cambridge University Press

Levy, M. and M. Salvadori (1987). *Why Buildings Fall Down*, New York: W.W. Norton

Martin, S, and D. Parker (1997). *The Impact of Privatisation: Ownership and Corporate Performance in the UK*, London: Routledge

Millward, R. and D.M. Parker (1983). 'Public and Private Enterprises: Comparative Behaviour and Relative Efficiency', in R. Millward, D. Parker, L. Rosenthal, M.T. Summer and N. Topham, *Public Sector Economics*, Harlow: Longman, pp 199-274

Niskanen, W.A. (1971). *Bureaucracy and Representative Government*, Chicago: Aldine-Atherton.

Okun, A. (1975). *Equality and Efficiency: The Big Tradeoff*, Washington: Brookings

Oxley, H., M. Maher, J.P. Martin, G. Nicoletti, and P. Alonso-Gamo (1990). 'The Public Sector: Issues for the 1990s', *Working Paper* No 90, Paris: OECD

Roberts, H. (1990). 'Performance and Outcome Measures in the Health Service', in M. Cave, M. Kogan and R. Smith (eds), *Output and Performance Measurement in Government: The State of the Arts*, London: Jessica Kingsley, pp 86-105

Rossi, P.H. and H.E. Freeman (1993). *Evaluation, A Systematic Approach*, London: Sage

Stiglitz, J.E. (1988). *Economics of the Public Sector*, Second Edition, New York: Norton

Tomkins, C.R. (1987). *Achieving Economy, Efficiency and Effectiveness in the Public Sector*, Edinburgh: ICAS

Vickers, J., and G. Yarrow (1988). *Privatisation: An Economic Analysis*, London: MIT

Vickers, J., and G. Yarrow (1991). 'Economic Perspectives on Privatisation', *The Journal of Economic Perspectives*, Vol 5, No 2, pp 111-132

Wildavsky, A. (1964). *The Politics of the Budgetary Process*, Boston: Little, Brown

2

The Process and Management of Appraisals and Evaluations[1]

RICHARD BOYLE

Overview

The emphasis in subsequent chapters will be on exploring the various methods and techniques available for appraisal and evaluation. However, if appraisal and evaluation are to be seen as useful, attention must also be paid to how the process of conducting appraisals and evaluations is managed.

In the early days of evaluation studies, there was a view that when evaluators presented their reports or findings to decision-makers, these findings would automatically be used to improve effective policies or programmes or to discontinue ineffective ones. But evaluation studies have not often been used in such a clearcut manner. This has led to some disillusionment about the usefulness of conducting appraisal and evaluation. However, such disillusionment may sometimes be based on limitations in the understanding of the interaction between evaluation studies and decisions. In this chapter, the emphasis is on exploring the process of conducting appraisals and evaluations. The aim is to examine what needs to be done by the evaluator and the evaluation sponsor, at the various stages of evaluation – pre, during and post-evaluation – in order to ensure that there is an effective link with decision-making. The steps needed to control the quality of appraisal and evaluation studies are also explored.

The activities to encourage evaluation use discussed in this chapter, essentially at the micro level, take place within a broader context. At this macro or governmental level, the development of evaluation demand and an evaluation culture is crucial to institutionalising evaluation in the decision-making process (Boyle, 1997a). Without this grounding of evaluation practice as a key element of governance, individual evaluation studies may be successful but evaluation activity as a whole is likely to be peripheral.

Influencing use – the political setting of appraisal and evaluation

Evaluation that results in immediate action is an example of *instrumental use*. Evaluation that results in the questioning of particular assumptions or the way a programme is thought of, is an example of *conceptual use* (Rossi and Freeman, 1993).

The early literature on evaluation focused on immediate and significant instrumental use. Later, however, evaluators discovered that evaluation use was more likely to be incremental and longer-term. This reflects the reality of decision-making, which tends to be of an incremental, pragmatic nature. The approach used, the findings, and the conclusions arrived at gradually come into currency among the many groups and interests that make up a particular policy 'domain', affecting the terms of the debate, the language in which it is conducted, and the ideas considered relevant to its resolution.

Also, evaluators have become more aware of the fact that the actual process of conducting an evaluation can itself have a significant impact on the programme under scrutiny, almost regardless of the findings of the evaluation. It is frequently noted by evaluators and sponsors that having an evaluation carried out is useful in helping programme staff clarify what they are about, in increasing awareness among different stakeholder groups of their own concerns and those of other groups, and in identifying strengths and weaknesses. Rigorous thinking is stimulated in a way that might not happen if evaluation did not go ahead.

However, not all use is positive. The evaluation literature includes reference to the defensive use of evaluation, where interest groups use an evaluation to try to maintain a programme, and to the destructive use of evaluation, where the purpose of an interest group or groups is to kill off a programme, or part of it (Patton, 1987). Evaluation takes place in a political setting.

Weiss (1975) notes that political considerations intrude into evaluations in three major ways:

- The policies and programmes with which evaluations deal are the creatures of political decisions. Programmes emerge from the process of political negotiation and bargaining, and attached to them are the reputations of legislative sponsors, the careers of administrators, the jobs of programme staff, and the expectations of clients and other interest groups.

- Because evaluation is undertaken in order to feed into decision-making, its reports enter the political arena. Factors at work here go far beyond programme effectiveness and efficiency. The development of coalitions, the values prevailing at a particular time, the repaying of political debts and other factors are all taken into account when making decisions.

- Evaluation itself has a political stance. It makes implicit political statements: the determination of goals is a political process; evaluation methodologies are not value-neutral tools – choices between different methods can significantly affect the outcome of a study; conclusions drawn from analysis of the data invariably reflect particular biases and value judgements.

All these factors combine to ensure that evaluation is not an objective, scientific exercise, the findings from which will be accepted and used where necessary for change. As Ross and Cronbach (1976) have dramatically stated:

> Far from supplying facts and figures to an economic man, the evaluator is furnishing arms to a combatant in a war with fluid lines of battle and transient alliances; whoever can use the evaluators to gain an inch of terrain can be expected to do so ... The commissioning of an evaluation ... is rarely the product of the inquiring scientific spirit; more often it is the expression of political forces.

In this context, evaluators have a difficult task in trying to conduct an evaluation while at the same time being aware of the potential implications and importance of the evaluation findings to a wide range of groups. In order to facilitate the use of evaluations in this setting, the evaluator and evaluation sponsor must give some thought to managing the pre-evaluation stages, the evaluation study, and the evaluation study follow-up; and seeing to it that quality control mechanisms are put in place to ensure the quality of the evaluation study.

The pre-evaluation stage – getting ready for the evaluation

It is not uncommon to come across references to evaluation studies which have been methodically carried out, to a high standard of quality, only to be dismissed by the evaluation sponsors for not answering the questions which are important to them. At times, this may be a defensive reaction in the face of negative findings. However, it may result from a lack of dialogue between the evaluator and the sponsor or from a poor specification of what is required at the outset.

Four key factors need to be addressed at the stage of preparing for an evaluation: deciding why and when to evaluate; determining the parameters of the evaluation; selecting an evaluator; and setting terms of reference.

Deciding why and when to evaluate

A key aspect of the decision to evaluate is whether the evaluation is conducted to judge the merit of the programme under scrutiny or whether the evaluation is intended to improve the programme under scrutiny. Scriven

(1967) has termed these two types of evaluation summative and formative evaluation:

- *Summative evaluation* enables a judgement to be made about the effectiveness of a policy, programme or project, and under what conditions it is likely to be effective in other situations or places.

- *Formative evaluation* aims to improve the effectiveness of the activity under scrutiny. There is no attempt to generalise the findings beyond the context of the study.

In practice many evaluations will contain both summative and formative elements, with a bias towards one or the other.

Evaluation is possible at any stage in the life of a programme: ex-ante, on-going, and ex-post. The implications of the timing of the evaluation are that it affects such matters as the most appropriate methods to use and the reaction of various interest groups to the evaluation findings.

Determining the parameters of the evaluation

Having decided to proceed with an evaluation, the parameters for the evaluation must be set. In particular, thought needs to be given to the purpose which the evaluation is intended to serve, the scope of the evaluation in terms of what will and what will not be investigated, and the type of study to be undertaken. The aim is to ensure that the evaluation questions asked are relevant and useful. Three very broad kinds of purpose have been suggested for which evaluation information can be useful (Rossi and Freeman, 1993):

- *Programme conceptualisation and design* – for example, to assess the need for a new programme and determine the most appropriate form such an intervention might take

- *Monitoring of programme implementation* – for example, to assist programme managers carry out their day-to-day activities as effectively as possible; to show whether the stated intent of a programme has in fact been carried out, and to indicate if the target population is being reached

- *Assessment of programme utility* – programme utility comprises two aspects, firstly, programme impact: the degree to which the programme causes desired changes, together with its unintended effects; and secondly, programme efficiency: the benefits of the programme in relation to its costs.

The purpose of an evaluation is closely tied to who is commissioning the evaluation, as this influences the evaluative questions asked. The sponsor of an evaluation is usually the primary intended user. This point is crucial in that evaluations can serve the needs of multiple users, but if the evaluation is to maintain focus it is vital that the needs of the primary users are identified, made explicit at the commissioning stage, and seen as paramount. As Chelimsky (1987) has stated:

> ... the ability to serve multiple users is always constrained by the need for an evaluator to answer the precise questions posed by the primary users, and the need for conclusiveness of the answers given to match those users' particular information needs.

A clear idea of the purpose of the evaluation is crucial to its success. At the pre-evaluation stage, it is important that the information needs of the primary intended users are identified and used to frame the evaluation questions to be addressed. The evaluation should be designed around the users' specific information needs and questions. However, this is not to say that the evaluation takes one particular perspective as the only legitimate one. Rather, it is to be clear about the perspective from which a particular evaluation is being undertaken. If conducting an evaluation from the point of view of programme management, it is important that this is clearly stated from the beginning, but it is also important to recognise that alternative perspectives exist, such as those of clients or the funders of a programme.

Selecting an evaluator

The choice of evaluator – internal versus external, private versus public sector based etc – is a complex process dependent particularly on the resources available for the evaluation and the purpose of the evaluation. Where the evaluation has an accountability focus or involves a number of stakeholders with potentially conflicting views, the appointment of an evaluator external to the programme has a number of advantages. This does not guarantee independence – evaluators bring along their own particular biases and a range of influences may act on evaluators – but it is more likely to create a climate where the evaluation has a chance of succeeding. Internal evaluators, on the other hand, can produce credible information in a timely manner in situations where the emphasis is on formative evaluation and where programme improvement is the goal (Sonnichsen, 1994).

Setting terms of reference

To set the foundations for evaluation, several factors must be taken into account. Table 2.1 summarises the main items that should be considered for inclusion in the terms of reference for an evaluation.

Table 2.1: Outline of items to be included in the terms of reference for an evaluation

---

Introduction – What is the background to the programme? Who wants the evaluation? Who are the main stakeholders in the programme and in the evaluation?

Purpose of the evaluation – What is the intended use of the evaluation? Who are the intended users? What questions do they want addressed?

Scope of the evaluation – At what level of the programme is the evaluation to focus? Who are the stakeholders to be involved? What resources are available? What is the timescale?

Type of study – What type of study will most usefully address the evaluation questions? What is the most appropriate design for the evaluation, in broad terms?

Deliverables – Will interim and final reports be provided? What form will presentation take (written reports, oral briefings, seminar presentation and so on)?

Dissemination – What is the plan for disseminating results, including the target audiences to be reached, and the means and timing of dissemination?

Management issues – How will the study be overseen (informal liaison, steering group composed of main stakeholders etc)? How will access to information be secured for the evaluators?

Work done at the pre-evaluation stage has a significant impact on what follows. Whilst it cannot guarantee the success of an evaluation, time spent at this stage can provide clarification and a sense of direction. In particular, at the end of this process the sponsor and the evaluator should have a good understanding of the institutional and political context within which the evaluation is set.

Managing the evaluation study – carrying out the evaluation

Many and varied interests are affected by any evaluation. Some may be supportive of the concept of evaluation, seeing it as a way of clarifying issues, strengths and weaknesses. Others may be opposed to evaluation, concerned that they will be judged, perhaps on the basis of what they see as inappropriate criteria. The evaluator needs to be aware of, and take into account, these divergent interests when conducting the evaluation.

Guba and Lincoln (1984) note that each evaluation has gatekeepers who decide the extent to which they will be forthcoming. Formal gatekeepers have authority. Informal gatekeepers have influence. Both have the power to support or hinder an evaluation. Each stakeholding group has its own gatekeepers. It is important for evaluators to win the trust of these gatekeepers. Evaluators must therefore work at becoming established, and also at involving key stakeholder representatives in the evaluation. The latter task is usually done through the establishment of some form of steering group.

Patton (1987) has identified the purpose and composition of a steering group as key determinants in its success. The purpose focuses on different activities at different stages in the evaluation's progress. In the early stages, the steering group is particularly concerned with clarifying what the evaluation is about and in determining methodological options and approaches. Later on in the evaluation, the steering group is seen as a way of keeping people up-to-date on progress. In the final stages of the evaluation, the steering group is concerned with interpreting the data collected and providing guidance in the reporting process.

With regard to the composition of the steering group, the difficult task is to maintain a balance between involving everyone and not becoming so large as to be unworkable. The keys to the successful role of a steering group in an evaluation are firstly that the group represents the various constituencies with an interest in the evaluation, believes that the evaluation is worth doing, wants the findings to be relevant and useful, and plays an active role in progressing the study, and secondly that the group is very task-focused, spending time deliberating on substantive issues affecting the evaluation.

Focusing the evaluation – the role of goals and objectives

Once an evaluation is underway a critical task is to define the evaluation questions to be addressed. Evaluation questions are typically framed in the context of the goals and objectives of a programme. Evaluations are often assumed to answer the question 'to what extent has the programme made a difference?' To answer this question the evaluator must have some idea of how the programme was intended to make a difference. Yet there are significant difficulties in identifying goals and objectives. Of particular concern are two issues: how to translate broad objectives into 'measurable' objectives, and how to decide whose goals and objectives to take into account.

In terms of establishing measurable objectives, the evaluator often has to try to translate broad policy goals into clear, specific and measurable objectives which can be used to define the intended effects of the programme in order to help determine its impact. Here, goals are taken as broad statements of intent, usually non-quantitative in nature. Objectives provide operational statements of goals, specifying the effects of a programme in a measurable manner. A useful distinction drawn in the literature is between ultimate and intermediate objectives (H.M. Treasury, 1989). Ultimate objectives refer to the outcomes of a programme. Intermediate objectives are those which, if accomplished, lead to or contribute to the ultimate objectives.

Specifying measurable objectives leads the evaluator into difficult territory, particularly where there may be conflicting views about what the objectives of a programme are. In deciding whose objectives to study, determining the relevant objectives is far from a technical exercise. Patton (1986) has noted some of the practical difficulties associated with establishing goals and objectives, and the defensive manoeuvres associated with this process. In an effort to get away from such difficulties, several evaluation specialists have suggested alternatives to programme goal-based evaluation, such as using the information needs of stakeholders, and 'goal-free' evaluation, where information is gathered about the actual effects of a programme. In goal-free evaluation official goals are ignored, actual effects being evaluated against whether they meet demonstrated needs (Scriven, 1980).

However, in practice, no alternatives do away with goals and objectives. They replace them with the goals of other groups, or goals based on society's needs in the case of goal-free evaluation. It is better to accept that goals and objectives are central to evaluation and to face any problems that this may bring rather than trying to avoid dealing with goals and objectives. In particular, the issue of whose objectives are evaluated must be tackled.

Patton (1986) suggests that the key guide to the selection and determination of objectives for an evaluation is, 'What information is needed?' It is the purpose of the evaluation and the identified information needs of the main users of the evaluation which should help determine the setting of objectives for the evaluation. In pilot or innovative programmes, the evaluator also has a key role to play in helping those involved in the programme to come to an understanding of what the goals and objectives are, and to clarify what it is that the programme is about.

Focusing the evaluation – the role of performance monitoring

Performance monitoring refers to the ongoing examination of programme or project performance, and complements evaluation, which involves a periodic detailed scrutiny of performance. Performance monitoring can play a very useful role in evaluation, as performance monitoring data provides information for some activities and highlights where further information is needed. Evaluators can both draw on performance monitoring data and help improve monitoring systems. Performance monitoring is an essential element in the evaluator's toolkit, and is central to the success of public sector reform (Mayne and Zapico-Goni, 1997).

Performance monitoring data helps evaluation studies by providing information on two aspects of performance: the different dimensions of performance and the views of different stakeholders on performance (Boyle, 1997b).

With regard to the different dimensions of performance, there are three main aspects of performance which, internationally in the public sector, have gained prominence in recent years: output, quality and outcomes. Output measurements gauge the activities or services immediately produced by an organisation. Quality measurements are intended to facilitate assessment of the quality of outputs delivered. Outcome measurements reflect the impacts a service has on recipients and the wider community. When related back to inputs (staff time, financial resources etc), the dimensions of performance enable judgements to be made about the efficiency, quality and effectiveness of programmes (Boyle, 1997b).

With regard to the views of stakeholders on performance, a number of different views are possible, but likely to be central are the following:

- *The views of service users.* Ultimately, most services are provided for the benefits of users, and their views on performance are important in determining how well or how badly a service is provided. Defining users can be difficult at times in the public service, but a user perspective is important in judging performance.

- *The views of decision-makers.* The Oireachtas, cabinet and ministers all make policy decisions, and are affected by how well their decisions are implemented by departments.

- *The views of resource controllers.* Resource controllers aim to ensure that sound macro-economic management is in place, that overall levels of expenditure are contained within agreed limits, and that value for money is obtained from that expenditure.

- *The views of staff and management.* Improved performance requires that staff and management views on performance are obtained, and that the skills and competencies necessary for good performance are developed and used effectively.

A good performance monitoring system will provide balanced information across the different dimensions of performance and reflect the views of key stakeholders. As indicated, data provided can help the evaluator focus the evaluation and indicate gaps in information necessary to answer evaluation questions.

Method decisions

The means by which data are collected, analysed and interpreted is crucial to the success of evaluation studies. The information produced must be seen to be credible and useful if it is to have a positive impact. Findings must be backed up by trustworthy sources. The methods used, the interpretation put on findings, and how the findings were arrived at, are all likely to have a significant impact on how the evaluation is received.

There are two main methodological approaches to programme evaluation: scientific inquiry and naturalistic inquiry. In scientific inquiry, a distinction can be drawn between randomised experimental and quasi-experimental methods. In randomised experimental methods programme participants are randomly assigned to one of two groups, one receiving the programme and the other a control group not receiving the programme, with the difference between the changes to the two groups serving as the basis for the evaluation. In quasi-experimental methods, the control groups are matched to the programme group as closely as possible, but not by random allocation.

Naturalistic inquiry based evaluations typically focus in depth on relatively small samples, using observation, interviews and documentary analysis. The case study is the most common evaluation design in naturalistic inquiry.

The methodology chosen for an evaluation study can have a profound effect on the outcome of the study. For example, 'weaker' quasi-experimental designs (those without pre-test or control group) are more likely to show that a programme has had an impact than are more rigorous designs applied to the same programme.

The choice of method to be used in an evaluation, particularly between a quantitative or qualitative emphasis, is not an easy one. A contingency approach has been recommended by a number of practitioners. For instance, Rossi and Freeman (1993) suggest using the stage of performance development to help method decisions. When evaluating an existing programme, they recommend programme monitoring designed to improve programmes incrementally. When evaluating a new programme, they recommend discovery-oriented techniques, including needs assessment and case study. When evaluating pilot projects, they recommend methods for probing cause-and-effect relationships, including experimental and quasi-experimental methods.

Many commentators stress the need for the application of multiple methods. This may be an ideal approach, but given limitations of time and resources, selection will always be inevitable, at least to some degree.

Whatever the method or methods chosen, no methodology is perfect. Any method used can be subject to criticism. What is important for the relevance of the evaluation is that the people making use of the evaluation are happy with the methods and measures used and the approach adopted. Patton (1986) has indicated that this scenario is most likely to occur when users are actively involved in methodological decisions.

The main point to be made here is that decisions about what to measure and how to measure it are not simply technical options. Decisions such as these also need to take account of the range of potential views and to be based on the purpose of the evaluation. The needs of the main intended users of the evaluation should act as the guide when deciding on measurement options.

Developing a framework for analysis

The data generated in any evaluation study are voluminous, and some framework is required for analysing and synthesising the findings. Two broad alternative approaches can be used to provide an analytical framework: deductive and inductive.

In *deductive analysis*, the main variables are identified and specific research hypotheses decided before the data collection begins. This theoretical framework provides the basis for making sense of the data; does the data confirm or deny the hypotheses that were framed at the beginning of the evaluation? Statistical tests are used to help determine what is significant and meaningful in the data.

By way of contrast, in *inductive analysis* the evaluator tries to make sense of the situation without imposing pre-existing expectations. The search is for patterns and trends that emerge in the case(s) under study which identify the important variables, without deciding in advance what those important variables will be. The search for patterns is guided by the evaluation questions identified at the beginning of the study.

Whether by using inductive or deductive analysis, or a combination of the two, the aim is to provide a suitable framework for the analysis of data collected. This framework enables the evaluator to make sense of the data, in the light of the evaluation questions asked, and to translate that understanding to the evaluation users.

Planning for impact during use

The issues outlined in this section help ensure that maximising the impact of evaluation is kept in mind whilst the evaluation study is being carried out. A report produced by the European Social Fund (ESF) Programme Evaluation Unit (1995) identifies actions which the Unit sees as enhancing the impact of an evaluation report whilst the report is being prepared. Table 2.2 highlights these actions.

Table 2.2: Enhancing the impact of evaluations in the ESF Programme Evaluation Unit

The following actions if undertaken during the preparation of an evaluation report should enhance the impact of that report following its completion. The actions proposed emphasise the consultative nature of the evaluation process and the need to make information available on as wide a basis as possible if change is to be brought about.

- *Compile relevant circulation list while preparing the report.* This will ensure that the report is sent to the people who should read it, rather than waiting for requests to come from people who hear about the evaluation.

- *Identify relevant newsletters/journals.* Identifying the mechanism for communication to the players in a particular programme or organisation will allow the Unit submit an item for publication when the evaluation is complete.

- *Incorporate first responses into report.* This is a new approach which is being piloted in two evaluation reports. Essentially, it involves including in the report the first responses of the relevant decision-makers and players in the programme to the recommendations made. This practice, it is hoped, will have a very significant impact in facilitating consideration and debate on the issues raised in the reports.

- *Partnership on reports* It is also proposed to initiate a new procedure in the Evaluation Unit whereby any evaluator who is responsible for carrying out an evaluation has a nominated partner (another evaluator) with whom he or she can discuss ideas and who will assist in a practical way during the fieldwork stage.

Source: ESF Programme Evaluation Unit, *Impact of Evaluations*, 1995, p.13.

Managing evaluation study follow-up – the role of dissemination

Most evaluation studies result in a final report which summarises the findings and sets out any recommendations which may arise. However, whilst the final report is usually seen as a valuable document, many evaluators feel that leaving the presentation of findings till the final report is both too late and limits the potential audience for the evaluation's findings. If the findings are kept till the final report, and if they include a number of surprises, it is quite possible that the report will not be particularly well received, at least by those directly affected. As a consequence, it may have a limited impact or have unintended impacts. Also, final reports tend to be aimed at the sponsors of the study, and may not provide information useful to others involved in the programme, such as the staff or clients.

On-going feedback can be used to overcome such problems. Here, feedback is seen as part of the process of continuous thinking about a programme rather than a once-off information exercise. The evaluator feeds timely and relevant information into the programme during its operation, helping to improve the programme as it is implemented.

Interim reports serve a useful purpose. Interim reports can be useful in sharpening and focusing the minds of the evaluation sponsors; getting them to react to the study at an early stage rather than waiting for the final report. In this way, the evaluator can have more confidence that the final recommendations will be acceptable and realistic. Interim reports can play a useful role both in ensuring that there are no unwelcome surprises to the evaluation sponsor and in acting as a catalyst for discussions on findings to-date.

Final reports generally provide detailed descriptions of the evaluation's setting, design and data collection methods; present an analysis of the data; and include an interpretation of the findings, together with recommendations for action. It is common to have an executive summary, highlighting the main points made in the report. Tables, graphs and figures assist in illustrating the findings for the reader.

Another useful means of enhancing the impact of reports is the use of oral briefings, through seminars, workshops and so forth. Seminars can be very important in getting across the message of the evaluation. Written reports can be rather lengthy and perhaps intimidating for decision-makers who do not have a direct involvement with the evaluation. Seminars provide a more user-friendly means of learning about the study, and fit in well with the style of operating of officials. It is often easier for people to come along and listen for a couple of hours than to read for a similar period. Seminars also provide a means of interaction between the evaluators and potential users of the evaluation, allowing the exchange of ideas and the development of points made in the report. They help ensure that the evaluation has both a practical and a conceptual impact.

In all, the feedback and dissemination process indicates two distinct roles that evaluators can play. As formative evaluators, they may be facilitators of organisational change and development. As summative evaluators, they may act as judges of a particular programme. The nature of the role played affects the style and type of feedback and the dissemination which is most appropriate.

Dissemination of the findings of the evaluation is a key stage in the evaluation process and in determining the impact of the evaluation. Most evaluators and sponsors highlight the role of dissemination in determining a study's usefulness and relevance. However, it is rare to find dissemination plans built into the evaluation from the beginning of the process, or for a period of the evaluation to be set aside specifically for dissemination.

As with actions to be taken during an evaluation study, the ESF Programme Evaluation Unit (1995) has indicated actions to be taken after completion of the report to maximise the impact of their studies, as outlined in Table 2.3.

Table 2.3: Enhancing the impact of ESF programme unit evaluations – post report

---

The evaluation unit will track developments following the publication of the report. The relevant evaluator will maintain a watching brief related to the subject evaluated and report evidence of the impact the evaluation is having on an ongoing basis. This pro-active approach will involve the evaluation unit in ensuring good dissemination of reports and also in facilitating consideration by relevant organisations of the results of the evaluation.

- Circulate report to people on list developed during the evaluation.

- Circulate report to libraries, particularly those in all third level institutions.

- Provide summaries for the relevant journals/newsletters.

- Keep a record of who requests reports and if possible where the report was heard about.

- Workshops/discussion groups – In addition to the proposal to incorporate the first responses to evaluations in the report, a further option is currently being explored, that of holding small workshops/ discussion groups after the completion of the report, bringing together the key decision-makers and stakeholders for a presentation on the report and discussion of the implications of the conclusions and the recommendations.

Source: ESF Programme Evaluation Unit, *Impact of Evaluations*, 1995, p.14.

Ensuring the quality of evaluation studies

One of the many factors which influence the use made of evaluations is the trustworthiness of the results produced. Decision-makers are more likely to give credence to findings which they perceive to be high quality, rigorously sound and analytically thorough (Weiss and Bucuvalas, 1980). If the results can be vindicated after being subjected to detailed scrutiny, there is a greater possibility of their being influential than if questioning shows the findings to be suspect.

Assessing the quality of evaluation research involves setting quality criteria and standards for evaluators and establishing procedures for external assessment of quality.

Setting quality standards and criteria

The criteria for assessing the rigour of scientific-inquiry or quantitative-based evaluations has been well researched and documented in the evaluation literature (Rossi and Freeman, 1993). Four main criteria are usually cited:

- *Internal validity* – establishing a causal relationship. This criterion is concerned with proving whether or not x caused y. It is important in this process to identify and control possible extraneous confounding factors and to take account of design effects.

- *External validity* – establishing the extent to which a study's findings can be generalised across different settings, times, types of people and so on. This criterion is aimed at determining the extent to which the findings of a particular study may have applicability in other contexts.

- *Reliability* – (often referred to as replicability) refers to a study's consistency, predictability, stability and accuracy. The establishment of reliability for a study typically rests on demonstrating that the operations of the study, such as the data collection procedures and measurement techniques used, could be repeated, with the same results.

- *Objectivity* – requires a demonstration that a study is free of bias, values and prejudice.

Assessing the rigour of naturalistic inquiry or qualitative based evaluations is not as straightforward. There is less agreement about criteria and standards for qualitative evaluations, though some attention has been given to this issue in recent years (Patton, 1990; MEANS, 1996). The criteria applied to quantitative evaluations are not particularly helpful. Guba and Lincoln (1984) identify credibility and transferability as key criteria. These can be thought of as parallel criteria to internal and external validity.

Credibility focuses on establishing the match between the reality of the programme as perceived by the stakeholders and those realities as represented by the evaluator. This relies on stakeholders' reactions – saying in effect 'Yes, that rings true; that's the way it is.' The evaluator's role is similar to that of the investigative journalist – testing out people's understanding of the situation, saying 'This is how we see the situation; does it make sense to you?'

Transferability focuses on setting out all the working hypotheses for the evaluation, providing an extensive description of the time, the place, the context and the culture in which the evaluation was set. Then decision-makers can speculate in an informed manner on the likely applicability of the findings to other situations under similar but not necessarily identical conditions.

With qualitative type evaluations, the success of the studies depends on the following: using rigorous techniques and methods for gathering high quality data; checking out the findings with people involved with the programme under scrutiny to ensure their validity; and maintaining integrity in the study. Much attention focuses on the evaluator himself/herself, as the evaluator is much more obviously a factor in the study in qualitative than in quantitative evaluations. The evaluator must be, and must be seen to be, credible and competent. Therefore the evaluator must be aware of his or her own biases and perspectives and how these may affect fieldwork. The evaluator should carefully document all procedures so that others can review methods for bias, and be open in describing the limitations of the perspective presented.

External assessment of the quality of evaluations

External assessment of the quality of evaluation studies can also act as a useful check. Such external scrutiny can either be informal (e.g. peer review by colleagues) or formal (e.g. professional scrutiny of the findings by a panel of experts).

External scrutiny can act as a useful safeguard against evaluators becoming too closely involved or aligned with any particular interest group. It helps ensure that the evaluator maintains a neutral stance, keeping some distance from the programme under investigation. External assessors, or indeed evaluators themselves, can use checklists or frameworks to guide their quality assessment, such as that developed by MEANS (1996) for assessing the quality of evaluation reports.

Conclusions

This chapter has attempted to identify some of the key issues which must be managed if appraisal and evaluation are to be an integral part of the decision-making process.

In a wide ranging review of how public sector organisations learn from evaluations, Rist (1994) has identified six pre-conditions for effective learning:

- Governmental organisations appear more receptive to information produced internally than that which comes from external sources.

- There appears to be a positive correlation between the credibility of the source and the acceptance of the information. Information that comes into an organisation from an outside organisation that is not seen to be legitimate, or information that comes into an organisation without a legitimate inside sponsor, is information that is not likely to be accepted and acted upon. But an organisation will accept outside information when the source appears credible and nonconfrontational, and where benefits for the receiving organisation are evident.

- Learning is dependent not only upon how the organisation sees the supplier of the information, but also on how the organisation sees the internal receiver. If the internal receiver of the information is credible and speaks on behalf of the information coming from the outside, receptiveness will be greater.

- Inter-institutional scrutiny by government agencies set up to oversee other government agencies can have a significant impact if the organisations have developed a working relationship over time. The authority of some governmental institutions to force compliance and change in other institutions can generate a real, if at times begrudging, learning.

- Informal contact and a strategy of 'no surprises' establishes the level of interpersonal communication and trust necessary for the recipients of new information to incorporate that information into the organisation.

- Efforts to generate learning within an organisation have no conclusion. There is no finish line.

There needs to be continued and renewed efforts to manage the process of appraisal and evaluation so as to ensure that the findings are actively considered. This requires action both by evaluators and evaluation sponsors. Summarising the main points made in this chapter, Table 2.4 identifies the main actions which evaluators and evaluation sponsors need to consider, at each stage of the evaluation process. Only when these points are considered will appraisal and evaluation be seen as activities which are relevant and useful in the public sector.

Table 2.4: Actions by evaluation sponsors and evaluators to maximise the impact of evaluations

---

1 At the pre-evaluation stage

Actions by evaluation sponsors

- Decide on the appropriate balance between formative/developmental aspects of the evaluation and the summative/public accountability aspects.
- Determine the purpose and scope of the evaluation, and given some initial thought to the type of study to be used to produce the findings.
- Decide on the number of stakeholders to be actively involved in the evaluation, and the manner of this involvement.
- Weigh up the pros and cons of internal versus external evaluators. If putting the evaluation out to tender, consider a preliminary meeting with potential evaluators.
- Agree terms-of-reference with the evaluator, to act as an evaluation 'contract'.

Actions by evaluators

- Clarify the purpose and scope of the evaluation with the sponsor.
- Focus on the evaluation questions to be addressed, using the needs of the primary intended users of the evaluation as the guide.
- Agree terms-of-reference, including agreement on what will be delivered and a plan for dissemination of the findings.

Table 2.4: (continued)

---

2 *At the evaluation and post-evaluation stages*

Actions by evaluation sponsors

- Consider the establishment of a formal or informal steering group to oversee the evaluation, giving particular attention to the composition of the group and the working agenda.

- Agree with the evaluator the methodology to be used, ensuring that it will give answers to the questions to be addressed.

- Determine a dissemination plan to circulate the findings of the evaluation to those to be influenced, getting the findings into the policy arena of decision-makers, academics and interest groups concerned with the issue. Publish findings unless there are especially strong reasons not to do so.

- Make use of interim reports to ensure there are no surprises and to act as a catalyst for discussions on findings and likely recommendations.

- Encourage external professional scrutiny of the evaluation, by such means as peer review and public discussion, e.g. by experts in the policy field on methods and findings.

Actions by evaluators

- Spend time getting established with the various stakeholders involved in the evaluation, establishing independence and building up a relationship of trust.

- Where possible, establish clear, specific objectives. Be aware that objective setting is not simply a technical exercise, and that different stakeholders may have different objectives. Use the question 'What information is needed by the users of the evaluation?' to guide the selection and determination of objectives.

- Select appropriate methods and measures, using the purpose of the evaluation, and time and resource constraints as guides towards whether to put the emphasis on quantitative or qualitative methods. Involve users in methodological choices.

- Develop a framework for the study – based on either deductive or inductive analysis – to act as a guide in the collection, analysis and synthesis of data.

- Agree a dissemination plan with the sponsor, including on-going feedback during the evaluation, tailored reports for different stakeholders, and oral briefings for interested groups.

- Apply criteria and standards to assess the quality of the evaluation study. These criteria and standards will vary depending on whether the study has a quantitative or a qualitative bias.

- Develop an awareness of the political context of the evaluation – both the internal politics and the contextual politics – and develop strategies for managing relationships in this context.

NOTES

1   This chapter is largely derived from R. Boyle, *Making Evaluation Relevant*, 1993 – a research study commissioned by the Department of Finance, through its then Committee for Administrative Research (now the Committee for Public Management Research). The study was based on a review of the literature and on an analysis of the experience of a number of Irish public sector organisations.

REFERENCES

Boyle, R. (1993). *Making Evaluation Relevant: A Study of Policy and Programme Evaluation Practice in the Irish Public Sector*, Dublin: Institute of Public Administration

Boyle R. (1997a). *Evaluating Public Expenditure Programmes,* CPMR Discussion Paper No. 1, Dublin: Institute of Public Administration

Boyle, R., (1997b). *Developing an Integrated Performance Measurement Framework for the Irish Civil Service,* CPMR Discussion Paper No. 3, Dublin: Institute of Public Administration

Chelimsky, E. (1987). 'Linking Programme Evaluation to User Needs', in D.J. Palumbo (ed.), *The Politics of Program Evaluation*, London: Sage Publications, pp. 72-99

European Social Fund Programme Evaluation Unit (1995). *Impact of Evaluations*, Dublin: Department of Enterprise and Employment

Guba, E.G. and Y.S. Lincoln (1984). *Fourth Generation Evaluation*, London: Sage Publications

H.M. Treasury (1989). *Policy Evaluation: A Guide for Managers*, London: HMSO

Mayne, J. and E. Zapico-Goni (1997). 'Effective Performance Monitoring: a Necessary Condition for Public Sector Reform', in J. Mayne and E. Zapio-Goni (eds.), *Monitoring Performance in the Public Sector*, London: Transaction Publishers

MEANS (1996). *Quality Assessment of Evaluation Reports: A Framework*, MEANS Handbook No. 5, Brussels: European Commission, DG 16/G2 Evaluation Unit

Patton, M.Q. (1986). *Utilization – Focused Evaluation*, London: Sage Publications

Patton, M.Q. (1987). 'Evaluation's Political Inherency: Practical Implications for Design and Use', in D.J. Palumbo (ed.), *The Politics of Program Evaluation*, London: Sage Publications, pp. 100-45

Patton, M.Q. (1990). *Qualitative Evaluation and Research Methods*, London: Sage Publications

Rist, R.C. (1994). 'The Preconditions for Learning: Lessons from the Public Sector', in F.L. Leeuw, R.C. Rist, and R.C. Sonnichsen (eds.), *Can Governments Learn? Comparative Perspectives on Evaluation and Organizational Learning*, New Brunswick NJ: Transaction Publishers, pp. 189-205

Ross, L. and L.J. Cronbach (1976). 'Review of the Handbook of Evaluation Research', *Educational Researcher,* Vol. 5, No. 10, pp. 9-19

Rossi, P.H. and H.E. Freeman (1993). *Evaluation: A Systematic Approach*, London: Sage Publications

Scriven, M. (1967). 'The Methodology of Evaluation', in R.W. Tyler, R.M. Gagne, and M. Scriven (eds.), *Perspectives of Curriculum Evaluation*, Chicago: Rand McNally, pp. 39-83

Scriven, M. (1980). *The Logic of Evaluation*, Inverness, CA: Edgepress

Sonnichsen, R.C. (1994). 'Effective Internal Evaluation: An Approach to Organizational Learning', in F.L. Leeuw, R.C. Rist and R.C. Sonnichsen (eds.), *Can Governments Learn? Comparative Perspectives on Evaluation and Organizational Learning*, New Brunswick NJ: Transaction Publishers, pp. 125-41

Weiss, C.H. (1975). 'Evaluation Research in the Political Context', in E.L. Struening and M. Guttentag (eds.), *Handbook of Evaluation Research*, London: Sage Publications, pp. 13-26

Weiss, C.H. and M.J. Bucuvalas (1980). 'Truth Tests and Utility Tests: Decision-Makers' Frames of Reference for Social Science Research', *American Sociological Review*, Vol. 45, pp. 302-13

3

Financial Analysis of Commercial Projects

AIDAN HORAN

Introduction

Project evaluation seeks to ensure the most effective allocation and use of resources. It also provides high quality information and performance data to assist strategic decision-making in generating and evaluating options and devising project implementation and action plans.

As the frontiers of public service delivery continue to be redefined, there is an increased necessity to ensure that projects meet commercial/quasi commercial criteria such as medium-term projections of cash flows, profitability, efficiency, liquidity and solvency and also organisational working capital/treasury management policies. The commitment to allocate funds to a particular project needs to be analysed in terms of the ability of the project to sustain itself and remain in existence beyond the initial injection of funds.

In financial terms, projects will have precise quantified objectives which facilitate assessment both at the initiation of a proposal, at interim reviews, during implementation and at final assessment, by comparing budgeted results with actual outturns. The success of initiatives is dependent on competent management and, in particular, good financial management during the project stages.

Commercial project analysis assesses the underlying objectives of funded programmes such as product/service generation, cost recovery, wealth creation and economic development. The analysis then weighs up the investment strategies available to achieve the objectives of the programmes, evaluates the suitability, feasibility and acceptability of the different investment options and selects the most appropriate one.

The evaluation of a business proposal serves two main purposes: as an aid in assessing achievement of objectives and as a mechanism to assess financial and commercial viability.

The objective of this chapter is to consider project evaluation in the context of:

- published financial statements
- projected cash flow, profit and loss accounts and balance sheet
- cash flow, working capital and treasury management.

Published financial statements

In evaluating projects of a commercial nature, it is necessary to track the effect of project funding on the performance of the organisation.

Performance analysis examines the success of the business by appraisal of financial statements, i.e. the profit and loss account, the balance sheet and the cash flow statement.

The analysis involves:

- the consideration of profitability, efficiency (best use of assets), liquidity (ability to meet short-term obligations), solvency (ability to meet long-term obligations such as paying interest and servicing debt)
- the testing of key variables and assumptions in a business proposal
- the review of the external environment.

The objective of financial statements is to provide information to people both within and outside an enterprise about the financial position, performance and financial adaptability of the enterprise.

The profit and loss account or operating statement details the revenues for a period and the costs associated in generating these revenues.

The balance sheet details the assets and liabilities and financial position at a particular date.

The cash flow statement shows the inflows and outflows (generation and absorption) of cash under prescribed headings.

A well conceived business plan or proposal can draw together historical financial statements and projected statements based on key assumptions. These projections facilitate monitoring and control as they are the benchmarks against which to assess actual performance.

The format and presentation of published financial statements, i.e. profit and loss accounts and balance sheets, are dictated by the external reporting environment of organisations and companies. The two main elements in this environment are legislative provisions and prescribed or best practice.

Within state-sponsored companies, the main legislation is contained in the Companies Act 1963 and 1986, and in each company's parent legislation or act which may set down additional reporting requirements. Prescribed or best practice is promulgated by the Accounting Standards Board (ASB) and the accountancy profession generally in an effort to ensure accuracy, truth and fairness in the presentation of information to users.

The Companies Acts contain various legally-binding provisions on the presentation of financial statements. Failure to address these provisions may result in legal action against the organisation or company and a qualified audit report by the external auditor. The Companies Act 1986, which implemented the EC 4th Directive on company accounts, lays down specific formats for accounts, detailed disclosure notes and accounting policies. There are four alternative formats for profit and loss accounts and two alternative formats for balance sheets. The fundamental concepts of going concern, accruals, consistency and prudence are also incorporated. It is fair to say however that legislation cannot dictate for all circumstances in commercial practice and the very detailed accountancy rules and principles are left to the accountancy profession to prescribe.

The ASB is mandated to produce and issue accounting standards which are expected to be followed by the accountancy profession and its members. The ASB produces financial reporting standards (FRS) and its predecessor the ASC produced statements of standard accounting practice (SSAP). Increased awareness of the necessity for useful financial information which is objective, relevant, reliable, complete and comparable within and between organisations from period to period, has been the key task facing the accounting standards setting process.

The standards are not prescriptive but do incorporate generally accepted accountancy practices which have an expectation of being observed. Specific examples of standards which offer guidance on reporting of transactions are SSAP 12 'Accounting for depreciation', SSAP 4 'Accounting for government grants', FRS 3 'Reporting financial performance'.

In evaluating business performance as part of an overall appraisal of business plans and projects, it is important to effectively use the financial data contained in the published accounts (profit and loss account, balance sheet and cash flow statements) as well as management accounts and budgeted projections.

In analysing ratios, trends and comparisons from year to year and between businesses in the same industry, particular strengths and weaknesses will be apparent. An analysis of the external environment of the business will also help the evaluator in assessing opportunities and threats facing the business.

Comparison of the profit and loss account, which is prepared on an accruals basis, i.e. income and expenditure, with the strict cash flow will be an important indicator of how well credit policies and cash flow is managed in the business.

The published account formats are of greatest benefit in evaluation when the business plans and proposals are translated into projected final accounts for the medium and long terms (3-7 years).

The use of financial ratios, comparisons and trend analysis helps to clarify financial sustainability and viability as well as the ramifications of investment strategies. For example, a grant to a business for capital infrastructure will have a positive effect on cash flow, production or service capacity and earnings. If however the margins and profits remain static, the necessary internal funding and surpluses which are required for future investment will be absent and hence future viability may be in question. Recent examples in the state-sponsored sector such as Aer Lingus have highlighted the importance of getting the business plan and financial strategy right at an early stage.

Cash flow analysis

A cash flow forecast is a projected schedule of cash receipts and cash payments for forthcoming periods. It seeks to highlight the peaks and valleys of cash resources and to facilitate the prudent management of cash and the taking of corrective action to minimise liquidity problems.

A cash flow forecast, also known as a cash budget, should not be confused with a cash flow statement. A cash flow forecast seeks to predict future cash inflows and outflows, whereas a cash flow statement looks back and analyses the cash flows over the previous accounting period.

The forecast will facilitate cash management policies, ensuring that surplus cash does not lie idle or that adequate overdraft facilities are in place for use in difficult periods. The forecast is also useful in highlighting areas where payments need to be speeded up through tighter credit procedures, and where and at what stages large capital expenditure can be afforded which will usually be coterminous with the receipt of external funding, loans or grants.

The cash forecast also facilitates project monitoring and control because it represents a budget for the project, highlights the timing of inflows and outflows and focuses on short-term financing problems and the tools which management can use to overcome these problems. The forecast is an essential ingredient in overall project management.

Cash flow projections are necessary for discounted cash flow (DCF) analysis which will be described in later chapters. This analysis draws together costs, revenues, savings and interest rates to predict if a project has a positive or negative net present value (NPV).

However, as well as having a forecast of cash flows, the business will also like to predict or estimate profitability, liquidity and its overall financial position in a future period predicated on assumptions within the cash forecast. For this purpose a budgeted operating statement (a profit and loss account) and a budgeted statement of assets and liabilities (a balance sheet) will be prepared.

The main difference between these budgeted statements and the cash forecast is their basis of preparation. The cash forecast is prepared on a receipts and payments basis whereas profit and loss accounts and balance sheets are prepared on an income and expenditure basis, i.e. income is revenue earned in the period whether received or not, expenditure is costs incurred in the period whether paid for or not. Only in a strict cash business will both statements show the same results.

A detailed illustration of the linkage between these statements is presented later in the chapter.

Ratios and interpretations

The analysis and interpretation of financial statements at a particular date gives a static picture whereas ratios and trends over periods can give a valuable insight into trading performance, capital structures and financial policies and objectives.

In considering ratios, it is important to understand that a satisfactory ratio is dependent on the industry or market. Also the strategic and operational objectives will affect the ratios, percentages and trends. The evaluator must be aware of conflicting objectives such as increased turnover coupled with liquidity problems, due to a relaxation in credit terms, which may affect future viability.

Individual figures mean little to the evaluator. The main benefit comes from tracing relationships, percentages and ratios for more than one period, or comparing figures in a given period with those of similar oganisations or the industrial averages.

The main categories of ratios are: profitability, efficiency, liquidity and solvency. We will examine each of these in turn.

Profitability

Profitability ratios measure overall performance using return on investment ratios and cost control indicators in the form of gross and net profit ratios.

Return on investment ratios show the levels of return in the business, given the level of investment. Investment is usually defined as capital employed or shareholders' funds. Therefore the most common return on investment ratios are: return on capital employed (ROCE) and return on shareholders' funds (ROSF).

These ratios are stated as follows:

$$\text{Return on Capital Employed (ROCE)} = \frac{\text{Profit before Interest and Tax}}{\text{Capital Employed}}$$

$$\text{Return on Shareholders' Funds (ROSF)} = \frac{\text{Profit before Tax}}{\text{Shareholders' Funds}}$$

Whether looking at historical or projected final accounts, the return should be attractive compared with other long-term investment opportunities or deposit rates available to providers of capital.

The main indicators of cost control are net profit and gross profit percentages. These ratios will also indicate the margins obtainable by the business in order to build up surpluses and pay dividends.

The ratios are stated as follows:

$$\text{Net Profit Percentage} = \frac{\text{Net Profit}}{\text{Turnover}} \times 100$$

$$\text{Gross Profit Percentage} = \frac{\text{Gross Profit}}{\text{Turnover}} \times 100$$

The difference between these percentages indicates the level of expenses. Further review will highlight areas such as administration and distribution costs which may require better cost control measures.

Efficiency

Efficiency ratios measure the extent to which the business manages its working capital efficiently. The efficiency ratios emphasise the importance of converting stock into cash and the judicious use of credit facilities.

The key efficiency ratios are:

$$\text{Stock Turnover Period} = \frac{\text{Stock}}{\text{Cost of Sales}} \times 365 \text{ Days}$$

$$\text{Debtors' Days} = \frac{\text{Trade Debtors}}{\text{Credit Sales}} \times 365 \text{ Days}$$

$$\text{Creditors' Days} = \frac{\text{Trade Creditors}}{\text{Credit Purchases}} \times 365 \text{ Days}$$

In manufacturing operations and retail businesses the speed with which stock is sold is critical, particularly with perishable stock, e.g. stock in a super-market as opposed as that in a furniture store. Obviously stock turnover will be less of an issue in a service type business.

Debtors' and creditors' days look at the credit policy of the organisation, firstly in relation to the credit period allowed and secondly the credit period taken. A working capital management policy of quick stock turnover coupled with little or no credit allowed to customers while availing of maximum credit from suppliers will ensure adequate cash resources for short-term investment and so forth. A leading example is provided by the large supermarket chains. The policy of availing of maximum credit would need to be balanced against the possible discount foregone and the potential bad-will and other difficulties with creditors and suppliers.

In evaluating this area of financial performance there will be a direct correlation with credit control policies employed and projected stock, debtors' and creditors' ratios.

The symptoms of an overtrading position will be quickly evident in this area where increased turnover and tighter profit margins will be accompanied by increased investment in current assets, i.e. stocks and debtors.

Liquidity

Liquidity measures the extent to which a business can meet its short-term debts, such as creditors and bank overdrafts, from current assets.

The key liquidity ratios are:

$$\text{Current Ratio} = \frac{\text{Current Assets}}{\text{Current Liabilities}}$$

$$\text{Liquid Ratio} = \frac{\text{Current Assets (excluding stock)}}{\text{Current Liabilities}}$$

$$\text{Acid Test Ratio} = \frac{\text{Cash}}{\text{Current Liabilities}}$$

Liquidity focuses on the ability to meet obligations in the short term. The current ratio indicates the extent to which current liabilities are covered by current assets, i.e. assets which can be expected to be converted into cash within the same period. The acid test ratio indicates the immediate cash position to meet current liabilities.

Solvency

Solvency ratios indicate the way in which the business finances its long-term investment.

The key solvency ratios are:

$$\text{Gearing Ratio} = \frac{\text{External Debt}}{\text{Total Debt}}$$

$$\text{Debt Equity Ratio} = \frac{\text{External Debt}}{\text{Shareholders' Funds}}$$

The evaluation of solvency will focus on the appropriateness of the capital structure of the business and the ability of the business to meet its debts in the long term.

• Gearing example

A company at present has no external debt. It is financed by share capital of €100,000. The cost of a proposed project is €200,000 for which a bank loan or external finance is available at 8% interest.

The two options to finance the project are:

Option 1	Option 2
100% financed by loan	50%/50% funded by equity & loan
(High Gearing)	*(Medium Gearing)*

The forecast profits for three years are:

Year 1	€10,000
Year 2	€15,000
Year 3	€30,000

	Year 1	Year 2	Year 3
	€	€	€
Option 1: High Gearing			
Profits	10,000	15,000	30,000
Interest (200,000 × 8%)	16,000	16,000	16,000
Retained Profit / (Loss)	(6,000)	(1,000)	14,000
Option 2: Medium Gearing			
Profit	10,000	15,000	30,000
Interest (200,000 × 50% × 8%)	8,000	8,000	8,000
Retained Profit / (Loss)	2,000	7,000	22,000

It is clear from this example that there is a significant variation between the gearing options in the potential for shareholders' returns.

Overtrading and undercapitalisation

In evaluating business proposals, e.g. in a business expansion situation, an evaluator needs to take cognisance of common problems of overtrading and undercapitalisation.

Overtrading occurs in a business where the long-term capital structure is inappropriate to the level of operational activity. Rapid business expansion requires an increased investment in working capital and this may result in liquidity and short-term financing problems. Put simply, long-term business expansion with resultant increased investment in stocks and debtors should not be funded from short-term sources such as increasing creditors' days or obtaining a bank overdraft. Increasing creditors' days is a tempting method of finance, as creditors rarely charge interest. However, the risk of insolvency increases as the business may not be able to pay creditors on time.

Undercapitalisation may occur in situations where there are simply insufficient long-term resources available for capital investment. This implies an over-dependency on short-term working capital sources.

Illustration

The following information is extracted from the published accounts of Alpha Limited, a hypothetical manufacturing company:

	€000s
Fixed Assets	168
Stock	52
Debtors	118
Creditors	176
Bank Overdraft	20
Credit Sales	1,200
Cost of Sales	740
Gross Profit	460
Credit Purchases	725
Net Profit	48

Applying the ratios introduced in the previous sections we find:

Ratios

Stock Turnover	$= \dfrac{52}{740} \times 365 = 26$ Days
Debtors' Days	$= \dfrac{118}{1,200} \times 365 = 36$ Days
Creditors' Days	$= \dfrac{176}{725} \times 365 = 89$ Days
Current Ratio	$= \dfrac{170}{196} = 0.87$
Liquid Ratio	$= \dfrac{118}{196} = 0.60$
Sales/Fixed Assets	$= \dfrac{1,200}{168} = 7.14$
Gross Profit Percentage	$= \dfrac{460}{1,200} \times 100 = 38\%$
Net Profit Percentage	$= \dfrac{48}{1,200} \times 100 = 4\%$

These ratios indicate:

- A high level of dependency on short-term credit with a precarious liquidity position
- An underinvestment in fixed assets indicated by a high ratio of sales to assets
- A very tight net profit ratio with substantial expenses absorbing the gross profit
- A credit period of 36 days allowed to customers and 89 days taken from suppliers. This policy might be further relaxed to achieve higher sales levels with a consequent reduction in cash inflows to pay short-term debts and creditors.

Overtrading and undercapitalisation are symptomatic of a rapidly growing business. In considering funding alternatives in these situations the evaluator in addition to calculating historical ratios should look at projected accounts and the underlying assumptions.

Sensitivity analysis

Sensitivity analysis involves an examination of the key components, variables and assumptions affecting an investment project to assess how changes in each will or could affect the profitability or viability of the proposed project. By adjusting these variables individually and together the evaluator gets a sense of potential risks. In particular there will be risks if small fluctuations cause substantial changes in the overall projected performance of the project.

Illustration

A business investment proposal requires a capital injection of €500,000 with interest and capital repayment of €65,000 each year for 10 years.

	Existing	Projected Year 1	Projected Year 2
Sales	1,400	1,820	2,100
Cost of Sales[1]	800	1,040	1,200
Gross Profit[2]	600	780	900
Expenses	500	690	690
Net Profit	100	90	210

1. Assumption of an increase similar to sales

2. Reflecting a higher level of cost with new investment.

Sensitivity analysis looks at the key trends and variables, e.g. a 30 per cent sales increase in Year 1 and a 50 per cent increase in Year 2. The evaluator adjusts these variables to incorporate pessimistic and optimistic views of the future, e.g. growth of 25, 30, 35 per cent in Year 1 and 40, 50, 60 per cent in Year 2 and observes what happens to profit.

	Existing	Projected Year 1			Projected Year 2		
		25%	30%	35%	40%	50%	60%
Sales	1,400	1,750	1,820	1,890	1,960	2,100	2,240
Cost of Sales	800	1,000	1,040	1,080	1,120	1,200	1,280
	600	750	780	810	840	900	960
Expenses	500	690	690	690	690	690	690
Net Profit	100	60	90	120	150	210	270

The overall objective is to ensure adequate surpluses to make the repayments on the investment. It would appear from this example that after a poor Year 1 performance, there is a good likelihood of increased profits. The key question is 'How accurate are the assumptions?' The evaluator might also consider scenarios in which revenues, cost of sales and expenses figures fluctuate, and carry out sensitivity analysis accordingly.

In such analysis the efficient use of computer spreadsheet formulae and models would allow an evaluator considerable scope to amend the trends and the underlying assumptions and to consider the financial consequences of the investment.

Expected values

An alternative to sensitivity analysis is to use probabilities for certain events occurring and thereby to derive expected values. Prudent judgement and estimates are necessary and will be based on optimistic, pessimistic, and most likely outcomes, with their associated probabilities.

Illustration

A capital project is expected to yield the following returns for the next 3 years.

	Expected Profits (€)
Year 1	500,000
Year 2	750,000
Year 3	900,000

These estimates are based on current market conditions.

The evaluator considered historical trends and incorporated probability analysis into the proposal as follows:

	Optimistic (€)	Pessimistic (€)	Most Likely (€)
Year 1	800,000	100,000	500,000
Year 2	900,000	300,000	750,000
Year 3	1,200,000	700,000	900,000

The probabilities for the optimistic, pessimistic and most likely scenarios are: 20%, 30%, 50% respectively.

From this information it is possible to work out an expected value (EV) for each year to compare with the initial return projections.

Year 1	Probabilities	Expected Value (€)
800,000	.2	160,000
100,000	.3	30,000
500,000	.5	250,000
	EV	440,000

Year 2	Probabilities	Expected Value (€)
900,000	.2	180,000
300,000	.3	90,000
750,000	.5	375,000
	EV	645,000

Year 3	Probabilities	Expected Value (€)
1,200,000	.2	240,000
700,000	.3	210,000
900,000	.5	450,000
	EV	900,000

From this analysis it would appear that the initial estimated returns in Years 1 and 2, of €500,000 and €750,000 respectively, are high, with the largest discrepancy in Year 2, i.e. €105,000. This information provides further evidence with which to challenge the underlying assumptions of the project and to seek corroborative information to support an opinion on the project.

Financial benchmarks

Many analysts in looking at ratios and trend analysis seek to identify key financial benchmarks for particular industrial sectors. Unanimity about these benchmarks is difficult because issues like business position in the market, (start-up as opposed to long-established status), the stage of the product life cycle (development, growth or maturity), the advent and impact of technology and the range and diversity of corporate objectives will often frustrate agreement on ideal benchmarks.

However, a number of key measures and ratios, discussed earlier, can be examined in assessing effective or ineffective performance.

Profitability

The attractiveness of an investment is dependent on the return on capital employed (ROCE) which should be higher than secured returns with financial institutions or money markets. The higher the risk, the greater the return required. The returns on shareholders' funds (ROSF) draws on the concept of ROCE but in particular highlights the return to the shareholder after providing for other finance providers and would be compared with the dividend or profit retention policy of the business.

The gross profit and net profit percentage focus on margins derived from activity and sales and the difference indicates the proportion that indirect expenses consume of overall profits.

Efficiency

The efficiency ratios focus on working capital issues, in particular stock, debtors and creditors. Stock turnover varies between enterprises but the key measure is the length of the working capital cycle. The cycle reflects the length of time taken to convert stock into cash and is derived from:

Stock Turnover (in days) + Debtors' days – Creditors' days

These ratios also highlight the credit policy of the enterprise and the extent to which it avails of credit. For example, supermarkets are associated with very fast stock turnover, no debtors' and long creditors' days taken. This facilitates supermarket chains – the large ones in particular – to invest surplus cash on money markets in the short and medium terms, and the interest received/receivable is an integral element of their overall profitability.

Liquidity

The liquidity position assesses an enterprise's capacity to pay short-term liabilities when due by examining current assets and current liabilities. A ratio of less than 1 would highlight impending difficulties, should liabilities fall due.

Solvency

The analysis of solvency, based on gearing and debt ratios, is concerned with the ability of an enterprise in the medium and long term to service its long-term debts and improve the capital structure. Highly geared enterprises and companies carry a large annual interest burden which could be crippling in a recessionary period of the business.

Telecom Éireann's (TÉ) debt burden for the period 1990 to 1996 is detailed in the following table:

Year	Debt/Equity Ratio	Balance Sheet Debt £	P&L Interest Bill £	Retained Profits £
1990	3.0	1,069m	99m	65m
1991	2.9	1,053m	111m	44m
1992	3.0	998m	98m	33m
1993	2.5	996m	102m	11m
1994	2.2	939m	93m	39m
1995	1.9	862m	78m	12m
1996	1.4	703m	67m	66m
1997	.45	374m	43m	114m
1998	.18	172m	19m	108m

An integral element of the strategic alliance with KPN/TELIA is the extra long-term capital fund injection which will reduce interest payable in TÉ's profit and loss account and improve the overall TÉ balance sheet by a reduction in external debt.

A good portfolio mix of capital funds is important so as to ensure the most efficient use of resources. In the long term, however, increased dependence on outside sources makes the company vulnerable to receivership or liquidation if the market takes a downturn.

Case study

A state-sponsored company is considering a substantial investment in modern technology and equipment and has carried out an investment analysis using discounted cash flow techniques. The company feels that investment will result in higher turnover and decreased costs but it is anticipated that it will take 12 to 18 months from the completion date until the full benefit will be reaped.

In the intervening time, the installation of the equipment and associated construction costs will undoubtedly place an additional burden on short-term liquidity.

The estimated costs are as follows:

Description	Cost
Acquisition cost of equipment	€8.0m
Installation costs (using in-house staff)	€0.5m
Construction cost of facility (using an outside contractor)	€2.0m

The estimated completion date is 12 months from the date of commencement which is 1/10/99.

The company hopes to use short-term borrowings and retained profits and reserves to finance the installation and construction costs.

A project evaluator is asked to carry out a financial analysis of the proposed investment based on the projected financial statements produced by the company.

The financial statements are shown in the following tables:

Profit and Loss Account for year ended 30 September

	1998 €m	1999 €m
Turnover	8.137	8.713
Operating Costs	(4.650)	(5.436)
	3.487	3.277
Depreciation	(1.525)	(1.769)
Operating Profit	1.962	1.508
Other Income (Grant)	–	.225
Interest Payable	(1.021)	(0.927)
Profit before Taxation	0.941	0.806
Taxation	(0.314)	(0.274)
Profit after Taxation	0.627	0.532
Dividends	(0.318)	(0.266)
Retained Profit for Year	0.309	0.266
Revenue Reserves brought forward	1.201	1.510
	1.510	1.776

Balance Sheet as at 30 September

	1998 €m	1999 €m
Fixed Assets		
Tangible Assets	15.645	15.406
Current Assets		
Stock	.112	.101
Debtors	1.369	1.616
Cash	1.329	.804
	2.810	2.521
Creditors: Amounts falling due within one year		
Creditors	3.061	2.408
Dividends	–	.266
	3.061	2.674
Net Current Assets/Liabilities	(.251)	(.153)
Creditors: Amounts falling due after more than one year		
Loans and other external debt	(10.059)	(9.841)
	5.335	5.412
Financed by		
Share Capital	3.600	3.636
Revenue Reserves	1.510	1.776
	5.110	5.412
Capital Grants	.225	–
	5.335	5.412

Projected Financial Statements subsequent to investment are as follows:

Projected Profit and Loss Account for year ended 30 September

	2000 €m	2001 €m
Turnover	9.210	11.322
Operating Costs	(6.141)	(6.344)
	3.069	4.978
Depreciation	(1.913)	(2.701)
Operating Profit	1.156	2.277
Interest Payable	(1.411)	(2.133)
Profit before Taxation	(0.255)	0.144
Taxation	–	–
Profit after Taxation	(0.255)	0.144
Dividends	–	(0.100)
Retained Profit for Year	(0.255)	0.044
Revenue Reserves brought forward	1.776	1.521
	1.521	1.565

Projected Balance Sheets as at 30 September

	2000 €m	2001 €m
Fixed Assets		
Tangible Assets	24.434	21.328
Current Assets		
Stock	.213	.348
Debtors	1.616	1.841
Cash	–	1.602
	1.829	3.791
Creditors: Amounts falling due within one year		
Creditors	2.408	2.633
Bank Overdraft	1.108	–
Dividends	–	0.100
	3.516	2.733
Net Current Assets/Liabilities	(1.687)	1.058
Creditors: Amounts falling due after more than one year		
Loans and other external debt	(17.590)	(17.185)
	5.157	5.201
Financed by		
Share Capital	3.636	3.636
Revenue Reserves	1.521	1.565
	5.157	5.201
Capital Grants	–	–
	5.157	5.201

• Key ratios

The key efficiency ratios to emerge from the financial statements are:

	1998	1999
Debtors' Days	$\dfrac{1.369}{8.137} \times 365 = 61$ Days	$\dfrac{1.616}{8.713} \times 365 = 68$ Days
Creditors' Days	$\dfrac{3.061}{4.650} \times 365 = 240$ Days	$\dfrac{2.408}{5.436} \times 365 = 162$ Days

	2000	2001
Debtors' Days	$\dfrac{1.616}{9.210} \times 365 = 64$ Days	$\dfrac{1.841}{11.322} \times 365 = 59$ Days
Creditors' Days	$\dfrac{2.408}{6.141} \times 365 = 143$ Days	$\dfrac{2.633}{6.344} \times 365 = 151$ Days

Note: In the absence of credit purchases figure, operating cost figures were used.

The key trends over the period are set out in the following table:

Financial trends 1998–2001		
Detail	Outcome	
Turnover	+ 39%	$\dfrac{(11.322 - 8.137)}{8.137}$
Operating Costs	+ 36%	$\dfrac{(6.344 - 4.650)}{4.650}$
Interest Payable	+ 109%	$\dfrac{(2.133 - 1.021)}{1.021}$
Dividends	– 69%	$\dfrac{(.100 - .318)}{.318}$
Retained Profit	– 86%	$\dfrac{(.044 - .309)}{.309}$

• Schedule of ratios

The profitability, efficiency, liquidity and solvency ratios are set out in the following table:

	1998	*1999*	*2000*	*2001*
Profitability				
Operating Profit Percentage	24.1%	17.3%	12.6%	20.1%
Return on Capital Employed	12.9%[1]	9.9%	5.1%	10.2%
Efficiency				
Debtors' Days	61	68	64	59
Creditors' Days	240	162	143	151
Liquidity				
Current Ratio	.92	.94	.52	1.39
Acid Test Ratio	.43	.30	–	.59
Solvency				
Gearing	66%	65%	77%	77%
Other				
Shareholders' Funds				
Total Assets Ratio	27.7%[2]	30.2%	19.6%	20.7%

[1] $\dfrac{1.962}{10.059 + 5.110}$ [2] $\dfrac{5.110}{15.645 + 2.810}$

We can now use these ratios to analyse performance.

Profitability

The operating profit ratio and the return on capital employed projected for the year 2001 will not reach the levels of 1998 but it would be hoped that 2002 and beyond will bring greater returns. The elements contributing to ROCE can be further subdivided into:

$$\frac{\text{Operating Profit}}{\text{Turnover}} \times \frac{\text{Turnover}}{\text{Capital Employed}}$$

	(a) $\dfrac{\text{Operating Profit}}{\text{Turnover}}$	(b) $\dfrac{\text{Turnover}}{\text{Capital Employed}}$	Product (a × b)
1998	$\dfrac{€1,962}{€8,137} = \mathbf{24.1\%}$	$\dfrac{€8,137}{€15,169} = \mathbf{.536}$	12.9%
2001	$\dfrac{€2,277}{€11,322} = \mathbf{20.1\%}$	$\dfrac{€11,322}{€22,386} = \mathbf{.505}$	10.2%

This disaggregated analysis focuses on the underlying fall which is in the operating profit percentage. The fall has probably been caused by tighter profit margins and/or higher expenses.

The information shows that turnover increases have been matched by cost increases. Of particular note is the increase in interest payable which has more than doubled over the period. This is consistent with the reduction in dividends and retained profits by 69 per cent and 86 per cent respectively.

Efficiency

The company has a very lax credit policy inasmuch as it allows approx. two months credit. On the other hand the company itself avails of very long credit periods. Indeed we may say that there is substantial 'leaning on the trade'. Although the creditors' days have declined, there must be high levels of creditor and supplier dissatisfaction and this may be reflecting itself in higher costs of supplies to the company.

Liquidity

There is a significant improvement in the company's current and acid test ratios over the period. However, bearing in mind the substantial credit taking and the higher interest payments and debt levels, it is incumbent on the company to implement improved working capital management procedures.

Solvency

Solvency is the most difficult problem facing the company. The growing dependence on external debt makes it a highly geared company with a large interest and capital repayments burden to service.

The financial risk, with a gearing ratio of 66 oper cent rising to 77 per cent, is considerable and either some equity funding by way of share issue, exchequer funds or non-repayable grants might help the development of a more viable and sustainable operation.

The projected returns show the most favourable outcome but it is critical that the assumptions and estimates are examined thoroughly because, even using this favourable picture, the projected outcome is not encouraging.

Sensitivity and expected value analysis may confirm that the environment facing the company is difficult. However, it may be such that the company cannot sit and wait, but must be active in its investment strategy. The long-term view may be that reduced returns are better than receivership or liquidation.

Sensitivity analysis

As we have already seen, sensitivity analysis identifies the key variable elements within the financial information and considers the impact on the projected results of changes to these variables.

For example, using the 2000 and 2001 profit and loss accounts, we might analyse the effect when,

- turnover is 10 per cent less in 2000 and 15 per cent less in 2001,
- operating costs each year are 5 per cent greater than budget.

The analysis reveals the following:

	2000		2001	
	Projected	Adjusted	Projected	Adjusted
Turnover	9.210	8.289	11.322	9.624
Operating Costs	6.141	6.448	6.344	6.661
	3.069	1.841	4.978	2.963
Depreciation	1.913	1.913	2.701	2.701
Operating Profit	1.156	(0.072)	2.277	0.262

The table, by varying the underlying assumptions, indicates the volatility in performance of the investment. As part of the decision support techniques used by the evaluator, it also focuses on fluctuations and consequent material risks. For example, a projected profit of €3.433m over two years, necessary to service the capital investment, fell to an adjusted profit of €190,000.

Probability analysis and expected values

We have noted earlier that this analysis involves the assignment of probabilities to estimated key financial variables and the derivation of expected values for optimistic, pessimistic and most likely outcomes.

For example, using the 2000 and 2001 profit and loss accounts, the estimated turnovers with associated probabilities are as follows:

	2000			2001		
	Turnover	Prob.	Exp. Value	Turnover	Prob.	Exp. Value
Optimistic	10.11	.10	1.011	12.110	.15	1.817
Pessimistic	8.00	.30	2.400	9.400	.35	3.290
Most likely	9.21	.60	5.526	11.322	.50	5.661
			8.937			10.768

This would alter the operating profit as follows:

	2000		2001	
	Projected	Based on EV	Projected	Based on EV
Turnover	9.210	8.937	11.322	10.768
Operating Costs	6.141	6.141	6.344	6.344
	3.069	2.796	4.978	4.424
Depreciation	1.913	1.913	2.701	2.701
Operating Profit	1.156	0.883	2.277	1.723

The following table shows how alternative assumptions affect operating profit estimates:

	2000	2001
Projected Returns	1.156	2.277
Sensitivity Analysis	(0.72)	.262
Expected Values	.883	1.723

Illustrations: using plan assumptions

Business plan assumptions can be used to develop a set of projected financial statements which can then be analysed in terms of profitability, liquidity and efficiency. This analysis allows the evaluator to assess the extent to which a proposed investment is likely to achieve its financial objectives.

Business plan assumptions and projected financial position

Omega Ltd, incorporated one year ago, achieved a small profit on its activities. The company manufactures plastic moulds used by computer companies in packaging personal computers and printers, and is an import substitution product.

The company directors are now seeking industrial grant funding to develop and expand operations and to employ an additional five people. As part of the submission, they produce a business plan and projected statements of financial position.

Actual balance sheet and profit and loss account for 1999 are as follows:

Balance Sheet of Omega Ltd as at 31 December 1999		€000s
Fixed Assets		450
Current Assets:		
Stock	135	
Debtors	40	
	175	
Creditors: Due within one year		
Creditors	20	
Bank	120	
	140	
Net Current Assets		35
Creditors: Due after one year		(150)
		335
Capital		315
Retained Profit		20
		335

Profit and Loss Account of Omega for year ended 31 December 1999	€000s
Turnover	260
Cost of Sales	(182)
Gross Profit	78
Administration Expenses	(25)
Distribution Costs	(15)
Operating Profit	38
Interest Payable	(18)
Profit Before Tax	20
Taxation	–
Retained Profit	20

• Business plan assumptions

The assumptions underlying the business plan are:

Categories	Percentage change
Turnover	+ 60%
Cost of Sales	+ 60%
Administration Expenses	+ 15%
Distribution Costs	+ 30%
Interest	No Change
Estimated Taxation	30% of Profit
Stock Levels	No Change

• Additional information

A relaxation of credit policy will move the existing cash sales/credit sales split from 25/75 per cent to 10/90 per cent.

The cost of sales figure includes €100,000 staff costs and €50,000 depreciation.

It is anticipated that all costs are paid for within a month, except staff salaries and wages which are paid as incurred.

Interest is payable half yearly in arrears.

The investment sought is €100,000 and will be used to purchase additional equipment.

Assume original depreciation remains unchanged.

The company hopes to pay off all creditors quarterly with the intention of having no creditors outstanding at year end.

Preliminary Workings

	000s	% Change	Revised Amount 000s
Turnover	260	60	416
Cost of Sales (182) comprising:			
Staff	100	60	160
Depreciation	50	–	50
Creditors/Purchases	32	60	51
Administration Expenses	25	15	29
Distribution Costs	15	30	20
Interest Payable	18	–	18
Additional Depreciation on New Equipment	–	–	10

Turnover

Cash	25%	65	10%	42
Credit	75%	195	90%	374
		260		416

Debtors

$$\frac{40}{195} \times 365 \qquad 75 \text{ Days} \qquad (2^{1}/_{2} \text{ Months})$$

Assume a relaxation of credit period from 2·5 months to 3 months.

Constant Sales per quarter		*Cash Sales*	*Credit Sales*
Quarter 1	104	10	94
Quarter 2	104	10	94
Quarter 3	104	10	94
Quarter 4	104	10	94

Receipts in the first quarter = Cash Sales 10 + Opening Debtors 40 = 50

Receipts in each of the next three quarters = Cash Sales 10 + 94 (Previous Quarter Debtors) = 104

Closing Debtors (Quarter 4) = 94

Creditors

Opening Creditors   20

Creditors within Cost of Sales   51 (3 quarters @ 13 + last quarter @ 12)

Creditors Payments	71	
Quarter 1	33	(20 + 13) (Opening creditors + 1st quarter)
Quarter 2	13	
Quarter 3	13	
Quarter 4	12	

Quarterly Cash Flow Forecast

		Q1	Q2	Q3	Q4	Total
Receipts	Cash Sales	10	10	10	10	40
	Debtors	40	94	94	94	322
	Investment Grant	100				100
		150	104	104	104	462
Payments	Creditors	33	13	13	12	71
	Staff Costs	40	40	40	40	160
	Administration	7	7	7	8	29
	Distribution	5	5	5	5	20
	Interest	–	9	–	9	18
	Equipment Purchase	100	–	–	–	100
	Taxation	–	–	–	23	23
		185	74	65	97	421
Net Cash Flow		(35)	30	39	7	41
Opening Balance		(120)	(155)	(125)	(86)	(120)
Closing Balance		(155)	(125)	(86)	(79)	(79)

Projected Profit and Loss Account

Turnover	416
Cost of Sales	271 (160 + 50 + 51 + 10)
Gross Profit	145
Administration Expenses	29
Distribution Costs	20
Operating Profit	96
Interest Payable	18
Profit Before Tax	78
Taxation	23
Retained Profit	55

Projected Balance Sheet

Fixed Assets		490 (450+100-60)
Current Assets		
Stock	135	
Debtors	94	
	229	
Creditors: Due within one year		
Creditors	–	
Bank	79	
Net Current Assets		150
		640
Creditors: Due after one year		(150)
		490
Capital		315
Industrial Grant		100
Retained Profit		75 (20 + 55)
		490

Projected Cash Flow Statement

(In Accordance with Financial Reporting Standard No. 1)

Net Cash Inflow from *Operating Activities* (Note 1)	82
Returns on Investments and Servicing of Finance	
Interest	(18)
Taxation Paid	(23)
Capital Expenditure	
New Equipment	(100)
Acquisitions and disposals	–
Equity dividends	–
Management of liquid resources	–
Financing	
Industrial Grant	100
Changes in cash position	41
Reconciliation of net cash flow	
Opening Bank Balance	(120)
Closing Bank Balance	(79)
	41
Note 1	
Operating Profit	96
Depreciation	60
Increase Debtors	(54)
Decrease Creditors	(20)
Increase/Decrease Stock	–
Net Cash Inflow from Operating Activities	82

This illustration clarifies the difference between a cash flow forecast/budget and the prescribed FRS1 cash flow statement. The overall result will be the same but the manner of presentation and detail is quite different.

Analysis of projected financial position, Omega Ltd

The sales to fixed asset ratio is similar to other ratios we have encountered and assesses the level of turnover as a per cent of fixed assets employed. It considers the extent of trading or overtrading which may be occurring. Using the projected final accounts and the historical accounts given as part of the initial information, we can analyse and compare the financial performance indicators of Omega Ltd.

Schedule of Ratios

	Historic	Projected
ROCE	$\dfrac{38}{335 + 150} = 8\%$	$\dfrac{96}{490 + 150} = 15\%$
Net Profit %	$\dfrac{20}{260} = 7.7\%$	$\dfrac{78}{416} = 18.8\%$
Current Ratio	$\dfrac{175}{140} = 1.3$	$\dfrac{229}{79} = 2.9$
Debtors' Days	$\dfrac{40}{195} \times 365 = 75 \text{ days}$	$\dfrac{94}{374} \times 365 = 92 \text{ days}$
Sales/Fixed Assets	$\dfrac{260}{450} = .58$	$\dfrac{416}{490} = .85$

The projected results show a very strong performance for the year, with the main profitability indicators doubling and a substantial improvement in overall liquidity. Difficulties might arise in the area of debtor management and also stock holdings which appear very high relative to cost of sales. This may be due to a policy of buffer stocks or emergency stocks or stock piling of raw materials.

The main caveats concern the accuracy of projected revenue increases. Questions to be asked might include:

- Is the business plan supported by market research?
- Are the orders already in?
- Will margins be squeezed in order to sell the stock?
- Will performance be affected if the machinery or equipment is not in place for several months?
- Will the new staff need training with consequent reduction in overall productivity?

These questions could be analysed in terms of sensitivity analysis discussed earlier.

For example, we might ask what would be the effect of an increase in turnover of 40 per cent, assuming that costs and the proportional breakdown between credit sales and cash, remained as originally projected?

Initial Workings

Revised Annual Turnover = 364 (260 × 140%)
(10% cash = 36, 90% credit = 328)
Quarterly receipt from debtors = 82 (328/4)
Quarterly cash sales = 9 (36/4)

Revised Annual Cash Forecast/Budget

Receipts	€000s	
Cash Sales	36	
Credit Sales (Debtors)	286	(82 × 3) + 40 (i.e. original debtors)
Grant	100	
	422	

Payments (revised)		
Creditors	71 (20+51)	
Staff	160	
Administration	29	
Distribution	20	
Interest	18	
Equipment	100	
Taxation	8	
	406	

Overall Position	16	
Opening Balance	(120)	
Closing Balance	(104)	

The revised profit and loss account and balance sheet from this scenario would be as follows:

Revised Profit and Loss Account

	€000s
Turnover	364
Cost of Sales	271
Gross Profit	93
Administration Expenses	29
Distribution Costs	20
Operating Profit	44
Interest Payable	18
Profit Before Tax	26
Taxation	8
Dividends	–
Retained Profit for Year	18

Revised Balance Sheet

	€000s	€000s
Fixed Assets		490
Current Assets		
Stock	135	
Debtors	82	
	217	
Creditors: Due within one year		
Creditors	–	
Bank	104	
Net Current Assets		113
		603
Creditors: Due after one year		(150)
		453
Capital		315
Industrial Grant		100
Retained Profit		38 (20+18)
		453

Schedule of Ratios

	Actual	Original Projection	Revised Projection
ROCE	8%	15%	$7.3\% = \dfrac{44}{453 + 150}$
Net Profit %	7.7 %	18.8%	$7.1\% = \dfrac{26}{364}$
Current Ratio	1.3	2.9	$2.1 = \dfrac{217}{104}$
Debtors' Days	75 Days	92 Days	$91 \text{ Days} = \dfrac{82}{328} \times 365$
Sales/Fixed Assets	.58	.85	$.74 = \dfrac{364}{490}$

The revised projection carried out using some sensitivity analysis clearly shows that even with a 40 per cent increase in turnover, the main financial indicators have not improved; indeed some slippage has occurred.

Adjustments to some of the other key variables and components such as staff and other costs, interest and taxation could be incorporated and alternative projected outurns calculated.

Risk

This example highlights the area of financial and business risk which arises in an evaluation of a business proposal.

Financial risk represents the risk to contributors of ordinary share capital or other subordinated funds of having fixed charge or prior charge capital funds held by other lenders or agencies. The prior charge capital has first call on funds of the business or organisation in the event of winding-up. Indeed the fixed assets may have been used as security on debt from external providers who could as a consequence appoint a receiver in cases of non-payment of loan interest and capital.

The gearing ratio and debt equity ratio will highlight the external/internal capital split. The industrial grant, probably non-repayable, does not increase the financial risk.

Business risk on the other hand represents the risks associated with estimating revenues, costs and profits. The greater the possible variability in revenues and costs the higher the risk. The higher the incidence of fixed costs, the greater the susceptibility to wider fluctuations in profits when revenues change. The sensitivity analysis has indicated the variation in financial performance indicators under alternative scenarios and highlighted the business risk for Omega Ltd.

Risk and risk management are more fully treated in chapter six of this volume.

Review of ratios used in evaluation

The following table summarises the major ratios we have encountered in this chapter.

Ratio	Formula	Comment
Profitability		
Return on capital employed (ROCE)	$\dfrac{\text{Profit before interest and tax}}{\text{Capital Employed}}$	Common capital measure of overall business performance
Return on shareholders' Funds (ROSF)	$\dfrac{\text{Profit before tax}}{\text{Shareholders' funds}}$	Measure of return to shareholders
Net Profit Margin	$\dfrac{\text{Net Profit}}{\text{Turnover}}$	Profit as percentage of turnover
Gross ProfitMargin	$\dfrac{\text{Gross Profit}}{\text{Turnover}}$	Comparison with net profit margin shows level of expenses incurred.

Ratio	Formula	Comment
Efficiency		
RStock Turnover	$\dfrac{\text{Stock}}{\text{Cost of Sales}} \times 365$	Measure of success in turning over stock
Debtors' Days	$\dfrac{\text{Trade Debtors}}{\text{Credit Sales}} \times 365$	Indicator of credit period allowed
Creditors' Days	$\dfrac{\text{Trade Creditors}}{\text{Credit Purchases}} \times 365$	Measure of credit period taken
Liquidity		
Current Ratio	$\dfrac{\text{Current Assets}}{\text{Current Liabilities/ creditors due within 1 year}}$	Measure of ability of short term sources to pay current liabilities
Acid Test Ratio	$\dfrac{\text{Cash}}{\text{Creditors due within 1 year}}$	Critical indicator of ability to pay short term liabilities
Solvency		
Gearing Ratio	$\dfrac{\text{External Debt}}{\text{Capital Employed}}$	Measure of extent to which external debt is funding the business
Debt Equity Ratio	$\dfrac{\text{External Debt}}{\text{Shareholders' Funds}}$	Indicator of company financing

Another commonly used ratio, not included in the illustrations, is:

Interest Cover	$\dfrac{\text{Profit before Interest}}{\text{Interest Paid}}$	Indicator of ability to service debt.

Limitations of ratio analysis

The ratios and indicators discussed in this chapter highlight trends and issues for commercial organisations in project evaluation. However, they are not prescriptive. Ratios are a useful guide and will support information drawn from other sources in the organisation. The source of data for interpretation is usually the historical published accounts and these will not incorporate current and future developments of the business. It is also necessary to ensure that the ratios are computed in a consistent manner between periods to facilitate comparative analysis. Changing accounting policies by the business or between businesses will undermine the comparability of the financial indicators.

A ratio is a statement of a relationship between two figures and in analysing a changing ratio the evaluator must be clear about which figures are changing.

The main strengths of ratio analysis are the insight it gives into the change in the financial position of a business from one period to the next and also the basis for comparison it allows with similar companies and industry averages.

Pitfalls

In evaluating a proposal for funds, some pitfalls should be borne in mind.

- Over-reliance on a single customer or market or product; this has the obvious weakness of placing 'all the eggs in one basket'.

- Overtrading which is an attempt to achieve a high level of business activity, customer and market share, without the support of adequate long-term resources.

- High gearing which is over-reliance on debt funding indicated by a position of high prior charge, interest bearing capital to internally generated funds; such a financial position requires high annual interest payments no matter what the business performance.

- Creative accounting techniques such as variations in accounting policies, alterations in provisions in an attempt to show the most optimistic performance results of the business.

- Calibre of management; the experience and expertise of management, and the financial management policies and procedures they pursue, can be important to the performance of the business.

Treasury management and working capital

In the evaluation of proposed projects and programmes, in addition to considering the financial performance, the manner in which financial management is exercised will also have a fundamental effect on the success or failure of the proposal.

Two particularly relevant aspects of financial management are:

- Treasury management

- Working capital management.

Treasury management is the management of all money and capital transactions relating to the funding and cash resources of an organisation. It incorporates short, medium and long-term cash flow forecasting, borrowing and investment strategies of the business, as well as monitoring systems, reporting mechanisms and the allocation of responsibility and accountability within clear treasury management policies.

The objective of working capital management is to ensure that the business has adequate short-term financial resources to meet its requirements. This will involve ongoing analysis of current assets (debtors and stock) and current liabilities (short-term creditors). The turnover and efficiency ratios have already been explained. An efficient working capital management system will reduce the level of debtors and stock, ensure adequate funds to pay creditors, and make maximum use of surplus cash. Efficient working capital management is concerned with the balance between profitability and liquidity by not having surplus funds lying idle or foregoing investment opportunities or discounts from creditors.

Effective project evaluation and management will incorporate the benefits of good financial management by:

• providing prescribed guidelines within which projects are considered

• ensuring an effective control environment within which the project is carried out

• adopting policies and procedures over the project duration to facilitate the maximise drawdown of funds (from central sources) and ensure their efficient use

• facilitating the post-project-review through the completion of final accounts.

Conclusion

In this chapter we have analysed the various elements of commercial projects and business plans to show their usefulness to decisions on medium and long-term projects.

Financial performance measures are an integral element of initial evaluation and monitoring of projects. They play an important role in the management of limited resources to achieve value for money.

The chapter has discussed the main issues in terms of balance sheet, cash flow and profitability analysis and the interpretation of business information by including various illustrations to confirm the principles used in project decision-making.

A full review of the main ratios and their limitations helps to highlight both the technical knowledge and the judgement required in analysing data. Of course, the quality of the analysis depends on the quality of data which in turn depends on effective financial reporting, planning and control.

There is a wealth of published material dealing with financial analysis. A selection of readings which will help develop the issues raised in this chapter is given in the references which follow.

REFERENCES

Department of Finance (1994). *Guidelines for the Appraisal and Management of Capital Expenditure Proposals in the Public Sector*, Dublin: Department of Finance

Drury, C. (1996). *Management and Cost Accounting*, London: International Thomson Business Press

Institute of Chartered Accountants (Annual). *Accounting Standards*, Milton Keynes: Accountancy Books

Institute of Chartered Accountants (Undated). Handbook, Volumes 2 and 2A: *Accounting*, Dublin: Institute of Chartered Accountants

Jones, R. and M. Pendlebury (1996). *Public Sector Accounting*. London: Pitman

McLaney, E. J. (1991). *Business Finance for Decision Makers*, London: Pitman

Wood, F. (1993). *Business Accounting*, Vols 1 and 2, London: Pitman

4

Non-Financial Performance Measures

SYLVIA DEMPSEY

Introduction

Due to increased competition, particularly from abroad, many Irish manufacturing organisations are finding it difficult to compete on cost, even when employing mass production. In order to remain competitive, they are shifting towards world class manufacturing. Organisations involved in world class manufacturing compete by improving quality, by continuously introducing new products to the market and by responding quickly to the specific needs of their customers. As the focus of their operations changes, so too must the criteria for evaluating their success.

In the past the measures used to evaluate the success of organisations were mainly financial measures such as profitability, liquidity, efficiency, gearing and growth. An evaluation system based purely on financial performance measures worked well when the primary concern of manufacturing organisations was to reduce costs. If costs were reduced, then if nothing else changed, profit would increase. But these measures are no longer sufficient as they fail to assess the performance of world class manufacturing organisations. Modern evaluation systems need to place more emphasis on the non-financial factors critical to the success of manufacturing organisations. More and more emphasis is being placed on measures of quality, innovation and customer satisfaction, as these are the attributes required by Irish organisations to survive and prosper.

An evaluation system need not be based exclusively on either financial or non-financial considerations. To be fully effective, it should focus on both. It should support all the organisation's objectives. The financial measures, examined in the previous chapter, monitor the success of the organisation in achieving its financial objectives. Non-financial measures monitor the

88

progress of the organisation towards its other world class manufacturing objectives such as competitiveness, customer-orientation and market leadership.

Even though there is no clear consensus about which measures should be used, there is widespread recognition of the importance of integrating financial measures with measures such as defect rates, number of new products launched, time to market, order processing time and on-time delivery. An example of such an evaluation system is the balanced scorecard.

The balanced scorecard is a single page (or screen) report which is designed to focus the attention of top managers on the critical success factors of the organisation. It contains the main financial results of the previous period and supplements these with measures of current performance such as customer satisfaction and internal business success; it also contains measures that drive long-term performance such as innovation and learning. This chapter examines the performance measures that could be used by Irish manufacturing organisations, but similar measures could also be appropriate for service organisations.

Criticisms of traditional measures

The balanced scorecard was devised because of the inadequacies of traditional evaluation systems. In recent years, the financial performance measures traditionally used have been severely criticised. These criticisms can be grouped into four main areas.

Firstly, financial performance measures are internally focused. Little or no attention is paid to the environment in which the organisation operates (Drury 1996). Customers' preferences, competitors' actions and new technologies are ignored. Competitive manufacturing organisations need to be able to examine their performance in relation to all these factors. An examination of financial results may indicate that an organisation is achieving its financial targets at the moment. However, the organisation could still be outperformed by its competitors and gradually lose its market share. Therefore, external benchmarking measures are required if the organisation is to maintain its competitive advantage.

Secondly, financial performance measures are backward looking (Clinton and Hsu 1997, Vokurka and Fliedner 1995). They do not tell the full story. They are merely indicators of what has happened in the past (Clarke 1995). For example a report showing return on capital employed and return on investment is just reporting past results rather than explaining how these results were actually achieved. By the time the report is examined it is too late to take corrective action. Consequently, the examination of other measures which indicate current and possible future performance is essential.

Thirdly, financial measures of performance could encourage sub-optimal actions. Investments in marketing, research and development (R&D), training and capital assets are essential to long-term success. Short-term profits are easily increased by cutting the costs associated with these investments. To do so results in the achievement of financial targets now, at the expense of future success (Merchant 1985, Vitale and Mavrinac 1995, Richman 1995). Financial measures overemphasise short-term measures and thus discourage investment in the future of organisations. It is better that a balance is maintained between the achievement of short-term financial targets and long-term strategic objectives.

Finally, financial performance measures provide insufficient information to evaluate organisations that are committed to high quality standards, continuous innovation and customer satisfaction. When organisations invest in quality, innovation and flexible production techniques the result is better product design and reliability and quicker response to customers' requirements. These attributes are not monitored by financial measures (Vitale and Mavrinac 1995).

The development of an evaluation system that will assess the key attributes of world class manufacturing is required. Accordingly, attention moves away from past costs and profits, towards long-term investment in quality and innovation, in an attempt to remain competitive and meet customers' needs in the future (Kaplan 1983, Vitale and Mavrinac 1995).

Benefits of financial measures

Even though financial measures are criticised, many organisations rely on them to evaluate performance. There are several reasons for this. Firstly, accountants find it relatively easy to prepare financial measures. These measures are well understood and easily communicated within an organisation (Clarke 1995). Therefore there is a reluctance to change. Moreover, quality, innovation and customer satisfaction are inherently difficult to measure and this also contributes to the reluctance to change.

Secondly, financial measures are relatively inexpensive to prepare. Companies are legally obliged to prepare annual financial statements. Ratios such as profit margin and return on capital employed can be obtained directly from the annual financial statements (Merchant 1985). Measuring non-financial features of an organisation, such as responsiveness to consumers' needs, requires either additional resources or the reallocation of existing resources.

Thirdly, financial objectives such as profitability, liquidity and growth are among the primary objectives of almost every organisation. Even though they are highly criticised, financial measures do provide a good means of evaluating the achievement of these objectives.

Finally, shareholders and banks usually rely on financial measures to evaluate the performance of organisations. Consequently, it is natural that these are also the measures used for evaluation within the organisation. If an organisation does not excel in the measures used by its investors, it would find it difficult, if not impossible, to obtain funding for future ventures.

Financial measures, therefore, are simple and inexpensive to prepare. They assess financial objectives and provide key information to existing and potential investors. Financial measures would be sufficient if all the objectives of the organisation were financial objectives. However, achieving high quality standards, continuous innovation and customer satisfaction are also important objectives. Of course, financial success is important. However, it is success in non-financial objectives that will eventually contribute to long-term financial success. Therefore, both financial and non-financial objectives should be monitored.

Combination of financial and non-financial measures

An evaluation system should provide accurate feedback in a timely manner on the efficiency and the effectiveness of an organisation in meeting its strategic objectives (Cooper and Kaplan 1991). It is essential to measure financial performance, because cost control, cash flow, gearing and share price are obviously still important. These measures have been fully treated in the previous chapter. But financial measures can only provide a limited assessment of the efficiency and effectiveness of operations. A set of non-financial measures must also be examined.

The necessary set of financial measures is usually obvious; deciding on a set of non-financial measures can be more difficult. There is no optimal mix of non-financial measures; each organisation must find the mix that suits it best. Once a mix of measures is determined the organisation should not stick to it rigidly. It should be altered as the strategies, priorities or circumstances of the organisation change (Vokurka and Fliedner 1995).

Non-financial indicators

The purpose of an evaluation system is to evaluate the performance of the organisation in achieving its objectives. The evaluation system used affects the behaviour of managers and employees by guiding their actions (Keegan 1989). The measures used must motivate them to improve performance. Managers and employees ask themselves 'On which activities are we assessed?', and they do their best to excel in those activities (Eccles 1993, Clarke 1995). If the evaluation system does not measure the correct activities the managers may be channelled into taking the wrong actions.

To be successful in world class manufacturing, Irish organisations must compete by producing high quality, innovative products that are custom-made to the specific needs of customers. Consequently, evaluation systems should evaluate how well these organisations are performing in achieving these objectives (Kaplan 1983, Keegan 1989, Clarke 1995, Ramanathan and Schaffer 1995).

How can a manufacturing organisation measure the achievement of quality? Quality can be measured from both the organisation's point of view (internal measures) and the customer's point of view (external measures). The internal measures could include an examination of the volume of scrap and re-work, the defect rates, the types of defects and machinery downtime. The external measures could include the number of customer complaints, the volume of sales returns, the warranty expenses paid out, and the type of after-sale service required.

What measurements could be used to measure how innovative a manu-facturing organisation is? Innovation, in a manufacturing organisation, can be measured by monitoring such things as the advancement of the R&D department, the number of new products launched, the accuracy, speed and reliability of new product features compared to those of competitors, launch time and customer satisfaction (Kaplan 1994).

How can an organisation measure the extent to which customers' needs, are satisfied? Customers are not only interested in price. They are looking for 'value' (Kaplan 1994). Instead of just examining cost efficiency, an organ-isation should assess its efficiency in meeting its customers' expectations about such things as on-time delivery, quality, reliability, customisation, choice and after-sale service. An organisation can also measure its success in retaining its customers by monitoring the number of repeat orders, the number of customer complaints, the types of complaints and the volume of sales returns.

The balanced scorecard

Kaplan and Norton (1992) devised the balanced scorecard which is 'a set of performance measures that gives top management a fast but comprehensive view of the business'. It outlines some of the financial and non-financial performance indicators that could be included in the evaluation system of a modern organisation.

The balanced scorecard allows top managers evaluate performance from four different perspectives:

• *Financial*. How do the shareholders see the organisation? What do existing and prospective shareholders value in the organisation?

- *Customer*. How do the customers see the organisation? What do existing and prospective customers value from the organisation?

- *Internal business*. What must the organisation excel at in order to achieve the financial and customer objectives?

- *Innovation and learning*. Can the organisation continue to improve its products and services? Can it continue to create future value?

The balanced scorecard brings these four perspectives together, allowing top managers an overall view of the business. The scorecard forces them to look at the most critical indicators of current and future performance, without overloading them with too many measures (Kaplan and Norton 1992). Also, by bringing these different aspects of an organisation together it emphasises the link between the strategic objectives and the actual results (Clarke 1997).

For example, if short-term financial results deteriorate, the managers are in a position to look at the other perspectives to see if they have improved. Spending on improving quality, research and development, manufacturing processes, delivery times and customisation can all lead to reduced short-term performance but, in the long term, can improve competitiveness and contribute to future financial success. Alternatively, cutting such spending can enhance short-term financial performance to the detriment of long-term financial performance. The balanced scorecard thus enables managers to examine these trade-offs allowing them to see 'whether improvements in one area may have been achieved at the expense of another' (Kaplan and Norton 1992).

Financial perspective

The financial perspective evaluates how well the organisation has performed in creating value for its shareholders. Financial measures, though often criticised, form a section of the balanced scorecard for two reasons. Firstly, by examining the ratios which the current and prospective investors use to evaluate the performance of the organisation, financial measures ensure that the organisation looks at itself through the eyes of the shareholders. Secondly, measures of profitability, efficiency, liquidity and growth determine whether the past actions of the organisation have resulted in financial success. If the strategic operations of the organisation do not eventually result in improved financial performance, then they are not successful.

Customer perspective

The customer perspective evaluates how well the organisation has performed in creating value for its customers. To be successful in a competitive market,

Irish manufacturing organisations have to be customer driven. This section of
the balanced scorecard ensures that organisations look at themselves through
the eyes of their customers and that they monitor their performance in
achieving customer satisfaction.

What do customers want? They want responsive supplies, quality,
reliability and products custom-made to suit their needs. Is the organisation
achieving all of these goals? The only way to find out is to translate these
goals into measures and gauge the organisation's performance.

Internal business perspective

The internal business perspective evaluates how well the organisation has
performed in the processes required to achieve the financial and customer
objectives. An organisation must determine which core competencies are
required to ensure market leadership. Once it has determined its core
competencies, it must then specify measures for each. Measures of quality,
productivity and innovation are used in this section of the balanced scorecard.
If organisations excel in these, they will improve customer satisfaction.

Innovation and learning perspective

The innovation and learning perspective evaluates the effectiveness of the
organisation's innovation and learning processes. Irish manufacturing
organisations remain competitive by improving existing products and
processes and continually introducing new products to the market. The
competitive situation is always changing and continuous innovation and
learning is necessary to retain and enhance competitiveness (Newing
1994).

Creating a balanced scorecard

The balanced scorecard is used by many different types of organisation. Each
organisation has its own mission and strategic objectives. Therefore, the goals
and measures used in each organisation's scorecard will vary accordingly. It
is the responsibility of top management to design a scorecard that is suited to
its own needs. The first step is to define the mission of the organisation and to
develop the strategic objectives necessary to implement that mission. The
second step is to determine the goals that must be attained to achieve the
objectives. The final step is to devise measures to gauge the progress of the
organisation in attaining those goals.

The first step is the most important, but also the most difficult, part of
creating a suitable scorecard. Management must clearly define the mission

and translate this mission into meaningful strategic objectives. This involves bringing managers at each level of the organisation together, linking their individual objectives and gaining a consensus about the key objective necessary to achieve the mission of the organisation. This clarifies the mission of the organisation in the minds of all of the managers and illustrates to them the importance of integrating their individual operational and business targets into the overall mission.

Let us look at VCR plc, a hypothetical Irish company that manufactures video recorders for the continental European market. VCR plc was established in 1985 and up to the end of 1997 it manufactured standard video recorders. Its year-end results for 1997 show that, even though costs of production had been reduced (because of strict cost control procedures that were introduced in July 1996), sales volume fell dramatically, resulting in a significant drop in profits from previous years.

The management team of VCR plc met to discuss the possible reasons for the 1997 results and to come up with recommendations for the future. The sales manager was the first to volunteer his view:

'I'm out on the road every day meeting our customers and I know what the problem is. There is too much competition from abroad. The same types of video recorders are imported at a much lower price. What we need to do is to continue our cost cutting exercise. Then we can reduce our sales price. This in turn will lead to an increase in our sales volume and our profits will be back on track. Let's try to cut our production costs further.'

The production manager was shocked. The cost control procedures introduced in 1996 were successful and had reduced the production costs to a highly efficient level. He felt another solution would have to be found:

'I don't agree. We have cut costs as much as we can. Every month when the budgeted and actual figures are compared, we are attaining favourable labour rate and efficiency variances. There is no more room for cutbacks in my department. Perhaps more effort could be put into sales and marketing. Then our sales and profit figures would be better. It is you who are responsible for sales figures. We are doing the best we can – our productivity is up and our labour cost is down.'

The accountant had been working in VCR plc since it was established and had successfully initiated the cost control procedure in 1996. She decided it was time to voice her opinion:

'Okay, the profit figures are low and we need to do something radical to bring them back to the level they were in the early 1990s. I think we have to cut more costs. We had a similar problem before – profits were falling. We successfully cut costs and put our video recorder on the market at the lowest price ever. We became the leading manufacturers in Europe. We can do it again.

I have examined the production costs and there is nothing else we can do there. Let's look at our other costs and see if there is anything there we can cut. For example, our R&D costs and training costs are very high. We could afford cuts there. Those cuts would come straight off the bottom line. If we cut those, our profits would increase immediately.'

The manager of the R&D department did not like the idea, but it seemed to make sense. A new recruit in the accounting department had previously worked in Electro Ltd, an Irish electronics company involved in mass-production. It closed down because it could not compete with foreign electronics companies. Cost-cutting exercises had taken place, but were unsuccessful as it was impossible to compete with import prices. He decided to tell them what he thought:

> 'I experienced this problem in Electro Ltd. You must realise that the company cannot maintain its profitability in the future unless you produce a product that is competitive in the marketplace. And I don't just mean a competitive price. No matter how much you cut costs, it is still cheaper to make these standard products in other countries. If VCR plc continues to mass-produce, it will eventually start making losses. That's what happened in Electro Ltd.
>
> Why not find other ways of giving our customers value? Why don't we change over to producing video recorders that have innovative features that are not on the mass-produced ones? If the customers like these features, they will buy our product, even if it isn't the cheapest one on the market.'

The manager of the R&D department decided that this was her chance to defend her department and show that it could be used to make VCR plc more competitive in the future:

> 'Well, I have some ideas about how to make our video recorders more appealing to the market. First of all, I think we should have more variety in colour and shape. People like products that fit in with their colour schemes at home. Secondly, I think we could reduce the size of the video recorder, perhaps call it a "microcorder". Thirdly, I think we should invest money now in the development of a double tape-deck video recorder. The user could tape two programmes at the same time or watch a recorded programme while taping another. In fact, I have loads of ideas for developing a better quality product with innovative features that the customers will like, for example a voice recognition video recorder.
>
> I know that other companies could copy these ideas, but VCR plc could try to be the first to have new products on the market. We could then develop new ideas while the others are copying our old ideas. We could be the market leaders.'

The management team were impressed by these ideas and made three major decisions in an attempt to make VCR plc more customer-oriented. Firstly, it would carry out more market research and then try to adapt its existing video recorder to suit the customers' requirements. Secondly, it would try to improve both the quality of the products and the efficiency of the after-sales service. This would add value to existing products and make them more desirable to customers. Thirdly, a major investment in the R&D department would be necessary. Not only would VCR plc develop the video recorders the customers required now, but it would also research the viability of some other innovative ideas for the future.

The management team knew that these decisions would change the operations of VCR plc, so they decided to redefine the mission. When asked what the old mission statement of VCR plc was, no one could remember it. So they decided that a new mission statement was necessary. The new mission was 'to provide the market with a range of quality video recorders to suit the customers' needs'. The strategic objectives developed to implement this mission were: responsiveness to customer requirements, market leadership, continuous innovation, reduced defects, better quality and cost consciousness, while at the same time keeping the shareholders satisfied.

Once the strategic objectives were determined, it was then possible to set short-term goals to monitor how well the company was progressing. These goals would also ensure that the new mission statement would not be forgotten in the day-to-day running of the business. A balanced scorecard would be used to record the goals. It would contain financial measures focusing on short-term financial results of importance to shareholders and non-financial goals focusing on quality, innovation and customer satisfaction.

A meeting was called, at which the manager of each department was present. Each manager was asked to list the goals required of his or her department. All the lists were examined and the key goals necessary to achieve the overall strategic objectives of the company were chosen to be included in a balanced scorecard, which is shown in Figure 4.1. This scorecard would be examined by VCR plc's top management each month.

The 'financial results' section of VCR plc's balanced scorecard contained four goals that the finance department thought were important to the shareholders, namely profitability, efficiency, liquidity and growth. The finance department was satisfied that two or three ratios for each goal would be sufficient to ensure that VCR plc looked at itself through the eyes of the shareholders and retained its cost consciousness. Top management was glad to see a reduction in the number of financial measures. In the past they received a bound volume of financial results every month but they did not know what most of the figures meant and did not have the time to find out.

Just as the 'financial results' section of the scorecard looks at the company through the eyes of its shareholder, the 'customer satisfaction' section looks at the company through the eyes of its customers. This section contained four goals that the marketing, sales and customer complaint departments thought were important to the customers. These were: a responsive supply, quality and reliability, customisation, and, of course, price. One or two targets were decided for each of these goals. If these targets were met, then progression toward achievement of two of the strategic objectives of the company (responsiveness to customer requirements and higher quality standards) would be guaranteed.

Figure 4.1: VCR plc's first balanced scorecard

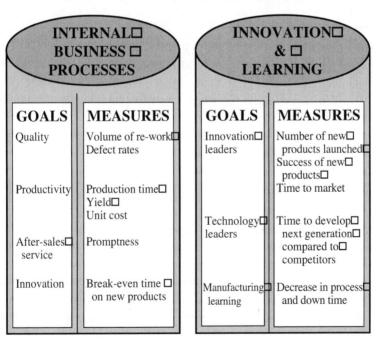

The 'internal business processes' section contained four goals that the production, R&D and after-sales service departments thought were vital if the strategic objectives of market leadership, continuous innovation, reduced defects, higher quality standards and cost effectiveness were to be met. These goals are high quality standards in production, retention of existing productivity levels, an efficient after-sales service and increased innovation.

The 'innovation and learning' section contained three goals, namely innovation leadership, technology leadership and manufacturing learning. VCR plc plan to remain competitive by improving existing products and manufacturing processes, and striving to be the first company to introduce new technology to the market. If it reached these goals then continuous innovation and responsiveness to customer requirements would be achieved.

We see from this example how a company, by dividing the evaluation system into four perspectives, can ensure that both the shareholders' and customers' views are considered, that quality and productivity are monitored and that innovation becomes one of its priorities. Together, the diverse measures used in the scorecard encourage movement towards the company's strategic objectives.

Strategy and the evaluation system

One of the advantages of the balanced scorecard is its ability to facilitate a review and update of the mission statement, strategic objectives and goals of the organisation (Butler, Letza and Neale, 1997). When the scorecard is being created, the mission statement and strategic objectives of the organisation are clarified and linked to short-term targets, and they are communicated throughout the organisation when the scorecard is put into operation.

Organisations operate in a volatile environment. Consequently their strategies must change to stay in line with the market. There is no point in examining past performance measures when it is the future that is important to the survival of an organisation.

Let us return to VCR plc. Each month the balanced scorecard was examined by the top management. This allowed VCR plc to investigate its progress towards its mission. In the 'financial results' section, it found that the profitability and liquidity positions had been adversely affected by the increased investments in market research, quality, customer service and innovation. Efficiency and growth (the other two measures in the 'financial results' section) had improved slightly.

In the 'customer satisfaction' section, order processing time and time to delivery had improved; sales returns, warranty claims and complaints also improved due to increasing quality levels; and the percentage of sales from custom-made products was rising slowly. Prices were still higher than those of the competitors, but VCR plc was confident that it was delivering value to its customers.

In the 'internal business processes' section, the volume of re-work remained at a low level; the reasons for defects were examined regularly resulting in a fall in defect rates; production time, yield and unit cost were maintained; after-sales service was more efficiently run; and break-even time for new products was still longer than targeted, but it was starting to improve.

In the 'innovation and learning' section, the number of new products launched, success of new products and time to market were all improving gradually; VCR plc seemed to be developing new products faster than its main competitor; even though process time and down-time had not improved, they were still at an acceptable level.

As anticipated, the investments in market research, quality and efficiency, and R&D had adversely affected the financial measurements in the short term. However, the other three sections of the scorecard had benefited from these investments. The management team was happy with the result. Nevertheless, the production manager had a suggestion:

'It is obvious that our new mission is a success. That is evident from the balanced scorecards of the last six months. On the production floor we have improved quality, reduced defect rates and volume of re-works, increased our product range and retained our productivity levels. As the manager of the production team, I am delighted with the progress.

However, the production team does not share my enthusiasm. It feels as if it had no say in these matters. The customers and the shareholders are kept happy but the employees are not considered.'

The management team was astonished that it had not thought of this before. It decided that in order to achieve its mission it was necessary to add 'the best interests of its employees' to the other strategic objectives of the company. This objective was translated into a goal, namely, 'staff satisfaction' and entered in the 'internal business processes' section of the scorecard. Two new measures were included in the scorecard to evaluate the success of VCR plc in reaching this goal, namely 'staff attitude survey' and 'number of employee suggestions'. Also, in the 'innovation and learning' section an additional measure, namely 'number of staff training days' was added to the manufacturing learning goal.

The team agreed that 'decrease in process and down-time', a measure to assess the achievement of manufacturing learning, was already included in the 'internal business processes' section under productivity. Therefore it was taken out to make room for the new, and more important, measures. Figure 4.2 shows the revised balanced scorecard.

Figure 4.2: The revised balanced scorecard of VCR plc

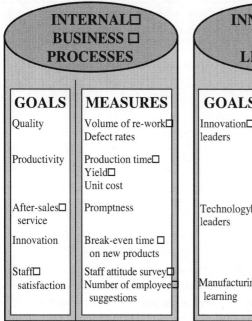

FINANCIAL☐ RESULTS

GOALS	MEASURES
Profitability	Net profit margin☐ Return on capital☐ employed
Efficiency	Stock turnover☐ Debtors' days☐ Creditors' days
Liquidity	Current ratio☐ Acid test ratio
Growth	Market share☐ Revenue growth☐ Profit growth

CUSTOMER☐ SATISFACTION

GOALS	MEASURES
Responsive☐ supply	Order processing☐ time☐ On-time delivery
Quality &☐ reliability	Sales returns☐ Warranty claims☐ Complaints
Customis-☐ ation	Percentage of sales☐ from custom-made☐ products
Price	Prices versus☐ competitors' prices

INTERNAL☐ BUSINESS ☐ PROCESSES

GOALS	MEASURES
Quality	Volume of re-work☐ Defect rates
Productivity	Production time☐ Yield☐ Unit cost
After-sales☐ service	Promptness
Innovation	Break-even time ☐ on new products
Staff☐ satisfaction	Staff attitude survey☐ Number of employee☐ suggestions

INNOVATION☐ & ☐ LEARNING

GOALS	MEASURES
Innovation☐ leaders	Number of new☐ products launched☐ Success of new☐ products☐ Time to market
Technology☐ leaders	Time to develop☐ next generation☐ compared to☐ competitors
Manufacturing☐ learning	Number of staff☐ training days

Conclusion

Cost reduction cannot be the main aim of Irish manufacturing organisations. If it were, they would not survive. In the global economy that exists today, manufacturing organisations, located in low wage-rate countries, can mass-produce products and supply them to the Irish market at a cost lower than even the most efficient Irish firms. Instead of competing on cost, Irish manufacturing organisations must use the skills and resources available to them to compete in other ways. Today's consumer looks for value. Irish manufacturers must continuously respond.

The expectations of the market are becoming more elaborate. Irish manufacturing organisations must invest both in innovation in order to improve their production techniques and in customer surveys in order to widen their product range. The improvement of production techniques reduces the use of routine methods of production that could easily be imitated by mass-producers in lower wage rate economies. Widening the product range satisfies the diversity of consumer needs.

The traditional financial evaluation systems of Irish manufacturing organisations are no longer adequate. New systems need to be devised to incorporate changing business strategies. These systems should include not only financial but also non-financial measures, such as measures of quality, innovation and customer satisfaction; measures which reflect the strategic objectives of the organisations.

This chapter illustrated how a balanced scorecard can be used to evaluate the performance of world class manufacturing organisations. Financial measures on their own do not focus managerial attention on the strategic objectives of the business. Indeed, they could guide management into making sub-optimal decisions. The balanced scorecard has at its core the mission and strategic objectives of the organisation. When examining the scorecard, top management is forced to evaluate the organisation's mission and strategic objectives and update them if necessary.

The successful implementation of a balanced scorecard requires the full support of top management based on an understanding that the non-financial measures are as important as the financial ones, and should not be sacrificed for short-term financial gains. Indeed, there is a strong case to use scorecard results as an input when determining managerial rewards.

An effective evaluation system, on its own, cannot guarantee success in the achievement of an organisation's strategic objectives. However, it can highlight the strengths and weaknesses of an organisation, place emphasis on the important aspects of the business, provide targets for managers, steer them towards the achievement of these targets and enable them to evaluate their success.

REFERENCES

Butler, A., S. R. Letza, and B. Neale (1997). 'Linking the Balanced Scorecard to Strategy', *Long Range Planning*, April, pp 242-53

Clarke, P. (1995). 'Non-financial Measures of Performance Management', *Accountancy Ireland*, April, pp 22-3

Clarke, P., (1997). 'The Balanced Scorecard', *Accountancy Ireland*, June, pp 25-6

Clinton, B. D. and K. Hsu (1997). 'Linking Manufacturing Control to Management Control', *Management Accounting*, September, pp 18-24

Cooper, R. and R.S. Kaplan (1991). *The Design of Cost Management Systems*, Englewood Cliffs: Prentice Hall

Drury, C. (1996). *Management and Cost Accounting*, London: International Thomson Business Press

Eccles, P. (1993). 'Planning for Improved Performance', *Management Accounting*, January, pp 53-4

Johnson, H. J. and R.S. Kaplan (1991). *Relevance Lost: The Rise and Fall of Management Accounting*, Cambridge: Harvard Business School Press

Kaplan, R.S. (1983). 'Managing Manufacturing Performance: A New Challenge for Managerial Accounting Research', *The Accounting Review*, Vol. LVIII, No. 4, October, pp 686-705

Kaplan, R.S. (1994). 'Management Accounting (1984-1994): Development of New Practice and Theory', *Management Accounting Research*, pp 247-60

Kaplan, R.S. and D.P. Norton (1992). 'The Balanced Scorecard – Measures that Drive Performance', *Harvard Business Review*, Jan/ Feb, pp 71-9

Keegan, D.P. (1989). 'Are Your Performance Measures Obsolete?', *Management Accounting*, June, pp 45-50

Merchant, K. A. (1985). 'Control in Business Organisations', Place Pitman, pp 91-120

Newing, R. (1994). 'Benefits of the Balanced Scorecard', *Accountancy*, November, pp 52-3

Ramanathan, K.V. and D.S. Schaffer (1995). 'How am I Doing?', *Journal of Accountancy*, May, pp 79-82

Richman, T. (1995). 'Performance Measurement', *Harvard Business Review*, July/-August, pp 10-11

Vitale, M.R. and S.C. Mavrinac (1995). 'How Effective is Your Performance Measurement System?' *Management Accounting*, August, pp 43-7

Vokurka, R. and G. Fliedner (1995). 'Measuring Operating Performance: A Specific Case Study', *Production and Inventory Management Journal*, First Quarter, pp 38-43

5

Appraising Capital Expenditure Programmes

PHILIP BYRNE

Introduction

The purpose of this chapter is to consider the most important techniques for appraising capital expenditure projects, namely, discounted cash flow (DCF) techniques. The chapter will treat the following: the principles of DCF, net present value (NPV), constant annual cash flows, relevant cash flows, internal rate of return (IRR), comparison of NPV and IRR, abandoning projects, sensitivity analysis, replacement theory, project control and evaluation.

The chapter will proceed by outlining basic principles and by using examples to illustrate important issues.

Underlying principles of discounted cash flow

Discounted cash flow is a capital expenditure appraisal technique founded on the concept of time value of money (TVM). People acting rationally prefer money now rather than in some future period of time or, in more formal language, they have a present value preference for money. The basis for this is that €100 now will be worth more than €100 in one year's time.

To understand the notion of TVM, we need to examine the workings of compound interest.

Example 1
An entrepreneur wishes to know the value of €20,000 invested at 10% compounded annually over four years. Suppose we invest €20,000 for four years at 10% per annum, then the compounded future value will be as follows:

Table 5.1: Compounded future values

End of year	Interest earned on investment	Total worth of investment
0	0	20,000
1	$20,000 \times 0.1 = 2,000$	$20,000 + 2,000 = 22,000$
2	$22,000 \times 0.1 = 2,200$	$22,000 + 2,200 = 24,200$
3	$24,200 \times 0.1 = 2,420$	$24,200 + 2,420 = 26,620$
4	$26,620 \times 0.1 = 2,662$	$26,620 + 2,662 = 29,282$

Thus, if you invest €20,000 at 10% compound interest for 4 years, your investment will be worth €29,282 in four years' time. Year 0 in the first column means that no time has yet elapsed. Year 1 means at the end of the first year and so on.

The values in this example could also have been calculated by using the following compound interest formula:

$$FV_n = PV_0(1+K)^n$$

Where FV_n = the future value of an investment in n years

PV_0 = the amount invested at the beginning of the period (year 0)

K = the rate of return on the investment

n = the number of years for which the money is invested.

Thus the calculation for €20,000 invested at 10% for three years is:

$$FV_3 = 20,000(1+0.10)^3 = 26,620$$

Therefore given the choice of receiving €20,000 or €26,620 in three years time we should be indifferent, as we have calculated that the value of €20,000 in three years time will be €26,620 if we invest it at 10%.

We can manipulate the compound interest formula to form the commonly used discounting formula which allows us to convert future cash flows into their present value.

$$PV_0 = \frac{FV_n}{(1+K)^n}$$

As can be seen from the foregoing, €1 received today is not the same as €1 received one year from now, because money received today can be used to earn interest over the coming year. Thus €1 in one year's time would be worth €0.9091 today if the interest prevailed at 10 per cent. This is derived as follows:

$$PV_1 = \frac{1.00}{(1+ 0.10)^1} = 0.9091$$

In Example 1, all of the year-end values are equal as far as TVM is concerned. Thus €22,000 received at the end of year 1 is equivalent to €20,000 received today and invested at 10 per cent (i.e. its present value). We can arrive at this value using the discounting formula as follows:

$$PV_1 = \frac{FV_1}{(1+ 0.10)^1}$$

$$PV_1 = \frac{22,000}{(1.10)^1} = 20,000$$

Net present value (NPV)

Net present value is the result when the initial investment is subtracted from the sum of net future cash flows of money discounted at the appropriate discount rate. If the NPV is positive, it is a financial management indicator of the financial worthiness of the project, and if negative, an indicator of the financial unworthiness of the project.

Establishing the financial worthiness of stand alone projects

Before a net present value can be calculated and analysed, the following steps must be followed:

- Establish the capital project's cash inflows and the possible savings for the enterprise. Examples of inflows are: project revenues, tax receipts, government grants and sale or scrap value of project assets. Examples of savings are: reductions in repair costs and in labour costs.
- Establish all the capital project's outflows. Examples of outflows are: initial investment, tax and working capital investment.
- Establish the life of the project.
- Establish the appropriate discount rate (rate of return). The discount rate is more commonly referred to as the cost of capital (i.e. cost of long-term borrowing).

The following example illustrates how to calculate NPV.

Example 2

Suppose the management of an enterprise is considering purchasing a certain type of machine. The machine which is estimated to have a 4-year life span, has an initial capital cost of €160,000, with a cost of capital of 10 per cent.

Inflows will occur as the machine is expected to achieve labour savings of €110,000 in Year 1 and €100,000 in the subsequent three years, and to have a residual/scrap value of €20,000 in the final year.

Outflows will occur because in addition to the initial investment of €160,000, the expected annual running costs are €50,000 per annum.

Table 5.2 allows us to establish the financial worthiness of the project by calculating the project's NPV. The positive NPV of €21,241 indicates a worthwhile project.

Table 5.2: Financial worthiness of a project

Year	Inflows	Outflows	Net Flow	Discount Factor	Present Value
	€	€	€		€
0	-	(160,000)	(160,000)	$\dfrac{1}{(1+0.10)^0} = 1.0$	(160,000)
1	110,000	(50,000)	60,000	$\dfrac{1}{(1+0.10)^1} = 0.9091$	54,546
2	100,000	(50,000)	50,000	$\dfrac{1}{(1+0.10)^2} = 0.8264$	41,320
3	100,000	(50,000)	50,000	$\dfrac{1}{(1+0.10)^3} = 0.7513$	37,565
4	*120,000	(50,000)	70,000	$\dfrac{1}{(1+0.10)^4} = 0.6830$	47,810
				Net Present Value (NPV) =	21,241

* €120,000 includes €20,000 for scrap value.

In order to calculate the NPV, it is very useful to set out the data in the above tabular format. Discount tables, which are presented in Appendix II at the end of this chapter, provide a very useful ready reckoner for establishing the discount rate for any period of time.

Constant annual cash inflows

When the annual cash flows are constant, the calculation is relatively simple. Example 3 illustrates this.

Example 3

An enterprise has the opportunity to invest €1,000 in a project which will yield cash inflows of €600 per year for three years. The minimum desired rate of return is 10 per cent. The enterprise wishes to know if it should invest in this project.

The discount factors when the cash flows are the same each year are set out in Appendix II at the end of this chapter. These tables are known as annuity tables or cumulative present value tables. If you refer to Appendix II you will see that the discount factor for three years at 10 per cent is 2.487.

Table 5.3: Net present value using annuity table

Annual Cash Inflow	Discount Factor	Present Value
€		€
600	2.487	1,492
	Less investment cost	(1,000)
	Net Present Value (NPV)	492

The total present value for the period is calculated by multiplying the cash inflow by the discount factor. It is important to bear in mind that Appendix II can only be used when the annual cash flows are the same each year.

The following example is a more sophisticated method of calculating NPV with the use of annuity tables.

Example 4

An enterprise is considering manufacturing a new product which would involve the use of both a new machine (costing €150,000) and an existing machine, which cost €80,000 two years ago and has a current net book value of €60,000. The latter machine has so far been under-utilised and has spare capacity to contribute to the manufacture of the new product.

Annual sales of the product are expected to be 5,000 units, selling at €32.00 per unit.

Unit costs are expected to be:	€
Direct labour (4 hours @ €2)	8.00
Direct materials	7.00
Fixed costs including depreciation	9.00
	24.00

The project is expected to have a 5-year life, after which the new machine would have a net residual value of €10,000. Because direct labour is continually in short supply, labour resources would have to be diverted from other work which currently earns a contribution of €1.50 per direct labour hour. Working capital requirements would be €10,000 at the outset rising to €15,000 by the end of the first year and remaining at this level until the end of the project, when it will all be recovered. The cost of capital to the enterprise is 20 per cent. The enterprise wishes to know the NPV and whether or not the project is worthwhile.

The relevant cash flows (which will be discussed in more detail in the following section) are as follows:

			€
•	Year 0	Purchase of the new machine	(150,000)
•	Year 5	Residual value	10,000
•	Years 1-5	Contribution from new product	
		5,000 units × €[32–(8+7))]	85,000
		Contribution foregone	
		5,000 units × 4 hours × €1.50	(30,000)

- The project requires €10,000 of working capital at the outset and a further €5,000 by the end of the first year. These cash outflows reduce the net cash flow for the period to which they relate. When the working capital tied up in the project is 'recovered' at the end of the project, it will provide an extra cash inflow (for example debtors will eventually pay up).

- All other costs, which are past costs, notional accounting costs, or costs which would be incurred anyway without the project, are not relevant to the investment decision.

- The NPV is calculated as follows:

Table 5.4: Net present value of net cash flow using present value and annuity tables

Year	Equipment	Working Capital	Contribution	Net cash flow	Discount factor at 20% cost of capital	PV of net cash flow
	€	€	€	€		€
0	(150,000)	(10,000)		(160,000)	1.000	(160,000)
1		(5,000)		(5,000)	0.833	(4,165)
1-5			55,000	55,000	2.991	164,505
5	10,000	15,000		25,000	0.402	10,050
				Net present value (NPV)		10,390

The NPV is €10,390 and the project is worthwhile.

Relevant cash flows

Investment decisions, like all other financial decisions, should be analysed in terms of the cash flows directly attributable to them. These cash flows include the incremental cash flows following commencement of the investment.

Before looking at the cash flows that should be included in any discounted cash flow (DCF) analysis, we should note those items that should be excluded.

- *Depreciation*. This is an accounting transaction, not a cash flow. Therefore depreciation charges should be excluded from DCF calculations. If profit figures after depreciation have been provided, the profits need to be converted into cash flows. This is done by adding back depreciation costs.

- *Apportioned fixed costs*. The cost of producing an item may include an apportionment of factory-wide fixed costs using some standard basis for absorption. These should be excluded. Fixed costs may appear as a cash outflow in a DCF calculation, but only if it is known that they will increase as a result of accepting a project. Fixed costs appear in a DCF calculation as a cash saving (inflow) if they will decrease as a result of accepting the project.

- *Book values of assets*. These are not cash flows and must be ignored.

- *Interest payments*. In most cases it can be assumed that the cost of interest has been taken into account by the discounting process. Interest payments should be ignored since to do otherwise would be 'double counting'.

- *Sunk costs*. Any sums that have already been spent or committed and cannot be influenced by the investment decision should be ignored.

The cash flows that should be included in the DCF calculations are those which are specifically incurred as a result of accepting the project and benefits, or losses, foregone as a result of not accepting the project.

Absolute and incremental cash flows

When deciding between two mutually exclusive projects, only one of which can be accepted, two approaches are possible:

- Discount the cash flows of each project separately and compare NPVs; or

- Find the differential (or incremental) cash flow year by year, i.e. the difference between the cash flows of the two projects. Then use the discounted value of those differential cash flows to establish a preference.

Either approach will lead to the same conclusion.

Example 5

Two projects, A and B, are under consideration. Either, but not both, may be accepted. The relevant discount rate is 10 per cent.

This example uses both approaches, namely, discounting each cash flow separately, and discounting relative (incremental or differential) cash flows.

The cash flows are as follows:

Time	Project A €	Project B €
0	(1,500)	(2,500)
1	500	500
2	600	800
3	700	1,100
4	500	1,000
5	Nil	500

Discounting each cash flow separately yields the following outcome:

Table 5.5: Discounting separate cash flows

Time	PV factor @ 10%	Project A Cash flow €	PV €	Project B Cash flow €	PV €
0	1.00	(1,500)	(1,500)	(2,500)	(2,500)
1	0.9091	500	455	500	455
2	0.8264	600	496	800	661
3	0.7513	700	526	1,100	826
4	0.6830	500	342	1,000	683
5	0.6209	Nil	Nil	500	310
NPV			€319		€435

Project B is preferred because its NPV exceeds that of A by €(435 − 319) = €116   €116

Discounting relative cash flows yields the following outcome:

Table 5.6: Discounting relative cash flows

Time	Project A	Project B	Incremental cash flow B-A	PV factor @ 10%	PV of incremental cash flow
0	(1,500)	(2,500)	(1,000)	1.00	(1,000)
1	500	500	Nil	0.9091	Nil
2	600	800	200	0.8264	165
3	700	1,100	400	0.7513	300
4	500	1,000	500	0.6830	341
5	Nil	500	500	0.6209	310
NPV of incremental cash flow					€116

In other words the net present value of the cash flows of project B is €116 greater than those of project A; therefore B is preferred. Both approaches give the same result but the latter provides a useful short-cut to computation when comparing two projects as long as it is known in advance that one must be undertaken.

Example 6
The following example is typical of problems relating to incremental cash flows.

An enterprise has decided to increase its productive capacity to meet an anticipated increase in demand for its products. The extent of this increase in capacity has still to be determined, and a management meeting has been called to decide which of the following two mutually exclusive proposals, A and B, should be undertaken. Each proposal has an expected lifetime of ten years.

The following information is available:

	Proposal A €	Proposal B €
Capital expenditure:		
Buildings	50,000	100,000
Plant	200,000	300,000
Installation	10,000	15,000
Net income:		
Annual pre-depreciation profits	70,000	95,000
Other relevant income/expenditure:		
Sales promotion (note (i))	–	15,000
Plant scrap value (note (ii))	10,000	15,000
Buildings disposable value (note (ii))	30,000	60,000
Working capital required over the project life	50,000	65,000

Notes:
(i) An exceptional amount of expenditure on sales promotion of €15,000 will have to be spent in Year 2 of proposal B. This has not been taken into account in calculating pre-depreciation profits.

(ii) The enterprise intends to dispose of the plant and buildings in ten years' time.

The discount rate is 8 per cent. The enterprise would like to know which of the alternatives is preferable.

Since the decision has been made to increase capacity (i.e. 'to do nothing' is not an alternative), the easiest approach is to discount the incremental cash flows.

The tabular approach is still appropriate, particularly as the project lasts for 10 years.

Table 5.7: Discounting incremental cash flows

Time		A €,000	B €,000	B-A €,000	8% Factor	PV €,000
0	Capital expenditure	(260)	(415)	(155)	1.00	(155)
0	Working capital	(50)	(65)	(15)	1.00	(15)
2	Promotion	–	(15)	(15)	0.8573	(12.860)
1-10	Net income	70	95	25	6.7100	167.75
10	Scrap proceeds	40	75	35	0.4632	16.212
10	Working capital	50	65	15	0.4632	6.948

Net Present Value (€,000) 8.05

The present value of proposal B exceeds that of proposal A by €8,050 at 8 per cent and therefore proposal B is preferred.

The foregoing example makes two assumptions. Firstly it assumes that the disposal value of buildings is realistic and that all other figures have been realistically appraised. Secondly it assumes that expenditure on working capital is incurred at the beginning of the project life and recovered at the end.

The incremental approach is effective in comparing two projects when one must be chosen. It may not, however, be reliable when neither project need be chosen. For example, if two projects both had negative NPVs the incremental approach would favour the project with the 'least negative' NPV. Of course, a manager with the freedom not to choose would in this case choose neither.

Internal rate of return (IRR)

For so-called conventional projects, i.e. those where a single cash outflow is followed by subsequent cash inflows, it is often useful to compute the internal rate of return (IRR) of the project. The internal rate of return is that discount rate which gives a net present value of zero.

It is sometimes known as the yield, or DCF yield, or internal yield, but these terms may lead to confusion and their use is not recommended.

In general, it is necessary to compute the IRR by trial and error, that is to compute NPVs at various discount rates until the discount rate which gives an NPV of zero is found.

The IRR can be thought of as the maximum rate of interest that can be paid on the finance for a project without making a loss.

Example 7
An enterprise wishes to make a capital investment of €1.5m but is unsure whether to invest in one of two machines each costing that amount. The net cash inflows from the two projects are as follows:

Time	1	2	3
Machine X (€,000)	900	600	500
Machine Y (€,000)	700	700	700

The enterprise wishes in the first instance to find the IRR of machine X.

At a discount rate of 10 per cent, the net present value is:

$$-\text{€}1,500,000 + \frac{\text{€}900,000}{1.10} + \frac{\text{€}600,000}{(1.10)^2} + \frac{\text{€}500,000}{(1.10)^3} = \text{€}189,707$$

The aim is to find the discount rate that gives an NPV of zero. Since the project has a positive NPV at 10 per cent, the later cash flows have not been reduced (discounted) enough and a higher discount rate must be chosen; try 20 per cent.

At a discount rate of 20 per cent the NPV is calculated as follows:

$$-\text{€}1,500,000 + \frac{\text{€}900,000}{1.20} + \frac{\text{€}600,000}{(1.20)^2} + \frac{\text{€}500,000}{(1.20)^3} = -\text{€}43,981$$

This is clearly closer to the IRR than 10 per cent, but not that close. One can continue to try discount rates between 10 and 20 per cent or else use a short-cut.

- NPV has fallen from a positive €189,707 to a negative €43,981 (by €233,688) as the discount rate has increased by 10% (from 10% to 20%). This is a fall of €23,369 per percentage point increase.

- To find the IRR the NPV needs to fall another €189,707.

- To achieve this, the discount rate must be increased by:

$$\frac{\text{€}189,707}{\text{€}23,369} = 8.12 \text{ percentage points}$$

- Therefore the IRR is 10% + 8.12% = 18.12%

This approach, known as interpolation, is one of a number of approaches that may be taken to calculating the IRR and is the only one to be considered here. The approach we have used can be generalised as follows:

$$IRR = A + \left(\frac{N_A}{N_A - N_B}\right)(B\text{-}A)$$

where
A = lower discount rate = 10%
B = higher discount rate = 20%
NA = NPV at rate A = €189,707
NB = NPV at rate B = −€43,981

Using this formula we derive the IRR for the foregoing example as follows:

$$10\% + \left(\frac{189{,}707}{189{,}707 + 43{,}981}\right)(20\% - 10\%) = 18.12\%$$

Figure 5.1: The NPV and the discount rate

Figure 5.1 illustrates in the case of example 7, the relationship between NPV and the discount rate along with the determination of IRR. It shows that the NPV is zero at 18.12 per cent which is therefore the IRR.

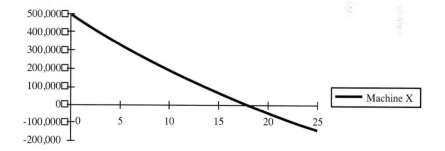

Net present value and internal rate of return

Different types of investment decision

We have considered two different DCF methods: NPV and IRR. When used to analyse a project, the decision is easily made:

- If a project has a positive NPV it should be accepted.

- If a project has an IRR greater than the required rate of return, accept it.

Since the two DCF methods are based on the same underlying principle – the time value of money – one would expect them to give identical investment decisions. This is not always so.

Different types of investment decision can be identified, namely decisions on

- single investment

- mutually exclusive investments

- projects with multiple yields.

The two DCF methods may not always give the same conclusion. The different types of decision are considered in turn.

- Single investment decision

When deciding only whether or not to accept a single capital project, no ambiguity arises. A project will be accepted if it has a positive NPV; if it has a positive NPV then it will have an IRR that is greater than the required rate of return. Figure 5.1 above illustrates the point.

- Mutually exclusive investments

Organisations may often face decisions in which only one of two or more investments can be undertaken; these are called mutually exclusive investment decisions. If NPV is used, the project with the highest NPV is chosen. If IRR is used, the project with the highest IRR is chosen. In these circumstances NPV and IRR may give conflicting recommendations. This is illustrated in the following example.

Example 8
An enterprise is considering two short-term investment opportunities, project A and project B, which have the following cash flows.

Project	Time	
	0	1
Project A (€,000)	(200)	240
Project B (€,000)	(100)	125

The enterprise has a cost of capital of 10 per cent and it wishes to find the NPVs and IRRs of the two projects. These are calculated as follows:

	NPV	IRR
	€,000	%
Project A: $-200 + \dfrac{240}{1.10}$	18.18	20
Project B: $-100 + \dfrac{125}{1.10}$	13.64	25

The IRRs could be found either by trial and error or by using the interpolation formula introduced above. It is easier to notice that project A, over 1 year, earns €40,000 on an investment of €200,000 (a 20 per cent return) whilst project B earns €25,000 on €100,000 (25 per cent).

Project A has the higher NPV whilst B has the higher IRR and there is clearly a conflict between the two methods.

This conflict can be seen in graphical form. If the NPVs of the two projects were calculated for a range of discount rates and a graph of NPVs against the discount rate plotted on the same axes it would look as shown in Figure 5.2.

Figure 5.2: NPV v Discount rate for mutually exclusive projects

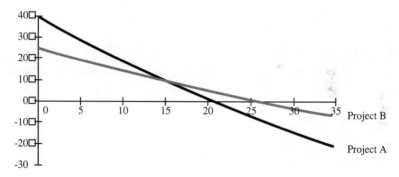

Each graph slopes downwards indicating that the NPV decreases as the discount rate increases for a 'conventional' project. The line representing project A starts at €40,000 (i.e. €240,000 – €200,000); the line representing project B starts at €25,000 (i.e. €125,000 – €100,000). The lines cut the horizontal axis in their IRRs of 20 per cent and 25 per cent and intersect at approximately 15 per cent. Project B has the higher IRR, whereas at the cost of capital of 10 per cent (in fact of any rate below 15 per cent) project A has the higher NPV.

Although NPV and IRR are based on the same principle of time value of money they are calculated in very different ways and there is no reason why they should give the same ranking for mutually exclusive projects.

Project A is preferred because it provides an incremental benefit of €4,540 (i.e. €18,180 – €13,640) over project B when discounted at 10 per cent.

In general, for mutually exclusive projects the NPV method is preferred to the IRR. The NPV method, by choosing the project with the greatest net benefit in current money terms, ensures the largest contribution to the value of an enterprise. The IRR method, as shown in the example above, can choose a project which will add less value than is possible to the enterprise. The IRR method does not take cognizance of the size of a project and may favour an unsuitably small project simply because of its higher rate of return.

• Projects with multiple yields
If mutually exclusive investments provide one reason why the IRR should not be used as a principal investment appraisal method, projects with multiple yields reduce IRR's status still further.

A weakness of the IRR method is that projects may either have no IRR or several IRRs as illustrated in the following example.

Example 9
Consider the following projects with cash flows over a three-year period.

Table 5.8: Projects with irregular IRR

Time	Project A	Project B	Project C
	€	€	€
0	(5,000)	(10,000)	(100,000)
1	2,000	23,000	360,000
2	2,000	(13,200)	(431,000)
3	2,000	(1,000)	171,600

An enterprise wishes to know the NPV of these projects over the range 0–40 per cent at 5 per cent intervals and to see the results on three separate graphs.

Table 5.9: NPVs at 5% intervals

Rate	0	5	10	15	20	25	30	35	40
NPV$_A$	1,000	447	(26)	(434)	(787)	(1,096)	(1,368)	(1,608)	(1,822)
NPV$_B$	(1,200)	(931)	(750)	(637)	(579)	(560)	(574)	(613)	(670)
NPV$_C$	600	162	0	(25)	0	19	0	(76)	(219)

The three graphs are shown below.

Figure 5.3: Project A

Project A is a 'conventional' project, with one outflow followed by several net inflows, and shows the expected pattern of NPV decreasing as the discount rate increases. Table 5.9 shows that project A has one IRR at just under 10 per cent.

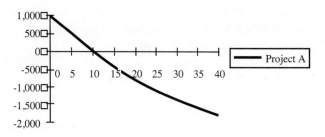

Figure 5.4: Project B

Project B has no IRR. Project B's cash flows could be described as unconventional with outflows of a significant size appearing at the beginning and end of the 'project' (which is always unprofitable but is least unprofitable at 25 per cent).

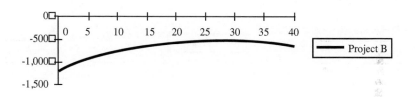

Figure 5.5: Project C

Project C's cash flows alternate between being outflows and inflows and the graph of the NPV and IRR alternatively falls and rises. Project C has three IRRs, at 10, 20 and 30 per cent.

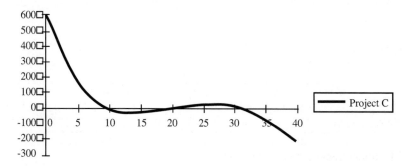

The feature of projects which causes the graph of the NPV and the discount rate to change from the standard shape, as shown by project A, is more than one 'change in sign'. Project A had an outflow followed by inflows (one change in sign), whereas project B had outflows, then inflows (a first change in sign), but then further outflows (a second change in sign).

There may be as many IRRs as there are changes in sign in the cash flows. Clearly project C has three changes in sign and has three IRRs, although project B has two changes in sign but no IRRs.

If project B's cash flows were adjusted to delete the last outflow then there would be two IRRs. We can call this scenario project D which can be represented graphically as follows.

Figure 5.6: Project D

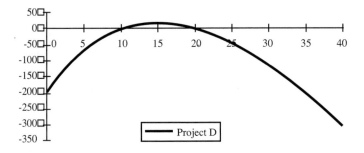

This type of cash flow pattern might occur with projects such as mining or oil exploration. An initial investment is followed by receipts from sales for a few years but at the end of the project the sizeable costs of reparations or shut-downs have a major effect on the project.

Clearly it is difficult to use the IRR method in these circumstances. Attempts can be made to modify the cash flows in such a way as to be able to find a single IRR without invalidating the analysis. However, this is cumbersome. Multiple yields merely provide further evidence that the NPV method is superior to IRR. Despite having several IRRs, projects will have only one NPV at the required rate of return.

Finally, we might note that the NPV method should be preferred in periods of interest rate volatility. Interest rate changes can easily be incorporated into NPV calculations. It is more difficult to allow for interest rate changes in IRR calculations because the IRR is based on an average rate of return over the life of a project.

Abandoning projects

Relevant costs and the decision to abandon

During our initial consideration of project appraisal, we noted that past costs were irrelevant to any decision about the future of a project. This remains true for those occasions when an enterprise has started a project and must decide whether it should continue with it or abandon it. The only relevant costs are future costs: these must be compared with future revenues to decide on viability or abandonment. Decision-makers in enterprises are often reluctant to abandon projects which are underway because it might reflect poorly on past decisions; however true this may be, it would be even worse to compound errors by making further poor decisions. Projects, therefore, must be kept constantly under review.

Cash flow patterns and the decision to abandon

We shall now consider two basic patterns of cash flow: firstly, negative cash flows followed by positive ones and secondly, a mixture of positive and negative cash flows throughout a project's life.

The first is the 'conventional' pattern where, for example, a factory is built and then used to manufacture goods which will recoup the outlay as in the following:

Table 5.10: Conventional cash flows

Period	0	1	2	3	4	5	6
Cash Flow €,000s	−500	−1,000	−200	+750	+600	+500	+400

In this example, it is unlikely that the project would be abandoned before period 3, unless it transpired that estimates of inflows were wildly inaccurate and that future cash flow expenditure would not be sufficiently covered by future cash inflows. When period 3 is reached, there would seem to be little point in abandoning the project, as it is expected to generate net inflows from then on.

It is, of course, important to keep estimates under review to gauge their accuracy. It would probably be fatal for the project, for instance, if at period 3 a net outflow of €100,000 was achieved instead of an expected inflow of €750,000, as this would clearly indicate that the estimated revenues were seriously inaccurate.

The second pattern, namely a mixture of positive and negative cash flows throughout a project's life, might take the following form:

Table 5.11: Positive and negative cash flows

Period	0	1	2	3	4	5	6
Cash Flow €,000s	−100	+150	−70	+60	+80	−100	+150

Such a flow might occur, for example, if substantial replacements were necessary in periods 2 and 5.

This project would not be abandoned immediately after a negative cash flow, if positive flows were expected in later periods. Thus, we would not abandon it in period 2 or 5. We would have to consider at period 1, whether we should proceed to period 3 or 4; and at period 4, whether we should proceed to period 6.

Factors in the decision to abandon

The following considerations must be taken into account in deciding whether to continue or abandon a project:

- The costs of proceeding with the project

- The revenues associated with the project

- Revenues which would arise if the project were abandoned

- Other projects, which may be either alternatives to the project under consideration, or more profitable uses of funds tied up in the project under review.

Each of these factors must be consciously assessed at each stage of a project's life, and if it is seen that abandoning the project would be more beneficial than proceeding with it, then a decision to abandon must be made.

Example 10

An enterprise with a cost of capital of 10 per cent is undertaking a capital project with estimated cash flows from the outset as in Table 5.10 above.

Assume that the enterprise has made an initial investment of €390,000 rather than the €500,000 forecast. It is approaching the end of the first year and €1m is just about to be spent. The managers are happy about the accuracy of the inflows originally forecast for periods 3 to 6 of the project. However, they now believe that the outflow in period 2 is more likely to amount to €450,000 rather than the original estimate of €200,000. The enterprise wishes to know whether the project should be abandoned before the €1m is spent.

Table 5.12: Net cash profile

Period	1	2	3	4	5	6
Cash flow €,000s	−1,000	−450	+750	+600	+500	+400
10% discount factor	1.00	0.9091	0.8264	0.7513	0.6830	0.6209
Present value (€,000)	−1,000	−409.1	+619.8	+450.8	+341.5	+248.36

The NPV is therefore €251,360, so the project still has a positive expected NPV and therefore should not be abandoned.

Sensitivity analysis

A notable problem with any capital investment decision is that the figure reached in any calculation (a positive or negative NPV) is only as reliable as the estimates used to produce that figure.

One way of providing useful supplementary information for an investment decision is to consider a range of figures for various estimates and establish whether these give positive or negative NPVs. This exercise, sometimes referred to as posing 'what if?' questions, is relatively easy to perform with spreadsheet packages. However, it is important to be able to determine what variations in estimates are reasonable and what are unlikely. This analysis is usually applied to one estimate at a time although it can be applied to each estimate simultaneously.

A more concise form of analysis takes each estimate in turn and assesses the percentage change required to change an investment decision. It is customary to apply the analysis to single estimates although, if any relationship between variables is known, it can be applied to groups of figures. It is this form of sensitivity analysis that is considered here.

Example 11

An enterprise is considering investing €500,000 in equipment to produce a new type of ball. Sales of the product are expected to continue for three years at the end of which the equipment will have a scrap value of €80,000. Sales revenue of €600,000 per annum will be generated at a variable cost of €350,000. Annual fixed costs will increase by €40,000 if this investment is accepted.

The enterprise wishes:
(a) to determine whether, on the basis of the estimates given, the project should be undertaken assuming that all cash flows occur at annual intervals and that the cost of capital is 15 per cent; and
(b) to find the percentage changes required in the following estimates for the investment decision to change:

- initial investment

- scrap value

- selling price

- sales volume

- cost of capital.

The first question can be answered with the aid of Table 5.13.

Table 5.13: Initial investment decision

Period	Cash flow	15% Discount €,000	Present value factor	€,000
0	Equipment	(500)	1.00	(500)
1-3	Revenue	600	2.28	1,368
1-3	Variable costs	(350)	2.28	(798)
1-3	Fixed costs	(40)	2.28	(91)
3	Scrap value	80	0.66	53

The NPV is therefore €32,000 and the project, on the basis of these estimates, should be accepted.

The second question requires the use of sensitivity analysis. In order to find the percentage change required in an estimate which would change an investment decision, we will calculate:

$$\frac{\text{NPV of the project}}{\text{PV of the estimate in question}}$$

- Initial investment

For the decision to change, the NPV must fall by €32,000. For this to occur the cost of the equipment must rise by €32,000. This is a rise of:

$$\frac{32,000}{500,000} \times 100 = 6.4\%$$

- Scrap value

If the NPV is to fall by €32,000, the present value of scrap proceeds must fall by €32,000. The PV of scrap proceeds is currently €53,000; it must fall by:

$$\frac{32,000}{53,000} \times 100 = 60.37\%$$

(This would bring the scrap proceeds down by 60.37 per cent to €32,000; the PV of the scrap proceeds would be €21,000, i.e. a reduction of €32,000.)

• Sales price

If sales price varies, sales revenue will vary (assuming no effect on demand). If the NPV of the project is to fall by €32,000, the selling price must fall by:

$$\frac{32,000}{1,368,000} \times 100 = 2.3\%$$

• Sales volume

If sales volume falls, total revenue and total variable costs fall; if the NPV is to fall by €32,000, volume must fall by:

$$\frac{32,000}{1,368,000 - 798,000} \times 100 = 5.6\%$$

• Cost of capital

If NPV is to fall, cost of capital must rise; the figure to which the cost of capital has to rise, that gives an NPV of zero, is the project's IRR. To find the IRR we can commence by calculating the NPV at say 17 per cent by using summarised cash flows. The net cash inflow is €210,000 (i.e. €600,000 – [€350,000 + €40,000]).

$$NPV\ (€,000) = -500 + [210 \text{ x } 2.21] + [80 \times 0.62]$$
$$= 13.7$$

The IRR is a little more than 17 per cent, possibly 18 per cent. Using the formula introduced earlier in the chapter we get:

$$IRR = A + \left(\frac{N_A}{N_A - N_B}\right)(B-A)$$

$$IRR = 15 + \left(\frac{32}{32 - 13.7}\right)(17-15)$$

$$= 18.5\%$$

The cost of capital would have to increase from 15 per cent to 18.5 per cent to cause the investment decision to change.

Replacement theory

The nature of replacement theory

Replacement theory is concerned with the decision to replace existing operating assets. The two questions to be answered are, When should the existing equipment be replaced? and What should be the replacement policy thereafter (i.e. the future replacement cycle)?

It is difficult to determine the replacement policy for existing assets in isolation, because that decision will be dependent on the cost of the future replacements, as will be demonstrated in the sections which follow.

Factors in replacement decisions

The factors to be considered include:

- Capital cost of new equipment. The higher costs of equipment will have to be balanced against known or possible technical improvements.

- Operating costs. Operating costs will be expected to increase as the machinery deteriorates over time. This is referred to as operating inferiority, and is the result of:

  – increased repair and maintenance cost
  – loss of production due to 'down-time' resulting from increased repair and maintenance time
  – lower quality and quantity of output.

- Resale value. The extent to which old equipment can be traded in for new

- Taxation and investment incentives

- Inflation. Both the change in the general price level, and relative movements in the prices of input and outputs.

Replacement techniques

There are various replacement techniques of which we will examine the lowest common multiple and equivalent annual cost approaches.

- Lowest common multiple (LCM)

The lowest common multiple is the smallest number divisible by each of two or more numbers: 12 is the lowest common multiple of 2, 3, 4 and 6. Using this method the lowest common multiple of the various replacement cycles is computed and the present value of costs over this period is calculated. Then the cost of the replacement cycles is compared, e.g. the cost of 3 × 2 year cycles is compared with 2 × 3 year cycles.

The method rapidly becomes unwieldy. For a machine which can be replaced every five or seven years the lowest common multiple is thirty-five years.

- Equivalent annual cost (EAC)

The neatest solution is to compute the present value of costs over one cycle and then turn it into an equivalent annual cost by the use of an annuity factor. Thus, the costs associated with any particular cycle can be considered as equivalent to having to pay this EAC every year throughout the cycle and throughout subsequent cycles. This will be made clearer by use of the following example.

Example 12

An enterprise must decide on replacement policy for vans. A van costs €12,000 and the following additional information applies:

Table 5.14: Trade-in allowance

Interval between replacement (years)	Trade-in allowance €
1	9,000
2	7,500
3	7,000

Table 5.15: Maintenance cost

Age at year end	Maintenance cost paid at year end €
Year of replacement	Nil
1	2,000
2	3,000

The enterprise wishes to know the optimal replacement policy at a cost of capital of 15 per cent. There are no maintenance costs in the year of replacement. In what follows, to simplify the calculation, we will ignore taxation and inflation.

It is assumed that a brand new van is owned from the beginning to the end of the cycle. We will now use the techniques introduced above.

- Lowest common multiple (LCM)

Since replacement is possible every one, two or three years the LCM is six and hence a 6-year period will be considered. First we will look at the case of replacement every year. The necessary information is laid out in Table 5.16.

Table 5.16: Replacement each year

Period	0 €	1 €	2 €	3 €	4 €	5 €	6 €
Capital cost (€)	(12,000)	(12,000)	(12,000)	(12,000)	(12,000)	(12,000)	(12,000)
Trade-in allowance (€)	–	9,000	9,000	9,000	9,000	9,000	9,000
Maintenance (€)	–	–	–	–	–	–	–
Net cost (€)	(12,000)	(3,000)	(3,000)	(3,000)	(3,000)	(3,000)	(3,000)
15% factor	1.0000	0.8696	0.7561	0.6575	0.5718	0.4972	0.4323
PV (€)	(12,000)	(2,608.80)	(2,268.30)	(1,972.50)	(1,715.40)	(1,491.60)	(1,296.90)

The NPV is therefore €(23,353.50).

Next, we consider the case of replacement every other year. The necessary information is laid out in Table 5.17.

Table 5.17: Replacement every other year

Period	0 €	1 €	2 €	3 €	4 €	5 €	6 €
Capital cost (€)	(12,000)	–	(12,000)	–	(12,000)	–	(12,000)
Trade-in allowance (€)	–	–	7,500	–	7,500	–	7,500
Maintenance (€)	–	(2,000)	–	(2,000)	–	(2,000)	–
Net cost (€)	(12,000)	(2,000)	(4,500)	(2,000)	(4,500)	(2,000)	(4,500)
15% factor	1.00	0.8696	0.7561	0.6575	0.5718	0.4972	0.4323
PV (€)	(12,000)	(1,739.2)	(3,402.45)	(1,315)	(2,573.1)	(994.4)	(1,945.35)

The NPV is therefore €(23,969.5).

In the case of replacement every third year, the necessary information is laid out in Table 5.18.

Table 5.18: Replacement every third year

Period	0 €	1 €	2 €	3 €	4 €	5 €	6 €
Capital cost (€)	(12,000)	–	–	(12,000)	–	–	(12,000)
Trade-in allowance (€)	–	–	–	7,000	-	–	7,000
Maintenance (€)	–	(2,000)	(3,000)	–	(2,000)	(3,000)	-
Net cost (€)	(12,000)	(2,000)	(3,000)	(5,000)	(2,000)	(3,000)	(5,000)
15% factor	1.00	0.8696	0.7561	0.6575	0.5718	0.4972	0.4323
PV (€)	(12,000)	(1,739.2)	(2,268.3)	(3,287.5)	(1,143.6)	(1,491.6)	(2,161.5)

The NPV is therefore €(24,091.7).

We can conclude therefore that annual replacement has the lowest present value of costs.

• Equivalent annual cost (EAC)
The costs incurred over a single cycle are computed and the equivalent annual costs are shown in Table 5.19.

Table 5.19: Equivalent annual cost

Replacement	NPV of a single cycle	Annuity factor	Equivalent annual cost $\dfrac{\text{NPV}}{\text{annuity factor}}$
Every year	$-€12,000 + \dfrac{9,000}{1.15}$ $= -€4,174$	0.8696	$\dfrac{-€4,174}{0.8696} = €4,799.9$
Every 2 years	$-€12,000 - \dfrac{€2,000}{1.15}$ $+\dfrac{€7,500}{(1.15)^2} = -€8,068$	1.626	$\dfrac{-€8,068}{1.626} = -€4,961.9$
Every 3 years	$-€12,000 - \dfrac{€2,000}{1.15}$ $\dfrac{-€3,000}{(1.15)^2} + \dfrac{€7,000}{(1.15)^3}$ $= -€11,405$	2.283	$\dfrac{-€11,405}{2.283} = -€4,995.6$

Comparing the three replacement choices, therefore, the optimal replacement period is every year (as it was in the previous instance).

Example 13
A company with cost of capital of 12 per cent wishes to determine the optimum replacement policy for its computers. Each computer costs €5,000 and can either be traded-in at the end of the first year for €3,000 (no maintenance cost paid) or at the end of the second year for €2,000 (€500 maintenance paid after one year). The company wishes to know the equivalent annual cost of each policy and which should be implemented. The calculation proceeds as follows:

Replacement every year:

$$\text{NPV of one cycle} = -€5,000 + \frac{€3,000}{(1.12)} = -€2,321.5$$

$$\text{Equivalent annual cost} = \frac{-€2,321.5}{0.8929} \qquad\qquad = -€2,599.9$$

Replacement every other year:

$$\text{NPV of one cycle} = \quad -€5,000 - \frac{€500}{(1.12)} + \frac{€2,000}{(1.12)^2} = -€3,852$$

$$\text{Equivalent annual cost} = \frac{€(3,852)}{1.69} \qquad\qquad = -€2,279.3$$

Therefore replacing every two years is the cheaper option.

Conclusion

In this chapter we discussed how DCF techniques can be used to appraise capital projects. These techniques are treated in greater depth in texts listed in the references below. The capital investment techniques must of course be considered within the overall process of project control. Project decisions involving capital expenditure will affect the direction and pace of an enterprise's future growth, or perhaps, its very survival. If a wrong decision is made, it will be difficult to correct, particularly where special purpose plant is involved.

Of all the decisions taken by management, those concerned with investment are the most crucial: once made, they may fix the future of an enterprise in terms of its technological status, cost structure and the market effort required. Once the product has been selected and the plant built, the enterprise is committed to the cost structure which accompanies them.

In order to control investment decisions, a capital expenditure committee may be formed, either as a sub-committee of the budget committee or as a separate meeting of the entire budget committee.

The functions of such a committee are to co-ordinate capital expenditure policy, appraise and authorise capital expenditure on specific projects and review actual expenditure on capital projects against the budget.

Capital expenditure requiring approval by the committee must be formulated by the managers. The amount of detail should be stipulated by the committee along the following lines.

- An outline of the project, including the budget classification and how it is linked, if at all, with other projects

- The reason for the expenditure – if a new project – and the departments affected along with an assessment of intangible benefits or disadvantages

- The amount of capital expenditure required (fixed and working capital), including a breakdown by budget periods, and an estimate of any work required within the enterprise

- A complete statement of incremental costs and revenue arising from the project, and the budget periods affected, along with an assessment of the effect of taxation

- The estimated life of the project

- An assessment of risks to which the project is sensitive – political, economic, competitive, natural hazards and so forth

- An identification of projects which are feasible alternatives along with comparative data

- The effect of postponement or rejection of the project.

Strict control of large projects must be maintained and the accountant must submit periodic reports to top management on progress and cost. A typical report would include such data as:

- Budgeted cost of the project, date started and scheduled completion date.

- Cost and over- or under-expenditure to date.

- Estimated cost to completion, and estimated final over- or under-expenditure.

- Estimated completion date and details of penalties, if any.

The capital expenditure committee will seek explanations for any over-spending that may have arisen. Where projects are incomplete and actual expenditure exceeds the authorisation, additional authority must be sought to complete the project. In so doing, the committee must consider the value of the project as it then stands and the additional value that will be gained by completing it, compared with the additional expenditure to completion.

A vital consideration is the adequacy of funds available. Where existing projects are overspending their allocation, other, perhaps more desirable projects may be delayed. When reviewing progress, therefore, the committee must consider the funds available, in the light of which it may become necessary to revise the order or priority in which funds are awarded to projects.

On completion of a project, an investigation should be undertaken to examine its profitability and compare it with the plan. Such investigations hold managers accountable and discourage them from spending money on doubtful projects. Moreover, it may be possible over a period of years to discern a trend of reliability in the estimates of various managers. If a similar project is undertaken in the future, the recently completed project will provide a useful basis for estimation.

REFERENCES

Anthony, R.N., J. Dearden and N.M. Bedford (1989). *Management Control Systems*, Illinois: R.D. Irwin

Bendry, M., R. Hussey and C. West (1996). *Accounting and Finance in Business*, London: Letts Educational

Brealey, R. and S. Myers (1991). *Principles of Corporate Finance*, Maidenhead: McGraw Hill,

Broadbent, M. and J. Cullen (1994). *Managing Financial Resources*, London: Butterworth, Heinemann

Clarke, P.J. (1994). *Accounting Information for Managers*, Dublin: Oak Tree Press

Drury, C. (1996). *Management and Cost Accounting*, London: International Thomson Publishing

Fitzgerald, R. (1992). *Practical Business Finance*, London: Kogan Page Ltd

Franks, J.R. and H.H. Scholefield (1979). *Corporate Financial Management*, Aldershot: Gower Press

Gadella, J.W. (1996). 'Post-Auditing the Capital Investment Decision', *Management Accounting*, November, pp 36-40

Glynn, J. (1987). *Public Sector Financial Control and Accounting*, Oxford: Basil Blackwell

Horngren, C.T., G. Foster and S.M. Datar (1997). *Cost Accounting, A Managerial Emphasis,* Englewood Cliffs: Prentice Hall Inc

Lucey, T. (1996). *Management Accounting*, London: D.P. Publications

Mott, G. (1991). *Management Accounting for Decision Makers*, London: Pitman

6

Risk Management in Capital Expenditure Appraisal

SYLVIA DEMPSEY

Introduction

The previous chapter used discounted cash flow techniques to evaluate capital expenditure projects. The annual future expected cash inflows (including potential savings) and outflows of a project were forecast and decisions were made based on these forecast figures. Any risk or uncertainty was ignored. In reality, the future expected cash flows of capital expenditure projects are not guaranteed; they are merely estimates of what is going to happen in future years. Therefore, there is a risk that the actual cash flows will differ from the estimates. Or, indeed, an investor may be aware that there is a range of possible outcomes, but is uncertain about which will actually occur. This chapter examines some of the popular approaches to incorporating this risk, or uncertainty, into the capital expenditure appraisal process.

The chapter is divided into three sections. The first examines how risk can be incorporated into the capital expenditure appraisal techniques that were outlined in the previous chapter. The approaches examined are: limited payback period, risk-adjusted discount rate, certainty equivalence and sensitivity analysis. The second section examines approaches that can be used to deal with risk when there is a range of possible outcomes and a probability can be assigned to each. In other words, there is partial uncertainty. This section also looks at ways in which risk can be quantified. The final section deals with complete uncertainty. It looks at situations where there is a range of possible outcomes, but the investor lacks knowledge of the probability of each of the outcomes. The three criteria examined in this section are the maximax criterion, the maximin criterion and the minimax-regret criterion.

Risk and capital expenditure appraisal

The riskiness of a capital expenditure project can be defined as the likely variability of the returns from that project. The more variable the likely returns, the riskier the project. In the previous chapter, techniques such as net present value and internal rate of return, were used to decide whether or not to proceed with capital expenditure projects and to decide between competing capital expenditure projects. Single estimates of each year's net cash inflows and outflows were forecast for each project. The variability of these figures was not considered. This section will re-examine these techniques, but this time incorporating risk. The first approach to be considered is the application of a time limit to the payback period technique.

Limited payback period

The most fundamental form of risk management is the application of a time limit to the payback period of potential capital expenditure projects. If an organisation has liquidity constraints and needs to make reasonably quick returns from its capital expenditure projects, then this method is particularly appropriate. There are two ways in which this method can be applied.

The first involves examining the net present value of a project within a certain time period. If the present value of the cash inflows exceeds the present value of the cash outflows within this period, the project is accepted. For example, a new machine, with an expected useful life of ten years, will only be purchased if the present value of its cash inflows (including potential savings) by, say, the fifth year, exceeds the present value of its cash outflows by that time. In other words, the machine is only purchased if it has a positive net present value at the end of the fifth year.

The second involves setting a payback period which is acceptable as a first test of a project. If the project passes this test, more sophisticated techniques will be used to assess its viability. For example, an enterprise may decide to use a payback period of six years as a 'first screening device' of all its potential capital expenditure projects. If there is a risk that a project will not recover its cash outlay within six years, then, without further analysis, it will be rejected. If the project is expected to recover the cash outlay within the six-year period, then other techniques will be used to investigate its viability. One such technique is the application of a risk-adjusted discount rate of return.

Risk-adjusted discount rate

An evaluator should add a premium to the discount rate if the risk associated with a capital expenditure project appears greater than that of typical projects undertaken by an enterprise. The use of this higher discount rate is based on the concept that investors expect higher returns from more risky projects, to compensate them for the extra risk. Therefore, the more risky the project, the higher the discount rate. By the same logic, if a project has less risk than the typical project, a reduction in the discount rate is appropriate.

An evaluator must choose an appropriate risk-adjusted discount rate for the more risky project, and use it in applying the net present value or internal rate of return techniques. When the net present value technique is used, the future expected cash flows are discounted at the risk-adjusted discount rate. If the net present value is positive, then management should accept the project. If the net present value is negative, it should reject the project.

When the internal rate of return technique is used, the 'hurdle' rate with which the project's internal rate of return is compared now becomes the risk-adjusted discount rate. If the internal rate of return is greater than the risk-adjusted discount rate, the management should accept the project. If the internal rate of return is less than the risk-adjusted discount rate, it should reject the project.

The risk-adjusted discount rate approach is commonly used as it is easy to apply and readily accepted by managers. However, this approach does not consider the specific risks of a project with enough rigour. Because a higher weighting of the risk-adjusted discount factor is used for more distant cash flows, this approach automatically assumes that the most distant cash flows are the most variable. This is not always correct. If the most probable variation in a project is the amount of the initial cost or the cash flows in the initial years, there is little point in using an inflated discount rate to discount the future cash flows. It may be more appropriate to adjust each of the present value cash flows according to their perceived variability. This is called the certainty equivalence approach.

Certainty equivalence

Using the certainty equivalence approach, each cash flow is adjusted according to its perceived risk, thus converting risky cash flows into riskless equivalent cash flows. The greater the risk of the expected cash inflow, the smaller the certainty equivalent value. The greater the risk of the expected cash outflow, the larger the certainty equivalent value.

For example an enterprise whose cost of capital is 10 per cent, is deciding whether or not to invest €100,000 in a new machine. If this new machine is purchased, operating costs are expected to fall by approximately €40,000 this year, and by approximately €30,000 in each of the two following years. The machine will be sold at the end of the third year for €33,000. Table 6.1 shows the calculation of the net present value (NPV) of the new machine before making any adjustments for risk.

The machine has a positive net present value (€8,488) and therefore seems to be a worthwhile purchase. However, the management of the enterprise believes that the estimated savings on the operating costs are optimistic. It believes that the savings this year could be as low as 90 per cent of the

estimated figure and that savings in the two following years could be as low
as 80 per cent and 70 per cent respectively of the estimated figures. The risk-
adjusted net present value is presented in Table 6.2.

Table 6.1: Net present value of new machine

Year	Cashflow/ saving (€)	Present value factor (10%)	Present value cashflow (€)
0	(100,000)	1	(100,000)
1	40,000	0.9091	36,364
2	30,000	0.8264	24,792
3	30,000	0.7513	22,539
	33,000		24,793
		NPV = 8,488	

Table 6.2: Risk-adjusted net present value of new machine

Year	Cashflow/ saving (€)	Present value factor (10%)	Present value cashflow (€)
0	(100,000)	1	(100,000)
1	40,000 × 90% = 36,000	0.9091	32,728
2	30,000 × 80% = 24,000	0.8264	19,834
3	30,000 × 70% = 21,000	0.7513	15,777
	33,000		24,793
		NPV = (6,868)	

The machine has a negative risk-adjusted net present value (–€6,868), and
the enterprise will not purchase it. This approach recognises that different
levels of risk can be associated with each of the cashflows. However, the
main disadvantage of this approach is the difficulty and subjectivity involved
in estimating the values of the variables. Consider for example a situation in
which an evaluator wishes to determine the viability of constructing a bypass
to avoid a busy town. Costs such as the construction of a motorway, bridges,
approach roads, flyovers, underpasses and interchanges are relatively easily

quantified. However, as elaborated in Chapter 9 below, the benefits, namely time saving, accident reduction, and fuel cost saving, are difficult to determine and to quantify. The next approach to be considered is sensitivity analysis, which attempts to overcome these estimation problems by testing a project's vulnerability to fluctuations in its most risky variable(s).

Sensitivity analysis

Sensitivity analysis, commonly called 'what if?' analysis, involves determining how the net present value, or internal rate of return, of a project is affected by changes in selected variables. In its simplest form, sensitivity analysis varies the value of the most risky variable, while holding the other variables constant, and calculates the revised net present value or internal rate of return. The revised and original net present values or internal rates of return are compared to assess the effect of the change. If the revised net present value is negative, or the revised internal rate of return is less than the 'hurdle' rate, when a minor change occurs in the most risky variable, the project should be rejected as it is too sensitive to this possible variation.

Another common approach to sensitivity analysis is to calculate by how much the most risky variable would have to change, before the net present value drops from a positive to a negative value, or the internal rate of return falls from being greater than to less than the 'hurdle rate'. The investor would then make a decision based on the likelihood of this level of change.

Sensitivity analysis is simple to use if only one variable is being adjusted. However, for large or important projects, it may be necessary to examine the effect of differing values for more than one variable. For example, some of the risks and uncertainties associated with potential projects may relate to changes in the external environment. Risks and uncertainties, such as volatile exchange rates and economic growth forecasts, are not project-specific. However, they may have direct impacts on the outcome of projects. Two approaches can be used in these situations.

The first, a variable-by-variable approach, assumes that each variable operates independently. A set of revised net present values, or internal rates of return, is calculated using each possible value of one variable (holding all other variables constant). These results would show the sensitivity of the project to this variable. The process is repeated for all other risky variables. The resulting set of net present values, or internal rates of return, illustrates the sensitivity of the project's outcome to each of the variables.

The second, a scenario approach, assumes that some variables are interdependent. Therefore, a set of net present values, or internal rates of return, is calculated for different scenarios. For example, in the case of the construction of a bypass, suppose an estimate is calculated for each of the benefits of time saving, accident reduction and fuel cost saving. The value given to the benefit of time saving is based on the cost to an employer of hiring labour. When travel time is saved, working time is increased, meaning more goods and services can be produced. The value given to the benefit of accident reduction is based on estimates both of hospital care and loss of output (based on gross national product) while the patient is undergoing treatment. The value given to the benefit of fuel cost savings is based on average fuel consumption per vehicle using the bypass compared to average fuel consumption of travelling through the town, in peak and off-peak periods.

Because of the difficulty in determining and quantifying each of the benefits, none of them can be known with complete certainty. For example, the total value of time saved varies with traffic growth and income growth. The total value of accident reduction varies with the cost of treatment and the contribution to gross national product. The total value of fuel cost saving varies with fluctuations in fuel price. The scenario approach to sensitivity analysis can be used to test the viability of the new bypass to possible variations in each variable. For example, the basic net present value, or internal rate of return, of the project can be calculated on the basis that there will be 2 per cent traffic growth, a fixed income level and fixed fuel prices. Next, revised net present values, or internal rates of return, can be calculated assuming that there will be 2 per cent traffic growth, 2 per cent income growth and fixed fuel prices. The exercise could then be repeated assuming that there will be 2 per cent traffic growth, 2 per cent income growth and 2 per cent fuel price growth. Each time, the adjusted net present value, or internal rate of return, is assessed to determine the viability of the project.

Sensitivity analysis gives information about possible outcomes under different circumstances, thus allowing a more informed appraisal process. It forces evaluators to recognise the risky variables in a project and the scenario approach recognises the interdependence of these variables. However, sensitivity analysis does not take into consideration the probability of the occurrence of any of the variables. This is examined in the next section.

Partial uncertainty and capital expenditure appraisal

Partial uncertainty exists when investors have expectations concerning the probable range of outcomes of a project, and, from past experience, can assign probabilities to each of these outcomes. Where this is the case, an expected value can be calculated for the project and the decision to accept or reject can be based on this value.

Expected value

The expected value approach allows each outcome to be weighted by the probability of its occurrence. The expected value of a project is the weighted average of all its probable outcomes. For example, suppose a service enterprise has sufficient surplus staff, and other resources, to provide an extra service over the next five years. The marketing manager estimates that there is a two in ten chance that this service will result in a net cash inflow of €10,000 per annum, a five in ten chance that it will result in a net cash inflow of €5,000 per annum and a three in ten chance that it will result in a net cash outflow of €7,000 per annum.

To calculate the expected value, each of the probable cash flows is weighted by the probability of its occurrence and the weighted cash flows are summed. The expected value per annum of providing this extra service is €2,400, calculated as follows:

$$V = €10,000 \left(\tfrac{2}{10}\right) + €5,000 \left(\tfrac{5}{10}\right) - €7,000 \left(\tfrac{3}{10}\right) = €2,400$$

The expected value (V) of €2,400 will not be the actual cash inflow for any single year (it will either be a cash inflow of €10,000 or €5,000, or a cash outflow of €7,000). Instead, it represents the long-term average cash inflow. Therefore, if the service is provided over five years, the enterprise will expect an additional cash inflow of approximately €12,000 (that is €2,400 × 5 years) for the period.

Calculating the expected value of a capital expenditure project can be complicated if there are two or more alternatives. If an enterprise has to choose between two or more possible alternatives, the calculation can be simplified by drawing a decision tree.

Decision tree

A decision tree is a graphical representation of capital expenditure appraisal. It illustrates the sequence of probable events and all the probable outcomes. Moreover, the computation of expected value is shown directly on the tree, so that each of its components can be easily understood.

For example, an enterprise has an opportunity to spend €30,000 on advertising a product that has a net cash inflow of €10 per unit sold. From past experience the management team arrived at a set of expectations. If €30,000 is spent on an advertising campaign, there is a twenty per cent chance that it will be very successful, resulting in sales of eleven thousand units. There is a sixty-five per cent chance that the campaign will be moderately successful, resulting in sales of eight thousand units. But, there is a fifteen per cent chance that the campaign will be unsuccessful and only four thousand units will be sold. If it does not advertise, there are equal probabilities (50%:50%) of selling six thousand units and three thousand units.

The decision is whether or not to spend €30,000 on the advertising campaign. The decision tree starts with two branches, as shown in Figure 6.1. One branch is labelled 'Advertise' and shows a cost of €30,000. The other is labelled 'Do not advertise' and shows a zero cost.

Figure 6.1: Decision tree – first step

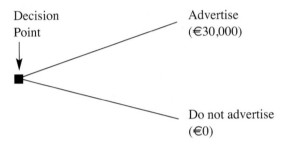

From the end of each branch, a sub-branch is drawn for each of the probable outcomes. On the top branch, the three sub-branches (that is, the three probable outcomes) are 'very successful' (sales of eleven thousand units), 'moderately successful' (sales of eight thousand units) and 'unsuccessful' (sales of four thousand units). On the bottom branch, the two sub-branches (that is, the two probable outcomes) are sales of six thousand units and three thousand units. The probability of each sub-branch is written on it and the cash inflow from the sales is written at the end of each sub-branch, as shown in Figure 6.2.

The cash inflow at the end of each sub-branch is then multiplied by the probability of that sub-branch occurring as shown in Figure 6.3. For example, looking at the top sub-branch, the cash inflow of €110,000 is multiplied by its probability (0.20) to give €22,000. To find the expected cash inflow of each of the alternatives (branches), add the weighted cash inflows of each of its sub-branches. As Figure 6.3 shows, if the enterprise advertises, the expected cash inflow is €80,000 (that is €22,000 + €52,000 + €6,000). If it does not advertise, the expected cash inflow is €45,000 (€30,000 + €15,000).

Figure 6.4 illustrates the deduction of the cost of implementing each decision from its expected cash inflow to find the expected value (V) of each alternative (branch). The enterprise will select the alternative with the highest expected value. If the enterprise advertises, the expected value is €50,000. If it does not advertise, the expected value is €45,000. Therefore it decides to spend €30,000 on the advertising campaign.

Figure 6.2: Decision tree – second step

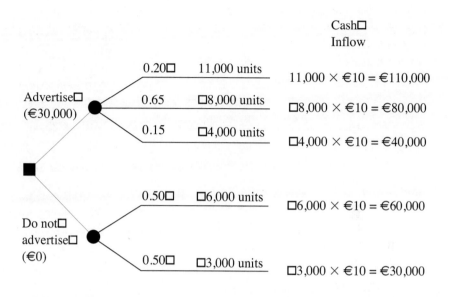

Figure 6.3: Decision tree – third step

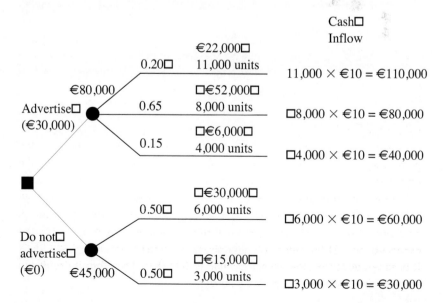

Figure 6.4: Decision tree – fourth step

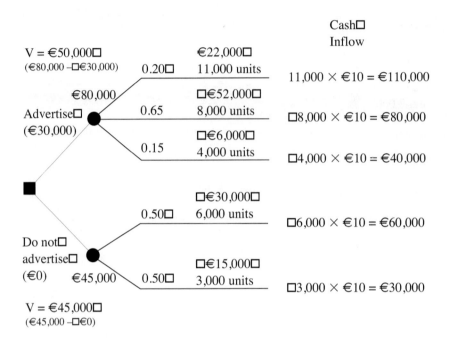

Where there are only a few probable outcomes, or a few alternatives to choose from, the decision tree is a clear illustration of the decision-making process. If the number of outcomes is large, or there are many alternatives to choose from, the decision tree can lose its clarity as it becomes unwieldy and complicated. A simulation approach, described in the following section, can be used instead. This approach provides a range of probable values for an investment's net present value or internal rate of return.

Simulation approach

The simulation approach involves constructing a model that imitates the performance of the project being appraised. Each of the variables of the capital expenditure project (for example initial outlay, cash inflows, cash outflows and asset life) is entered into a computer programme, along with probable values of each variable and the probabilities of their occurrence. The computer programme selects values at random and produces an estimated net present value or internal rate of return for the project. This process is repeated until a representative record of the project's probable outcomes is assembled.

The use of computer simulation is complex; it requires obtaining all the probable values of the variables and the probability of each occurring. It also involves a large input of time by analysts and consequently is expensive. Therefore simulation is only feasible for major projects. Another disadvantage of this approach, and all the approaches mentioned so far, is that it does not take the investors' attitude to risk into consideration. Two projects may have the same initial outlays and the same expected values, but the investor may still prefer one project to the other depending on his or her attitude to risk.

• Attitude to risk

A person may be either risk-averse, risk-seeking or risk-neutral. A risk-seeker is inclined to take risks, a risk-averse person is reluctant to take risks and a risk-neutral person neither seeks nor shuns risk. We can examine attitude to risk by means of an example where the management of an enterprise must choose between two competing investments, A and B. The details of these investments are shown in Table 6.3.

Table 6.3: Details of mutually exclusive investments A and B

Investment A		Investment B	
Probable returns	Probability	Probable returns	Probability
€10,000	0.1	€2,000	0.3
€1,000	0.6	€1,500	0.5
€100	0.3	€1,400	0.2
	1		1

The management team first calculates the expected value of each of these investments. This calculation is shown in Table 6.4.

Each of these investments has the same expected value (€1,630). However, that does not mean that they are equally desirable projects. The range of probable returns from investment A is from €10,000 to €100. Investment B has the same expected value, but its range of probable returns is only from €2,000 to €1,400. In the previous section, risk was defined as the variability of likely outcomes. Therefore, in general the smaller the range of probable returns, the smaller the risk associated with the project. Because investment A has a wider range of probable returns, it is more risky than investment B.

Different people have different attitudes to risk. A risk-seeker is most likely interested in the best possible result, even though the probability of its occurrence may be low. Therefore, in the example above, if the management of the enterprise is risk-seeking, it will most likely choose investment A, as the best possible return is €10,000 (even though the probability is only 0.1), whereas the best return from investment B is only €2,000.

Table 6.4: Calculation of the expected value of investments A and B

Investment A			Investment B		
Probable return(€)	Probability	Expected value (€)	Probable return (€)	Probability	Expected value (€)
10,000	0.1	1,000	2,000	0.3	600
1,000	0.6	600	1,500	0.5	750
100	0.3	<u>30</u>	1,400	0.2	<u>280</u>
		$V = €1,630$			$V = €1,630$

A person who is risk-averse would pick the least risky alternative. Therefore, in the above example, a risk-averse manager will most likely choose investment B. This is because, firstly, the range of returns from investment B is smaller than the range of returns from investment A; therefore it is more likely that the actual return will be closer to the expected value. Secondly, the worst possible return from investment B is €1,400 and from investment A is as low as €100. Finally, there is an 80 per cent chance (i.e. 0.3 + 0.5) of a return of at least €1,500 from investment B, whereas there is only a 70 per cent chance (i.e. 0.1 + 0.6) of a return of at least €1,000 from investment A. In general, enterprises tend to be risk-averse. Therefore the management team will most likely pick investment B.

A person who is risk-neutral does not look at the range of probable returns, but at the expected value. In the above example, if the management of the enterprise is risk-neutral, it is indifferent between the investments A and B, as they both have the same expected value.

The above example illustrates that decisions cannot be based purely on the expected value. The risk preference of the decision-maker and the risk of the project must also be taken into account. To be more useful, risk can be quantified. If competing projects have the same expected value, a measure called the standard deviation can be used to measure risk.

Standard deviation

Standard deviation, denoted by (sigma), is a measurement of the variation of the outcomes around the expected value. The lower the standard deviation of a project, the closer the actual return to the expected value. If two capital expenditure projects have the same expected value, a risk-averse manager will choose the project with the lower standard deviation, as that is the alternative with the least degree of uncertainty or risk. The formula used to calculate the standard deviation is as follows:

$$\text{Standard deviation} = \sigma = \sqrt{\Sigma(X-V)^2 P}$$

Where Σ = sum of
   X = probable return
   V = expected value
   P = probability of each return

In the above example, an enterprise has the opportunity to invest in one of two mutually exclusive investments, A and B. Both investments have the same expected value (€1,630). Tables 6.5 and 6.6 illustrate the calculation of their respective standard deviations.

Table 6.5: Standard deviation of investment A

Investment A					
Probable returns $X(\text{€})$	Prob-ability P	X P (€)	X – V	$(X-V)^2$	$(X-V)^2P$
10,000	0.1	1,000	8,370	70,056,900	7,005,690
1,000	0.6	600	–630	396,900	238,140
100	0.3	30	–1,530	2,340,900	702,270
		$V = \text{€}1,630$			$7,946,100 = \Sigma(X-V)^2P$
					$\sqrt{7,946,100} = \sqrt{\Sigma(X-V)^2P}$
					$2,818.88 = \sigma$

A risk-averse investor, when choosing between two investments which have the same expected value but different standard deviations, will choose the investment with the lower standard deviation. The standard deviations (σ) of investments A and B are €2,818.88 and €245.15 respectively. Therefore, even though the two projects have the same expected value (€1,630), the risk-averse manager will most likely choose investment B as it is less risky.

Table 6.6: Standard deviation of Investment B

			Investment B		
Probable returns X(€)	Prob-ability P	X P (€)	X – V	$(X - V)^2$	$(X - V)^2 P$
2,000	0.3	600	370	136,900	41,070
1,500	0.5	750	–130	16,900	8,450
1,400	0.2	280	–230	52,900	10,580
		V = €1,630			60,100 $= \Sigma(X - V)^2 P$

$$\sqrt{60,100} = \sqrt{\Sigma(X - V)^2 P}$$

$$245.15 = \sigma$$

Coefficient of variation

In the previous example, standard deviations were calculated and used to decide between two projects earning the same expected value. However, if the projects have different expected values, it does not make sense to simply choose the project with the lowest standard deviation. In such a situation, the standard deviation of each project must be divided by its expected value to find a comparable risk measure. This measure is called the coefficient of variation. The formula for the coefficient of variation is:

$$\text{Coefficient of variation} = \frac{\text{Standard deviation}}{\text{Expected value}} = \frac{\sigma}{V}$$

The lower the coefficient of variation of a project, the lower the risk associated with it. Consider an enterprise which can choose one of two mutually exclusive investments, A and C. As calculated in Table 6.7, the expected value of investment A, once more, is €1,630, and the expected value of investment C is only €210.

If the management of the enterprise is risk-seeking, it will most likely choose investment A, as there is a chance of making a highest possible return of €10,000 compared with €300 from investment C. If the management of the enterprise is risk-neutral, it will choose investment A, as it has an expected value of €1,630 compared with €210 from investment C. However, in general, the management of the enterprise will tend to be risk-averse and base its decision not only on expected return but also on risk.

Table 6.7: Expected values of investments A and C

Investment A			Investment C		
Probable returns(€)	Probability	Expected value (€)	Probable return (€)	Probability	Expected value (€)
10,000	0.1	1,000	300	0.3	90
1,000	0.6	600	200	0.3	60
100	0.3	30	150	0.4	60
		$V = €1,630$			$V = €210$

As in the previous example, the expected value of investment A is €1,630 and as shown in Table 6.5 the standard deviation is €2,818.88. Table 6.8 shows that the expected value of investment C is €210 and its standard deviation is €62.45.

Table 6.8: Standard deviation of investment C

Investment C					
Probable returns X(€)	Prob-ability P	$XP(€)$	$X - V$	$(X - V)^2$	$(X - V)^2P$
300	0.3	90	90	8,100	2,430
200	0.3	60	−10	100	30
150	0.4	60	−60	3,600	1,440
		$V = €210$			$3,900 = \Sigma(X - V)^2P$

$$\sqrt{3,900} = \sqrt{\Sigma(X - V)^2P}$$

$$62.45 = \sigma$$

A direct comparison is not possible between the two investments, as they have different expected values and standard deviations. What is needed is a relative measure of risk, that is a measure expressed as a percentage rather than in monetary terms. The coefficient of variation, calculated in Table 6.9, is used for this purpose.

The coefficient of variation of investment A is subject to greater variability than that of investment C. The risk-averse management team will pick the investment with the lowest coefficient of variation, which is investment C in this case.

Table 6.9: Coefficient of variation

	V	σ	σ/V (coefficient of variation)
Investment A	1,630	2,818.88	$\dfrac{2{,}818.88}{1{,}630} = 1.73\ (173\%)$
Investment C	210	62.45	$\dfrac{62.45}{210} = 0.30\ (30\%)$

In the foregoing, investors had expectations concerning the probable range of outcomes of a project and could assign probabilities to each of these outcomes. Risk was quantified and the risk-averse manager picked the project with the lowest coefficient of variation. However, when the probability of each outcome is difficult or indeed impossible to calculate, risk cannot be quantified.

Complete uncertainty and capital expenditure appraisal

Complete uncertainty is when the investor has knowledge of the possible outcomes but lacks any knowledge of the probability of each occurring. In situations of complete uncertainty, it is not possible to calculate the expected value or the coefficient of variation.

For purposes of illustration, consider a manufacturing enterprise that must choose between three new machines, A which is most suited to high output, B which is most suited to low output and C which is equally suited to high and low output. The profits from each machine in periods of low, medium and high demand are shown in Table 6.10.

Table 6.10: Illustrative profits from machines

	Low demand	Medium demand	High demand
Machine A	€200,000	€500,000	€800,000
Machine B	€900,000	€100,000	€1,000
Machine C	€250,000	€250,000	€250,000

Even though risk cannot be quantified, the machine that the management of the enterprise chooses will reflect its attitude to risk. To show this, we will consider some of the criteria that can be used, namely the maximax, the maximin and the minimax regret criteria.

Maximax criterion

The maximax criterion assumes that the investor is risk-seeking and will always look for the best possible outcomes. Using this criterion, the investor lists the best possible outcome of each alternative and then picks the alternative that gives the 'highest best' (the maximax) outcome.

Using the above example, if the management uses the maximax criterion, it identifies the maximum profit from each alternative and chooses the alternative with the greatest maximum profit. This process is illustrated in Table 6.11.

Table 6.11 : Application of the maximax criterion

Machine	→	Maximum profit	→	Maximax
A		€800,000		
B		€900,000		X
C		€250,000		

Using the maximax criterion, the management of the enterprise will purchase machine B as it gives a best possible profit of €900,000, whereas machines A and C only give best possible profits of €800,000 and €250,000 respectively.

The maximax criterion is too simplistic. It only looks at the best possible outcome from each alternative. In the above example machine B was picked because it gives the highest best possible profit. However, the fact that it could also give the worst possible result (a profit of only €1,000) was ignored. As such this criterion appeals only to risk-seekers and therefore is seldom used. In practice, investors tend to be risk-averse and are more inclined to use the maximin criterion.

Maximin criterion

The maximin criterion assumes that the investor is risk-averse and will always look at the worst possible outcomes. Using this criterion, the investor lists the worst that can possibly happen for each alternative and then picks the alternative that gives the 'least worst' (the maximin) outcome.

Using the above example, if the management of the enterprise uses the maximin criterion, it identifies the minimum profit from each alternative and chooses the alternative with the largest minimum profit. Table 6.12 illustrates this process.

Table 6.12 : Application of the maximin criterion

Machine	→	Minimum profit	→	Maximin
A		€200,000		
B		€1,000		
C		€250,000		X

If the management of the enterprise uses the maximin criterion, it will purchase machine C, as it gives a minimum profit of €250,000, whereas machines A and B give minimum profits of €200,000 and €1,000 respectively.

The maximin criterion is more realistic than the maximax criterion for capital expenditure appraisal, but again it is very simplistic. Its main fault is its total lack of consideration for anything but the worst possible outcome from each alternative. As such it adopts an extremely conservative attitude to risk.

Minimax regret criterion

The minimax regret criterion is slightly more complex than the previous two criteria. This criterion is based on protecting the investor against making excessive mistakes. Once the outcome is known, the investor may regret not having picked another alternative.

In the above example, if the management of the enterprise had decided to purchase machine A and the demand was low, it would regret its decision. Had it invested in machine B, it would have made a profit of €900,000 instead of making a profit of only €200,000 from machine A.

Regret is represented by the difference between the actual payoff and the payoff that could have been received if the investor had known which level of demand would occur. The aim of the minimax regret criterion is to minimise the maximum possible regret.

If demand is low, the management of the enterprise would have wished it had chosen machine B. Had it chosen machine B, it would have no regret. Had it chosen machine A, it would have regret of €700,000 (€900,000 – €200,000). Had it chosen machine C, it would have regret of €650,000 (€900,000 – €250,000).

If demand is medium, the management of the enterprise would have wished it had chosen machine A. If it had chosen machine A, it would have no regret. Had it chosen machine B, it would have regret of €400,000 (€500,000 – €100,000). Had it chosen machine C, it would have regret of €250,000 (€500,000 – €250,000).

If demand is high, the management of the enterprise would have wished it had chosen machine A. If it had chosen machine A, it would have had no regret. Had it chosen machine B, it would have had regret of €799,000 (€800,000 – €1,000). Had it chosen machine C, it would have regret of €550,000 (€800,000 – €250,000).

Each of these scenarios is illustrated in Table 6.13.

Table 6.13: Regret table

	Low demand	Medium demand	High demand
Machine A	€700,000	€0	€0
Machine B	€0	€400,000	€799,000
Machine C	€650,000	€250,000	€550,000

From Table 6.13, the management team chooses the alternative with the lowest maximum regret. This process is illustrated in Table 6.14.

Table 6.14 : Application of the minimax regret criterion

Machine	→	Maximum regret	→	Minimax regret
A		€700,000		
B		€799,000		
C		€650,000		X

In this example, if the management of the enterprise uses the minimax regret criterion, it will purchase machine C, as it gives a least 'worst regret' of €650,000, whereas machines A and B give a 'worst regret' of €700,000 and €799,000 respectively.

Again this criterion is simple to use, but it is extremely cautious. If possible the management of the enterprise should attempt to assign probabilities to the different levels of demand. This would enable it to calculate the coefficient of variation of each alternative, as shown earlier in this chapter.

Conclusion

Where risk or uncertainty exists in capital expenditure appraisal, the investor has three possible options. First, the risk or uncertainty can be completely ignored. Unfortunately, this is often the option that is chosen, even though it is only appropriate where the risk or uncertainty is immaterial. Second, risk or uncertainty can be incorporated in the capital expenditure appraisal process. This chapter dealt with this option. Third, attempts can be made to reduce the risk or uncertainty. This can be achieved by obtaining more information or more accurate information.

This chapter illustrated how risk and uncertainty can be incorporated into the appraisal process. A distinction was drawn between risk, partial uncertainty and complete uncertainty, and relevant approaches were examined for each. The methods of dealing with risk and uncertainty vary according to the circumstances. For example, if the probability of each probable occurrence is available, it would be inadequate to use the maximin criterion to select between alternatives; instead the calculation and comparison of the coefficients of variation would be a more appropriate approach.

If the management of an enterprise obtained perfect information, then it could make decisions with complete confidence that it had selected the best alternative and all risk and uncertainty would be removed from the capital expenditure appraisal process. In practice, it is highly unlikely that perfect information will be available. Market research or past experience can sometimes provide reasonably accurate information, but this information could be wrong.

Any additional information that indicates which events are most likely to occur will reduce risk and uncertainty, but this information will be available at a cost. Before investing in this additional information, the enterprise must therefore calculate its expected value. The expected value of information is the difference between the expected value of a project if the information is not obtained and the expected value if it is. The enterprise will most likely obtain the additional information if the cost of obtaining it is less than its expected value.

Much has been written on risk and uncertainty. Most management accounting, finance and economics textbooks devote some attention to this topic. The following references are some of the texts referred to in the writing of this chapter and would form a suitable basis for further reading.

REFERENCES

Baumol, W. J. (1972). *Economic Theory and Operations Analysis*, London: Prentice/Hall

Begg, D., S. Fisher and R. Dornbusch (1994). *Economics,* London: McGraw-Hill

Bodie, Z., A. Kane and A. J. Marcus (1989). *Investments,* Boston: Irwin.

Brealey, R. A. and S. C. Myers (1991). *Principles of Corporate Finance*, London: McGraw-Hill

Brigham, E. F. and J. L. Pappas (1972). *Managerial Economics*, Illinois: The Dryden Press

Broadbent, M. and J. Cullen (1994). *Managing Financial Resources*, London: Butterworth-Heinmann

Brown, C. V. and P. M. Jackson (1990) *Public Sector Economics*, Oxford: Basil Blackwell

Drury, C. (1992). *Management and Cost Accounting*, London: Chapman and Hall

Musgrave, R. A. and P. B. Musgrave (1989). *Public Finance in Theory and Practice*, London: McGraw-Hill

Pearce, D. W. (1983). *Cost-Benefit Analysis*, London: MacMillan

Stiglitz, J. E. (1988). *Economics of the Public Sector*, London: W. W. Norton

Watts, B. K. R. (1992). *Business and Financial Management*, London: Longman

7

Value for Money Auditing

FRANCIS McGEOUGH, AIDAN HORAN

Introduction

The purpose of this chapter is to give an overview of value for money (VFM) auditing. The chapter will commence by discussing the role of the Comptroller and Auditor General (C&AG) and the implications of the Comptroller and Auditor General (Amendment) Act 1993. It will then examine the role of VFM auditing in local government. Next it proceeds to examine the role of the auditor and to outline the steps in conducting a VFM audit. The chapter will conclude by reviewing some key issues and by looking in some detail at audits conducted by the C&AG and the Local Government Audit Service (LGAS).

Comptroller and Auditor General (Amendment) Act 1993

The Comptroller and Auditor General (Amendment) Act 1993 gives specific powers to the C&AG to conduct VFM audits. These audits are separate to the financial audits also conducted by the C&AG. A separate unit has been set up within the C&AG's office to conduct VFM audits. Section 9 of the act outlines the new role of the C&AG in relation to VFM audits. The relevant parts of section 9 are as follows:

(1) The Comptroller and Auditor General may ... carry out such examinations as he considers appropriate for the purpose of ascertaining
   (a) whether and to what extent the resources of the Department, person or fund
      (i) have been used, and
      (ii) if acquired or disposed of by the Department, person or fund, have been so acquired or disposed of, economically and efficiently, and
   (b) whether any such disposal has been effected upon the most favourable terms reasonably obtainable.
(2) ... the systems, procedures and practices employed by the Department or person concerned or the manager of the fund concerned for the purpose of enabling the Department or person or the manager of the fund to evaluate the effectiveness of its or his operations may be examined by the Comptroller and Auditor General.

(3) ... the Comptroller and Auditor General may, in carrying out examinations under this section, make such comparisons, including comparisons of systems, procedures and practices, as he considers appropriate.

(4) Where the Comptroller and Auditor General proposes to make any examination under this section, he may, at his discretion, seek the views of the committee of Dáil Éireann established under the Standing Orders of Dáil Éireann to examine and report to Dáil Éireann on the appropriation accounts.

In summary, the C&AG can conduct an audit to verify if assets have been acquired, used or disposed of economically and efficiently. The C&AG cannot specifically audit for effectiveness but can examine if procedures have been put in place by an organisation to examine/monitor its own effectiveness.

The terms economy, efficiency and effectiveness are not defined in the legislation. The definitions introduced in chapter 1 of this volume and set out below are in line with those used by the C&AG's office:

- *Economy* – minimising the cost of goods or services having regard to the appropriate quality. It is important to note that economy is not about buying at the cheapest price. The quality required must be specified and then the aim is to acquire these resources at the lowest price. Therefore, the first step has to be a specification of the technical requirements. Once these have been specified, the organisation acting economically should aim to acquire the resources at the lowest price.

- *Efficiency* – maximising the output of goods or services from the resources used to produce them. Therefore, efficiency looks at the relationship of outputs to inputs. Organisations should aim to optimise this input/output relationship. This can be done by maximising output for a given level of inputs or by minimising the inputs for a given level of output.

  Establishing efficiency pre-supposes that inputs can be calculated, for example, cost of staff, materials, number of hours worked; and that outputs can be identified. Output of services can be defined on a unit basis, for example, miles of road repaired, operations completed or application forms processed.

- *Effectiveness* – the relationship between the intended results and the actual results of programmes, projects and policies. In other words are the objectives of the organisation being achieved? An organisation is effective if it achieves its objectives.

Local Government (Financial Provisions) Act 1997

Concern to pursue and monitor value for money has grown throughout the 1990s. Section 7 of the Local Government Act 1991 placed an obligation on local authorities to use resources in the most 'beneficial, efficient and effective' way. A value for money unit of the Local Government Audit Service (LGAS) was set up in the Department of the Environment and Local Government which worked closely with local authorities and produced a number of reports.

In 1996, the policy document *Better Local Government* (Department of the Environment, 1996a) proposed that VFM auditing in local government have a comparable legal status to that conferred in the Comptroller and Auditor General (Amendment) Act. It also proposed strengthening the role of the VFM Unit.

In 1997, the Local Government (Financial Provisions) Act provided legal status for VFM auditing in local government and for a Local Government (Value for Money) Unit.

Section 14 of the Act provides for the Local Government (Value for Money) Unit which can carry out studies and make recommendations on steps to be taken to:

(a) secure the provision by local authorities of services in a more economical, efficient and effective manner,
(b) improve the manner in which local authorities are managed.

Section 15 of the Act bears a close resemblance to section 9 of the Comptroller and Auditor General (Amendment) Act. It states:

(1) A local government auditor may, in the course of an audit of the accounts of a local authority or at any other time, carry out such examinations as he or she considers appropriate for the purpose of ascertaining
  (a) whether and to what extent the resources of the local authority
    (i) have been used, and
    (ii) if acquired or disposed of by the local authority, have been so acquired or disposed of, economically and efficiently, and
  (b) whether any such disposal has been effected upon the most favourable terms reasonably obtainable.
(2) ... a local government auditor may examine the systems, procedures and practices employed by a local authority for the purposes of enabling the local authority to evaluate the effectiveness of its operations.
(3) ... a local government auditor may, in carrying out examinations under this section,
  (a) make such comparisons, including comparisons of systems, procedures and practices, as he or she considers appropriate, and
  (b) (i) examine the extent to which a local authority has implemented, or is implementing, recommendations made to the Minister by the personnel of the Unit
    (ii) to the extent that those recommendations have been, or are being, implemented by the local authority, examine the measures taken by it for those purposes.

The role of the auditor

It is the responsibility of management to ensure that the organisation is delivering value for money. The auditor has a major role to play in supporting management in this role. This can be done in two ways: firstly by examining the structures in place to ensure that the organisation is able to deliver value for money and secondly by actually conducting VFM audits.

The internal auditor is appointed by an organisation's management to fulfil the role of independent internal appraiser. The internal auditor helps ensure the safeguarding of the assets of the organisation, compliance with internal control systems and adherence to the policies and procedures set by management. In fulfilling this role the internal auditor is not just a 'whistle blower' but also assists management with assessment of overall policy and the achievement of objectives.

External audit involves the independent examination and expression of opinion on financial statements in compliance with relevant statutory or regulatory requirements by an evaluation from outside the organisation. In the public sector the C&AG and the LGAS must meet specific requirements when assessing the accuracy, validity and probity of financial statements.

The traditional audit examines an organisation's systems, assesses key controls, carries out tests for compliance with the controls, comments on any weaknesses and produces a report. This approach is widely practised and understood. To be well accepted, VFM auditing must proceed with clear objectives, scope and parameters.

The external auditor must be careful when evaluating effectiveness not to question policy. To do so would mean taking on a 'political' role. The making of policy is the role of an organisation's elected representatives and senior management.

Therefore, the external auditor would question whether objectives of the policy are clearly stated, if alternative means of implementing the policy were examined, if sufficient and reliable data were available to evaluate progress, whether remedial action had been taken if objectives were not achieved and if objectives remained valid in the light of changing circumstances.

The external auditor can draw attention to deficiencies in the answers to the above questions but the overall policy cannot be questioned.

Management must put the structures in place to facilitate the achievement of value for money. The auditor's role is to advise on the necessary structures and at a later stage to review these structures to ensure that they are robust enough to help deliver value for money. The necessary structures can be examined under a number of headings:

- *Policy formulation*. The clear statement of objectives allows performance to be monitored. The objectives need to be reviewed on a regular basis to ensure that they are still relevant.
- *Information system*. Information is the key to monitoring performance. Such information needs to be timely and accurate. The necessary information will come in the form of performance indicators.
- *Management and operational control of resources – accountability*. It is insufficient just to clearly state objectives and collect information on how well these objectives are being met. Management needs to be held accountable for the achievement or non-achievement of objectives. Performance indicators must be integrated into the decision-making processes in the organisation.
- *Inter-organisational comparisons*. Performance indicators on their own are of limited benefit. Where possible, organisations should compare their performance indicators with those of similar organisations. A comparison between organisations should help to identify areas for further investigation. Again, these comparisons should be part of the decision making process in the organisation.

When the review of structures has been completed, the auditor should be able to assess the organisation's ability to deliver value for money.

Conducting a VFM audit

Selecting potential areas

The subject of a VFM audit must be carefully chosen. Given the complexity of public sector organisations there is a danger that the area chosen could be too large for a full audit. Additionally, the limited resources available determine that the areas chosen should be those most likely to yield high levels of benefit to the organisation.

A systematic search for potential areas should question whether there are areas where managers suspect or are aware of problems; for example, are there excessive amounts of rent arrears? Such a search would also ask whether successful studies have been conducted elsewhere. If studies have been conducted in other organisations which have indicated good or bad practice, we can use these studies to examine practices in the organisation on which we are focusing. It is also necessary to assess the degree of risk involved. Risk brings the potential for poor value for money though of course it should be noted that high expenditure does not necessarily mean high risk.

By systematically reviewing an organisation, the auditor should be able to identify a number of areas involving risk which are worthy of further investigation. The auditor might query whether expenditures are high or low compared to other organisations, if significant individual transactions have occurred such as the sale or purchase of a major asset or the awarding of a substantial contract, whether new services are being offered and reviewed to ensure that the objectives are being achieved, if there are areas of high spending or areas where expenditure has increased significantly over the past few years and whether there have been major changes in recent years either in the organisation, in its services or the way they are delivered, or in its environment.

Objectives and scope

An organisation moves from its mission statement to clear objectives. The organisation can then verify its progress against these objectives. If the objectives are being achieved, then the organisation can be said to be effective. The Strategic Management Initiative in the Irish public sector has facilitated the agreement of clear mission statements, objectives, strategies and action plans.

VFM cannot ignore the importance of effectiveness. Because it is the most difficult to audit, there may be a tendency to ignore it. However, no assessment of value for money is complete without regard to effectiveness. Economy and efficiency in the execution of programmes is insufficient if the programmes are not meeting the authorities' objectives. In order to assess effectiveness it is necessary first to determine and specify objectives and second to assess performance against these objectives so that appropriate adjustment can be made or remedial action taken. However, if these objectives are vaguely stated, then they will be of no benefit in evaluating effectiveness.

The following vaguely worded objective is quoted in the C&AG's (1994) VFM report on the LEADER programme: 'The principal objective ... is to organise, co-ordinate, and promote local development initiative.'

Because of the vagueness of this statement it would be very difficult to evaluate progress. Objectives need to be examined against the following criteria sometimes summarised by the acronym SMART. Objectives should be:

- *specific* – the objectives should be broken down into tangible form; for example, instead of referring to local development initiative the objectives might be stated in terms of number of jobs created and increase of income levels in the locality.
- *measurable* – targets must be set into the objectives so that we can monitor progress.
- *achievable* – the targets set must be capable of being achieved.
- *realistic* – the targets set must not be over-optimistic. However, they should not be formulated too loosely.

- *time bounded* – time targets should also be set. Targets can be set for the short, medium and long term.

Therefore, taking the vague objective about local development outlined above, we can try to break it down into its sub-component objectives which meet the above criteria. For example, one objective of local development is job creation. The specific objective of a programme might be to create 500 jobs in each of the next two years. This could be done by creating awareness of the incentives available and supporting all viable proposals.

By breaking down the objectives and stating them explicitly, the effectiveness of a programme can be evaluated. The organisation can establish a series of indicators under the headings of economy, efficiency and effectiveness to monitor on a regular basis its progress in achieving this objective.

Indicators of economy might include advertising costs, costs per meeting held, staff costs, and other costs.

Indictors of efficiency might include number of applications per meeting, time to process applications, cost per application, and size of grant per application.

Indicators of effectiveness might include number of jobs created (this indicator is to some extent outside the control of the programme because it will be affected by the economic environment), number of people aware of the available incentives, and satisfaction with the way the proposals were assessed.

Properly defined objectives for and scope of a study help to clarify the approach to be taken and reduce ambiguity. For example, an objective to establish the costs of a community-based health programme is relatively specific. But still we need to be clear about what we mean by costs.

The scope of the study should define costs as a combination of either direct staff costs and non-pay costs; direct pay, non-pay and corporate management staff costs; or direct costs, corporate management staff costs and other corporate costs such as the use of facilities.

In a similar vein, the scope of the study can establish boundaries for the study. For example, do we mean just community-based health service, or something wider such as community-based with occasional institutional places. The scope, therefore, focuses on the part or element of the service to be reviewed.

Table 7.1 illustrates how objectives and scope might be set for the audit of a sports facility. Table 7.2 and 7.3 show the objectives and scope for two VFM studies undertaken by the C&AG.

Table 7.1: Sports facility

Scope

The project will concentrate on the sports centre and all-weather pitches. It will establish full costs and revenues for financial year 1998 and will assess utilisation over that period by customer type and category, e.g. adult, child, employed, unemployed, member and non-member.

Assessment of management systems will include corporate control, planning and budgeting as well as performance monitoring.

The project will review competitor prizes and facilities as part of a bench-marking exercise.

Objectives
- To determine full costs and revenues relating to the provision of sports facilities
- To assess management controls in the sports centre
- To determine the rate of utilisation of sports facilities
- To review the charging policy and the price structure for sporting facilities.

Table 7.2: Emergency ambulance service

Scope

This value for money examination was undertaken to establish the extent to which the emergency ambulance services are provided efficiently and economically.

Objectives
- To determine whether the emergency ambulance services are efficient in responding to emergency calls
- To determine whether the emergency ambulance services are provided economically
- To determine whether resources are used efficiently by the emergency ambulance services, consistent with maintaining rapid response times
- To determine whether a national strategy for the provision of effective, efficient and economic emergency ambulance services has been developed and implemented.

Table 7.3: Consultancies in the civil service

Scope

The examination was concerned with all consultancies undertaken in all government departments in the period 1994 to 1996. It set out to establish the extent of the use of consultants in the civil service and to what degree the impact of the consultancies is being measured.

Objectives
- To determine the cost of consultancies in the period 1994 to 1996 and the purpose for which consultants were engaged
- To assess whether the need for consultants was properly assessed and other options fully evaluated
- To determine whether consultancy services were acquired in the most economical manner
- To determine whether the consultancy projects were managed efficiently
- To review the extent to which the outputs of consultancy projects were utilised.

The objectives and scope outlined in these tables provide useful guidelines. Of course, each audit requires specifically designed objectives and scope. The case-studies below give further examples of objectives and scope.

Data gathering and analysis

When the objectives and scope have been agreed the evaluation can move forward to data collection and analysis. The most common data gathering techniques include:

- Examination of files and documentation for information on programmes and projects
- Literature searches and reviews
- Surveys and questionnaires which systematically collect data from target populations.

The most common data analysis techniques include the following:
- Bench-marking, which entails comparing an organisation's methods, procedures and processes with other organisations believed to operate at or near best practice levels. Organisations may combine to act as bench-marking partners in a confidential manner, in order to facilitate comparisons and critical evaluation
- Focus groups, which are comprised of customers and other stakeholders brought together to provide feedback about and insight into the quality and level of services provided

- Before-after studies which compare programme proposals or services before and after implementation of an initiative.

Having gathered and analysed the data the auditor will be in a position to consider the resources consumed in terms of financial costs, staff involvement and use of equipment and infrastructure. The establishment of causal relationships and the corroboration of findings will allow the auditor to draw conclusions and make recommendations.

Initial investigation

The aim of the initial investigation is to conclude whether a full investigation should proceed and if so to recommend the objective of the full investigation and the tasks to be carried out. The initial investigation would involve interviewing senior managers to get their perspective on the issues involved. The investigation would proceed by reviewing the objectives and examining how success in achieving them is measured. Next the auditor might examine staffing levels, the mix of staff and the relationship between staffing levels and level of activity over recent years. Also as part of the investigation the auditor might review the organisation chart and the job descriptions. It would, of course, be necessary to read any reports, internal or external, produced on the area of activity under audit. The auditor should conduct a detailed review of costs or other statistics, for example, performance indicators such as number of invoices processed per hour. Where possible these should be compared with indicators in other organisations. It is also useful to interview people in the area under audit. They may have their own ideas on what needs to be done.

When the initial investigation is completed the auditor should be in a position to decide on the area(s) for full investigation. The auditor should also be able to draw up the terms of reference and a work programme for a full investigation.

Full investigation

The processes under discussion are reasonably well structured but a degree of flexibility should also be allowed for. Because the auditor is dealing with people, a sensitive and sympathetic approach is required. Hence the need for flexibility.

A structured approach to the full investigation might involve the following:
- *Input-based* reviews which are largely concerned with statistical analysis and comparisons including the use of performance indicators to evaluate economy and efficiency

- *System-based* reviews which are largely concerned with the process of turning inputs into outputs. These reviews look at areas such as staffing levels and duties, organisation structures and procedures and activity levels. They may also help to answer issues raised by the input-based review
- *Output-based* reviews which are concerned with policy objectives, the activities to achieve these objectives and the use of performance indicators to measure the effectiveness of the policies.

The first two types of reviews are concerned with economy and efficiency. The third type of review is concerned with effectiveness.

Input-based reviews

Input-based reviews are concerned with examining inputs (i.e. costs and other resources) used to produce the outputs (i.e. goods or services such as application forms processed). Performance indicators are a useful tool for the auditor; they can be compared to other similar organisations. However, a higher or lower figure than the comparable organisation(s) does not in itself indicate a better or poorer performance. For example, higher costs than the average may be due to the provision of a higher level of service as a result of a policy decision. Therefore, such comparisons are not an end in themselves but are a way of identifying possible areas for further investigation as part of the system-based review.

When making comparisons with other organisations, it is important that we compare like with like. In the UK, the Audit Commission has developed 'families' of local authorities and health authorities which are similar in terms of area covered, population and demographics. This makes the comparison more meaningful. However, the caveat that such comparisons only identify areas of further investigation still applies.

System-based reviews

A system-based approach looks at staffing, organisation structures, procedures and activity levels. These reviews are often a follow-on to areas identified by the input-based review. As part of the review the auditor might query the objectives of the area under review, how success is measured and what corrective action is taken. The review would ask whether the organisation's systems and structures allow management to exercise control over the organisation's resources. It would also be important to assess why the work is done and why it is done the way it is, whether costs can be reduced without impairing service, and whether the service levels can be changed.

In conducting a system-based review the auditor would examine the nature and purpose of each activity/function in the area under audit, the costs involved, the organisation structure and the procedures in place especially if there are any bottlenecks, the duties and workloads of each staff member and the activity levels in the area under audit.

The necessary information can be obtained by examining the existing records (e.g. work files, accounts, work returns), administering written questionnaires, interviewing management and staff and by direct observation or, where appropriate, through activity sampling (i.e. by taking a sample of units and following them through the various processes to see what conclusions can be drawn. These conclusions can then be extrapolated for the whole area of activity).

Output-based reviews

Output-based reviews are concerned with effectiveness. The auditing of effectiveness presupposes the existence of clearly stated objectives. The external auditor should not be concerned with appropriateness of the policy. An output-based review needs to enquire whether objectives are well defined and communicated to management and staff. The review needs to find out if performance indicators have been put in place to monitor progress on the achievement of the objectives and if the indicators are prepared accurately, on time, regularly and to the appropriate level of detail. The review should also check whether appropriate corrective action, if required, has taken place. It is also necessary to enquire whether alternative ways of delivering the service have been considered and whether management have considered the appropriateness of the service in the light of changes in the environment.

Essentially the auditor is examining if the organisation has the structures in place to monitor its effectiveness. If the structures are not in place, then the auditor should report this fact. The auditor may develop the audit to include the review of outputs and the development of performance indicators to monitor progress on the achievement of the objectives.

Another way to monitor effectiveness is through the use of user surveys whereby a sample of users is interviewed for opinions on different aspects of the service provided. This technique has to be used carefully and considerable thought must be given to the sample size and to designing questionnaires that are free of bias. It is an expensive technique to use.

Choice of approach

In deciding on the approach to be adopted, key questions must be asked. In examining the input-based and system-based approach, these questions are: Can inputs and outputs be measured? Is the process clearly established? Is the activity to be repeated?

Depending on the answers to these questions, a decision can be made on whether to use an input-based or system-based approach. If the answer to all three questions is yes, then either approach can be used. If the answer to the second question is no, then only an input-based approach can be used.

In evaluating effectiveness a few key questions need to be asked, namely, Are the objectives clearly identified and ranked in importance? Can progress towards the achievement of the objectives be objectively assessed? Is there a link between the service target levels and the achievement of the organisation's objectives?

If the answer to the first question is no, then measuring effectiveness becomes very difficult. If the answer to the third question is no, then evaluation of achievement becomes very subjective.

The audit process: key questions

A full investigation by an auditor would include a more detailed review of the following: objectives and how success in achieving them is measured, financial and other controls used within the organisation, organisation structure, staffing levels, workload and costs. The investigation would also review each procedure/activity within the organisation by asking whether it is necessary, if it can be carried out more efficiently and if costs can be reduced without impairing service. In Table 7.4 important issues which arise in the process of investigation are outlined.

These questions are illustrative. Every audit is unique and requires specifically designed questions. We will see some of these questions in the case-studies which follow.

Case studies

A number of VFM studies conducted by the C&AG have been published. By end-1998 the C&AG had produced over 25 reports; these are listed in the appendix to this chapter.

The value for money unit of the LGAS has compiled a number of studies (Department of the Environment 1996b) covering areas such as purchasing, advertising, insurance, parking charges, photocopying costs, machinery yards, energy efficiency, property management and public lighting.

In this section we will outline two studies, one by the C&AG and the other by the LGAS. The studies give an insight to how evaluators deal with the practicalities of assessing value for money.

Table 7.4: Key questions in audit process

Evaluating capital expenditure controls

- *Approval procedure* – responsibility for all aspects of the projects should be clearly laid out and communicated.
- *Appraisal* – a full scale appraisal of the financial and non-financial costs and benefits needs to be conducted.
- *Control* over project implementation – adherence to schedule, design and budget needs to be monitored. What controls were in place? Were problems highlighted? Were they corrected?
- *Review* – each project should be reviewed after completion. Can the organisation learn from the experience? What new controls, if any, need to be put in place?

Land and property management

- Are the objectives of the organisation clearly defined?
- What controls are in place to cover the acquisition, disposal and retention of land and property?
- Is the information on land and property adequate and up-to-date?

Charges for services

- How was the level of charge decided on?
- How often is it reviewed?

Evaluating revenue expenditure controls

- How is the budget prepared? Is it incremental or zero-based budgeting?
- How is expenditure controlled? What monitoring procedures are in place?
- Is the effectiveness of the arrangement reviewed on a regular basis?

Evaluating purchases

- Is there a central purchasing department?
- Are there limits placed on who can order what value of materials?
- Is the objective of purchasing to meet user requirements or provide the most economic service?

Manpower planning

- Is the workload translated into manpower needs in terms of skill, grade and location?
- Are current manpower resources in terms of skill and age profile sufficient to meet current or future demands?
- Is there an action plan to meet any gaps identified? Who is responsible for implementation? Who monitors and how?
- Is there a regular review of productivity and efficiency?
- Are vacancies critically evaluated prior to giving authorisation to fill them?

Energy management

- What is the current level of expenditure?
- Have the housekeeping arrangements, especially in relation to maintenance, been reviewed?

Insurance arrangements

- Is there a full record kept of what is insured? What is the level of cover? Are valuations updated on a regular basis?
- Are these arrangements reviewed frequently?

Evaluating the procedures for managing current assets

- How quickly are debtors billed? What procedures are in place to collect monies owed?
- How quickly are claims for grants submitted?
- How quickly are creditors paid? Is the organisation making best use of credit terms?
- Are accurate records of stocks kept? How do stocking and demand levels compare?

LEADER programme

This was a study undertaken by the Comptroller & Auditor General. The overall objective of the LEADER I programme was to create a self-sustaining rural community through local development action groups. These groups are responsible for developing and implementing business plans.

The business plans are drawn up by each group in accordance with the local community's own priorities and resources. A total of €34.6m was paid out to sixteen LEADER groups. These groups were selected from thirty-four applicants.

For projects to be funded, the EU required that public funds should at least be matched by private investors. The two main categories of projects were rural tourism (mainly self-catering/B&B accommodation) and small enterprises.

The purpose of the VFM audit was to assess the efficiency of the administration of the programme, and examine how the effectiveness of the LEADER programme is evaluated. Any lesson learned from the VFM audit would be of use on the LEADER II programme.

The LEADER programme was administered at 3 levels:

- The Department of Agriculture administered the scheme at national level in terms of funding, monitoring and controlling the groups and liaison with the EU.
- A monitoring committee reviewed and if necessary, revised the programme.
- Each group was responsible for selecting projects by way of implementing its business plan and for the proper distribution of funds.

The audit approach was to interview personnel, review records including EU guidelines, business plans and evaluation reports, and examine a sample of four LEADER groups.

Key questions

The auditors posed a variety of questions. For example, to assess effectiveness they asked whether clear objectives had been set by each group against which outcomes could be measured. Mostly, however, the questions dealt with administration of the programme at each level, namely the Department of Agriculture, monitoring committees and groups.

The questions posed by the auditor about the Department of Agriculture were: How many personnel were devoted to administering the scheme? What resources were devoted to on-site inspections? How many on-site inspections took place? What returns were made by the groups? How prompt were these?

Do these returns allow proper accounting for expenditure in conformity with EU rules? Were the groups able to draw down the funding from the Department? How efficient was the Department in drawing down funds from the EU?

At the level of the monitoring committees the key questions were: How many people were on the committee? How were decisions made? What decisions were made in relation to revising the scheme?

The questions posed at group level were: How were projects selected, inspected and assessed? Were there cost overruns? Was expenditure properly vouched? Were projects evaluated after completion? Did LEADER overlap with other schemes?

Key findings

In assessing effectiveness the audit found that the objectives of the groups which were examined were very vague. For example: 'The principal object-ive ... is to organise, co-ordinate and promote local development initiative.'

As noted above, the vagueness of the objective makes it very difficult to evaluate the effectiveness of the LEADER programme.

Other objectives such as the development and empowerment of local communities are also extremely difficult to measure directly. However, output indicators such as public meetings held, number of workshops held and number of persons trained could be used. The economic benefits of LEADER could be evaluated by the number and type of jobs created and the increase in the level of income in the area.

The audit also found that due to delays in the submission of monthly reports and their compilation into an overall report, the drawdown of funds was delayed.

In assessing administration, the audit found that at the Department of Agriculture level the number of personnel devoted to administration was the equivalent of four full-time staff and that the inspection activity was the equivalent of three quarters of a full-time staff member.

It transpired that no formal record of visits by the Department of Agri-culture was kept. The number of inspections depended on the time pressures the inspectors were under. The five inspectors were also responsible for a number of other schemes. A formal record of dates and outcomes for each group visit should have been kept so that areas of risk could be focused on.

The monthly returns by each group were not completed consistently, were often delayed and the sheer size of the reports made it very difficult to re-input the reports into the Department's computer system.

EU rules require that expenditure be analysed by fund. The monthly return did not conform to this requirement and the Department had to undertake this analysis before the final payment from the EU was made.

The audit noted that there were delays between the commitment of funds to projects and the actual spending of funds. This created problems with records which made it difficult to conduct thorough assessments.

The absence of detailed records made inspection very difficult. Inspection was conducted by a locally appointed and based person who would verify that expenditure was related to the project approved and that the costs were reasonable. The audit found that the inspectors appointed in many cases did not have the relevant experience. Inspectors often had a conflict of roles as inspectors and project facilitators. Indeed in many cases no record of the inspection was kept.

The lack of a clear breakdown of the individual elements made it very difficult to monitor expenditure. In some cases payments were made before invoices were presented. In a number of cases there was no evidence to indicate whether all the necessary tax clearance certificates had been received.

Two of the groups intended to conduct a post-completion evaluation. In the absence of a set of project targets against which to compare the outturn, this would be very difficult.

The auditor found that there was some overlap between LEADER and other initiatives. However, no evidence was found of projects receiving funding from a number of sources. This overlap could be reduced by devolving some of the administration to groups such as the county enterprise boards.

At the monitoring committee level the audit found that 40 people were on the committee. Each group had one representative and decisions were made by consensus. This limited the committee's ability to control the programme. In particular, the need for consensus made it difficult to reallocate funds if groups were falling behind in spending funds.

At the group level the audit found that in three of the four groups visited, projects receiving aid had been promoted by board members or by people closely connected to board members and that projects were funded which were specifically excluded. Many projects which were grant aided had no formal record on file of the elements of the project, the likely outputs or the cost components. Assessment was often informal, with no report.

The audit featured in this case-study clearly identified important issues. Of course, each VFM audit will require its own approach. In general, however, the structured approach of the VFM audit as evidenced in the case-study will help ensure that the audit is effective.

Machinery yards

This was a study undertaken by the Value for Money Unit of the Local Government Audit Service. Local authority machinery yards store plant, machinery and vehicles used for work on roads, sanitary services and housing. A machinery yard provides machinery in sufficient quantity for routine and emergency tasks, at lower cost than if it were hired and, indeed, where it might not be available from commercial operators.

The purpose of the VFM study was to evaluate operational procedures, review policy on machinery replacement, establish the extent to which machines are hired by local authorities and make recommendations on how local authorities could better manage machinery stocks.

The audit approach consisted of a detailed questionnaire sent to nine local authorities on a pilot basis. The information gathered was used to produce a draft report which was circulated to all county councils and county borough corporations. The councils and authorities were asked to compare the findings in the draft report with the practices operating in their authorities, to detail any differences and to supply details of significant statistics for inclusion in the final report.

The final report compared the results obtained and suggested best practice improvements in a number of areas.

Key Questions

The questions pursued by the report were grouped in sections including additions/disposals, leasing, hiring of machinery, charge-out rates, wages and salaries, operating costs, overheads and workshop costs and credits.

The key questions about additions and disposals were: When is a decision made to replace a machine? What purchasing procedures are in place? What procedures are in place for the disposal of machines?

The study enquired into leasing costs and terms and posed questions about hiring of machinery such as, How much was spent on hiring machinery? What causes machinery to be hired? What type of machinery was hired?

On the question of charge-out rates the report asks, What is the charge-out rate per hour? How is this made up in terms of material, labour and overheads?

The study enquired into salary and wage costs (for drivers, general operations, workshop staff, stores staff, administrative staff and engineering staff), operating costs (fuel, oil, tyres, repairs etc) and overheads (travel expenses, motor insurance, employers' liability insurance, road tax, pensioners of retired staff etc).

Key questions about the workshop concerned the number of employees, purchasing policy and the charge-out rate per hour.

Key Findings

The report produced the following key findings and recommendations.

- *Additions and disposals of machinery.* The report noted that it may be more economical to purchase machinery second-hand than to buy new or even to hire. It emphasised the need for information which identifies the optimum time to replace machinery, for example by comparing the reduced depreciation charge as a machine gets older with the increasing maintenance costs. A comprehensive recording and reporting system would allow above-average expenditure, for example on maintenance and running costs, to be identified and investigated. The report recommended that local authorities when replacing old machines should auction them so as to be free to purchase replacements 'for cash' at the lowest price.

- *Hired machinery.* Local authorities hire machinery for several reasons: to meet requirements during periods of peak demand, to avail of specialist machines, when it is cheaper to hire, and when the required machine is not available.

  The report found that much of the expenditure on plant refers to plant not normally purchased by local authorities. Over a quarter of the expenditure was for hire of plant such as lorries, tractors and vans normally operated by local authorities. There were many instances where similar machines were hired at different rates; this was due to the non-availability at particular times of the lowest quoted machine.

  The report found that some machinery was on hire on a continuous basis and recommended that local authorities seek special terms or discounts for machinery hired in this fashion. In some cases it may be cheaper to purchase rather than hire machinery. The report found that none of the pilot authorities formally considered the correct mix between ownership and hire. Generally where levels of activity are low it should be cheaper to hire because of the existence of fixed costs such as depreciation, insurance and road tax which exist regardless of activity. As levels of usage increase the fixed cost per unit of activity decreases, eventually reaching a point where it becomes cheaper to purchase than to hire. The report recommended that local authorities increase the level of management information in order to make decisions about the optimum mix between ownership and hire.

- *Charge-out rates.* Charge-out rates were estimated by the pilot authorities once a year, based on costs and levels of activity. Authorities treated replacement costs in different ways including: direct purchase, contribution to a replacement fund, a depreciation charge and actual lease repayments. Generally, machines and vehicles were charged out on an hourly basis with no distinction between working time, standing time or travel time. In most cases authorities did not share machinery even where there were several authorities in the same locality or city. The report argued that machinery yards ought to be in a position to provide machinery at rates competitive with those of commercial operators.

- *Machinery expenses account.* The report found that labour costs were largely accounted for by drivers and fitters. Drivers worked substantial overtime and one authority suggested that drivers work a set number of hours a year with time off during slack periods to compensate for excess hours worked during busy periods. The report indicated possible industrial relations problems with such an arrangement.

Some authorities allocated specific machines to specific drivers on the presumption that they would take more care of 'their' machines. The report noted that this arrangement carries the danger of inflexibility and idleness when machines are being repaired.

The report examined the ratio of fitters to drivers and found that the authorities with the oldest machines had the highest fitter-to-driver ratios and that those with the most modern machinery had the lowest ratios.

Authorities differed in the way they treated the type and apportionment of overheads charged to the machinery expense account. The report called for an investigation of the treatment of overheads so that, for example, the machinery yard is not allocated the insurance costs applicable to other machinery, such as library vans, within an authority. The report noted that an overburdening of the machinery expense account with overheads would lead to high charge-out rates compared to commercial rates and that this might lead to user-sections preferring to hire from commercial companies.

Local authorities provide workshops for the maintenance and repair of machinery. The report recommended an appropriate internal costing system so that when workshops carry out work for sections other than the machine yard the relevant sections are properly charged.

- *Overview.* The report developed several themes. It emphasised the need to base decisions on costing systems, recording and reporting systems, and information. It identified and queried differentials in rates, such as hiring rates. The report was vigilant for opportunities for complementarity and sharing in service delivery and for the availability of special terms and discounts where there was a high volume of purchases. It noted the need for clarity and standardisation in financial procedures. Finally, the report highlighted the use of analysis to determine optimal resource use, for example in determining the balance between old and new machines and between ownership and hiring. These themes are central to value for money and prompt questions which can be applied in many other areas of enquiry.

Conclusion

As a result of greater demand for public services, limits on the availability of funding and the need to demonstrate accountability, organisations have to ensure that they are getting value for money from the funds they are spending. The C&AG (Amendment) Act 1993 and the Local Government

(Financial Provisions) Act 1997 give legal backing to this objective. VFM audits can be conducted on various activities in an organisation. We have examined how these areas can be chosen and how to conduct a VFM audit. We have also outlined VFM audit case studies conducted in Ireland by the C&AG and the LGAS. These can help us to identify areas for further review.

The pursuit of value for money involves the outlining of the organisation's mission statement, breaking this into SMART objectives and establishing performance indicators to monitor progress. The fundamental issue is that the organisation is constantly questioning and reviewing the way it operates, i.e. What service is being provided? Why is it being offered? Can it be offered in a different way? The auditor has a key role to play in this process both as a facilitator and a means of ensuring that a mission statement, objectives and performance indicators are in place and are being monitored.

The second role of the auditor is to conduct a VFM audit. This involves the selection of potential areas for auditing. Each area selected is investigated initially to see if it would be of benefit to the organisation to conduct a full investigation. A full investigation can be input-based, system-based or output-based. In many ways VFM audits adopt a common sense approach. They help to raise questions about the amount of money being spent and what is being achieved with that money. In so doing, VFM audits can contribute significantly to improving performance, maximising the use of scarce resources and increasing accountability.

The evaluation of value for money has a number of benefits for an organisation. It facilitates and promotes better strategic and operational decision-making, enhances management responsibility and accessibility, allows assessments of the achievement of objectives, promotes better use of resources and highlights the importance of the customer or service user. Clearly, therefore, VFM reviews are an important element in the strategic management of organisations.

APPENDIX

Reports on Value for Money Examinations by the Comptroller and Auditor General

1994
1 The Leader Programme

1995
2 Energy Management in the Health Service
3 Garda Transport
4 Gas Interconnector Project
5 Management of Telephone Facilities in the Civil Service
6 Regional Development Measures
7 FEOGA Borrowing
8 Means Testing

1996
9   Gulliver: The Irish Tourism Information and Reservation System
10 Planning of Second Level School Accommodation
11 The National Museum at Collins Barracks
12 Procurement in Universities
13 Ordnance Survey
14 The Irish Genealogical Project
15 Administrative Budgets in the Irish Civil Service
16 Arterial Drainage of the Boyle and Bonet Rivers

1997
17 The Development of the Integrated Short-Term Schemes Computer System
18 Management of Inland Fisheries
19 Prescribing Practices and the Development of General Practitioner Services
20 The Emergency Ambulance Services
21 Value Added Tax Collection and Control

1998
22 Consultancies in the Civil Service
23 The Administration of Supplementary Welfare Allowances
24 The Provision and Management of Industrial Property
25 Administration of Premium and Headage Grant Applications

REFERENCES

Bates, J. (1993). *Managing Value for Money in the Public Sector*, London: Chapman and Hall

Butt, H. and B. Palmer (1985). *Value for Money in the Public Sector: the decision-maker's guide*, Oxford: Blackwell

Buttery, R. and R. Simpson (1986). *Internal Audit in the Public Sector*, Cambridge: Woodhead-Faulkner

Comptroller and Auditor General (1994). *Report on Value for Money Examination: Department of Agriculture, Food and Forestry – The LEADER Programme*, Dublin: Stationery Office

Comptroller & Auditor General (1997). *Report on Value for Money Examination: Consultancies in Civil Service*, Dublin: Stationery Office

Comptroller & Auditor General (1998). *Report on Value for Money Examination:* The Emergency Ambulance Service, Dublin: Stationery Office

Coombs, H. and D. Jenkins (1991). *Public Sector Financial Management*, London: Chapman and Hall

Department of the Environment (1996a). *Better Local Government: A Programme for Change*, Dublin: Stationery Office

Department of the Environment (1996b). *Value for Money Studies on Local Authorities*, Studies Nos 1–10, Dublin: Stationery Office

Glynn, J. (1985). *Value for Money Auditing in the Public Sector*, Englewood Cliffs: Prentice Hall

Jones, P. and J. Bates (1990). *Public Sector Auditing: practical techniques for an integrated approach*, London: Chapman and Hall

Price Waterhouse (1983). *Value for Money Auditing Manual: the investigation of economy, efficiency and effectiveness in local government*, London: Gee and Co

Venables, J. and K. Impey (1988). *Internal Audit*, London: Butterworth

8

Cost Benefit Analysis

MICHAEL MULREANY

Introduction

Cost benefit analysis is the most important technique for project appraisal in the public sector. In chapter 5 we considered the appraisal of commercial projects. There are many common elements in both approaches and where this occurs the reader will be referred to the principles and techniques first introduced in chapter 5.

In classical microeconomic theory the market system leads to maximum efficiency: producers minimise costs, society maximises output, consumers maximise satisfaction and any redistribution of output could not increase one person's satisfaction without reducing that of another.

Would that things were so perfect. In practice, there are many market failures (e.g. see Stiglitz 1988). One such failure is due to externalities or spillover effects, i.e. certain 'goods' and 'bads' which are not allocated by the market system. For example, 'bads' such as environmental pollution or traffic congestion are not generally taken into account in the production of or the demand for market products.

Welfare economics goes beyond the market system to consider the effects of externalities and more generally to analyse how successfully society is achieving certain objectives which may not be attainable by the free play of market forces.

The main technique for using welfare economics in practice is cost benefit analysis. In essence, cost benefit analysis attempts to evaluate what the market system omits; its perspective is that of society. Cost benefit analysis attempts to evaluate on a common monetary scale the costs and benefits of all the marketed and unmarketed consequences of projects and to estimate the net social benefits.

Cost benefit analysis allows quantified social costs and benefits to be incorporated into the appraisal of investments. Of course the appraisal and

177

subsequent investment decisions will be based on a combination of the social along with the underlying market-valued costs and benefits.

Generally, cost benefit analysis is conducted 'ex-ante' – it appraises projects before they are undertaken. The appraisal can be used to answer such questions as, Should a project be undertaken? and If so in what form and at what scale? The basic rationale behind cost benefit analysis is the pursuit of economic efficiency. Once government has decided on the sectoral distribution of public money then cost benefit analysis can indicate how best it can be allocated among the various investment opportunities in any sector.

The procedure of cost benefit analysis

The theory of cost benefit analysis has its roots in nineteenth-century welfare economics. The practice has developed mostly in the twentieth century and particularly in the areas of transport and water related projects. The scope of cost benefit analysis has been extended to include areas as diverse as training programmes and health care and medical procedures.

In Ireland, cost benefit analysis has developed from the late 1960s especially in the area of transport and also in areas such as drainage (see Blackwell 1991). The high levels of investment in physical infrastructure in the late 1980s and 1990s combined with public concern over safety and environmental damage has led to a fresh momentum to cost benefit analysis studies and to some renewal of interest in methodological issues (e.g. Honohan 1998, Gray 1995).

The procedure followed in cost benefit analysis consists of several steps. Exactly how the steps are identified will inevitably give rise to some dispute. Here we will adopt the approach outlined by the Department of Finance as stated in the Public Capital Programme 1984 (Department of Finance 1983).

According to this outline, economic and/or financial appraisals should contain the following elements:

- A clearly defined set of objectives for the project
- A statement of alternatives that would meet the objectives
- A statement of the constraints (*viz.* technological, physical, financial and statutory) that impinge on the project, together with a listing of those alternatives that do not fall within the constraints
- In respect of each chosen alternative:
  - A list of the benefits and costs expected over the economic life of the project and underlying assumptions
  - A quantification of the benefits and costs in cash flows or economic flows as appropriate
  - A statement of projected cash flows or a cost/benefit balance sheet, as appropriate

- A calculation of the decision criteria (net present value, cost/benefit ratio, internal rate of return, maximum effectiveness at least cost) and a test for sensitivity to changes in key variables
- Identification, and whenever possible quantification, of the distributional effects of the costs and the benefits
- An assessment of the pay-back period (where appropriate)
- A recommendation as to the preferred alternative.

This is a reasonably succinct outline of the steps, from defining objectives to making a decision or recommendation. The Department of Finance (1994) and the Community Support Framework Evaluation Unit (1999) have produced more detailed guidelines for the appraisal of capital expenditure proposals in the public sector. We will refer to these as we proceed.

Defining objectives

We have discussed in the previous chapter the importance of setting and specifying objectives. Here we will add some points of direct relevance to project and programme appraisal.

Objectives should be made as explicit, precise and amenable to measurement as possible. For example, in a flood control project an objective stated in the form 'to reduce flood damage by €A in area B by year C' is vastly preferable to the form 'to reduce flood damage'. Similarly for a literacy programme an objective in the form 'to increase reading scores' is much weaker than in the form 'to increase reading scores by X among group Y by year Z.' Such a formulation allows the possibility of identifying alternative ways to meet the objective and facilitates assessment of the costs and benefits of each alternative. It also clarifies for whom the benefit is intended which in turn enables consideration of potential 'gainers' and 'losers'.

The definition of objectives is closely bound-up with the definition of the project itself, i.e. with the specification of the boundaries of the project and the resources to be allocated. For example, the definition of a project to upgrade a stretch of rail should clarify what is included and excluded. Are train stations and adjoining car parks to be included or excluded?

Finally, in this brief discussion of objectives we might recall from chapter 1 that some projects and programmes have multiple objectives. Where this is the case, in order to have effective resource allocation and appraisal the objectives should be both explicit and prioritised.

Identifying alternatives

Properly specified objectives may facilitate the identification of alternatives but care is still needed. The alternatives either of doing nothing or of minimal intervention are often overlooked, yet these are often feasible alternatives.

The inclusion of the 'do-nothing' option requires care in drawing inferences. For example, if the option of an urban road building programme can be shown to be preferable to doing nothing then the reflex inference may be to go ahead and put the programme in place. But all we know is that the programme is better than nothing; perhaps it would be better to choose just part of the programme or a different alternative such as improved public transport.

The Department of Finance (1994) cautions against any presumption that public sector responses are the only available ones and indicates that alternatives involving or relying on the private sector should also be considered. The Department suggests that, where appropriate, different scales of the same response should be included as separate alternatives. It also suggests that any conflict that may occur between certain alternatives and existing policies be referred to decision-makers who might then wish to review the policies.

A standard caveat in the analysis of alternatives is to be vigilant for the manipulation of options intended to present a particular one in a favourable light. The one-time US Secretary of State, Henry Kissinger put the point as follows: 'I have seen it happen ... that when one asks for choices one is always given three: two absurd ones and the preferred one.' One would expect higher standards from Irish public servants.

Constraints

Constraints take several forms and it is important to identify which are relevant in any particular appraisal.

Budgetary constraints are familiar. Constraints on expenditure may take the form either of set amounts to be fully spent, or sums to be spent with discretion up to a maximum, or a requirement that a certain percentage of expenditure be self-financed. The form of the constraint will influence the appraisal; for example, where there is discretion to spend up to a maximum, considerations of opportunity cost are particularly relevant.

There is a natural tendency to think of budgetary constraints as targets for restraints on expenditure, but targets may also apply to revenue. Such is the case, for example, where enterprises are given targets for profit.

Environmental constraints may take the form of natural terrain or of geological deposits which must be protected. Input, or physical constraints, may take the form of unavailability of supply, inelasticity of supply or technological incompatibility of inputs. Input constraints may apply to raw materials, labour, skills, information technology and so forth. Technical constraints arise where there is a technically limited number of ways in which to produce a good or deliver a service.

Legal constraints are common. They may limit the activities of organisations, types of land-use, rights of access, pricing options and so forth. Administrative constraints may also exist as when there are staff, skills or information technology shortages which limit what can be processed through the administrative system.

This is quite a formidable list and not an exhaustive one. There may be policy constraints requiring consistency with existing decisions on policy or investment. Or there may be distributional constraints intended to favour certain regions or income groups; this is an issue to which we will return later in the chapter. At this juncture, however, we have established the variety of the constraints and their importance for project appraisal.

Identifying costs and benefits

The relevant costs and benefits of projects may be direct, indirect, tangible or intangible or some combination of these. For a road project, for example, identification would include a listing of the resources used such as concrete, tarmac and labour and the benefits such as time saved, reduction in traffic fatalities and so forth. We would also list effects on property prices, local businesses, quality of the landscape and so forth.

Additionality, deadweight and displacement

Important concepts to bear in mind when identifying and listing costs and benefits are additionality, deadweight and displacement. Additionality and deadweight are closely related and refer to the net impacts of programmes and projects. Deadweight occurs when part of a public expenditure programme confers benefits on recipients other than those intended. For example, in the case of a publicly funded programme to promote business start-ups, some participants may in any event have started their own businesses. For these, the programme is not strictly needed and they represent deadweight. Viewed in another way, in terms of additionality, the benefit should be measured net of any start-ups that would have occurred in the absence of the programme.

Displacement occurs when the creation of a positive project or programme output leads to a loss of output elsewhere. For example, a grant-aided leisure facility may displace a commercially funded one or graduates from a job training programme may displace people from employment.

Categorising costs and benefits

Musgrave and Musgrave (1984) provide a useful categorisation of costs and benefits as exemplified in Table 8.1. The categorisation is rehearsed here to highlight some key distinctions between types of costs and benefits.

Table 8.1 Types of costs and benefits

		Irrigation Project	
		Benefits	Costs
Real			
• *Direct*	tangible	Increased farm output	Cost of pipes
	intangible	Beautification of area	Loss of wilderness
• *Indirect*	tangible	Reduced soil erosion	Diversion of water
	intangible	Preservation of rural society	Destruction of wildlife
Pecuniary		Relative improvement in farm equipment industry	

The main distinctions to be drawn are:

Real and pecuniary

Real benefits are those derived by the final consumer. They add to the welfare of society and can be set against the real cost of resources used. Pecuniary costs and benefits derive from changes in relative prices in secondary markets. For example, the improvement of a road may lead to increased earnings for roadside restaurants. However, these earnings are not a net gain to society; rather they are gains to particular businesses which, at least in part, are likely to be offset by reduced food purchases and restaurant earnings elsewhere. Generally, therefore, pecuniary costs and benefits are not included in the economic evaluation of costs and benefits.

Direct and indirect

Real costs and benefits can be sub-classified as direct (primary) or indirect (secondary) in relation to the main objectives of projects or programmes. For example, an education programme may be directly aimed at increasing the earning power of a certain cohort of schoolleavers but may have the secondary effect of reducing delinquency.

Tangible and intangible

Tangible costs and benefits are those which can be valued by the market; intangible costs and benefits are those which cannot. In the example in Table 8.1 the tangible cost of water pipes is set alongside the intangible cost of loss of wilderness and the tangible benefit of increased farm output alongside the intangible benefit of beautification of the area. Intangible costs and benefits give rise to measurement difficulties to which we will return.

The foregoing are the more obvious distinctions. Others include the distinction between final and intermediate, i.e. between the provision of goods directly to consumers and the provision of goods as inputs to the production of other goods; and between inside and outside, i.e. between costs and benefits which occur within the area where the project or programme is undertaken and those which occur outside the area.

An important question to emerge from this categorisation and discussion of costs and benefits is, How far should the analysis go in pursuing costs and benefits? Analysis itself imposes costs and it would be unwise to incur such costs in pursuit of minor impacts of projects or programmes which are being evaluated.

Transfer payments

In identifying costs and benefits two pitfalls in particular must be avoided. Firstly, transfer payments should be excluded. Taxation provides some good examples. A private enterprise in assessing a project will view tax as an expense and look for net profits on the bottom-line. From society's point of view, however, taxation transfers part of the project's benefit from the enterprise to other members of society. In cost benefit analysis as a general rule, it is gross, not net, profit which is relevant. An exception to this arises with foreign direct investment: for outward investment the taxation of profit paid abroad must be deducted because this part of the benefit accrues abroad. For inward investment the taxation of profits is reckonable as a benefit but the part of the profit remitted to the parent company cannot be included as a benefit.

Another example of transfer payment arises when a project affects indirect tax revenues and unemployment benefit. If for instance, a project, by affecting employment levels or consumption, leads to additional payments of unemployment benefits and reductions in indirect tax revenues there is no effect on real resources. However, there are redistributions of money through the exchequer. These redistributions are more properly the subject of exchequer cash flow analysis than cost benefit analysis.

Double-counting

The second major pitfall in identifying costs and benefits is double-counting. In our discussion above of the distinction between real and pecuniary benefits we considered the case of improvements to a road which confer benefits on roadside restaurants. This scenario could easily be extended to benefits to garages on the road, effects on adjoining land and so forth. As a general rule, these types of benefit are not additional and are not included in cost benefit analysis. This is partly because of offsetting reductions in profitability for garages and restaurants on other roads. Even if this were not the case, however, the increased profitability is due to more journeys being taken than before the road improvement rather than extra satisfaction gained by consumers from using the restaurants and garages.

Another example is where a new rail line, or the upgrading of an existing rail line, leads to an increase in the prices of houses conveniently located to the line. Increases in house prices are due to the additional benefits of quicker and easier access to jobs, shopping or entertainment venues. These benefits are estimated in cost benefit analysis. To count the rise in house prices as well would be double-counting; the rise in house prices being the capitalised value of the stream of future benefits of quick and easy access.

In essence, in cost benefit analysis every attempt is made to eliminate transfer and distributional items from the appraisal and to count the additional output arising from any given investment as opposed to the increase in value of existing assets.

Valuing costs and benefits

When costs and benefits have been identified the next step in cost benefit analysis is valuation in common units by use of prices. If market prices exist which accurately reflect the cost and benefits to society then the process of measuring values is relatively straightforward.

Market prices and social values

But market prices may sometimes embody distortions which make them poor indicators of social costs and benefits. Or, as is often the case with public sector output, goods and services may be untraded and no market price may exist. We will examine both of these scenarios.

The classic reason why market prices may not reflect social costs and benefits occurs in imperfect competition where prices are higher and output is lower than in competitive conditions. Imperfect competition entails production where the consumer's willingness to pay does not equal the cost of an extra unit of output; consumers willing to pay more than the cost of the extra unit of output are not supplied and hence market prices are poor indicators from a social point of view.

Taxes on expenditure are included in market prices and are another reason for divergence between market prices and social costs and benefits. Government intervention to support prices, as when the prices of certain agricultural products are artificially raised, will also create a divergence. So will tariffs, import controls and subsidies.

A divergence between private and social cost may occur where there is unemployment. An extreme case is where a project hires workers who have been unemployed and drawing unemployment benefit hitherto and who could be expected to remain unemployed in the absence of the project. The unemployment benefit is a transfer payment which we have established should be ignored for the purpose of analysis. In this extreme case there is no output foregone by society due to employing workers on the project. The workers are drawn from among the unemployed and not from other projects so the opportunity cost is zero. Prest and Turvey (1965) in their still authoritative review of cost benefit analysis stated, 'when there is an excess of supply at the current market price of any input, that price overstates the social cost of using that input.' In the example just considered the market price, namely the wage paid to workers on the project, overstates its social opportunity cost.

At the heart of the analysis of costs in cost benefit analysis is the attempt to measure the use of real resource while excluding transfer payments. Opportunity cost gives the real cost of resource withdrawal from other uses and is therefore central to cost benefit analysis.

On the benefits side, evaluation in monetary terms assumes that the value of a project to an individual is equal to his or her willingness-to-pay for it and that the social value of the project is the aggregation of individual values.

The concept of willingness-to-pay raises issues of consumer surplus namely the difference between what a consumer actually pays for a good or service and what he or she would have been willing to pay. If I pay a €1 toll to cross a bridge but would have been willing to pay €3 then my consumer surplus is €2. Consumer surplus is used as a measure of welfare changes. A measure of the gross benefit of a project is got by adding the consumer surplus to the market price where the latter is either a good reflection of social value or adjusted to be a good reflection, as we will see below.

The absence of market prices

The first of the two scenarios introduced in this section was where market prices give a misleading measure of social opportunity cost. The second, to which we now turn, is where market prices may not exist at all.

Market prices do not exist where there are public goods, externalities and intangibles. Public goods such as defence are not marketed; they are supplied collectively and the willingness-to-pay of individuals cannot be ascertained. Similarly there are difficulties in arriving at values for the elimination of negative externalities such as noise or for the appraisal of intangibles such as scenic value, the value of life, historic value, prestige, the value of loss of wilderness, the value of a sense of security and so forth.

In the absence of market prices, information on value can be obtained by questionnaires and by a range of relatively recently developed methodologies such as contingent valuation, described in chapter 10 of this volume. Of course, using questionnaires to ascertain the public's willingness-to-pay for the benefit of a project runs the gauntlet of people misrepresenting their preferences in order to influence the result of the analysis.

Value of time

A common way to value untraded goods is by analysing markets in which close substitutes are sold. As we will see in chapter 9, time savings are the largest benefits of most transportation projects. Time savings can be valued at the cost of employing users of the completed projects – their wages plus the overheads borne by employers including pension and national insurance contributions. Assumptions play a vital role in such valuations. In this case the key assumptions are that the value of a person's output is at least equal to the cost of employing him or her and that a saving in time will allow production to increase by a corresponding amount. In practice, there are real difficulties in valuing time; different people have different abilities to vary the time they work and hence to use time saved in travel. Different destinations are more conducive to work. Hence, for example, time saved in getting from an office to an airport is not the same as in getting from an airport to an office.

Leisure time is valued more cheaply than work time but it gives rise to even greater difficulties of estimation. Leisure time is valued by analysing how much people are willing to pay for time savings when alternative means of transport are available – one slower and cheaper and the other faster and more expensive. The alternative means of transport include walking, cycling, car, bus, train and so forth.

A common problem which arises with savings of both working and leisure time is that the time savings in individual journeys may range from seconds to a few minutes. When a large number of individual journeys are aggregated the time savings look very significant. For most people, however, the saving of a minute or two does not significantly add to work output or enjoyment of leisure. The aggregate figure, therefore, may give an excessive valuation.

Value of life

The most controversial aspect of cost benefit analysis is the attempt to value human life. Distasteful as this may seem it is inseparable from the analysis of many projects especially transport and healthcare projects. A moralist might well condemn such valuation; an economist obliged to give advice on expenditure decisions which affect road safety or the treatment of disease must grapple with it.

Zerbe and Dively (1994) provide a review of the methods of life valuation and the issues that arise, in which they comment that:

the value placed on a human life depends on the purpose of the evaluation. In war the value placed on the lives of enemy soldiers is usually negative. The value generals place on the lives of their own men seems to be the opportunity cost of other uses of their lives to win the war. In some cases, lives may be valued *ex post* (after the fact) for the purpose of compensation. In other cases, lives may be valued *ex ante* (before the fact) for the purpose of preventing death and injury. Lives may be seen in the abstract where the names of the individuals are not known, such as when investments are made in highway guard rails as a way to save lives. Alternatively, lives may be seen in the particular where the names of the individuals are known. ... These contrasts illustrate that valuing lives does not lend itself to a simple and direct approach that applies in all circumstances.

The most common approach to life valuation is that used by the courts to decide on awards for wrongful injury or death. Based on foregone earnings, it estimates the value of a life as the lifetime contribution to national output expressed in present values. This method assumes that people's earnings are a good reflection of what they add to a society's production. This assumption is untenable in some cases.

A more significant criticism is that this method does not distinguish between lifetime production and the value of life. Bearing this distinction in mind is an antidote to indirect inferences from this method that, for example, a well-paid person's life is more valuable than a poorly-paid person's or that one's life has no value after retirement.

The approach to valuation of life preferred by economists is to estimate the willingness-to-pay for additional safety or the willingness-to-accept payment for bearing additional risk to life. The foregone earnings approach only roughly conforms to this view because a person's earnings may greatly differ from the amount he or she would pay for additional safety, or accept, to bear additional risk.

An alternative method which does recognise risk is based on wage premiums. This method estimates the value of life by analysing how much extra income is needed to compensate people for an increase in risk to life. Some occupations are riskier than others and people working in these occupations earn a risk premium. Risk premiums can also be discerned in consumer choices whether it be the choice whether or not to smoke, drive a fast car or consume foods about which there are health scares.

There are difficulties also with this method. People may be either poorly informed about the risks they face or may pay little heed to the information they have. A person's wealth also has a big influence: a poorer person will in general be more likely than a rich person to accept a wage premium for accepting greater risk.

A final method of valuing life is the most recent. It uses questionnaire studies to gain information about behaviour under risk. This is the contingent valuation approach which is treated more fully in the context of environmental evaluation in chapter 10 of this volume.

It is to be expected that there will be difficulties in estimating a value for human life. These difficulties can be extended to the need to allow for the quality of life, not just the number of lives. We will return to issues concerning the value of life in chapters 9 and 11 in this volume. Whatever the difficulties, the valuation of life must proceed if projects which entail risks to life are to be evaluated.

Shadow prices

In this section we have discussed two broad scenarios that arise in the valuation of costs and benefits; one is where market prices provide a poor guide to social values and the other is where market prices do not exist. In both cases it may be necessary to construct artificial prices known as shadow prices (sometimes the term 'surrogate price' is used where market prices do not exist). For example, the wage rate may be taken as the shadow price of travel time. We have already seen that in conditions of high unemployment the market price, or wage, of employing people on a project may overstate the social opportunity cost. In such cases it can be argued that the market wage be replaced by a lower shadow price.[1]

The construction of a 'shadow price' is complex not least because it is difficult to trace the full consequences of a project. The Department of Finance (1994) sensibly states that:

> market prices are generally reliable and, normally, verifiable. They generally provide the appropriate basis for valuing a project's costs and benefits; they should be used, unless there are clear and convincing reasons that they are inappropriate and also that it is possible to derive shadow prices using a sound means of calculation.
>
> If shadow prices are used, market prices, if available, should be applied also. If the analysis on both bases leads to differing conclusions, reliance should be placed on results using shadow prices only where it can be clearly justified.

Of course, where market prices do not exist the estimation of a shadow or surrogate price may be unavoidable. It may, for example, be possible to estimate a surrogate price for the benefit derived by an area from the provision of extra policing by analysing the increase in house values as a result of an increase in the sense of security.

Present values

When the costs and benefits relevant to a project have been expressed in monetary terms they must be converted into present values. Money has a time value: costs and benefit accruing in various future years are different when viewed from the present. A hundred euro which accrues next year is not the same as a hundred euro today. By stating costs and benefits in present value terms we can meaningfully compare them.

An obvious reason to prefer a given sum of money immediately is the desire to spend rather than defer consumption. But a person may also prefer the money immediately in order to accumulate interest: if the interest rate is 5 per cent then the €100 will grow to €105 in a year. By compounding interest (i.e. by multiplying by $(1 + i)n$ where i is the rate of interest and n the number of years) we can trace the value of money into the future. In ten years time €100 invested at five per cent will be worth €162.89 and in 50 years it will grow to €1,146.74. This is due to the effects of interest rates and not inflation: even if inflation is zero the growth in investment will occur.

Adopting a different perspective we can ask what is the present value of €105 due in one year's time. If the interest rate, or in this context the discount rate, is five per cent then the answer obviously is 100. In general terms the present value V of a given amount S accruing n years from now can be stated as

$$V = \frac{S_n}{(1 + i)^n}$$

or

$$V = Sn \left[1/(1 + i)^n \right]$$

The expression $[1/(1 + i)^n]$ is known as the discount factor. Discount factors will have values between 0 and 1. The further into the future a cost or benefit accrues, the lower the discount factor. Also the higher the discount rate the lower the discount factor. Appendix II shows discount factors for different values of n and i.

Using the discount table in Appendix II we see that, at a five per cent discount rate, €100 receivable in 10 years time is worth €61.39 now and if receivable in 25 years time it is worth €29.53. Put another way, a person who today invests two sums, one of €61.39 and the other of €29.53 will receive sums of €100 in 10 years and again in 25 years time.

In general, a project with benefits occurring early and with deferred costs is preferable to one with early costs and deferred benefits. With capital projects, however, the returns tend to accrue over a period of time and the costs, although they also occur over time, tend mostly to occur in the early years. The appraisal of capital projects is extensively treated in chapter 5 of this volume.

The social discount rate

The discounting process outlined above is equally applicable to commercial and non-commercial, or social, cost benefit analysis. However, things are not that simple. We need to ask what rate should be chosen with which to discount future costs and benefits and whether the same rate can be used for commercial and non-commercial projects.

For long-term projects the choice of discount rate may be critical: a project which is attractive at a five per cent rate may be dismissed at a ten per cent rate. In general, as the rate of discount increases, projects with early net benefits will appear more favourble than projects whose net benefits occur further into the future.

However, at any given time there exist many different rates of interest. For example, different rates apply depending on the duration of a loan, the purpose for which it is required, the security offered and the track-record of the borrower. These factors affect the cost of capital which along with other considerations such as the risk-profile of investment, contribute to the choice of discount rate for commercial projects.

Much greater care is needed in selecting discount rates for non-commercial, or social, cost benefit analysis. Market interest rates are not appropriate for several reasons. People tend to be short-sighted about future costs and benefits which affect them and tend to prefer current consumption. This preference affects not only the efficiency of private investment but also may affect the wider society. By reflecting private rather than social rates of time preference the market interest rate takes inadequate account of future generations. We can expect the market rate to be above the social rate of time preference. Therefore, discounting by the market rate will attach a lower than appropriate value to future benefits to society.

From the point of view of social cost benefit analysis, market rates are also suspect because built into them tends to be a premium to cover risk. Investment in the public sector is generally less risky than in the private sector; the public sector is, for example, in a better position to spread risks (Brown and Jackson 1990). This is another reason why the market rate may exceed the social discount rate.

The use of different discount rates for public and private sector projects may give rise to its own problems. Care must be exercised that the use of different rates does not favour poorer quality public sector projects at the expense of better private sector ones.

If circumstances merit the use of a social discount rate the question which arises is: which rate? In theory, probably the best rate to use is the opportunity cost of capital. Funds used in public projects are obtained either from the private sector, via tax or borrowing, or within the public sector by diverting funds from other projects. In each case the funds have alternative returns which could be earned. However, rates of return vary from one type of investment to the next and in practice it is difficult to get a weighted average of all the rates of return for all the displaced uses of the funds.

An alternative approach attempts to construct a social rate of time preference to reflect society's evaluation of the relative merits of present rather than future returns. This approach takes the perspective of society as a whole in valuing future returns. The previous approach takes the perspective of a given point in time and values the resources transferred from other uses. Both approaches are likely to create practical difficulties of estimation.

The solution most easily applied to these problems is to use the yield on long-term government bonds. A government borrowing rate of this type gives a reasonable proxy for the risk-free (i.e. free of the risk of default) rate of interest appropriate to public sector investments.

The Department of Finance (1994) has recommended that the same basic discount rate, usually called the test discount rate, should be used in all cost-benefit and cost-effectiveness analyses of public sector projects. The test discount rate recommended was five per cent in real terms. This means that, before discounting, all nominal flows of costs and benefits should be deflated by the expected level of price inflation.

Decision criteria

Assuming that we can identify and quantify all the costs and benefits relevant to a number of projects, what criterion should we use to choose between them?

Undiscounted measures

Undiscounted measures do not take account of the time value of money. Consequently, although they give some guidance in choosing between projects they cannot be relied upon. The measures are: payback period; proceeds per unit of outlay; average income on book value of investment.

- Payback period

This is the period from the beginning of the project to the point where net value of production equals the amount of the capital investment. This is an uncomplicated indicator of how long it takes to recover an initial investment and has some appeal when projects have a high degree of risk. Lucey, McCabe and McHugh (1995) found that, consistent with evidence from the UK, payback is the most popular method of investment appraisal among Irish firms.

There are some obvious drawbacks of this measure for the ranking of projects. Firstly, it does not take account of earnings after the payback date. Consider two projects both of which require a capital investment of €1 million. If project A earns €2 million in the first year and project B earns €1 million then project A will be preferred. However, this would be a wrong choice if in subsequent years project A earns €1 million and project B earns

€2 million per annum.

The second weakness is the neglect of the timing of proceeds. We know that money has a time value and that the earlier benefits are received the more valuable they are. The payback period measure does not take account of this.

• Proceeds per unit of outlay

This method ranks investments by dividing the total net value of production by the total investment. Once again, this approach neglects timing by failing to distinguish between money today and money in the future.

A variation of this method is the average annual proceeds per unit of outlay. This begins by dividing the total net value of production by the expected life of the project in years, thereby yielding an average of the annual proceeds which is then divided by the original investment.

This refinement fails to solve the problem of timing. It does not consider the span of time over which benefits accrue. Hence it will not distinguish between projects which earn money early from those that earn it later.

• Average income on book value of investment

The book value of an investment is the value after subtracting depreciation. This measure states the ratio of average income to the book value. Although this is a useful measure of the performance of a firm it is inadequate as an investment criterion because, yet again, it fails to take account of the timing of the stream of benefits.

Discounted measures

These methods allow for the time value for money. A brief outline of the main methods follows; more detail can be found in chapter 5 of this volume.

• Net present value

This criterion is based simply on whether the sum of discounted gains exceeds the sum of discounted losses. The costs and benefits are estimated for each year of a project's life, the costs are subtracted from the benefits and the net benefits are expressed at their present value.

Thus the discounting process is applied just once to the net benefit stream. Alternatively, but more onerously, both the cost and benefit streams can be separately discounted and then the costs subtracted from the benefits. Either way the use of the NPV criterion requires a decision about the appropriate rate of discount.

At the chosen rate of discount if the net present value (NPV) is positive then a project should be accepted. If the NPV is zero then the decision-maker is indifferent about the project and if the NPV is negative then the present value of the benefit stream will be insufficient to recover the investment and the project will be rejected.

Projects with positive NPVs enable efficient allocation of resources and represent an improvement to the welfare of society.

When choosing between mutually exclusive projects, i.e. when the acceptance of one excludes the acceptance of any others, NPV is the preferred criterion. The projects are ranked according to the NPVs and the project with the highest positive NPV is chosen.

The NPV criterion is less successful in ranking alternative independent projects, i.e. projects which are not mutually exclusive. The decision criterion is to accept all independent projects with positive NPVs. However, this creates difficulties in providing a ranking for order of implementation. For example, a small but highly attractive project may have a lower NPV than a large but only moderately attractive one. The NPV criterion does not register such differences and will accept both projects as long as each has a positive NPV and there are sufficient funds with which to proceed.

Notwithstanding this difficulty, the NPV criterion is satisfactory from the point of view of efficient resource allocation, the welfare of society and because it is free from problems associated with alternative discounted measures to which we now turn.

• Internal rate of return

The internal rate of return (IRR) is the maximum rate of interest that a project can afford to pay for the resources used which allows the project to cover its investment and operating expenses and still break-even. The IRR is the discount rate which will make the NPV of a project equal zero. An IRR of 15 per cent means that at a discount rate of 15 per cent the project just breaks even; in other words it could earn back all the capital and operating costs incurred and pay 15 per cent for the use of the money in the meantime.

The IRR approach is based on a cut-off rate, or target rate of return, which is a pre-determined rate which usually approximates the opportunity cost of the funds to be invested. For independent (i.e. not mutually exclusive) projects the IRR approach will accept all projects with an IRR greater than the cut-off rate.

There are however several difficulties with the IRR approach. There are difficulties in using the IRR to rank projects, either independent projects subject to capital rationing (i.e. where there is an expenditure constraint) or mutually exclusive projects. The IRR compares the return on a project to the opportunity cost of funds; it does not compare performance across several projects. It is possible for two projects to have the same IRR and therefore the same ranking but because the incidence of their costs and benefits are timed differently, they may have different rankings when net benefits are discounted to present value using a common rate such as a social discount rate or a market rate.

The IRR has other, sometimes exaggerated, difficulties. Some projects can generate multiple IRRs and create obvious difficulties about which one to use.

In general, the NPV criterion has several advantages over the IRR criterion. In practice the IRR continues to be used partly because it can be calculated without the need to select a discount rate in advance, which as we have seen creates its own difficulties.

- Cost-benefit ratio

This is the ratio of discounted benefits to discounted costs. Using this approach independent projects will be accepted if the ratio exceeds one.

This method is relatively simple to apply but ranking of projects, whether independent projects subject to an expenditure constraint or mutually exclusive projects, can lead to wrong choices. For example, project A may have a slightly higher benefit-cost ratio than project B but project A may be small-scale and project B may be large-scale with greater capacity to generate future benefits.

In the final analysis each of the foregoing discounted measure is useful. However, the drawbacks associated with the IRR and benefit-cost ratio approaches favour the NPV criterion as the most reliable.

Uncertainty and risk

Up to now we have assumed that measured costs and benefits are known with certainty. Where this is so, the NPV criterion can show the relative efficiency of projects. But for cost benefit analysis conducted *ex ante*, costs and benefits are estimates which are subject to change. For example, a cost benefit analysis of a transport project is based on estimates of future physical flows, such as traffic, and relative values, such as fuel prices.

There are many ways to allow for uncertainty; some relatively uncomplicated and others highly sophisticated. For example, a relatively uncomplicated way to deal with uncertainty about the life of equipment, perhaps because of technological change, is to reduce the estimated life of the project.

Another easy-to-apply approach is to increase the discount rate. This will most heavily reduce the present value of projects where significant benefits accrue more remotely into the future. This approach is not always appropriate. Stiglitz (1988) argued that the most common mistake in dealing with uncertainty is the inappropriate use of higher discount rates. If, for example, a project has uncertain costs which will occur at the end of its life then discounting at a higher rate will reduce the present value of costs and make the project more attractive. To guard against this possibility the flow of net benefits could first be adjusted for risk by use of a risk premium and then present values could be calculated by using the regular discount rates.

A more sophisticated approach is to take each uncertain variable and assess the probability, say high, medium and low, of a number or values occurring. Each stated value could then be assigned a probability weighting based on the likelihood that it will occur. An NPV could then be calculated for every combination of stated value and each NPV could be ascribed a probability measure leading to a probability distribution of NPVs. For example, for a given project there may be a 65 per cent chance that the NPV lies in the range €5 million and €10 million, a 20 per cent chance that it lies between €10 million and €15 million and so forth.

Whatever its sophistication this approach bears an important *caveat*: it depends on the informed judgement of analysts in assigning probabilities.

Finally we will consider what in practice is the most useful method for dealing with risk and uncertainty, namely sensitivity analysis. This involves recalculating the NPV in line with changes to the values of important parameters or assumptions.

These parameters include the discount rate, the physical quantities of inputs and outputs, the shadow prices of inputs and outputs and the project life span. In particular the NPV will often critically depend on the discount rate chosen.

Sensitivity analysis allows the analyst to discover to which parameters or assumptions the NPV is most sensitive. When these have been found then the analyst can attempt to refine estimates of the parameters and, once the project is started, project managers can attempt to monitor or guide carefully these parameters.

Sensitivity analysis is an effective means of dealing with uncertainty. But sensitivity analysis is just part of the decision process. In assessing each uncertain outcome the decision-maker must be conscious of his or her attitude to risk. For example, people may be risk-averse or risk-loving. Approaches to dealing with risk such as maximin and minimax-regret criteria are dealt with in chapter 6 of this volume and will not be treated here.

Distributional issues

Cost benefit analysis attempts to select projects and policies which are efficient in their use of resources. It assumes implicitly that the existing distribution of income is an acceptable one. We have seen earlier in this chapter that values in cost benefit analysis are partly measured by willingness-to-pay. This in turn depends on ability-to-pay which of course is based on the distribution of income.

The calculation of NPVs makes no allowance for the distribution among people of costs and benefits. If one person is made better-off by €200 and another is disadvantaged by €100 then this is regarded as a net gain for society because in principle it would be possible for those who gain to compensate those who lose and still be better-off than heretofore. This is a potential compensation criterion which we will discuss later in the chapter.

However, there are cases where redistribution is an explicit objective of public expenditure. Even when there are no explicit objectives the effects of public projects may be so large as to affect distribution in a way that cannot be ignored.

One way to take account of distributional issues is to attach weights to the benefits and costs accruing to different people. The relevant population could be divided into different income groups and if, for example, the government felt that benefits accruing to low-income groups were of greater value than similar benefits accruing to high income groups then additional weights could be assigned so as to amplify the benefits accruing to the low-income groups.

In practice, there are many problems with the use of distributional weights and they are seldom used. The problematic questions include: How are groups to be defined? How is the impact on the groups to be evaluated? and, of course, What weights should be used?

An alternative to the use of distributional weights is to compare measures of inequality both without and then with the project. Discussion of inequality measures is beyond the scope of this chapter but an examination of these measures in the context of cost benefit analysis can be found in Stiglitz (1988).

Deciding between alternatives

An efficient allocation of resources requires that investment should continue until its marginal benefit equals (or, less precisely, approximates) its marginal cost.

This is illustrated in Table 8.2 which is adapted from Eckstein (1967). It shows flood damage prior to government intervention and then for four progressively bigger flood protection projects which are, of course, mutually exclusive.

Project A appears attractive: it has a benefit-cost ratio of €6 million to €3 million, i.e. 2:1, the best for any of the projects, and a net benefit of €3 million. However, project B is an improvement on project A because for an additional €7 million there is additional benefit of €10 million; the net benefit of project B is €6 million. Project C represents yet a further improvement because for a marginal cost of €8 million there is a marginal benefit of €9 million; the net benefit of project C is €7 million. With project C we have the nearest approximation of marginal costs and marginal benefits. Project C represents the most efficient allocation of resources: moving beyond it to project D would entail a marginal cost of €12 million but a marginal benefit of only €7 million and a net benefit of just €2 million.

Table 8.2: Flood control projects

Project	Annual cost	Average annual damage	Benefit (reduction in damage)	Net benefit	Marginal cost	Marginal benefit
Before project	0	38	0	0	0	0
Project A	3	32	6	3	3	6
Project B	10	22	16	6	7	10
Project C	18	13	25	7	8	9
Project D	30	6	32	2	12	7

The logic of equating marginal cost and marginal benefit is familiar from the microeconomic theory of the firm. It provides a guideline for decision-making in cost benefit analysis. In practice, where there are large indivisible projects, fine marginal adjustments are not possible. The underlying logic, however, remains, namely to maximise the net benefit.

A second example which is adapted from Musgrave and Musgrave (1984) is illustrated in Table 8.3 which presents information about seven alternative independent road projects. Decision-makers must choose which projects to pursue within a budget of €700 million.

In deciding which projects to pursue within the budget of €700 million we can turn to several decision rules.

Firstly, we could rank projects by their benefit-cost ratio and use this ordering to choose projects within the budget constraint. From Table 8.4 we see that using this approach, projects D, A, E and C would be chosen at a cost of €630 million. Project B which is next in the ranking cannot be included because at an additional cost of €145 million it would breach the budget constraint. Applying the benefit-cost ratio approach, therefore, will provide gross benefits of €1,049 million and net benefits of €419 at a cost of €630 million, leaving €70 million unspent.

Table 8.3: Project selection under fixed budget

			€million		
Project	Costs	Benefits	Net Benefits	Benefit-cost ratio	Benefit-cost ranking
A	200	400	200	2.0	2
B	145	175	30	1.2	5
C	80	104	24	1.3	4
D	50	125	75	2.5	1
E	300	420	120	1.4	3
F	305	330	25	1.1	6
G	125	100	−25	0.8	7

Secondly, we could apply the rule of maximising net benefit. By trial and error we can find that projects D, A, E and B maximise net benefit. With this approach gross benefits are €1,120 million, net benefits are €425 million, the cost is €695 million and €5 million is unspent.

Thirdly, we might adopt a decision rule to minimise the amount left unspent. This approach would select projects A, B, D and F thereby yielding gross benefits of €1,030 million and net benefits of €330 million at a cost of €700 million with nothing left unspent.

The costs and benefits associated with each of the decision rules are set out in Table 8.4.

Table 8.4: Decision rules – costs and benefits

	€ million				
Decision rule	Projects selected	Benefits	Costs	Net benefits	Amount unspent
Benefit-cost ratio	D, A, E, C	1,049	630	419	70
Maximum net benefit	D, A, E, B	1,120	695	425	5
Minimum left unspent	D, A, B, F	1,030	700	330	0

Table 8.4 clearly shows that the approach of minimising the amount left unspent can be dismissed: it spends more and buys fewer net benefits than the other approaches. The benefit-cost ratio approach is attractive because it chooses projects which yield the highest return per euro spent.

However, as we would expect, the best decision is to maximise net benefits. This approach costs €65 million more than the benefit-cost ratio approach but buys €71 million more benefits thereby yielding €6 million more net benefits.

Cost effectiveness analysis

A full cost benefit analysis is a painstaking activity. In particular, there are difficulties in estimating benefits. This is due both to problems in assigning money values to certain benefits and to the tendency for benefits to accrue further into the future than costs.

Cost benefit analysis enables comparison of alternative projects or programmes even when they are not aimed at common objectives. Hence cost benefit analysis estimates for education, healthcare, housing and transport projects might be compared. Such comparisons are fraught with difficulties and doubts about whether like is being compared with like.

Cost effectiveness analysis is an alternative to, indeed some would say a type of, cost benefit analysis. Unlike cost benefit analysis it does not entail the conversion of costs and benefits to a common money measure. Instead cost effectiveness analysis assesses the effectiveness of projects and programmes in relation to the monetary value of costs.

Cost effectiveness analysis is used where benefits are hard to value in money terms or when the total expenditure available to a project is fixed or when the output from alternative projects is expected to be similar.

If an objective is clear, for example to increase reading scores (or convert smokers to non-smokers or reduce road fatalities etc) by amount x in group y by time z, then cost effectiveness analysis allows projects to be compared and ordered.

Cost effectiveness analysis can also be used to compare the costs of achieving different degrees of an objective. For example, if the objective is to reduce a certain type of mortality then the additional costs of successive reductions in that type of mortality due to different policy interventions can be estimated. This might help identify reasonably large reductions in mortality for relatively small additional costs.

If there are multiple benefits or outputs then some element of subjective preference by decision-makers is necessary. This might take the form of placing the benefits on a scale from say 1 to 10. The ratio of scaled outputs or benefits to costs could then be compared.

Cost effectiveness analysis is, in effect, a variation of cost benefit analysis which is based on the same principles and uses the same methods. In cost effectiveness analysis the NPV approach is applied to the stream of costs, both the capital and the recurring costs.

Cost effectiveness analysis has weaknesses. Although it can help clarify the most effective way to achieve an objective within an expenditure limit, it cannot assist in selecting the optimal expenditure level for a project. It can compare the relative costs of different options for achieving an objective but is not, in itself, sufficient for deciding whether or not to proceed with a project. Cost effectiveness analysis tends to compare a more narrow range of variables than cost benefit analysis and is not as useful as cost benefit analysis in comparing marginal costs and marginal benefits.

Private and public sector cost benefit analysis

Private enterprises continually assess new investment opportunities. In so doing they will consider their objectives, identify alternative means of achieving the objectives, assign money values to inputs and outputs, assess the costs and benefits and estimate profitability.

Social cost benefit analysis tries to apply in the public sector the type of decision that would be made if private sector markets worked properly. Cost benefit analysis in the public sector differs from the private sector in certain key respects. It takes account of externalities such as effects on the environment and generally adopts a wider perspective than private sector appraisal. Public sector projects may also differ in having concerns about and objectives in the area of income distribution.

Social cost benefit analysis may adjust market prices where they exist or substitute proxy prices where no market prices exist. It does so with a view to promoting efficient allocation of resources for society. Thus social cost benefit analysis may attempt to value untraded and indeed intangible goods such as time saved, life saved, peace and quiet and so forth.

Social cost benefit analysis may also differ from private sector appraisal in the choice of discount rate. The rate of discount for cost benefit analysis in the public sector may be lower than the rate applied in private appraisals either because government wishes to place a higher value on future benefits than would be the case with commercial rates or simply because government may borrow more cheaply than private enterprises.

There is no scope here to enter a discussion of private sector investment and its analysis. The principles of private sector investment analysis have been treated in earlier chapters and interested readers may wish to pursue treatments such as those by NESC (1998) and Lucey, McCabe and McHugh (1995).

Criticisms and drawbacks of cost benefit analysis

Cost benefit analysis is an application of welfare economics. It is predicated on the belief that society's welfare is promoted through people's estimation of what things are worth to them. Values are established by people's willingness-to-pay for things they want or their willingness to accept payment to put up with things they do not want.

There are two broad purposes for which cost benefit analysis is used. Firstly, in the case of public sector investment, it is used to identify the most efficient project or programme from among possible alternatives. In Ireland, cost benefit analysis usually takes this form. Secondly, it is used to evaluate government intervention in the private sector such as road safety programmes, environmental regulations, the deregulation of commercial services and so forth.

Cost benefit analysis is subject to criticism at the technical and procedural level and at a more conceptual level.

We have considered drawbacks of a technical nature throughout this chapter. They arise all along the line: there are problems of estimation surrounding future output and prices, shadow prices, surrogate prices, consumer surplus, willingness-to-pay, risk and uncertainty, opportunity costs and so forth. There are hazards in the choice of discount rate and investment criterion (NPV, IRR, cost-benefit ratio) for public sector projects and of the weights to be applied for distributional purposes. There is a need for vigilance about double-counting and consciousness about the inherent errors and incompleteness in much economic data.

There are also inherent difficulties in economic analysis: unlike laboratory conditions, economic projects do not always afford the opportunity to examine outcomes both with and without an intervention.

In a similar vein, there are problems of the scope of analysis. For example, should an analysis of urban railways include the car parking facilities? Alternatively, if an analysis of the costs and benefits of by-passing a town estimates a certain level of net benefit, is this a meaningful number if a consequence of the bypass is partly to move a traffic bottleneck on to the next town?

There are also wider issues to consider. The use of different discount rates in public and private sectors has an associated danger that some public sector projects may displace other more worthy private sector projects. Alternatively the use of cost benefit analysis to select one project, say a town by-pass on a busy inter-city route, in preference to another, say a town by-pass between two moderately busy regional centres, may be based on the higher value of time saved on the former. However, by proceeding with the former the decision-makers may be compounding regional inequity.

In making comparisons it is also worth bearing in mind that it is more convincing to compare like with like. Hence it is more acceptable to compare one option for road-building with another rather than to compare the building of a hospital with a school.

Drawbacks of a technical nature are well known to economists. Indeed, economists are accustomed to identifying and dealing with these drawbacks. Economic analysts are often first to highlight drawbacks but usually within the context that the analysis will proceed and drawbacks will be dealt with as best possible. Whether or not cost benefit analysis should be used at all is a separate issue which arises at a more conceptual level.

Criticisms, at a conceptual level, of cost benefit analysis take several forms. There are criticisms of the assumptions on which it is based. For example, there are reservations about whether people's willingness-to-pay should be the appropriate standard for policy decisions. There are criticisms also of the potential compensation criterion, i.e. that a project is worthwhile if the gainers could compensate the losers and still be better-off. This, the Kaldor-Hicks criterion, is derived from the Pareto criterion which holds that the best policy or course of action is that which benefits some people without causing losses to anyone. The Kaldor-Hicks potential compensation criterion causes difficulties by not being concerned about who gains and who loses nor about whether the compensation is actually paid. A project might pass the cost-benefit test if it conferred €1,000 on the well-to-do in society and imposed €900 costs on the low-paid. But this is an extreme scenario.

There are also objections based on whether certain policy problems can be meaningfully reduced to costs and benefits. For example, policies which involve life or the environment may be seen by some as too important to be formulated by market-type rules for efficiency and effectiveness. There may be reservations that placing a price on life will diminish its value in people's minds. These are understandable reservations; yet when policies which save lives are being analysed costs and benefits are stubbornly relevant.

There are also a host of criticisms based on the objectivity, or the perceived lack of objectivity, of cost benefit analysis and on the use of subjective judgements. There are questions about whether analysts, with their positivist training and professional socialisation, can be objective in identifying project goals, costs and benefits; and there are reservations about whether analysts, particularly if retained by commercial enterprises, can be objective in conducting cost benefit analysis and interpreting results.

Another source of criticism is based on what some believe to be the inappropriate extension of economic reasoning to the social or political domain where there may be lack of data, sudden changes in policy or project content, multiple objectives and so forth.

The foregoing criticisms are clearly important. They indicate the limits and weaknesses of economic evaluation. In the final analysis, however, they are not sufficient to make cost benefit analysis redundant. Used with care and acknowledging its inherent limits and imprecision, cost benefit analysis does provide a relatively coherent and disciplined approach to decision-making in practice. It is certainly preferable to arbitrary decision-making and to decision-making based on assumptions and values which are not open to scrutiny.

Conclusion

In this chapter we have reviewed the main issues that arise in cost benefit analysis. It is not intended as a comprehensive review and the interested reader may wish to pursue other issues in the chapters which follow and in Appendix III of this volume. Much greater depth can be found in a range of texts including Brent (1996), Layard and Glaister (1994), Mishan (1982), Ray (1984), Squire and van der Tak (1975), Walshe and Daffern (1990) and Zerbe and Dively (1994). There are also many case-studies of cost benefit analysis in practice such as the classic study in the UK of the Victoria underground railway line (Foster and Beesley 1963) and the analysis of the Naas bypass in Ireland (Barrett and Mooney 1984).

Cost benefit analysis is an important aspect of evaluation. It is the most developed and soundly based means to evaluate the efficiency of public sector programmes. It helps discipline decision-making in the public sector when market forces do not exist to penalise poor decision and reward good ones.

It has been said that everything is economics but economics isn't everything. Similarly, cost benefit analysis isn't everything in public sector decision-making. Projects which would be selected by cost benefit analysis may not be politically acceptable. This is as we would expect in democratic society. Cost benefit analysis, is however, available to decision-makers requiring a rational, coherent and comprehensive way to evaluate public projects and programmes.

NOTES

1. The Community Support Framework Evaluation Unit (1999) in their proposed working rules for cost benefit analysis state that shadow prices should be used when market prices do not reflect opportunity costs due to some clearly identified market failure. Hence, for example, labour costs should be included at market prices unless there is a clearly identified case for an alternative approach. Even then, according to the proposed working rules, the shadow wage used should not be less than 80 per cent of the market wage and there should be a sensitivity analysis based on a shadow wage of 100 per cent.

REFERENCES

Barrett S. D. and D. Mooney (1984). 'The Naas Motorway Bypass – A Cost Benefit Analysis', *Quarterly Economic Commentary*, January, 1984, pp 21-34

Blackwell, J. (1991). 'Efficiency and Effectiveness in Public Investment Appraisal', in T. P. Hardiman and M. Mulreany (eds) *Efficiency and Effectiveness in the Public Domain*, Dublin: Institute of Public Administration

Brent, R.J. (1996). *Applied Cost-Benefit Analysis*, Cheltenham: Edward Elgar

Brown, C.V. and P. M. Jackson (1990). *Public Sector Economics*, Fourth edition, Oxford: Basil Blackwell

Community Support Framework Evaluation Unit (1999). *Proposed Working Rules for Cost-Benefit Analysis*, Dublin: CSF Evaluation Unit

Department of Finance (1983). *Public Capital Programme 1984*, Dublin: Stationery Office

Department of Finance (1994). *Guidelines for the Appraisals and Management of Capital Expenditure Proposals in the Public Sector*, Dublin: Department of Finance

Eckstein, O. (1967). *Public Finance, Second Edition*, Englewood Cliffs: Prentice-Hall

Foster, C. D. and M. E. Beesley (1963). 'Estimating the Social Benefit of Constructing an Underground Railway in London', *Journal of the Royal Statistical Society*, vol 126, pp 46-58

Gray, A. W. (1995). *EU Structural Funds and other Public Sector Investments: A Guide to Evaluation Methods*, Dublin: Gill and Macmillan

Honohan, P. (1998). *Key Issues of Cost-Benefit Methodology for Irish Industrial Policy*, Dublin: Economic and Social Research Institute

Layard, G. and S. Glaister (1994). *Cost Benefit Analysis, Second Edition*, Cambridge: Cambridge University Press

Mishan, E. J. (1982). *Cost Benefit Analysis: An Informal Introduction*, Third Edition, London: George Allan and Unwin

Musgrave R. A. and P. B. Musgrave (1984). *Public Finance in Theory and Practice*, Maidenhead: McGraw-Hill

Prest, A. R. and R. Turvey (1965). 'Cost-Benefit Analysis: A Survey', *Economic Journal*, vol 75, pp 685-705

Lucey, B. M., P. McCabe and G. McHugh (1995). 'An Analysis of the Investment Appraisal Practices of Irish Companies', *IBAR*, vol 16, 1995, pp 101-114

NESC (1998). *Private Sector Investment in Ireland*, Dublin: National Economic and Social Council

Ray, A. (1984). *Cost-Benefit Analysis: Issues and Methodologies*, Baltimore: The Johns Hopkins University

Squire, L. and H. van der Tak (1975). *Economic Analysis of Projects*, Baltimore: The Johns Hopkins University Press

Stiglitz, J. E. (1988). *Economics of the Public Sector*, Second Edition, New York: Norton

Walshe, G. and P. Daffern (1990). *Managing Cost Benefit Analysis*, London: Macmillan

Zerbe, R. O. and D. O. Dively (1994). *Benefit-Cost Analysis: In Theory and Practice*, New York: Harper-Collins

9

The Evaluation of Transport Projects[1]

OWEN P. KEEGAN

Introduction

The need has long been recognised for an acceptable appraisal framework for evaluating public investment programmes and for promoting efficient choices in the allocation of scarce public resources between competing programmes and projects. An appraisal framework is essential for the optimal allocation of public expenditure, including expenditure on transportation. While progress has been made in evaluating major transport investment programmes and in developing techniques for selecting between competing projects, significant work remains to be done.

In Ireland, the transportation sector has been to the fore in the development and application of public expenditure evaluation/appraisal techniques. As far back as 1961, O'Keeffe proposed the application of cost benefit analysis (CBA) in the allocation of road expenditure in Ireland (O'Keeffe, 1961). By 1966, the then Department of Local Government had partly accepted this approach and was advocating a change from the then system of allocating funding for roads on the basis of historic provision towards a system based on traffic volumes (Department of Local Government, 1966). In 1971, the Dublin Transportation Study contained a CBA of its proposals (An Foras Forbartha, 1971). Through the 1970s and 1980s, while there was no systematic policy of appraising transport projects some major road and rail projects were subjected to CBA. More recently, the major transport investment proposals contained in the report of the Dublin Transportation Initiative have also been subjected to detailed evaluation including CBA (Steer, Davies, Gleave, 1994).[2]

In recent years there has been an increasing recognition that a special approach is required for the appraisal of public sector transport projects. This is because of the key role of the transportation sector in economic and social development and the special nature of the arrangements that exist for the delivery of transport services including a number of different modes, different operators (both public and private), different levels of competition, complex subsidy regimes and so forth. Given the very significant costs involved in the provision of transport infrastructure and the demand for new investment there has always been a need to develop a basis for allocating scarce resources between competing projects.

The dominant role of the state and more recently of the EU in financing transportation projects has increased the pressure for better project evaluation and appraisal. Finally, the fact that time savings which constitute the major benefit of transport projects can be more readily measured and valued than the benefits of most other major public investment projects has also assisted the development and application of evaluation techniques to transport projects.

The evaluation of any transport project generally involves a number of different assessments. A detailed technical assessment dealing with the engineering/design approach to the project is usually required, together with an assessment of the project's environmental impact. In addition, depending on the nature of the project, a detailed financial appraisal and/or an economic appraisal will usually be required. A financial appraisal assesses the cost of the project and how it is to be financed, the revenue stream it will produce and the return that will be achieved on the capital invested. It also considers the impact of the project on the cash flow, the profit and loss account and the balance sheet of the enterprise. An economic appraisal identifies and attempts to measure the economic costs and benefits of the project. In the case of most road infrastructure projects and increasingly in the case of rail infrastructure projects, the emphasis in project evaluation is on the economic appraisal of the project using CBA.

This chapter focuses on a number of key issues that arise in the application of CBA to transportation projects in Ireland. These are:

- *Methodological issues:* the derivation of parameter values for the value of time, for accident cost savings and for vehicle operating cost savings; the choice of discount rate and the problems associated with forecasting traffic.
- *Environmental issues:* the treatment of environmental impacts in CBA studies.

Given the increasing reliance on CBA in the evaluation of transportation projects it is important that there should be a broader understanding of the issues that arise in deriving parameter values and in choosing a discount rate. Since traffic forecasts play a critical role in the calculation of benefits associated with transportation projects some understanding of the issues that arise in this area is also important.

A major criticism of most CBA studies is their failure to take explicit account of environmental impacts. The growing interest in measuring and valuing the environmental impacts of transport investments has been driven by the belief that if scarce resources are to be allocated efficiently and equitably, then it is essential that environmental effects be explicitly considered along with other costs and benefits. This chapter outlines both the progress that has been made in this area and the considerable obstacles that remain to be overcome.

To dispel any suggestion that the application of CBA to transport projects is purely a mechanical or technical process the chapter finishes with a consideration of suggested CBA application rules derived on the basis of the author's personal experience in both undertaking and reviewing CBA studies of transport projects in Ireland.

Before addressing these issues it is necessary to consider the CBA approach to project appraisal and to explain why it is appropriate for some but not necessarily all transport projects. CBA is essentially a set of techniques designed to ensure efficiency, from an economic welfare perspective, in the allocation of scarce public investment resources. An investment is considered desirable where the economic benefits exceed the economic costs and the potential therefore exists for beneficiaries from the investment to fully compensate losers and still be better off. CBA requires costs and benefits to be assessed from the perspective of the economy as a whole. The profit maximising enterprise which is usually concerned only with private costs and benefits will choose the project which contributes most to total profits at the margin. However, for public infrastructure projects the objective is the maximisation of social/economic welfare which requires the interests of society as a whole to be taken into account. This in turn requires estimation of positive and negative externalities generated by the project, in addition to its direct benefits and costs. Compared with financial appraisal, CBA substitutes social benefit for the revenue of the enterprise and social or opportunity cost for the cost to the enterprise.

Some indication of the scale of the external costs of transport is given in a European Commission Green Paper (EU Commission, 1995).

Although there is a large uncertainty surrounding cost estimates of individual externalities and costs vary significantly across and within modes, time and place of use, the order of magnitude of the total costs – which is broadly comparable to the total direct contribution of the inland transport modes to GDP – is so large that policy action is definitely warranted.

The EU Commission indicated rough estimates of the external costs of transport as a percentage of GDP as follows – air pollution (excluding global warming): 0.4 per cent, noise: 0.2 per cent, accidents: 1.5 per cent and congestion: 2.0 per cent. The Commission also indicated that over 90 per cent of these costs relate to road transport.

While major road investments may yield modest savings in road maintenance costs they do not generate income streams and cannot therefore be appraised on financial grounds. Even in cases where a toll is imposed on a road, financial appraisal is considered inappropriate for the following reasons:

• CBA measures the benefit to consumers in terms of the increase in 'consumer surplus' (i.e. the maximum amount a consumer would be willing to pay for a given quantity of a good less the amount he or she actually pays). However, to capture these benefits in the form of toll revenue on a road project would require the imposition of a toll on each user equivalent to the maximum amount he or she would be willing to pay, which in turn would reflect the value of the time savings to each user. In practice, of course, a uniform toll is imposed on all users in a particular category (e.g. private cars). Thus toll revenue will always be less than the increase in 'consumer surplus' that results from a new road facility.

• The provision of a new road facility will usually result in a diversion of traffic from other parts of the road network, resulting in benefits (e.g. reduced travel time, fewer accidents etc.) to other users of the network who do not pay any toll.

• Toll revenue will not reflect the full economic effects of accident savings and beneficial environmental impacts.

CBA is also applied in the case of other transport projects (e.g. investment in rail, port and airport projects) where it usually supplements more traditional financial appraisal. Since investments in these areas generate income in the form of additional revenue from user charges it is sometimes argued that financial appraisal on its own should be sufficient. However, just as in the case of toll roads, there are arguments in favour of the application of CBA to these projects. The primary advantage of the general application of CBA to all transport infrastructure projects is that this approach should ensure consistency in project selection between projects involving different modes. This is important if scarce public resources available for investment in transport are to be allocated efficiently and overall economic welfare maximised.

At the same time there are arguments for preserving a strong commercial focus in the evaluation of certain transport infrastructure projects, especially where competitive markets now exist. One consequence of the effective deregulation of road haulage, inter-urban bus services and air and sea transportation services in Ireland is that competitive markets now operate in areas which were previously characterised by monopoly or near monopoly conditions. Special care is required in the application of CBA where competitive markets exist and where grant aid is being sought for a project. Such grants could lead to distortionary impacts on competition.

Similar considerations arise in the case of investment in ports because of the increasingly commercial and competitive nature of the port sector. It is not at all clear that investments in additional port capacity or in improved handling facilities generate benefits that cannot be captured in the form of additional revenue or cost savings by port operators. Because of doubts about the existence and scale of externalities associated with port projects and the need to avoid interfering in competitive markets, the evaluation of port projects should be based primarily on financial appraisal.

It is worth noting that in the UK there has been a reluctance to embrace CBA of rail projects unreservedly. It is argued that comparisons of cost between public road and public rail projects are distorted because rail costs include the maintenance cost of the permanent way whereas road costs do not include road maintenance. While the case for subsidising rail transportation is strong given the net positive externalities it generates, there is the drawback that subsidisation often leads to inefficiencies, to services that are not matched to demand, to a lack of innovation and to poor cost control. Objectives for appraisal of rail investment in the UK, set out below, reflect these competing pressures:

- There is a requirement that service improvements as a consequence of major investments should be funded out of additional fare revenue and operating cost savings. An exception is made in the case of urban rail and light rail schemes where it is argued that the benefits of major investments exceed the additional fare revenue likely to be generated.

- Subsidies are payable in respect of new schemes which reflect the value of external benefits (e.g. less road congestion).

- There is a presumption in favour of maintaining existing non-commercial services.

These policy objectives have resulted in a range of appraisal techniques from commercial appraisal to CBA to a combination of both approaches being applied to rail projects in the UK.

Parameter values, the discount rate and traffic forecasts

The main costs and benefits associated with transport investment projects which are valued in CBA are set out in the Table 9.1.

Table 9.1: Summary of major costs and benefits associated with transport investment projects

Costs	Benefits
Capital cost	Time savings (e.g. business, commercial and leisure)
Delays during construction	
	Reduction in the number and severity of accidents
	Reduction in vehicle operating costs
	Net savings in maintenance costs

The value of time savings

Most transport infrastructure investments reduce travel times and increase the reliability of transport services. In the UK studies indicate that on average time savings account for over 75 per cent of the quantified benefits of major road improvement schemes. Valuing time savings is a critical element in CBA analysis of all transport infrastructure projects.

The cost of travel time can be regarded as having two distinct elements – an opportunity cost reflecting the value of the activity which would otherwise be engaged in, and a disutility element reflecting the characteristics of the journey itself as experienced by the traveller and including discomfort, waiting time, walking etc. The value of time savings to drivers/passengers depends therefore on how the opportunities made possible by the saving in time are used (e.g. whether for the purpose of increased production or for leisure).

Studies of the value of time generally distinguish between travel for business and working purposes on the one hand and travel for non-working purposes on the other. Various categories of non-working time savings such as commuting time, personal business time and pure leisure time are sometimes identified separately. Since many factors are known to influence the value of time including the purpose of the trip, its length, the amount of time saved, the mode of travel, characteristics of the traveller (e.g. age, income), whether time is saved in vehicle or in waiting, the certainty of the time saving, the time of day and whether the traveller has the opportunity to work in the course of the journey, it may not be appropriate to have a single value of time.

The normal approach in seeking to take account of all these factors that influence the value of time is to estimate a standard value of in-vehicle working time and to derive a series of modifiers which reflect consumer preferences in respect of the most significant influencing factors (e.g. travelling conditions, uncertainty and the activity value of waiting time). However, it is clearly not feasible to take account of all the personal factors surrounding an individual trip. The calculations must deal, as it were, with the average, or representative, user.

'In-work' time is a resource, the opportunity cost of which is the value of the other activities for which the time would be used. 'In-work' time savings are normally valued at the average wage rate for the workers whose time is saved, plus an allowance to cover the cost to the employer of hiring labour (i.e. overheads and employment taxes). It is important to appreciate that this approach is subject to a number of qualifications as follows :

- Individual employees will not behave as if they personally accepted this valuation of time. Thus the application of an average estimated value of 'in-work' time may result in either an over- or under-estimation of the value of time savings.

- Imperfections in the labour market may mean that the value in other uses of travel time saved may be less than the average wage rate. In an economy characterised by high and persistent unemployment, the wage rate may not reflect the economic cost of labour because of labour market inflexibilities which prop up wages. In these circumstances it might be argued that a more appropriate measure of savings in working time would be the opportunity cost of labour.

- The approach also assumes that resources released due to travel time savings will be converted into increased output. However, monopolistic labour market practices, limited possibilities for substitution between labour and capital, and divergences from the profit maximising assumption of the behaviour of firms may prevent this happening.

- Travel time is treated as a disutility, although in some cases travel time may be used productively (especially on a train or plane journey). In addition, the value the employee may place on journey time is not considered.

- Time saved in the transport of freight may be more valuable than the wage cost of the driver. Faster and more reliable delivery leads to other savings including reduced spoilage, reduced inventory costs, and more efficiency which employers may value at a higher rate than the wage of the driver.

Traditionally a single value of time has been applied for savings in 'in-work' time although, where different groups can be clearly identified, account is sometimes taken of variations in wage rates. For example, business travellers' time is more expensive than that of the average of the working population and if the higher salaries of business travellers represent a greater contribution to the output of the community as a whole then there may be a case for valuing the 'resource cost' element of business travellers' time savings at a higher rate. In some countries mode-specific values of 'in-work' time savings are derived reflecting the average earnings of travellers on the various transport modes.

There is no economic argument for excluding freight time savings from CBA studies although there is a question whether time saved in the transport of freight is necessarily more valuable that the wage cost of the driver. The main difficulty lies in valuing freight time savings. The MVA Consultancy (1987) quotes one study which examined the practices of transport operators using the Humber Bridge in England and concluded that the operators' valuation of travel time was of the order of the wage rate. This is an area where more research work would be very valuable.

Non 'in-work' time savings are the property of the traveller and it is, therefore, his or her own valuation of the combined opportunity cost and disutility which gives the basic value for this time. Values for the various categories of non-working time were traditionally derived from the 'observed preferences' revealed in people's actual travel choices. The main advantage of observed or 'revealed preference' information is that it shows actual behaviour whereas even the most carefully designed social survey data can only show hypothetical choices. However, the revealed preference approach can only be used where there are real trade-offs between time and money for alternative modes or routes. It cannot be used for potential trade-offs and this has proved a constraining factor.

More recently values of non-working time have been derived from 'stated preference' social surveys designed to elicit preferences for expenditure on various forms of travel compared to other potential expenditures within and outside the transport sector. One advantage of the stated preference approach is that it is easier to investigate the influence of different factors (e.g. age, household income, inherent characteristics of the various transport modes etc.) which affect the value of time.

A major study of travel time savings was undertaken for the Department of Transport in the UK using a combination of revealed and stated preference surveys (MVA Consultancy, 1987). As part of this project six major surveys of travellers were undertaken. Information was obtained from respondents on journey purpose, household income, household size and composition, employment status and age. The surveys were analysed to reveal the effect of these personal and household characteristics on the value of time. The major conclusions of the study were as follows:

- Household income was the most important single influence on people's valuation of time. Values of time increased with income, reflecting both a greater ability as well as willingness to pay for time savings at higher incomes.

- The study provided support for the notion of variations in the value of time by transport mode. The estimated values of time were higher for modes which were faster and more expensive and the influence of income on value of time became stronger with faster modes. The consultants recommended that mode specific estimates of the value of time be used.

- Retired people tended to have lower values of time than people in the working age groups (16-60 years) in the same household and income bands, and some studies showed that students also had slightly lower values, which may be income related. No significant differences were found in the values of time for men and women.

- In general, employment status had little effect on people's value of time after allowance had been made for the influence of income. The effect of unemployment on people's value of time showed up through lower incomes and not as a direct effect of their having more spare time available.

- *A priori* it seems reasonable that commuting should be distinguished from other non-work travelling and that the value of commuting time should be higher for a number of reasons, including greater time constraints on journeys to work, the fact that the conditions in which commuting trips are made are usually worse in terms of comfort, congestion etc. and the fact that for some people journeys to work may reduce the amount of time spent working. While one or two of the surveys identified some differences in the values of time for different non-work trip purposes, most surveys indicated little effect. In general, higher values of time were found to be associated with a need to keep appointments or make connections with other transport services and with journeys made more frequently,

- The evidence from the various surveys of the impact of car occupancy on drivers' valuation of time was conflicting. Some surveys indicated significantly higher values of time when there were passengers in cars and others revealed no significant effects of occupancy.

- The stated preference surveys of car drivers suggested that values of time were higher for congested road conditions compared with free flow (25 per cent to 40 per cent higher values were found), although this effect was not confirmed by the revealed preference studies. These higher values might reflect driver stress or indicate a reaction to uncertainty of journey times in heavy traffic. The stated preference surveys of the other modes generally identified a sensitivity to uncertainty of arrival time.

- A whole range of other factors such as time of day, day of week, possession of a company car, variability of working hours, and length of journey only made a small contribution towards explaining the variations in values of time in some of the studies.

- Urban bus surveys suggested that people valued walking time at about twice that of time spent in vehicles. This may reflect both a disutility associated with walking and the cost of walking time. Time spent waiting for public transport, and unscheduled time delays resulting from late running of public transport were both valued more highly than scheduled in-vehicle time.

Revealed preference and stated preference estimates of the value of time reflect 'behavioural' values of time (i.e. the money that an individual would be prepared to pay to save a unit of time for himself or herself). In CBA studies the appropriate value of time to be used is the amount of money that the state would be willing to pay to save a unit of time for the individual. This is likely to differ from behavioural values of time because of misperceptions by the individual, the impact of taxation and subsidies which cause the cost affecting the individual to diverge from the true resource cost, a difference in time horizons between the individual and the state and a concern by the state for income distribution effects. It is appropriate that the state should modify behavioural values of time, especially given the state's concern with income distribution issues.

A departure from the 'equity' principle in the valuation of non-work time saving could result in investment measures which would increase the relative wealth of the better-off members of society by valuing their time savings more highly. A further argument for the application of 'equity' values for non-work time savings is that studies have shown that, in terms of utility, extra travelling time is as inconvenient to low income people as to high income people; it is merely that the latter are more able to afford the cost of avoiding such inconvenience. For similar reasons it is generally the practice to use a single standard value for project appraisal and not to make allowance for variations in the value of time for different income groups and modes.

The approach currently being adopted for valuing time savings in the appraisal of transport investments in the UK can be summarised as follows:

- Separate in-work and non-working time savings are estimated.
- The same value for all non-working time journeys (commuting, shopping, holidays, educational etc.) is used.
- Non-working time values are up-dated in line with changes in real GDP per head.
- Where time is spent waiting for a transport connection the value of time savings is increased (usually doubled).
- Where transport changes will have an impact on the time spent walking then these walking time savings are valued at twice the in-vehicle time savings. Walking time values are applied to all pedestrian journeys whether part of a wider journey by public transport or not. Walking time values are also assumed to apply to cyclists where their journey times and convenience are likely to be affected.
- Small and large time savings and the cost of journey time increases, where they occur, are valued at the same rate.
- The same values of time are used for urban and rural areas.

In Ireland, the usual approach has been to estimate values for working time savings based on average earnings and national income and expenditure data. Non-working time savings are usually valued at a fixed proportion of the wage element of the working time rate with an adjustment for the proportion of indirect taxes (net of subsidies) in consumers' expenditure.

The value of accident savings

Transport investments can be expected to contribute to savings in accidents in a number of ways including the following:

- by encouraging transfers to a safer mode
- by providing new and safer infrastructure, e.g. through the provision of motorways
- by removing hazards on existing infrastructure
- by reducing the level of exposure, e.g. by reducing the actual kilometres travelled.

Typically, in appraisals of road improvement schemes, accident savings account for up to 20 per cent of the total quantified benefits.

The central problem in valuing transport safety involves placing a monetary value on a human life and on human suffering. There can be an understandable reluctance on both moral and ethical grounds, to do this.

However, if appropriate weighting is to be given to safety considerations in resource allocation between different transport projects and if the optimal trade-offs between safety and financial costs and other advantages and disadvantages of projects are to be made, then safety effects must be explicitly weighted and evaluated along with other cost and benefits. While the moral or ethical reluctance to place a monetary value on a human life is understandable, any decision to ignore benefits in this area would penalise projects which might save life or limb relative to ones which would not.

It is important to remind ourselves that we are not required to place a value on a specific life which could or could not be saved through a transport investment – a kidnapped millionaire may well be willing to pay to the limit of his or her wealth when facing a death threat. What is involved in a transport investment is the reduction in the statistical risk of a fatality or an injury. It is perfectly rational to ask what value is to be placed on reducing the risk of an event which is undesirable. At a practical level, this value cannot logically be either zero or infinity.

The traditional approach to evaluating personal accident costs was to estimate the value of the 'lost production' of the accident victim due to death or injury. An estimate of economic effects such as medical and police costs and vehicle damage was usually added and sometimes a subjective assessment for pain, grief and suffering of the victim and relatives was also included. The major objection to the foregoing 'gross output' approach is that it values safety on the basis of current and future levels of income and output whereas most individuals probably value safety on the basis of their aversion to the prospect of their own and others' death and injury *per se*. More recently there has been a change towards valuing transport safety on the basis of 'willingness to pay' with revealed and stated preference data being used to collect information on the value of a reduction in accident risk.

Under the willingness to pay approach to the valuation of safety, the amounts that those affected would individually be willing to pay for (typically small) improvements in their own and others' safety are determined. These amounts are then added to derive an overall value for the safety improvement concerned – a reflection of what the safety improvement is 'worth' to the affected group, relative to the alternative ways in which each individual might have spent his or her limited income. The adoption of this approach goes some way towards recognising that an individual is not a mere factor of production.

One consequence of the move towards the willingness to pay approach based on revealed and stated preference data is that there have been significant increases in the estimated value of a statistical life. However, there are methodological and practical difficulties in implementing this approach. The 'irrational' behaviour of car drivers in relation to safety (e.g. when not wearing seat belts) appears to conflict with revealed preference valuations on safety.

Jones-Lee (1990) reported the results of a series of studies which valued a 'statistical life' for transport risks and noted other studies which derived values of statistical life from observed wage premia for risk in labour markets. These studies generally involved the use of multiple regression analysis to control for the variety of other factors, besides job risk, that can be expected to influence equilibrium wage rates in labour markets. In broad terms the estimates of the value of a statistical life produced in these studies were consistent with the findings of the transport risk studies.

Accident rate reductions can often be anticipated and included in the calculation of benefits. However, there are severe practical difficulties in applying CBA methodology to accident cost savings in practical situations. For example, historical records of accident rates on particular segments of the road network may only be available in a rough categorisation of accident severity. Typically, the records will distinguish fatalities, injuries, and material damage. Fatalities are rare, and most network segments would never have had a fatality. But since measures of the severity of the other accident categories are not really feasible, two segments with the same apparent accident rate may in truth have very different safety characteristics.

The proper allowance to be made for accident reduction will depend on engineering judgement in many instances – a bend may be a dangerous bend even if the historical data are not capable of demonstrating high accident frequency and severity. High accident rates may also be due to driver behaviour, ambient conditions, or other factors which are not amenable to rectification through physical road improvements.

In some transport modes, historical records provide no guidance whatever. Most airports in the world, including airports which are quite busy, have never had an accident on takeoff or landing. Such accidents as do occur may be due to pilot error, equipment failure or other factors unrelated to infrastructure investment. Thus improvements which enhance safety may have to be evaluated from a probabilistic perspective: the likelihood of an accident is reduced by an improvement, even where the historical records show that no accident has ever occurred.

Vehicle operating cost savings

For road investments, there are well-established procedures for reckoning the savings in vehicle operating costs which may be expected to arise from network improvements. Some schemes will shorten journey times, either by shortening the distance to be travelled or by enhancing level of service. All relevant links in the network need to be considered – a by-pass will improve journey times for those using the 'old' route, for example. The main items of savings will include fuel, oil, tyres, maintenance and depreciation. Standing charges, which do not vary with the volume of usage, should be ignored. They include road tax, insurance, and the opportunity cost of the capital used to buy the vehicle. Some improvements can yield economies in fleet size which should be taken into account. For example, predicted passenger loads for an inter-urban bus or road freight operator might require a smaller fleet consequent on a major network upgrading.

Indirect taxation is a major element in vehicle operating costs, especially for road transport, where tax is as much as 60 per cent of the retail price of petrol in some European countries. Taxes are a transfer of resources between sections of society as a whole, and should be ignored in a social cost-benefit analysis. Direct taxation is treated differently to indirect taxation – gross pay is the measure of output foregone to society through lost working-time. But a gallon of petrol is really worth less than the price actually paid by the motorist.

The traffic engineering literature contains a range of empirical studies of the impact of road improvements on vehicle operating costs, allowing for savings due to such factors as better road surfaces and gradients. In non-road modes, similar considerations apply. An improved railway line will cut journey times and may also lead to fleet economies. In the case of sea and airports, the point-to-point journey times of vehicles are not, of course, directly affected by port improvements, but turnaround times may be reduced. Thus the probability of a ship having to wait for a berth is cut when an additional berth is constructed. Equally, when an airport widens a runway, the incidence of bad weather diversions for certain aircraft types should fall, and the probabilities can be calculated from meteorological and operating data. Improvements in air traffic control and in the technology of both airports and aircraft which increase the ability to operate safely in adverse conditions will have the same type of impact.

The discount rate

Discounting procedures are needed to compare costs and benefits over time, in a way which reflects the preferences of consumers and taxpayers for enjoying benefits earlier and incurring costs later. In private market transactions the justification for discounting reflects two factors – the productivity of capital and the time preference of individuals. Because of the former, a borrower who invests in a capital asset can expect to end up with more in value than he or she started with and will be in a position to pay interest to anyone who lent the resources in the first place. On the consumer side it is clear that consumers would prefer to consume a unit today than to defer consumption for a year. Many public sector decisions incorporate a judgement, implicit or explicit, about the importance of the more distant future relative to the present or near future. There are good reasons to presume some preference, by those affected by a public sector activity, for benefits to be sooner rather than later and for costs to be later rather than sooner.

Some measure of people's preferences is given by the real return which they are willing to accept on government bonds. Over the past twenty years the real yield on long-term Irish government debt has averaged approximately 3 per cent. The Department of Finance recommends a real discount rate of 5 per cent for use in public sector project evaluation (Department of Finance, 1994). Some observations on this rate are as follows:

• Five per cent is a low rate in absolute terms. It is a rate which is appropriate for a liquid, government-backed security, rather than for project finance.

• Investing in an index-linked government security is just about the lowest-risk project which can be imagined.

• The application of a uniform rate to all projects regardless of risk may not be appropriate unless the riskiness of projects is taken into account explicitly in the appraisal.

There are reasons for viewing bond yields as the lower limit rather than a mean estimate of the time preference of individuals. Not all individuals are net savers. Some are net borrowers and personal borrowing rates are generally above the long-term bond yield. There are also uncertainties about future returns to individuals. Some individuals will be dead or too infirm to enjoy extra income as much as they would today and their time preference will exceed the 'risk free' yield on long bonds.

Apart from a very general risk of some catastrophe such that the longer-term benefits (and costs) of any investment made now might not materialise, there are ordinary risks associated with all public projects (e.g. implementation risk and risks about future demand levels) which suggest that the discount factor should exceed the 'risk free' yield on long bonds. However, there are also arguments why the social rate of discount should be below the market rate. Reliance on individuals' time preference could result in society allocating too little to investment if the discount rate is too high. In addition, too high a discount rate may also have undesirable environmental implications since the future exploitation and consumption of natural resources, both renewable and non-renewable, will be assigned a low value.

A high discount rate reduces the importance given to resource depletion and environmental damage in the future. In public projects financed out of taxes the risk is spread over a much larger population and this has led to suggestions that for these projects the risk premium should be excluded from the discount rate. There is another objection to including a premium in the discount rate to take account of risk: with a higher discount rate a greater weight is given to costs and benefits closer to the present and a lower weight to costs and benefits in the distant future; this procedure may (but does not necessarily) favour low risk projects and penalise high risk ones.

Overall the discount rate recommended by the Department of Finance is probably reasonable (if somewhat low) for use in the case of transport projects so long as risk is dealt with explicitly in the appraisal process, by modelling a range of possible outcomes based on different cost and traffic volume forecasts.

Traffic forecasts

Traffic forecasts play a key role in CBA studies. The evaluation of economic costs and benefits and the appraisal of environmental impacts depend on forecasts of the amount and pattern of traffic using the new network compared to the existing one. For the purpose of estimating the benefits of a transport project future traffic should be divided into three basic types as follows:

- *Normal traffic*. This is the traffic that would have occurred without the investment. It benefits from the full reduction in operating costs and from the full time savings.

- *Diverted traffic*. This is traffic diverted to the new or improved facility from other facilities of the same mode or from other modes. The benefit to this traffic is the difference between future transport costs on the old route/facility and the new one. Traffic diversion depends not on relative economic costs but on actual financial costs including non-transport charges.

- *Generated or induced traffic*. The third type of traffic is that which did not previously exist and is generated as a consequence of the lowering of transport costs. It is not appropriate to apply the full reduction in costs to this traffic since the traffic would not have materialised without the reduction in costs.

It is important that a robust and acceptable methodology is used to derive forecasts of overall traffic broken down into the different components. Where models are used to forecast traffic they should be subject to appropriate validation.

There has been considerable debate in the UK over the existence and scale of induced traffic associated with major road improvement schemes. Road traffic forecasts have traditionally been estimated on the basis of expected trends in economic growth, the costs of car ownership and the costs of car use. Account was generally taken of induced traffic only in particular cases (e.g. estuary crossings). However, it has been argued that the provision of additional road capacity itself encourages travellers to travel more or further.

An expert report by the Standing Advisory Committee on Trunk Road Assessment (1994) which examined this issue concluded that induced traffic does occur, probably quite extensively, although its size and significance is likely to vary widely in different circumstances. The report noted that induced traffic is likely to be of greatest consequence in cases where a network is operating at or close to capacity, where traveller responsiveness to changes in travel time or costs is high (e.g. where trips are suppressed by congestion and then released when the network is improved) and where the implementation of a scheme can cause significant changes in travel costs. The Committee recommended that the appraisal of road schemes should be carried out within the context of economic and environmental appraisal at a strategic area-wide level and that account be taken of induced traffic through variable demand methods which recognise congestion constraints. The issue of induced traffic is relevant in Dublin where planned transport investments may facilitate increased private car usage with negative environmental impacts.

The treatment of environmental impacts

A major criticism of CBA is its failure to take explicit account of environmental impacts. Transport infrastructure projects can have positive or negative environmental impacts. Positive impacts occur, for example, when road and rail projects take traffic away from congested town centres. Negative impacts include noise associated with a new airport development, or with a new urban motorway. The application of cost benefit analysis to the environment is treated in detail in Chapter 10. This section considers specific issues which apply to transportation and the environment.

The main environmental impacts associated with investments in inter-urban transport infrastructure in Ireland are as shown in Table 9.2.

Environmental impacts are externalities since they do not usually affect the users of the new facility to any great extent. Other externalities are associated with the use of land and water resources and the production of solid waste as part of the construction and abandonment of roads, rail lines etc. Another type of environmental externality is the visual intrusion created by transport infrastructure. This affects residents or landowners rather than transport system users. Road schemes may pass through environmentally sensitive areas, and may be visually intrusive. Electric rail projects involve unsightly overhead gantries. These 'disbenefits' are notoriously difficult to quantify but are nonetheless real.

Table 9.2: Main environmental impacts of transport infrastructure projects

• Noise	Associated with road traffic and to a lesser extent with rail and air traffic.
• Air pollution	Associated with all transport modes to different degrees.
• Impact on neighbourhoods and on farmland and wildlife habitats	Associated with road investments and to a lesser extent with other transport investments.

In recent years there has been increasing recognition that the transport sector generates environmental externalities which impose costs on society as a whole and that transportation investments often magnify the incidence of these externalities. For example, in developed economies it has been estimated that the transport sector accounts for approximately 75 per cent of carbon monoxide emissions, for between 40 per cent and 50 per cent of emissions of nitrogen oxides and hydrocarbons and for significant proportions of the emissions of particulates and sulphur oxides. Given the sheer size of the transport sector in developed economies it is hardly surprising that it has a significant impact on the environment. In addition, since travel is highly income elastic, the size of the transport sector is likely to increase as incomes rise, and this has implications for the scale of associated environmental impacts in the future.

Significant progress has been made in recent years in environmental benefit estimation/damage assessment using revealed and stated preference studies of people's willingness to pay. Benefit estimation describes the process whereby monetary values are placed on the advantages that accrue to society from improvements in the natural and built environment. Damage assessment describes the obverse: placing monetary values on losses to society from environmental deterioration.

The main techniques used in valuing noise and air pollution impacts and other environmental externalities involve the use of hedonic property price indices. This approach to benefit estimation assumes that if different locations have different environmental attributes there will be observed differences in property prices. The methodology involves examining the revealed preferences of people in the housing market when they trade-off the noise/air pollution attributes of different properties against their prices. Statistical techniques are available to identify how much of an observed property price differential is due to a particular environmental difference and to infer from this how much people are willing to pay for an improvement in environmental quality. However, as might be expected the approach is fraught with methodological difficulties. The approach ignores the considerable transaction costs in the housing market and the infrequent turnover in the housing stock due to this and other factors. In addition, there are doubts about the capacity to allow for changes in all other factors that influence house prices.

An alternative approach is contingent valuation which asks individuals directly what they would be willing to pay for an environmental benefit or what/how much they would be willing to accept to tolerate an environmental cost. The aim is to elicit valuations which are close to those that would be revealed if an actual market existed. However, there are doubts about the accuracy of the contingent valuation approach because of the biases that can arise.

Evidence from the USA quoted by Button (1990) on the value of traffic noise nuisance using hedonic techniques, suggests a decline of between 0.08 per cent and 0.88 per cent of the house price per unit change in Leq (a measure of continuous sound levels) in a number of American cities. Somewhat higher values were found in Canada and Switzerland. Similar ranges of values were found in the context of aircraft nuisance. However, a UK study showed that while properties in areas affected by the noise of aircraft using Manchester International Airport had lower market values than those in other parts, the whole of the difference could be attributed to neighbourhood and other characteristics of the properties (Pennington, Topham and Ward, 1990). There is evidence from US studies that for seven large North American cities the percentage fall in property values for a 1 per cent rise in air pollution is in the range of 0.01 per cent to 0.22 per cent with part of the variation explained by the nature of the pollution.

The conclusion reached by the OECD is worth quoting (Pearce, Markandya, 1989):

> Overall we take the view that environmental pollution in the form of air pollution, noise nuisance and water quality deterioration has significant effects on the property values on which they impinge. The overwhelming evidence of the empirical studies supports this conclusion. The accuracy with which we can quantify such effects is, however, much more debatable. There are many reasons for thinking the numbers can only be orders of magnitude. ... It is also our opinion that this matter of fuzziness is not one that will be resolved by better measurement or better statistical techniques: it is inherent to the problem being considered.

And again:

> Also there has been considerable improvement over the last ten years in the quality
> of the data used and in the analytical techniques used. These improvements have
> resulted in a greater awareness of the accuracy of the estimates. It has now become
> clear that, even with the best techniques at our disposal, this accuracy remains quite
> low and that estimated costs ... could be out by a substantial margin in either
> direction.

The impact of transport developments on property values can be double edged. The noise and air pollution are a nuisance, but there may be an offsetting locational premium in being near the transport facility. Some people find it convenient to be near an airport, and studies of property values near airports have found both positive and negative effects. It is generally accepted that residential properties along the DART route in Dublin command a premium price.

The impact of noise, or air pollution, will depend on the location of any project. There will normally be a presumption that environmental impacts from noise, noxious odours and the like will be most significant in urban areas where substantial numbers of people will be affected. In rural areas, there will simply be fewer people to be adversely affected. But rural projects can have significant impacts on visual amenity, which might not be a concern in some urban areas.

In the UK, in appraisals of transport infrastructure projects, environmental considerations are not generally given monetary values. However, they are taken into account in the appraisal process. The factors considered are traffic noise, visual impact, community severance, agriculture, heritage and conservation areas, ecology, disruption due to construction, pedestrian amenity, the view from the road, and driver stress. In the case of some factors the effects are quantified. For example, in the case of noise, estimates are made of the number of properties that will experience at least a 3 decibel change compared with existing noise levels. The assessment also identifies who actually experiences the adverse environmental impact (e.g. travellers, property owners etc.) so that distributional effects can be considered. It is especially important in assessing emissions to include the upstream emissions in the production of the fuel source (e.g. in oil refineries or power stations).

The valuation of environmental externalities involves greater quantification difficulties than the other main elements in transport project appraisal. Given existing knowledge in this area we must accept that it is not feasible to value the environmental impacts of transport infrastructure projects with a view to incorporating these impacts into the CBA process. Clearly, however, environmental impacts cannot be ignored. Environmental Impact Statements are required for certain larger projects, and should be considered alongside the factors quantified by the cost-benefit analysis. In other cases the principal environmental aspects should be identified and their significance assessed.

CBA application rules

While the bulk of this chapter has concentrated on technical aspects of the application of CBA to transport projects, the fact that CBA is more than a technical process cannot be overemphasised. Adler (1987) remarks as follows: 'The appraisal of a project is not a mechanical process; a high degree of analytical ability and a broad imagination are required.'

The following application rules deal with some of the critical issues that arise in applying CBA to transport projects. They are intended to assist in preparing, reviewing and interpreting CBA studies.

The definition of a project for analysis purposes

Considerable care needs to be taken in the application of CBA to transport infrastructure projects, to ensure that the project is a meaningful unit for evaluation purposes and that it is properly defined. In particular, the unit of analysis (i.e. the project) should be specified so as to distinguish projects from programmes. All ancillary sub-projects which are essential to the achievement of the benefits of the main project should be included. Unfortunately this is frequently not the case in Ireland.

In the transportation area, developed countries will tend to be permanently engaged in programmes of investment in the various modes of travel. It is possible to evaluate these programmes, as a whole, and to conduct CBA evaluation of the entire investment package. But this can be highly misleading, to the extent that the programme consists of individual, stand-alone elements, which may not be equally desirable, or may not be equally urgent. It is best to break the programmes down into a series of self-contained projects, and to conduct CBA at the level of the project. To construct a motorway from Dublin to Galway is not a project; it is a programme. We know that traffic volumes along the route vary enormously, and that, while extra motorway capacity may be needed soon on certain sections, it will not be needed for decades, if ever, on other sections. Thus it makes sense, in evaluating road investments, to reduce the unit of analysis to a length of road that has uniform traffic volumes, or to a town by-pass, and this is the standard practice in Ireland. A good example is the Naas Bypass study (Barrett and Mooney, 1984).

However, it is likely that the improvement to one section of a road will, by simulating new traffic, affect other sections and account should be taken of these network impacts. For example, the opening of a new stretch of motorway will result in reduced transit times on that section. However, part of these savings may be dissipated by increased congestion on other sections of the route. This should be taken into account.

Even in the case of a route with uniform traffic it may be appropriate to split the project. For example, a route could go through some easy terrain and then through some difficult terrain. It might be appropriate to split the project into two projects, because the costs will differ, even where we expect the benefits to be uniform. The time-savings may justify the cost in easy terrain, but may not do so in difficult terrain.

Sometimes the true project may be bigger, rather than smaller, than it seems. If a new suburban rail or light rail facility cannot realise the benefits of traffic growth without extra car-parking (e.g. a 'park and ride' facility) or a feeder bus service, then the cost of the car park and/or the feeder bus service is part of the rail or light rail project. Similarly a port access road might be required to capture the full benefits of a major port project. Again the cost of a project involving the development of quality bus corridors should include the cost of the additional enforcement that will be required to ensure their effectiveness. The test should be that a project's costs must include everything needed to realise the benefits of the project, regardless of who meets these costs. Most CBA studies of transport projects in Ireland can be criticised on the ground of poor project definition.

Timing of a project

It is important to experiment with alternative starting dates in applying CBA to transport infrastructure projects. Even if a project shows an adequate return if commenced immediately, it may still not be a priority for inclusion in the programme of immediate works. There may be other projects which show a higher immediate return, and delay may not worsen the return on some projects at all, or may even improve it. The premature provision of transport infrastructure capacity in advance of traffic growth will always tend to put a project in this category. It is therefore always worthwhile to experiment with a range of future years as alternative starting points for any particular project. Unfortunately, it is the exception rather than the rule in CBA studies of transport projects in Ireland that consideration is given to alternative starting dates.

Alternatives to a project

Probably the most critical element of the application of CBA to transport infrastructure projects is the definition and analysis of alternatives to the project under consideration. Adler (1987) comments as follows: 'The most serious mistakes in project appraisal do not arise from the application of erroneous statistical techniques but from inadequate analysis of alternatives and results.'

The options of closing a route, of discontinuing a transport service, of developing an alternative mode, of using a cheaper technology (e.g. diesel instead of electricity powered suburban rail), or of simply doing nothing, should always be amongst the options considered in evaluating transport investments. However, even 'doing nothing' needs to be articulated carefully. In developed countries, and in the context of ongoing traffic growth, doing nothing may well mean deferral for, say, five or ten years. This deferral can itself be evaluated by considering the differential stream of costs and benefits that it implies.

The alternative could be to discontinue, either forthwith or at some future point, a particular service or route. The option of discontinuation is not normally considered in the case of certain transportation investments, where there is no feasible alternative method of catering for the traffic volumes. But this is not universally the case. It is feasible to discontinue regional air services, or off-peak bus services, or to close lightly-patronised rail lines. It may or may not be desirable, but that is a matter for CBA to establish. Whenever proposals for upgrading arise in these cases, the option of discontinuation should be regarded as the base case scenario.

Consideration of alternatives is especially important in transport investment because of the existence and extent of competition within and between modes. For example, the proposal to build a new regional airport has an alternative, namely to do nothing, which would see the relevant traffic volumes catered for by other airports or by bus, rail, or car. In considering the costs and benefits of a new airport, or extensions or improvements to an existing one, the impact on other facilities and modes needs to be explicitly taken into account. Where freight or public transport passengers need to be moved between A and B, a full CBA of a proposed investment in any mode must consider the relative merits of all modes for carrying the anticipated traffic, including bus, rail, air, truck, or inland waterway as appropriate.

It is common in CBA studies in Ireland for alternatives to be selected by the project promoters or their consultants which are so implausible that one can only assume they were selected for the sole purpose of making the preferred project appear attractive by comparison. CBA studies prepared by or on behalf of project promoters most often fail because inadequate attention is given to alternatives or because appropriate alternatives are not considered.

Technology choice and frequency in public transport

Private transport modes, such as car or truck, have the advantage of continuous departure times at the option of the user. The only transport modes used by the public which offer continuous departures are taxis and hired vehicles or craft. Users of public transport, in planning their journeys, must accordingly rely on timetables of published departure schedules. The only exception is in urban systems where frequency is so high that customers do not feel the need for timetables – DART approaches these frequencies as do certain bus routes.

In Ireland, rail services between the principal cities and towns offer frequencies of 3 or 4 departures a day in many cases. Even frequencies up to 10 or 12 a day, which are not found in Ireland, mean that people will rely on timetables. There is evidence from many studies that improvements in frequency in these circumstances will help to generate increased patronage. So will shorter transit times, of course. The potential frequency on any route will depend on the choice of mode and the choice of technology. Thus the bus mode offers the prospect of greatest frequency, but at some cost in terms of transit time, while within the rail mode, large, locomotive-based technologies will offer lower frequency than lighter, smaller railcars. The impact of these choices, through frequency, on passenger demand, needs to be taken into account in projecting patronage.

The time horizon and residual values

It is common in transport projects, to use time horizons of 25 or 30 years, perhaps with some ascription of residual value to the project's capital stock in the terminal year. At discount rates as low as 5 per cent (real), however, the present value of €1 of benefits or costs in year 25 is still 30c, and, particularly where benefit streams are expected to grow rapidly, there may be a case for using a longer time horizon.

Residual values, after a 30-year lifetime, will tend to be low or zero for many kinds of transport infrastructure, depending of course on volumes of planned maintenance spending. But where rolling stock or other equipment has to be acquired through the life of the project, the residual values will be more significant. There is a case for developing a common approach to both the time horizon and the determination of residual values for use in all CBA studies of transport projects.

The avoidance of double-counting

When user benefits have been fully accounted for, care should be taken to avoid double-counting through the inclusion of other projected occurrences which are induced by these user benefits.

It is sometimes argued that transport investments can have a sufficiently large impact on the available transport links as to alter the spatial pattern of economic development in a region or country. Examples are rare in developed countries, where transport investment programmes are ongoing and incremental in nature. But there are exceptions such as the Channel Tunnel.

In Ireland, some projects have been mooted from time to time which, it is claimed, would have such a large impact as to promote regional development objectives. In the late 1980s, there was some discussion of a motorway route linking the South West to the North West as a tool for stimulating the economic development of the West. Similar considerations have been raised in connection with the upgraded Dublin-Belfast rail link, and with some regional airport schemes. In evaluating such schemes, it is important not to double-count benefits, for example by ascribing value to the time-savings of users, and then ascribing a further and separate value to developmental stimuli which these savings are believed likely to induce.

An additional consideration is that transport links between, say, metropolitan areas and remote regions will not always have a uni-directional impact on the pattern of development. There are examples in the literature of such links facilitating greater, rather than less, concentration of economic activity. These may be exceptions, but the issue is complex, and intuitive notions can mislead.

Another frequent problem with CBA studies is that items are sometimes included erroneously as benefits, particularly when the CBA is too heavily influenced by project promoters. For example, the wage bill during construction is sometimes mentioned as a positive feature of the project, even though it is a cost rather than a benefit! Indirect economic benefits of a macro-economic character are also sometimes attributed to transportation projects. Thus a new road which links into a less developed region may be said to yield benefits in terms of a higher rate of economic development for that region. However, these effects may be fully captured by the calculation of direct user benefits and their inclusion separately will almost always involve double counting.

Capital investment as a substitute for other policy interventions

One direct consequence of the availability of EU assistance in Ireland in recent years has been the increased emphasis on investment projects in the transportation area and the consequential expansion in the scale of transport investment programmes.

There is a danger that because of the availability of additional funding, investment projects will be seen as the only method of achieving desired benefits. This is especially likely to be the case where service provision is in the hands of state-owned monopolies. It is important to ensure that the potential contribution of more effective management and market deregulation as substitutes for capital investment are not ignored.

The impact of grant-aid

Because of the availability of EU assistance for transportation projects it is sometimes argued that only the domestically-financed portion of the capital costs of a grant-aided project should be evaluated, on the basis that the EU finance is somehow 'free'. By extension it is occasionally argued that given the availability of 'free' money a less rigorous approach to project evaluation will suffice. Even if this is not explicitly argued it is often implicit in the approach to the CBA study.

However, since the opportunity cost of EU funding is the return that could be obtained by investing the finance in another project there is no basis for making allowances for the source of finance and certainly no basis for adopting a less rigorous approach in the case of EU financed projects.

Parameter values

In the absence of detailed government guidelines, it is usually left to consultants undertaking CBA studies to prepare their own estimates of the parameter values to be used to define the project, to determine what alternatives will be examined, to prepare a time horizon for the analysis and to determine the treatment of residual values. It would be preferable if an external agency (e.g. the Department of Finance) were to specify the parameter values to be used in CBA studies of all projects involving public expenditure, just as they specify the discount rate to be applied. Consideration might also be given by the Department to commissioning research studies of the value of time and of accident and vehicle operating costs in order to derive better parameter value estimates. Finally, guidelines on the approach to be adopted in forecasting traffic are required to ensure greater consistency in approach in CBA studies.

In conclusion, one must emphasise the need for exercising caution and judgement in preparing, reviewing and interpreting CBA studies. This need is all the greater in Ireland where CBA evaluations are usually prepared directly by the project promoter or by consultants acting on the promoter's behalf and where the government has not required compliance with detailed guidelines. There is significant scope for the misuse of CBA. In these circumstances it is hardly surprising that many CBA studies of transport projects in Ireland give the impression of having been carried out retrospectively to justify the promoters' preferred project rather than as part of an objective project selection process.

NOTES

1 This chapter draws on an earlier paper by Keegan and McCarthy (1994)
2 An overview of developments in the application of appraisal techniques to road projects in Ireland is contained in a report by Casey (Casey, 1986).

REFERENCES

Adler, H. (1987). *Economic Appraisal of Transport Projects*, Baltmore: John Hopkins

An Foras Forbartha (1971). *Dublin Transportation Study*, Dublin: An Foras Forbartha

Barrett S. D. and D. Mooney (1984). 'The Naas Motorway Bypass – A Cost Benefit Analysis', Article in *ESRI Quarterly Economic Commentary*, January, pp. 21-34

Button, K J. (1990). 'Environmental Externalities and Transport Policy', *Oxford Review of Economic Policy*, Vol. 6 No. 2, pp. 61-75

Casey, J. J. (1986). 'A Review of the Value of Time and Car Ownership Forecasts', Unpublished Paper (RT 326). Dublin: An Foras Forbartha

Department of Finance (1994). *Guidelines for the Appraisal and Management of Capital Expenditure Proposals in the Public Sector*, Dublin: Department of Finance

Department of Local Government Dublin (1966). *Arterial Roads Needs Study*, Dublin: Department of Local Government

EU Commission (1995) *Towards Fair and Efficient Pricing in Transport*, Green Paper Luxembourg: COM (95) 691 Final

Jones-Lee, M.W. (1990). 'The Value of Transport Safety', *Oxford Review of Economic Policy*, Vol. 6, No. 2, pp. 39-60

Keegan, O. and C. McCarthy (1994). 'CBA Parameter Values and Application Rules', Paper Prepared under the Technical Assistance Programme of the Operational Programme on Peripherality, Dublin: DKM Economic Consultants

MVA Consultancy; Institute for Transport Studies, University of Leeds; Transport Studies Unit, University of Oxford (1987). *The Value of Travel Time Savings*, Newbury, Berkshire: Policy Journals

O'Keeffe, P. (1961). 'Economic Aspects of Road Improvement in Ireland', Paper Presented to the Institute of Civil Engineers of Ireland, Dublin: Institute of Civil Engineers

Pearce D. W. and A. Markandya (1989). *Environmental Policy Benefits: Monetary Valuation*, Paris: OECD

Pennington, G., N. Topham and R. Ward (1990). 'Aircraft Noise and Residential Property Values Adjacent to Manchester International Airport', *Journal of Transport Economics and Policy*, Vol. 24, No. 1, pp. 49-59

Standing Advisory Committee on Trunk Road Assessment (1994). *Trunk Roads and the Generation of Traffic*, London: HMSO

Steer, Davies, Gleave, in association with McHugh Consultants (1994). *Dublin Transportation Initiative: Final Report*, Dublin: Stationery Office

10

Evaluation and the Environment

J. PETER CLINCH, FRANK J. CONVERY

Introduction

We tend to judge the value of items or activities by the amount of money we pay to acquire or experience them. A loaf of bread or an evening at the theatre can be valued by the price we have to pay for them. The fact that we buy the loaf and pay for the theatre ticket indicates that, for us, the experience of eating and enjoying are worth at least the price we pay. However, much of what we enjoy is not directly mediated through markets. We fall in love without putting a price on it, we enjoy a joke with a friend without demanding payment, we walk in the uplands without having to pay a price for admission, we enjoy looking at an old building and having it 'anchor' our sense of place and time without paying the owner for the privilege.

In many situations, it is not logical nor is there a need to place a value on such dimensions of our lives. Indeed, the very attempt to do so may be highly detrimental. Putting a 'price' on friendship, for example, may undermine it, in the same way that pre-nuptial agreements may induce a sense of the transient in a nominally perpetual commitment. But sometimes choices must be made when it would be useful to be able to provide some values where none are readily available. For example, if a choice has to be made between the planting of two woodland types, such as broadleaves or conifers, on a particular site, the market values for wood outputs can be assessed relatively easily, but the implications for carbon fixing and therefore global warming, for landscape quality, for biodiversity and for water quality are all unvalued in markets. If reasonably credible estimates of market-type values could be derived for what can be categorised as 'non-market' outputs it would help to clarify the implications of choices. Indeed, in a decision-making system where monetary value is perforce regarded as the prime performance indicator, unless there is such valuation there is a tendency for non-market outputs to be ignored in the decision-making process and this can lead to incorrect decisions.

This issue is of central concern in regard to environmental endowments. Environment can be defined as that part of our existence which we somehow share in common. However, that which belongs to all, in a sense belongs to no one. It is this common property characteristic of environmental assets which results in their destruction. In the absence of property rights, that which Garrett Hardin (1968) so brilliantly, if somewhat over-simplistically, characterised as the 'tragedy of the commons' occurs. Everyone has free access and the system does not value conservation and so the incentives lead to destruction. The neoclassical economic paradigm says that the market has failed, resulting in a scarce and therefore valuable asset, the environmental endowment, being destroyed. This is because no market exists which can reflect the environment's scarcity value as a price and therefore this value is not reflected in the incentives which users and others face. The solution favoured by most economists is to create markets by some combination of the assignment of property rights, the imposition of charges and taxes which reflect scarcity value, and the encouragement of a market in tradeable permits. The market failure rationale is developed more formally later in this chapter. The point here is to recognise that the absence of values is inimical to good decision-making.

In this paper, we show how economists are attempting to address this problem by firstly considering the problem of market failure in greater detail. We then provide a framework within which the economic value of environmental assets may be analysed. A number of techniques for assessing non-market values are then outlined. In addition, we address some other aspects which must be considered when evaluating the environment or projects or policies which affect the environment. These include whether the discount rate to be applied to environmental projects should be different from the market discount rate, how cost-benefit rules can be modified when evaluating a project which will cause the irreversible destruction of a natural asset, and the role of non-market valuation in the assessment of sustainability.

The values and market prices discussed below are a product in part of the existing income distribution. If the distribution of income changes, prices will change, and so will non-market values. In addition, the estimates of values are made at the margin. The plausibility of the techniques described depends in part on the fact that most things remain the same, with the implicit assumption that there is no paradigm shift in values, power, income and the like over the time period of assessment.

Market failure

The rationale for the consideration of environmental values in economic evaluation was formally recognised in 1936 when the US Flood Control Act introduced welfare economics into public decision-making by deeming flood control projects to be desirable 'if the benefits to whomsoever they may accrue are in excess of the costs'. This distinguished financial appraisal where the only costs and benefits of a project considered are those faced by the private agent (such as an individual or firm), from cost benefit analysis where the costs and benefits of a project are considered to be those faced by society as a whole. The divergence between these costs and benefits results from what is known as market failure.

As a result of market failure, certain adjustments must be made when evaluating the costs and benefits of a project to society. For instance, shadow prices are used in place of market prices where there are considered to be distortions within the economy which render certain prices invalid as indicators of social opportunity cost (Drèze and Stern, 1994). These distortions include monopoly power, indirect taxes and subsidies (unless they are correcting for some other form of market failure) and unemployment. However, in relation to the environment, the key manifestations of market failure are externalities and public goods.

Baumol and Oates (1988) provide the following formal definition for the existence of an externality: 'An externality is present whenever an agent's utility or production relationships contain real (non-monetary) variables whose values are chosen by other agents without attention to the effects on the first agent's utility.'

More simply, an external cost is a cost resulting from an activity which is not borne by the agent engaging in that activity and an external benefit is a benefit which results from an activity which is appropriated by someone other than the agent engaging in that activity. Examples of external costs can be found at local level such as fish kills from water pollution by farming, at regional level such as the damage to crops and buildings by acid rain resulting from sulphur emissions, and at global level such as the costs of global warming which result from the burning of fossil fuels. Examples of external benefits include the landscape benefits of a forest plantation and carbon sequestration and oxygen production from the world's forests. Most externalities feature 'non-rivalry' in consumption. For example, air pollution (an external cost) which is harmful to the population living in a town is likely to be equally harmful to each individual even if the population were to suddenly double.

A public good exhibits non-rivalry and non-excludability in consumption. For example, if a group of tourists stop to take a look at an attractive landscape, the value of that landscape will not be reduced should other tourists also view the same landscape but, in addition, it is not possible to exclude certain tourists from viewing the landscape; it is thus a public good. In some cases public goods can exhibit rivalry in consumption past a certain point. For example, a public park is usually thought of as a public good. However, as more people use it, congestion may set in after a certain point, thus reducing the value of the experience to each user. This type of a good is known as an 'impure' public good. Since it is impossible to exclude individuals from consuming a public good, it is normally provided by the state or local government.

When an external cost results from some activity, there is a divergence between the cost to society (social cost) and the cost to the individual undertaking that activity (private cost), i.e.

$$\text{Social cost} = \text{Private cost} + \text{External cost}$$

Similarly,

$$\text{Social benefit} = \text{Private benefit} + \text{External benefit}$$

When an activity is appraised financially, external costs and benefits are excluded from the analysis. However, a proper cost benefit analysis should adjust for all forms of market failure including the existence of externalities and public goods. In the case of a public good this can be done using what is known as the total economic value framework. The evaluation challenge is to develop estimates of external benefits and costs which reflect as closely as possible the values which would have been yielded by market forces if the latter existed.

Why bother with environmental valuation?

There are two main reasons for engaging in environmental valuation. Firstly, if we want to charge a polluter for emitting pollution or to compensate the victims of pollution, the existence of credible values facilitates a coherent debate regarding charges and compensation. Secondly, where projects and policies are being evaluated, and decisions must be made, if there is a significant component of the project which involves the imposition of external costs, or the generation of external benefits, then some estimate of the values of these 'non-market' aspects is an essential element in assessing whether the project is worthwhile from the point of view of society.

It is important to note the difference between environmental impact assessment (EIA) and 'non-market' valuation. EIA is a cluster of techniques for estimating the physical implications for the environment and the effect of environmental change on human well-being whereas 'non-market' valuation is a cluster of techniques which provides market values for these effects and thus allows the environmental effects to be compared with other costs and benefits. In other words 'non-market' valuation is a necessary component of cost benefit analysis (CBA). A useful analytical tool in CBA is known as the total economic value (TEV) approach.

Total economic value (TEV)

The TEV approach expands the traditional neoclassical concepts of value to include option value and existence value. An environmental asset has both 'use' and 'non-use' value. Use value can be broken down into actual use value and option value.

Use value

Actual use value is derived from the actual use of the asset, and is composed of direct use value such as timber from a forest and indirect use value such as the value that would be yielded to inhabitants downstream should the forest reduce flooding.

The notion of option value is more complex. Friedman (1962) had suggested that, if a national park closed down when run by a profit maximising entrepreneur because gate receipts would not cover operating costs, this is not a failure of the market. However, Weisbrod (1964) pointed out that this decision would ignore an option value, i.e. people would be 'willing to pay something for the option to consume the commodity in the future' since 'there is no practical mechanism by which the entrepreneur can charge non-users for this option'. Thus, 'user charges are an inadequate guide to the total value of the park'. In his seminal piece *Conservation Reconsidered*, Krutilla (1967) defined option demand as 'a willingness to pay for retaining an option to use an area or facility that would be difficult or impossible to replace and for which no close substitute is available. Moreover, such a demand may exist even though there is no current intention to use the area or facility in question and the option may never be exercised.' Option value[1] can be broken down into a number of components (Pearce and Turner, 1990): the value individuals place on the preservation of an asset so that they may have the option of using it in the future (value of future options for the individual), the value they attach to preserving the asset because it can be used by others[2] ('vicarious value'), and the value they attach to preserving the asset so that future generations have the option of using it ('bequest value'). Thus, total use value is defined as follows:

Total use value = Direct use value + Indirect use value + Option value

where

Option value = Value of future options for the individual
+ Vicarious value + Bequest value

Non-use values

Non-use values are 'existence' values. Existence values reflect the benefit to individuals of the existence of an environmental asset although those individuals do not actually use the asset. These values may exist due to sympathy for animals and plants and/or some human approximation of the intrinsic value of nature, i.e. this value reflects a sense of stewardship on the part of humans towards the environment. Evidence of these values is shown in the willingness of people to contribute to charities which preserve wildlife. While many of the donors are unlikely to ever see these animals in the flesh, they value the fact that they exist. Krutilla (*op. cit.*) first introduced the concept of existence value: 'there are many persons who obtain satisfaction from mere knowledge that part of wilderness North America remains even though they would be appalled by the prospect of being exposed to it.' There has been some disagreement regarding existence values. McConnell (1983) sees the concept as 'far fetched' and states that 'existence value occurs only insofar as bequest or altruistic notions prevail', thus conferring on it a use value. However, it is clear that individuals often contribute to animal charities not because they want animals to be preserved for others or for future generations but because they gain utility themselves from knowing that the animals are being preserved. Thus, following Krutilla's definition, existence value is classed as a non-use value such that total economic value is defined as follows:

TEV = Actual use value + Option value + Existence value

It is important to note that the TEV approach attempts to encapsulate all aspects of a resource which enter into the utility functions of a human, i.e. it is anthropomorphic. Thus, it does not attempt to find an intrinsic value for the environment where 'intrinsic' means the value that resides in something which is unrelated to human beings altogether (Pearce and Turner, *op. cit.*) However, it does attempt to include the intrinsic value which humans bestow on nature.

There is no agreement on the exact breakdown of the values in the TEV framework. However, the important issue in CBA is to account for all these values as best as possible.

A forestry example

Taking the example of an afforestation project, the TEV might be composed of the value of: the timber (T), the sequestering and storing of carbon, thereby reducing greenhouse gasses in the atmosphere (G), restriction of water flow (W_f), water pollution resulting from the 'scavenging' and deposition of air pollutants by the tree and pollution from forestry practice (W_p), recreation (R), wildlife habitat (A), aesthetic/landscape value (L).

In this case, the benefit of afforestation is measured by:

$$B = T + G + W_f + W_p + R + A + L$$

Some of these components may be negative, i.e. external costs are included as negative benefits.

In order to assess the efficiency of an afforestation project using CBA, the costs of the inputs into afforestation would then be subtracted from these benefits.

Non-market valuation methods

Since externalities are not captured within markets, they do not have an obvious 'price' which can be included in a CBA. Thus, what are known as 'non-market' valuation methods must be used to calculate some of the components of TEV. We outline below a number of techniques for estimating these non-market values.

All of these techniques use consumer surplus measures to value non-market costs and benefits. This involves estimating the aggregate willingness to pay to capture benefits [Hicksian compensating variation (CV)] or to avoid costs [Hicksian equivalent variation (EV)] or aggregate willingness to accept compensation for costs (CV) or to forego the benefits (EV).

These methods include:

- *Production function approaches*, whereby we value a non-market output by the value of the loss of (or addition to) production as a result of that output
- *Hedonic pricing*, whereby the value of the non-market output is approximated by estimating the change in the market value of a traded good which is attributable to that output
- *Travel cost,* whereby the value of a non-market asset (e.g. a forest park) is approximated by the willingness to pay of individuals for admission to the asset on the basis of the costs incurred in travelling
- *Contingent valuation*, whereby those actually or potentially affected by the provision of a non-market good are asked to place a value on it.

Production function approaches

Production function approaches are indirect methods of valuing externalities. Environmental goods often enter into firms' and households' production functions, e.g. a fishery combines water quality (q) with purchased inputs (x), labour (l) and capital (k) . Where F is the output of fish, the production function would take this form:

$$F = f(l, k, x, 1,)$$

Thus, if a factory causes a deterioration in water quality, F will be reduced (assuming $\partial F/\partial q > 0$)[3]. This cost can be estimated in two ways:

- By the cost of the increase in other inputs which would be necessary to achieve the same level of output after the reduction in water quality as before (defensive expenditures/avoided cost approach) or by the cost of restoring the damage done, e.g. restocking a river (replacement cost)
- By the value of productivity changes, i.e. the value of the lost output of fish (dose-response functions).

Avoided cost and replacement cost approaches

If there is a deterioration in water quality, defensive expenditures may be necessary to reduce the impact on productivity. These expenditures can be used as a proxy for the cost of the damage to the water supply. In most of the literature, this is expressed from another point of view, i.e. the benefits of an improvement in environmental quality can be measured by the defensive costs avoided, hence it is known as the avoided cost approach. If the productivity after defensive expenditures is equal to the productivity prior to the deterioration of the quality of the water, then the defensive expenditures give a reasonable approximation of the external cost imposed by the activity which causes the pollution. If productivity with defensive expenditures is less than productivity prior to the deterioration in water quality then this approach underestimates the external cost. If the defensive expenditures result in benefits other than the maintenance of productivity, e.g. if for some reason they were to improve the quality of the fish, then this approach would overestimate the external cost. Hanley and Spash (1993) conclude that in most cases the avoided cost approach is likely to provide a lower bound on willingness to pay for environmental quality.

The replacement cost approach measures the cost imposed on society through the degradation of an environmental asset by the cost of replacing or restoring that asset. This approach tends to underestimate damage costs since it is usually impossible to restore something to exactly its original state. In the less usual case of an asset being replaced by a more valuable asset, e.g. a small building being burned down and a new larger building being erected in its place, then the replacement cost would overestimate the cost of the damage.

The replacement cost approach is often a poor proxy for externalities because there is no necessary linkage between the costs of restoration and the benefits lost. Take the case of a fish farm which is wiped out by siltation caused by deforestation upstream. The costs of restoring the fish farm may be several times the cost of relocating the business elsewhere. The latter cost is more relevant as an estimate of the external cost of deforestation.

Dose-response functions

Hanley and Spash (*op. cit.*), from which this explanation is adapted, provide a clear outline of dose-response methods. These methods seek a relationship between environmental quality variables and the output level of a marketed commodity. They take natural science information and include it in an economic model. There are three approaches:

- *The traditional model.* Taking the example of an externality manifesting itself in damage to an agricultural crop, the traditional model multiplies yield changes based on current area in production by the current price of the crop. This assumes that resource use and prices (and therefore consumer surplus) remain constant. Therefore, for the answers to be legitimate, it is necessary to assume that any reduction in yield will leave prices unaltered.

- *Optimisation models.* Optimisation models consist of linear programming models and quadratic programming models. These are normative models which are specified as cost-minimising or profit-maximising models. In linear programming, changes in environmental quality can be simulated by using biological dose-response functions to alter the quantity of output produced from the set of inputs required for each production activity. The disadvantages of these models is that they require large data sets and it is not unusual for considerable discrepencies to exist between model solutions and the real world. This can be due to either mis-specification of the model or the inaccuracy of the assumption of optimality in the real world.

- *Econometric models.* Econometric models resolve some of the problems just mentioned since they rely upon historical data. However, the institutional setting is taken as given and the models cannot capture changes in technology that have not been captured in the data.

In conclusion, while the accuracy of the traditional approach relies on very strict assumptions, it is the most simple dose-response approach and it requires very little data. While optimisation and econometric models are more sophisticated, they require larger data sets and depending on the way in which responses are modelled, widely varying estimates emerge.

Hedonic pricing

The hedonic pricing method (HPM) developed by Griliches (1971) and Rosen (1974) is used to estimate the implicit prices of the characteristics which differentiate closely related products (Johansson, 1993). The value of an asset is measured by the stream of benefits which flow therefrom. This is best explained using an example. The value of a forest park will be partially reflected in the difference in price between a house beside the park and one further away from the park. However, in addition, the price of the house is likely to be a function of a number of other variables. The first stage is to estimate an equation of the form (Pearce and Turner, 1990):

property price = f (property variables, neighbourhood variables, accessibility variables, environmental variables)

The extent to which changes in the environmental variable (the forest park) 'explains' changes in the property price can be estimated by multiple regression. The willingness of people to pay for the environmental commodity can then be derived. Aggregate consumer surplus is calculated by summing across all households. Thus, the absence of prices for environmental assets can be overcome by disaggregating the market price of a private good; in this case, by disaggregating the house price function.

Travel cost

The travel cost method (TCM) uses costs of travel to an environmental asset as a proxy for the value of that asset. This was first proposed by Hotelling but first used by Clawson in 1959 (see Clawson and Knetsch, 1966). Using this method, demand for a recreation site can be measured by the costs of travel to that site. Take, for example, a single recreation site that can be reached by individuals in a certain area. The area can be divided into a number of zones according to distance from the site, zones A and B, for example, with B being further from the park. By surveying those attending the site from the zones in question, estimates are made of the number of trips per capita and the average cost of travel which includes the direct costs of people's travel to the site such as petrol, depreciation of their car etc. and the opportunity cost of the trip, i.e. time. Sets of observations like these can be used to estimate a 'distance decay curve' for trips. This curve is negatively sloped such that the further away from the forest a community is situated, the higher the cost and the fewer the visits, all else being equal. Average consumer surplus from a visit to the recreation site from areas A and B is calculated from the curve and total aggregate willingness to pay for the forest is given by total consumer surplus plus actual travel cost.

Contingent valuation (stated preference) method

The contingent valuation method (CVM) is the only direct non-market valuation approach. The CVM collects information on preferences by asking households how much they are willing to pay for some change in the provision of a public good, or the minimum compensation they would require if the change was not carried out (Johansson, 1993). The advantage of the CVM is that, unlike other methods, it can elicit option and existence values. In addition, it can measure Hicksian consumer surplus directly.[4] The CVM is the most controversial of all non-market valuation methods. Therefore, it is worth exploring the methodology and the controversies surrounding the method in some detail.

History of CVM

According to Hanemann (1992) the CVM was first suggested by S. V. Ciriacy-Wantrup in 1947 although its significance was not immediately appreciated. In 1958 the United States (US) National Park Service was the first to use the CVM when a survey of outdoor recreational activities was undertaken on their behalf which elicited the willingness to pay a site entry charge to publicly owned recreation areas. In 1961, Davis (1964) carried out the second contingent valuation (CV) study when he used a survey to value hunting in the Maine woods.[5] Up until the mid 1980s, the CVM did not stand out from other non-market valuation measures. Since then, however, this method has become the most widely used approach for valuing public goods and there has been an explosion in the number of CV studies (Mitchell and Carson, 1995).

CVM steps

A CV study consists of the careful selection of a representative sample of the population whose valuation of a public good is being elicited. The interview technique is then selected (face-to-face, telephone or mail) and a questionnaire is developed. This questionnaire contains (Mitchell and Carson, 1989) the following:

- A detailed description of the good being valued and the hypothetical circumstance under which it is made available to the respondent, i.e. the researcher constructs a hypothetical market which is communicated to the respondent in a realistic scenario including a plausible method of payment.

- Questions which elicit the respondent's willingness to pay for the good being valued. These are constructed to facilitate the valuation process.

- Questions about the respondent's characteristics (e.g. age and income), preferences relevant to the good being valued (e.g. how concerned or interested is the person in the environment), and his or her use of the good. This information is used in a regression equation for the good. If these variables 'explain' the individual's valuations, as the theory would suggest, then this is a partial test of reliability.

The study is pre-tested using a pilot survey and then the full survey is carried out. The mean and median willingness to pay or accept can then be calculated and the results generalised to the population.

Appropriate welfare measures: willingness to pay vs. willingness to accept

There are two key problems in choosing an appropriate consumer surplus measure. Firstly, there is the theoretical observation that willingness to pay (WTP) and willingness to accept (WTA) can differ in size. Secondly, it has been observed that respondents to CV questionnaires react differently to each approach. Willig's classical work (1976) showed that the difference between WTP and WTA should be relatively small in most cases and while Willig's results were for price changes, Randall and Stoll (1980) extended these results to cover quantity changes where expenditures on the good were a small proportion of income. They suggested that, in CV experiments, the difference between WTP and WTA should not be more that 5 per cent. However, empirical studies still showed a large divergence between WTP and WTA measures. The following possible reasons as described by Mitchell and Carson (1989) may explain this divergence:

- *Rejection of WTA property right.* This occurs when respondents do not accept the property right implied by the question. For example, they may refuse to 'sell' the environmental asset at any price, regarding this as unethical. More frequently, individuals do not see the property right as plausible. For example, they may be asked how much compensation they would accept for the deterioration of air quality in their area. However, if they have never been compensated for environmental damage in the past, they may see this as implausible. This tends to result in 'protests' and/or infinite bids.

- *The cautious consumer hypothesis.* Under conditions of uncertainty, risk-averse individuals will offer smaller WTP amounts and larger WTA amounts than they would under certainty.

- *Prospect theory*. According to prospect theory, the value function from a neutral position is steeper for losses than for gains, i.e. people value a loss more highly than a gain since the former is considered the loss of a 'right' and the latter is considered only as a 'bonus'.

Criticisms of the contingent valuation method

Up to the mid-1980s, the bulk of the research on the CVM had been carried out in agricultural economics departments in the 'state' universities in the US, where the fields of resource and environmental economics developed. However, the lack of interest on the part of 'mainstream' economists quickly disappeared in the aftermath of the Exxon Valdez oil spill in Alaska in 1989 when the state and federal governments decided to undertake a contingent valuation study to assess the magnitude of the damages. Whereas the government assembled a group of resource economists to carry out the CV, the Exxon Corporation hired a panel of economists mainly from outside this discipline in an attempt to prove that the CVM was an unreliable method for valuing natural resource damage (Mitchell and Carson, 1995). A book of the papers produced by the Exxon economists was published in 1993 (see Hausman, 1993 and also Diamond and Hausman, 1994). The main criticisms of the CVM relate to sources of bias.

Sources of bias:

- *Free-riding and strategic bias*. Samuelson (1954) suggested that the individual has an incentive to understate his or her WTP for a public good on the understanding that others will pay for it and that therefore he or she will benefit from its provision in any case. On the other hand, the individual may engage in strategic behaviour to raise the mean bid by overstating his or her WTP on the basis that the level of provision is subject to the size of the mean bid. Brookshire et al (1976) test for and reject strategic bias while the results from Rowe et al (1980) suggest that WTP bids are a good reflection of true valuations. While experiments suggest free-riding does occur, it appears to be less prevalent than standard neoclassical theory would predict (Bateman and Turner, 1993).

- *Hypothetical bias*. Critics of the CVM suggest that the hypothetical nature of the market renders the answers invalid. Bishop and Herberlein (1979) showed a significant difference between hypothetical WTA for duck hunting licences and their true WTA when offered 'real' money. However, Mitchell and Carson (1989) show that the significance of the difference relied on the truncation decisions in the original analysis, i.e. the authors' assumptions regarding the length of the distribution of WTP/WTA. Further studies suggest that actual and hypothetical WTP differences are much smaller than in the case of WTA due largely to the rejection of the WTA property right as explained above. Duffield and Patterson (1991) show that hypothetical willingness to contribute to charitable organisations is higher than actual contributions. However, the authors suggest that the differences are small enough for CV to be used to estimate real WTP. Evidence produced from a study comparing hypothetical WTP for strawberries with actual purchases (Dickie et al, 1987) was reinterpreted by Diamond et al (1993) as showing that the CV approach tends to systematically over-estimate quantity demanded at each price. However, Arrow et al (1993) qualify the results in two ways: firstly, the quality of the survey was poor and secondly, it is going too far to conclude that systematic overestimation means that CV can tell us nothing about the demand for strawberries.

- *Part-whole (mental account) bias.* Some authors testify that results from CV studies are invalid as they are inconsistent with rational choice. Several authors have found that WTP does not increase with the size of the good. Kahneman (1986) found that there was no significant difference between WTP for the clean-up of lakes in a small area of a province and WTP for the clean-up of all the lakes in the province. This 'embedding' effect was also shown by Kahneman and Knetsch (1992) by giving one sample group a more inclusive public good and the other sample group a less inclusive good. The results showed no significant difference between the mean WTP for each good. The authors proposed that this is due to a 'warm glow' whereby people are contributing because they feel good about improving the welfare of society. Thus, WTP does not measure their true valuation of the good. A number of other papers have also demonstrated this phenomenon (e.g. Desvousges et al, 1993 and Diamond et al, 1993). Smith (1992), Hanemann (1994) and Mitchell and Carson (1995) have argued that Kahneman and Knetsch's findings result from poor instrument design and poor information (see 'General responses to the critics' below).

- *Information bias.* One of the most controversial issues in CV relates to the quantity of information which is supplied to the respondent. It should go without saying that if individuals are given incorrect information, the use of their responses in making policy decisions is invalid. The more disputed claim is that the provision of more information elicits a higher WTP. Willingness to pay is likely to be a function of information but, if adequate information is provided, information bias should not be an overriding problem. Another criticism of CV surveys is that they often provide only vague descriptions of the good in question (this has also been a criticism of the CV studies carried out by economists wishing to demonstrate the flaws of the CVM).

- *Payment vehicle bias*. Choice of payment vehicle, e.g. an increase in taxes or a contribution to a 'fund', has been shown to influence WTP (see Desvousges et al, 1983 and Navrud, 1989). It is therefore suggested that controversial payment methods be avoided and that the payment vehicle should be the one which is most likely to be used in reality. The method of payment should also be such that the respondent is aware of the substitutes for the public good in question. This is important due to the criticisms of opponents of the CVM who question the large mean WTP figures for environmental improvements that emerge from CV studies. They ask whether individuals would really be willing (or able) to pay similarly large amounts if asked to pay for all environmental improvements. In addition, there is a common criticism that respondents do not consider their budget constraints when stating their WTP if the payment vehicle is unrealistic. Arrow et al (1993) state that 'to date very few CV surveys have reminded respondents of the very real economic constraints within which spending decisions must be made'.

- *Bid level bias*. There are a number of ways of eliciting bids in CV studies (Hanley and Spash, 1993):

  - *As a bidding game*. The interviewer asks the individual whether he or she will pay a specified amount. If the respondent says 'no', the interviewer lowers the amount until he or she says 'yes'. If, in the first instance, the respondent says 'yes' then the amount is raised until he or she says 'no'. This approach often results in a large number of 'protests' since some respondents find this 'auctioning' of a public good either unethical or unrealistic. It also can suffer from what is known as 'starting point bias' whereby the initial bid suggested influences the WTP of the individual. Mitchell and Carson (1989) suggest that the provision of a starting point reduces the effort people put into making their choice of WTP.

  - *As an open-ended question*. Individuals are asked their maximum WTP with no value being suggested to them. Respondents tend to find it difficult to answer questions of this type when they have no experience of trading in the commodity in question. Open-ended CV studies are subject to 'free-rider' bias much more than the other approaches.

  - *As a payment card*. A range of values is presented on a card which helps respondents to calibrate their replies. This is less problematic than the bidding game. However, in some instances respondents also may find the approach rather unrealistic. This approach can produce 'anchoring bias' whereby the respondent assumes that the 'correct' valuation is one of the values on the card and therefore he or she is reluctant to go outside that range.

- *As a closed-ended referendum*. This approach is also known as 'take-it-or-leave-it' or 'dichotomous choice'. The sample is split into sub-samples and a single payment is suggested to which the respondent must agree or disagree. A different amount is presented to each of the sub-samples. This is the most incentive-compatible approach. However, the analysis of binary responses requires more sophisticated econometric techniques and larger samples. Sometimes the question is followed up by a higher or lower offer depending on whether the answer to the first question is 'yes' or 'no'. This is called the double bounded dichotomous choice approach. The dichotomous choice approach may be subject to anchoring bias if the payment amounts chosen do not cover the full range of WTP. In addition it may be subject to 'yea-saying' whereby individuals may just say 'yes' in order to avoid having to think carefully.

• *Interviewer bias*. The interviewer may intentionally or unintentionally put pressure on the respondent to give particular answers to questions. This is most common in face-to-face surveys.

General responses to the critics

Hanemann (1994) criticises the papers referred to in Diamond and Hausman (1994) and Hausman (1993) for the weakness of the CV studies they use to back up their claims of the inappropriateness of the CVM. He states:

> None uses in-person interviews. Many are self-administered. Most use open-ended questions. None is cast as voting. Many ask questions with a remarkable lack of detail. Several seem designed to highlight the symbolic aspects of valuation at the expense of substance. The Exxon surveys were designed and fielded in great haste, with little pre-testing, just at a time when federal agencies were gearing up for natural resource damage regulations. The only way to justify this is to make the tacit assumption that, if contingent valuation is valid, details of its implementation should not matter. This is fundamentally wrong: measurement results are not invariant with respect to measurement practice in *any* science.

Mitchell and Carson (1995) explain two misconceptions about contingent valuation that arise in the debate regarding the validity of the CVM. Firstly, they reprimand the critics of the CVM for failing to realise that a CV question involves much more than just asking a respondent to express a WTP for some good. Asking respondents whether they are willing to pay £50 for cleaner air is an 'attitudinal' WTP question. Neither the payment vehicle nor the good are specified clearly. A CV question measures 'behavioural intention' by setting out the specific details of the good which is being sold to the respondent, how the good would be provided, and how the good would be paid for. Mitchell and Carson (*op. cit.*) criticise Kahneman and Knetsch (1992) for presuming that an attitudinal WTP question is a sufficient basis upon which to test the reliability of CV. In one experiment Kahneman and Knetsch ask one sample of Vancouver residents how much they would be willing to pay 'to improve sport fish stocks in British Columbia fresh water' and ask the other sample 'how much they would be willing to pay to improve sport fish stocks in Canada fresh water'. They do not explain the meaning of 'fish stocks' and 'fresh water', the size of the improvement, how long the improvement would be maintained, who will provide the good, how it will be provided, when it will be provided, and how the respondents will pay for it. It is not surprising therefore that respondents give quick and not so meaningful answers. Studies that test the CVM using attitudinal as distinct from behavioural surveys are not a reasonable basis upon which to discount the CVM.

The second observation made by Mitchell and Carson is that all CV surveys are not equally reliable and that therefore it is not reasonable to choose surveys selectively in order to criticise the method. This amounts to asserting that CV results are averse to CV practice.

Guidelines for the contingent valuation method

With such conflicting views on the validity of the CVM, the US National Oceanic and Atmospheric Administration (NOAA) convened a blue ribbon panel of experts (known as the NOAA Panel) to deliberate on all the evidence produced and to answer the question: 'Is the contingent valuation method capable of providing estimates of lost non-use or existence values that are reliable enough to be used in natural resource damage assessments?' (Portney, 1994). This was chaired by Nobel prize winners Kenneth Arrow and Robert Solow and had four other members.[6] The panel reported its findings in 1993 (Arrow et al, 1993) and drew the overall conclusion that:
'CV studies can produce estimates reliable enough to be the starting point for a judicial or administrative determination of natural resource damages – including lost passive value.'

The report suggests that, so long as the study is well designed, the CVM is a reliable tool. In this regard they issued a comprehensive set of 'best practice' guidelines for the carrying out of such studies including details regarding sample size and type, non-response and protests, the interview method, reporting, pre-testing, the elicitation format, the payment method, the description of the programme or policy concerned, bid curve estimation and aggregation issues. The requirements are very detailed and rigid. However, it is important to bear in mind that the NOAA panel's guidelines are for CV studies which are to be used in natural resource damage assessment. Mitchell and Carson (1995) note that these guidelines set a 'very high' and 'very costly' standard. They suggest that the extent to which the guidelines must be adhered to will depend on the importance of the policy question being examined.

Other stated preference methods

Other stated preference methods include contingent ranking and choice experiments. A choice experiment values a good as a function of the attributes of that good. These experiments can be used to place an economic value on individual attributes of which they are a part. Limitations of scope preclude further consideration of other stated preference methods in this chapter.

Discounting and the environment

In undertaking economic evaluation, account must be taken of the fact that costs and benefits arise at different time periods. Thus future costs and benefits must be discounted so that they can be compared with present costs and benefits (B). Having calculated the costs (C) and benefits of a project, it is necessary to compare them in present value terms. Where r is the discount rate, the net present value of the investment is the sum of benefits less costs across all time periods (from $t = 0$ to T), i.e.

$$NPV = \sum_{t=0}^{T} \frac{(B_t - C_t)}{(1 + r)^t}$$

The project is accepted if and only if,

$$NPV > 0$$

Problems with discounting

There have been a number of controversies surrounding the choice of discount rate. There are some general arguments regarding the measurement of the discount rate and the difference between the market rate of discount and the social rate of discount (the rate at which society as a whole would wish to discount the environment) which are beyond the scope of this chapter.[7] However, in relation to the environment, discounting tends to be controversial in the eyes of many environmentalists because it rules out certain projects they would see as desirable and encourages certain activities they would see as undesirable. For example, it encourages more rapid exploitation of resources, discourages certain long-term projects such as the planting of broadleaved forests, reduces the costs of potential damage in the long run such as the consequences of global warming.

Worrell (1991) summarises three schools of thought concerning the use of discounting:

- Provided externalities are included in the CBA, and the preferences of future generations are accounted for by sustainability constraints, discounting provides an accurate picture of consumer behaviour. Sustainability criteria would maintain a constant stock of natural capital or provide compensation for environmental damage either by implementing other environmental (shadow) projects or by replacing natural capital with man-made capital (see 'sustainability' below).[8]

- Alternatives to straight-forward discounting should be used. One such method, known as the modified discounting method, allows new individuals in new generations to discount costs and benefits from the start of their lives and this effectively reduces the discount rate.[9] Another approach is to disaggregate the determinants of the discount rate (time preference, diminishing marginal utility of income, etc.) and explicitly include their individual effects separately in analyses.

- Discounting is unacceptable and counter to sustainable resource use and therefore a zero discount rate should be used.

The choice of discount rate is most important. However, since economists have been unable to provide a definitive figure for the social rate of discount let alone resolve the issues which arise in relation to the environment, it has become something to be chosen rather than something that is measured (Heal, 1981), and as Leslie (1989) states, 'all views on discount rates are opinions'. In reality, the discount rate used to assess government projects is chosen via the political system.

Irreversibility and sustainability

Krutilla-Fisher algorithm

In their seminal work, *The Economics of Natural Environments*, John Krutilla and Anthony Fisher (1985) consider the example of the economic evaluation of a proposed hydro-electric dam to be built on a wilderness area which has value in its natural state. They considered the necessary changes in project investment rules where a project would result in an irreversible change, i.e. where damage could not be rectified. Pearce and Turner (1990), from which this discussion is adapted, provide a succinct summary of the analysis of Krutilla and Fisher. In carrying out a cost benefit analysis of the development of the site, it is necessary to consider the present value of the development benefits of the site $[PV(B_D)]$, the development costs $[PV(C_D)]$ and the net opportunity cost of development, i.e. the present value of the benefits of preservation $[PV(B_P)]$ and the direct cost of preservation $[PV(C_P)]$. The traditional cost-benefit rule approves the development if,

$$[PV(B_D) - PV(C_D)] > [PV(B_P) - PV(C_P)]$$

However, this rule does not distinguish between a decision which is reversible and a decision which would result in the irreversible destruction of an environmental asset. The Krutilla-Fisher algorithm adjusts the rule to reflect irreversibility by treating the benefits foregone as part of the costs of development, by assuming preservation benefits increase over time at a rate g as the natural environment becomes more scarce, and by including an offsetting discount factor k which represents technological decay such that the development benefits are likely to be reduced over time (Pearce and Turner, *op. cit.*).

Supposing the costs of development are €1 and arise in the current time period and the development benefits amount to €D per annum, then where r is the discount rate, the present value of development is

$$PV(D) = -1 + \int_0^\infty De^{-rt}\, dt = -1 + \frac{D}{r}$$

The opportunity cost of development is the present value of per annum preservation benefits (P), i.e.

$$PV(P) = \int_0^\infty Pe^{-rt}\, dt = \frac{P}{r}$$

and thus the net present value of development is,

$$NPV(D) = -1 + \frac{D}{r} - \frac{P}{r}$$

According to the traditional cost-benefit rule, $NPV(D)$ must be positive for the project to be worthwhile so the project goes ahead if,

$$(D - P) > r$$

Introducing a discount factor k which represents technological decay reduces development benefits over time such that development benefits at time t are given by

$$D_t = D_0 e^{-kt}$$

and including the growth rate g in the 'price' of the natural asset (over and above inflation) which reflects the increasing scarcity of environmental assets such that the preservation benefit at time t is given by

$$P_t = P_0 e^{gt}$$

gives a new expression for the net present value of development,

$$NPV(D) = -1 + \int_0^\infty De^{-(r+k)t} dt - \int_0^\infty Pe^{-(r+k)t} dt = -1 + \frac{D}{r+k} - \frac{P}{r-g}$$

For $NPV(D)$ to be positive and for the project to be accepted under this modified rule, the following expression must hold,

$$\sqrt{D} > (\sqrt{P} + \sqrt{k+g})$$

and thus the higher is the discount rate r, the lower are the development benefits, all else being equal. The lower is r, the stronger is g in making preservation benefits more attractive, all else being equal. This modified cost-benefit rule allows for a greater weighting of the benefits of preservation when a decision to destroy an environmental asset is irreversible. For example, if P is 0.4 and $k + g = 0.02$, then, from the above expression, $D = 0.5989$, such that the ratio of D to P is 1.50. Thus, for the project to pass the modified cost benefit test, development benefits must be 50 per cent higher than preservation benefits.

Uncertainty can be built directly into the decision-making rule (as opposed to indirectly by using sensitivity analysis) by requiring the net present value of development to be greater than some positive number.

Sustainability

Valuation of non-market effects has become considerably important in the assessment of sustainability. There is an emerging consensus that traditional measures of economic performance such as gross domestic product (GDP) and gross national product (GNP) are not adequate measures of well-being. They do not measure at all, or they measure only very obliquely, much that is of central importance to well-being, such as safety, literacy, health and environmental gains or losses, and though they value an annual flow of goods and services produced, they give no indication about what is happening to stocks. Thus a country can seem relatively prosperous as it harvests its natural forests; large annual flows of goods and services are being produced and valued in markets, but the stock on which the flow is predicated is being depleted. This depreciation of the stock is not captured in the traditional measures of economic performance.

Pearce and Atkinson (1995) have developed an interesting means of categorising countries to indicate whether or not they are on sustainable development paths. They make a distinction between 'weak sustainability', the constant capital rule, whereby an aggregate capital stock no smaller than the present one is passed on to the next generation, and 'strong sustainability', whereby, in addition to conserving the aggregate capital stock, that component of the aggregate capital stock characterised as 'natural' is not diminished.

They apply the weak sustainability rule to a number of countries as follows: for each country analysed, they take estimates of the rate of depreciation of natural capital (sometimes called resource rent) and of 'made' capital, and compare these with the rate of savings. If the rate of depreciation of natural and 'made' capital drawn down exceeds the rate of savings, then the country is not re-investing sufficient to 'replace' the natural and 'made' capital draw down, and fails the 'weak sustainability' test. If a country has a higher savings rate than the rate of depreciation of natural and 'made' capital, then it passes this test. The results for a few countries are shown below.

Table 10.1: Weak sustainability test results for selected countries

Country	Rate of saving	Rate of depreciation of made capital	Rate of depreciation of natural capital	Net saving rate
	(i)	(ii)	(iii)	(i) − [(ii) + (iii)]
Japan	33	14	2	17
Poland	30	11	3	16
Costa Rica	26	3	8	15
Netherlands	25	10	1	14
USA	18	12	3	3
Mexico	24	12	12	0
UK	18	12	6	0
Malawi	8	7	4	−3
Nigeria	15	3	17	−5
Ethiopia	3	1	9	−7
Burkina Faso	2	1	10	−9
Madagascar	8	1	16	−9
Mali	-4	4	6	−14

Source: Pearce and Atkinson, 1993

In order to estimate the rate of depreciation of natural capital, they had to estimate the value of as much as possible of the non-market outputs provided by such capital. Valuation of non-market outputs is therefore a necessary concomitant towards identifying whether we are on a sustainable path.[10]

Conclusions

Much that sustains us physically, socially and spiritually is not mediated through markets. In particular, environmental endowments, being defined as assets held somehow in common, are not readily integrated into markets. Increasingly, however, markets are being viewed as the arbiters in the allocation of resources and in the measurement of well-being. If something does not have a price, a perception can emerge that it does not exist and/or is not important. To help ensure that non-market goods and services in general, and environmental goods and services in particular, can command the requisite degree of attention and resources, a wide range of techniques has been developed to generate non-market values. In this chapter we have attempted to provide the reader with a sense of the rationale for including these values in the evaluation process, the techniques for so doing and some of the other issues which should be considered when undertaking a cost benefit analysis. While the techniques require a degree of sophistication in derivation and application and a certain leap of faith that the proxy measures do indeed adequately mimic markets, they can make an important contribution to ensuring that we do not neglect to see the true value of the environment.

NOTES

1 The reader is referred to an excellent exposition on option value by Bishop (1982).
2 In the late eighteenth century, Adam Smith in his *Theory of Moral Sentiments* (1790) drew attention to this 'sympathy principle' (Kriström, 1990).
3 $\partial F/\partial q$ is a calculus convention meaning a change in F with respect to a change in q.
4 Thus, actual willingness to pay and willingness to accept is measured.
5 Some authors suggest that this was the first CV study.
6 Edward Leamer, Paul Portney, Roy Radner and Howard Schuman were the other members of the panel.
7 Interested readers may wish to consult Lind et al, 1982.
8 see Pearce et al, 1989 and Markandya and Pearce, 1988 for further details.
9 See Kula, 1988a, 1988b, 1989, Bateman, 1989, Rigby, 1989 and Hutchinson, 1989 for further details.
10 Readers interested in this area may wish to consult an excellent paper by Pezzey (1992).

REFERENCES

Arrow, K., R. Solow, P. R. Portney, E. E. Leamer, R. Radner and H. Schuman (1993). 'Advance Notice of Proposed Rulemaking, Extension of Comment Period and Release of Contingent Valuation Methodology Report', *Federal Register*, Vol. 58, pp 4601-14

Bateman, I. (1989). 'Modified Discounting Method: Some Comments – 1' *Project Appraisal*, Vol. 4, No. 2, pp 104-06

Bateman, I. J. and R. K. Turner (1993). 'Valuation of the Environment, Methods and Techniques': The Contingent Valuation Method, in R. K. Turner (ed.), *Sustainable Environmental Economics and Management*, London: Belhaven Press

Baumol, W. J. and W. E. Oates (1988). *The Theory of Environmental Policy*, 2nd edn., Cambridge: Cambridge University Press

Bishop and Herberlein (1979). 'Measuring Values of Extra-Market Goods: Are Indirect Measures Biased?' *American Journal of Agricultural Economics*, Vol. 61, pp 926-30

Bishop, R. C. (1982). Option Value: An Exposition and Extension, *Land Economics*, Vol. 58, no.1, pp 1-15

Brookshire, D. S., B. C. Ives, and W. C. Schulze (1976). 'The Valuation of Aesthetic Preferences', *Journal of Environmental Economics and Management*, Vol. 3, pp 325-46

Clawson, M and J. Knetsch (1966). *Economics of Outdoor Recreation*, Baltimore: Johns Hopkins University Press

Davis, R. K. (1964). 'The Value of Big Game Hunting in a Private Forest', in *Transactions of the Twenty-ninth North American Wildlife Conference*, Washington DC: Wildlife Management Institute

Desvousges, W. H., F. R. Johnson, R. W. Dunford, K. J. Boyle, S. P. Hudson and K. N. Wilson (1993). 'Measuring Natural Resource Damages with Contingent Valuation: Tests of Validity and Reliability', in J. A. Hausman (ed.), *Contingent Valuation: A Critical Assessment*, Contributions to Economic Analysis 220, Amsterdam: North Holland

Desvousges, W. H., V. K. Smith and M. P. McGivney (1983). *A Comparison of Alternative Approaches for Estimating Recreation and Related Benefits of Water Quality Improvements*, Report no. 30-05-83-001, US Environmental Protection Agency, Washington DC

Diamond, P. A. and J. A. Hausman (1994). 'Contingent Valuation: Is Some Number Better than No Number?' *Journal of Economic Perspectives*, Vol. 8, No. 4, pp 3-17

Diamond, P. A., J. A. Hausman, G. K. Leonard and M. A. Denning, (1993). 'Does Contingent Valuation Measure Preferences? Experimental Evidence', in J. A. Hausman (ed.), *Contingent Valuation: A Critical Assessment*, Contributions to Economic Analysis 220, Amsterdam: North Holland

Dickie, M, A. Fisher, and S. Gerking, (1987). 'Market Transactions and Hypothetical Demand Data: A Comparative Study', *Journal of the American Statistical Association*, Vol. 82, pp 69-75

Drèze, J., and N. Stern (1994). 'Shadow Prices and Markets: Policy Reform', in R. Layard and S. Glaister (eds.) *Cost-Benefit Analysis*, 2nd edn., Cambridge: Cambridge University Press

Duffield, J. W. and D. A. Patterson. (1991). 'Field Testing Existence Values: An Instream Flow Trust Fund for Montana Rivers', Paper presented at annual meeting of American Economic Association, New Orleans, January, 1991

Friedman, M. (1962). *Capitalism and Freedom*, Chicago: University of Chicago Press

Griliches, Z. (1971). *Price Indexes and Quality Change*, Cambridge: Harvard University Press

Hanemann, W. M. (1992). Preface, in S. Navrud (ed.), *Pricing the European Environment*, Oslo: Scandinavian University Press

Hanemann, W. M. (1994). 'Valuing the Environment through Contingent Valuation', *Journal of Economic Perspectives*, Vol. 8, No. 4, pp 3-17

Hanley, N. and C. Spash. (1993). *Cost-Benefit Analysis and the Environment*, Aldershot: Edward Elgar

Hardin, G. (1968). 'The Tragedy of the Commons', *Science*, Vol. 168

Hausman, J. A. (ed.) (1993). *Contingent Valuation: A Critical Assessment*, Contributions to Economic Analysis 220, Amsterdam: North Holland

Heal, G. M. (1981). 'Economics and Resources', in R. Butlin (ed.), *Economics of Environmental and Natural Resource Policy*, Boulder: Westview Press

Hutchinson, R. W. (1989). 'Modified Discounting Method: Some Comments – 3', *Project Appraisal*, Vol. 4, No. 2, pp 108-09

Johansson, P.-O. (1993). *Cost-Benefit Analysis of Environmental Change*, Cambridge: Cambridge University Press

Kahneman, D. (1986). 'Comments', in R. G. Cummings, D. S. Brookshire and W. D. Schulze (eds.), *Valuing Environmental Goods*, Totwa: Rowman and Allenhead

Kahneman, D. and J. L. Knetsch. (1992). 'Valuing Public Goods: The Purchase of Moral Satisfaction', *Journal of Environmental Economics and Management*, Vol. 22, pp 90-4

Kriström, B. (1990). *Valuing Environmental Benefits using the Contingent Valuation Method – An Econometric Analysis*, Umeå Economic Studies No. 219, Umeå: University of Umeå

Krutilla, J. V. (1967). 'Conservation Reconsidered', *American Economic Review*, Vol. LVII, No. 4, pp 777-86

Krutilla, J. V. and A. C. Fisher (1985). *The Economics of Natural Environments*, Second Edition, Washington DC: Resources for the Future

Kula, E. (1988a). 'Future Generations: The Modified Discounting Method', *Project Appraisal*, vol. 3, no. 2, pp 85-88

Kula, E. (1988b). *The Economics of Forestry: Modern Theory and Practice*, London: Croom Helm

Kula, E. (1989). 'Modified Discounting Method: Rejoinder', *Project Appraisal*, Vol. 4, No. 2, pp 110-12

Leslie, A. J. (1989). 'On the Economic Prospects for Natural Management in Temperate Hardwoods', *Forestry*, Vol. 62, pp 147-66

Lind, R. C., K. J. Arrow, G. R. Corey, P. Dasgupta, A. K. Sen, T. Stauffer, J. E. Stiglitz, J. A. Stockfisch and R. Wilson (1982). *Discounting for Time and Risk in Energy Policy*, Washington DC: Resources for the Future

Markandya, A. and D. Pearce (1988). 'Natural Environments and the Social Rate of Discount', *Project Appraisal*, Vol. 3, No. 1, pp 2-12

McConnell, K. E. (1983). 'Existence and Bequest Value', in R. D. Rowe and L. G. Chestnut (eds.), *Managing Air Quality and Scenic Resources at National Parks and Wilderness Areas*, Boulder: Westview Press

Mitchell R. C. and R. T. Carson (1995). 'Current Issues in the Design, Administration and Analysis of Contingent Valuation Surveys', in P.-O. Johansson, B. Kriström and K-G. Mäler (eds.), *Current Issues in Environmental Economics*, Manchester: Manchester University Press

Mitchell, R. C. and R. T. Carson (1989). *Using Surveys to Value Public Goods: The Contingent Valuation Method*, Washington DC: Resources for the Future

Navrud, S. (1989). *The Use of Benefits Estimates in Environmental Decision Making: Case Study on Norway*, Paris: OECD

Pearce, D. and G. Atkinson (1995). 'Measuring Sustainable Development', in D. Bromley (ed.), *Handbook of Environmental Economics*, London: Basil Blackwell

Pearce, D. W. and C. Nash (1981). *The Social Appraisal of Projects*, London: Macmillan Press

Pearce, D. W. and R. K. Turner (1990). *Economics of Natural Resources and the Environment*, Hemel Hempstead: Harvester Wheatsheaf

Pearce, D., A. Markandya and E. B. Barbier (1989). *Blueprint for a Green Economy*. London: Earthscan

Pezzey, J. (1992). *Sustainable Development Concepts: An Economic Analysis*, World Bank Environment Paper No. 2, Washington DC: World Bank

Portney, P. R. (1994). 'The Contingent Valuation Debate: Why Economists Should Care', *Journal of Economic Perspectives*, Vol. 8, No. 4, pp 3-17

Randall, A. and J. R. Stoll (1980). 'Consumer's Surplus in Commodity Space', *American Economic Review*, Vol. 70, No. 3, pp 449-55

Rigby, M. W. (1989). 'Modified Discounting Method: Some Comments – 2', *Project Appraisal*, Vol. 4, No. 2, pp 107-08.

Rosen, S. (1974). 'Hedonic Prices and Implicit Markets: Product Differentiation in Pure Competition', *Journal of Political Economy*, Vol. 82, pp 34-55

Rowe, R., R. d'Arge, and D. Brookshire (1980). 'An Experiment on the Economic Value of Visibility', *Journal of Environmental Economics and Management*, Vol. 7, pp 1-19

Samuelson, P. (1954). 'The Pure Theory of Public Expenditure', *Review of Economics and Statistics*, Vol. 36, pp 387-89

Smith, V. K. (1992). 'Arbitrary Values, Good Causes and Premature Verdicts', *Journal of Environmental Economics and Management*, Vol. 22, pp 71-89

Weisbrod, B. A. (1964). 'Collective-Consumption Services of Individual-Consumption Goods', *Quarterly Journal of Economics*, Vol. 78, pp 471-77

Willig, R. D. (1976). 'Consumer's Surplus Without Apology', *American Economic Review*, Vol. 66, No. 4, pp 587-97

Worrell, R. (1991). *Trees and the Treasury: Valuing Forests for Society*, Godalming: World Wide Fund for Nature

11

Economic Evaluation in Health Care

FERGAL LYNCH

Introduction

Health care markets are substantially different from those for many other commodities. They are not generally competitively organised; they are subject to highly imperfect information; demand on the part of individuals is unpredictable; and there is at least some scope for supplier-induced demand.

Since much health care is funded either by the state or through private insurance, neither the demanders nor suppliers may have a significant incentive to contain costs or to limit demand. According to traditional economic theory, this *third party* payment system results in demand beyond the level of both productive and allocative efficiency[1].

Figure 11.1 contrasts the markets for 'ordinary' commodities, in which consumption will occur at the point where marginal benefits equal marginal cost (i.e. Q1), with the market for health care where, assuming full payment by a third party, consumption continues right up to the point where marginal benefits have been exhausted, i.e. Q2.

Figure 11.1: Contrasting usage of health care with other commodities

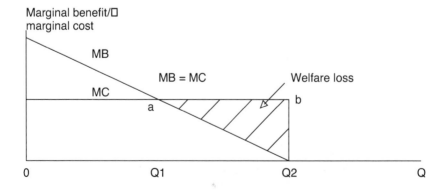

The *welfare loss* to society is illustrated by the shaded area abQ2, in which health care has been supplied well beyond the point where the marginal cost of its production begins to exceed the marginal benefits derived from it.

This is not to suggest that health care markets are entirely different from those for all other commodities. A number of other markets are also subject to imperfect information, monopoly power, uncertainty of demand and a substantial third party payment system. Nonetheless, health care has a higher incidence of these differentiating characteristics than most other markets.

Quite apart form the elements of health care that make it significantly different from any other markets, another marked characteristic is the apparently widening gap between expectations and supply. Thwaites (1987) illustrated the difference between the health care market's ability to provide services for the population and the resources available.

Figure 11.2: Widening gap between expectations and resources

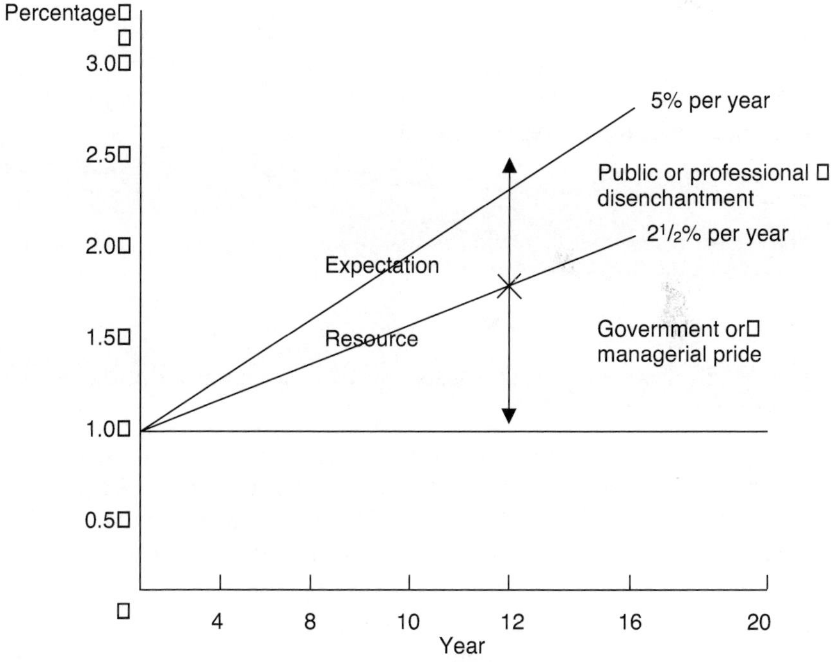

Source: *British Medical Journal*, adapted from Thwaites (1987)

Such a framework helps to underline the importance of establishing rational and (as far as possible) objective ways of determining priorities in health care. Economic evaluation offers an important tool to aid decision-making in heath care. This article explores the main applications of economic evaluation to health care, discussing the main uses to which it can be put and the challenges involved in doing so.

As in all other areas of evaluation, the application of appraisal techniques to health care must be seen as an aid to, rather than as a substitute for, other forms of decision-making. It would be wholly misleading to suggest that economic appraisal can offer clear-cut or ready-made answers that immediately justify implementation. Instead, economic evaluation in health care helps decision-makers formulate a series of relevant questions and encourages judgements and assumptions, which would otherwise be made implicitly, to be made explicitly.

Perspective of the evaluation

It is important to be clear about the perspective from which an economic evaluation is to be carried out. In health care, a programme or a form of treatment could be analysed from the viewpoint of

- the individual patient
- a definable group of clients (e.g. the elderly)
- the provider (hospital, doctor or another professional) or
- society as a whole.

The widest perspective is obviously that of society as a whole, and is often the preferred point of reference. Robinson (1993a) notes two implications of the societal approach:

- It usually involves placing a value on items not normally priced by the market.
- Some costs (or savings) must be excluded from the evaluation because they merely represent transfers of resources from one part of society to another. This might arise in the case of income maintenance payments to, say, the disabled. Although a cost to government, they are a transfer of money within society.

The main approaches to evaluation

These are four main approaches to economic evaluation in heath care. Moving from the least to the most complex, these are cost minimisation analysis (CMA), cost effectiveness analysis (CEA), cost utility analysis (CUA), and cost benefit analysis (CBA).

Which of the four methods to use depends on the nature of the question being asked and the type of information available for analysis. To date, CMA and CEA have been the more popular methods in health care, but in recent times there has been a growing use of CUA. Practical and theoretical difficulties have hindered the extensive use of CBA, but notwithstanding this some of its main principles can be of substantial assistance in an economic evaluation.

CMA is generally applicable where the outcomes of alternative options are considered likely to be very similar. Then it is primarily a matter of identifying the best-cost option. CEA is required where outcomes between options are expected to differ and a quantification of those outcomes is therefore required.

CUA reflects a growing concern to evaluate the benefit (or utility) offered to patients by alternative treatments or programmes in health care. It attempts to take account of the quality improvements brought by health care interventions in a way that is not possible under CMA or CEA. Finally, CBA focuses on whether a programme of treatment offers a net benefit to society by measuring benefits and costs in a single unit of value, usually money. It differs from the three other methods by evaluating the overall gain to society as a whole.

Cost minimisation analysis (CMA)

In some cases it may be clear that the results produced by different options in health care, such as alternative treatments for a particular condition, are very similar. If so, the main question to answer in an economic evaluation is, Which option can be implemented at least cost? A cost minimisation analysis is appropriate in these circumstances since the relative success of alternative options is assumed to be the same.

However, it is important to establish that outcomes will, in fact, be very similar. Otherwise a CMA based on an inaccurate assumption about results of alternative options will be misleading.

Drummond et al (1987) argue that 'a full economic evaluation through cost minimisation analysis requires some evidence on which to believe that outcome differences of the alternatives are nonexistent or unimportant'.

Ideally CMA studies should be performed alongside, or immediately after, supporting clinical trials which establish the close similarity of outcomes between alternative options. A practical difficulty may arise here, in terms of availability of data or ease with which an appropriate set of trials can be carried out. CMA may therefore have to rely on previously collected evidence, medical opinion or assumptions about results from earlier studies.

Applications of cost minimisation analysis in health care are most often found in choosing between alternative medical treatments or sites of medical treatment. Examples include analysis of treatments for minor conditions such as hernia, haemorrhoids and varicose veins. Drummond et al describe studies in these areas, where the choice may be between day surgery and traditional in-patient care. There are many other potential uses of CMA in the area of treatment alternatives; the key prerequisite to its use is that the outcomes are expected to be very similar.

CMA need not be confined to decisions concerning alternative treatments. It can also be applied to questions of how best to achieve a given objective at least cost. If, for example, it is decided to make a 'meals-on-wheels' type service available to non-ambulant elderly people in their own homes, there may be different options for doing so. One is by grant-aiding an existing voluntary organisation for the elderly, while another is by utilising employees of the local health authority or board. A third option is to contract with a private catering firm to supply and serve the meals.

In each case the outcome (meals delivered directly to the homes of a selected dependent population) could be expected to be the same, but the cost of providing the service would probably vary between options. While most CMAs are directed towards decisions regarding the relative cost of alternative treatments, the meals example underlines that the scope of this type of analysis can be much wider.

CMA can be applied not only to potential new areas, but also to existing programmes. A CMA on alternative ways of providing a service can be applied to programmes already in operation. The analysis would scrutinise the way in which a service is currently being provided, compared with a number of alternative options.

It is in this area that economic evaluation is perhaps under-used in posing often awkward questions about the performance of existing programmes or services compared with different methods of achieving the same result. Appraisal techniques can therefore offer a valuable means of reviewing services already in operation. They need not be confined to new programmes or treatments.

Cost effectiveness analysis (CEA)

Cost effectiveness analysis is used when both the costs *and* results of alternative options are expected to vary. Thus it takes the appraisal a step further than CMA by quantifying changes in outcome as well as in cost. It is important, however, that the varying outcomes can be measured in common units; otherwise it is not possible to compare the results of different options.

CEA is a popular method for comparing alternative treatment regimes; outcomes can be measured in terms of standard indicators that are present in all cases treated. For example, alternative treatments of renal failure can be compared in terms of life years gained, or for hypertension in terms of blood pressure. The costs – and marginal costs – can of course also be compared.

The value of CEA in these cases is that it can take account of differing results from alternative treatments, while at the same time comparing costs. Treatments for varicose veins may have varying outcomes in terms of side-effects, recuperation time and duration of improvement in condition, but these factors can be taken into account in a CEA. When a common unit of output has been established, such as

- life years gained from a renal treatment
- number of positive cases detected by a screening programme
- post-operative infection rate using alternative methods of surgery
- degree of mobility after a set period following orthopaedic surgery
- proportion of cases in which complications were avoided

then the resource implications of each alternative treatment can be expressed in terms of a *cost per unit output*.

A number of valuable studies have been carried out using CEA. Robinson (1993b) notes a series of CEA studies in which useful conclusions were drawn regarding the relative performance of alternative treatments. Among these are Boyle et al's (1993) study of neonatal intensive care for very low birthweight babies, in which the author compared results prior to the introduction of neonatal intensive care with those after its introduction and measured costs in the context of additional lives saved.

Other uses of CEA, as reported by Robinson (1993b), include an evaluation of Pap tests (smears taken for the detection of cervical cancer) by Mendelblatt and Fahs (1988) and a study by Oster and Epstein (1987) of antihyperlipaemic therapy in the prevention of coronary heart disease. Both studies use an estimate of the cost per life saved as the unit of measurement. Robinson lists a number of other studies in which the unit of measurement varies from number of pain-free days to number of successful diagnoses (using alternative diagnostic strategies), to the number of episodes of fever cured and deaths prevented.

Many studies measure cost effectiveness in terms of just one of the above indicators or criteria. However, a potential disadvantage arises in this approach. The single measure chosen may conceal or distort variations within the alternative options under review. For example, a study of different treatment regimes which focuses on a single measure of abatement in a condition, such as blood pressure, might miss another important outcome factor, such as patient discomfort during treatment.

With this in mind, some studies use a multi-dimensional approach, taking account of a greater number of outcome measures. Thus Percival and Setty's (1992) study of day surgery versus in-patient treatment for cataract surgery used a set of measures of effectiveness namely operative and post-operative infection; visual acuity after three to six days following surgery and again ten weeks to six months after surgery; and a survey of patient satisfaction.

The use of a set of cost-effectiveness measures is valuable where there is concern about how meaningful a single measure would be. However, it creates difficulties in assessing the overall cost-effectiveness of competing options where the results do not consistently favour one option. In Percival and Setty's study virtually all of the indicators pointed towards day surgery over the in-patient alternative, making the conclusions clear-cut. Nevertheless, studies which find the results produced by different options to be more finely balanced face a difficult task in reaching conclusions. They can still, however, advance the decision-making process by pointing to the differing results from the measures chosen. At the very least, judgements can then be made about the relative priority of each measure chosen, with the decision-making process being influenced accordingly.

To date, the discussion of CEA has been concerned mainly with its application to clinical trials and alternative treatments for a given condition. However, as in the case of CMA, its potential in health care extends well beyond decisions of this nature. CEA can be used to examine the relative cost-effectiveness of existing programmes or services compared to alternative options. It might, for example, be applied to evaluating the most cost-effective way of providing residential care for a group of elderly people in a specific catchment area. A CEA study might compare the relative performance, or the marginal cost, of existing homes for the elderly owned by a health board, with that of homes operated by voluntary organisations grant-aided by the health board. In each case, the measure of output might be judged in terms of, for example, client satisfaction.

Similarly a CEA approach could be used where a health board is allocated a pre-determined amount of money to reduce waiting times for a given speciality. Thus the question facing decision-makers would be to identify the most cost-effective means of spending €500,000 to reduce waiting times in the health board's catchment area for, say, orthopaedic procedures. The measure of output in this case is reduction in waiting times. The options for achieving this might include contracting with another health board with excess capacity, employing additional staff on a temporary basis in its own area, or switching the use of a ward and facilities from another speciality to orthopaedics. This is but one example of how the use of CEA can extend beyond individual treatment options or other medical-related decisions.

CEA provides another example of economic evaluation as a useful aid to decision-making. It can provide a rational and objective means of judging between alternatives but it should not be seen as the exclusive basis of making a decision.

An important consideration in all of the CEAs presented above is that they do not question the desirability of achieving specified objectives. Neither do they question the level of priority that should be attached to the objectives. For example, CEA does not determine whether it is appropriate to devote resources to reducing orthopaedic times; it is concerned only with identifying the most cost-effective means of doing so. Similarly, a CEA does not question whether the €500,000 allocated to orthopaedics might more appropriately have been devoted to a competing purpose, such as waiting times in another speciality, to rehabilitation services for the disabled, or to any other health care service.

This limitation is not a serious disadvantage. Instead it can be regarded as an important element of the framework within which CEA operates. Failure to take account of the fact that CEA does not question the underlying desirability of the objective under consideration will lead to invalid inferences about the evaluation's conclusions. Since CEA sets out only to determine the most cost-effective option of achieving a particular objective, it should not be taken as a validation of the priority of achieving that objective above all others.

Cost utility analysis (CUA)

Background

We have seen that cost effectiveness analysis (CEA) is useful in clarifying choices by taking account of differing results from alternative options and estimating a cost per unit of output. However, if decisions have to be taken regarding the priority to be attached to alternative programmes or treatments, i.e. if a choice must be made between different service areas, then CEA is less helpful. This is because the units of output from the competing programmes are likely to differ. It would be difficult, using CEA, to choose between, say, a service for the elderly and a treatment protocol for premature babies, because the units of output being measured would differ greatly.

In the case of residential service for the elderly, the unit under examination might be client satisfaction, while in the case of premature births it could be specific mortality or morbidity indicators.

CEA is therefore less useful in setting priorities between competing programmes or interventions; its strength lies in identifying the most cost-effective means of achieving an objective after priorities have been set. An increasing emphasis in health care is on assessing the health and social gain,[2] i.e. the added benefit brought about by the health services. Under this approach, it is not sufficient to establish that a programme is cost-effective, or that the money allocated to a service was devoted to the purpose for which it was intended. It is necessary, in addition, to examine the extra benefit or utility brought about by the intervention under review.

CUA and quality of life

Cost utility analysis (CUA) is a means of measuring the utility conferred by treatments on patients in terms of improved quality of life. This is a technically difficult and often controversial approach to economic evaluation, but it offers significant advantages in clarifying the implications of alternative options. It attempts to be explicit about valuations made implicitly in the absence of such appraisals; decisions about the relative priority of projects are made in any event. By estimating the improvements in quality of life brought about by a health care intervention, and the cost of that improved quality, CUA can inform decision-makers in the setting of priorities. As in the case of CEA and CMA, it is intended primarily as an aid to decision-making by clarifying the implications of choosing alternative options.

Application of CUA: the QALY

CUA uses measures of the utility placed on different states of health and on varying degrees of social functioning. A number of such measures has been devised, including the Nottingham Health Profile, the Rosser Index and the Oregon Demonstration Project described in Robinson (1993c). All are directed towards quantifying the value placed by individuals on varying indicators of quality of life. CUA takes these a step further by estimating the costs involved in programmes or treatments which aim to improve that quality of life.

The Quality-Adjusted Life Year (QALY) is one of the most widely used measures of quality of life in CUA. It comprises both a qualitative measure of quality of life and a quantitative estimate of life years. It can then express treatments or other health care interventions in terms of a cost per QALY gained. The marginal cost per QALY can, of course, also be calculated. A fuller outline of QALYs is provided by Gudex and Kind (1988).

The Rosser Index has been used in the calculation of QALYs in the UK. The index describes states of health in terms of two dimensions – disability and distress. Eight levels of disability are described in increasing stages of deterioration from no disability to unconscious as shown in Table 11.1.

The eight levels of disability and four categories of distress are then combined to produce a matrix of 32 possible states of health. Rosser interviewed a selected set of doctors, nurses, patients and volunteers in good health to establish their views on the relative severity of each of the 32 states of health compared with each other. The results were expressed in an index ranging between 0 = dead and 1 = perfect health.

Table 11.1: Levels of disability

I	No disability
II	Slight social disability
III	Severe social disability and/or slight impairment of performance at work. Able to do housework except very heavy tasks
IV	Choice of work or performance at work very severely limited. Housewives and old people able to do light housework only but able to go out shopping.
V	Unable to undertake any paid employment Unable to continue any education Old people confined to home except for escorted outings and short walks and unable to go shopping Housewives able to perform only a few simple tasks
VI	Confined to a chair or wheelchair or able to move around in the house only with support from an assistant
VII	Confined to bed
VIII	Unconscious

Source: Kind, P., R. Rosser and A. Williams (1982)

Four levels of distress are defined by Rosser:

Table 11.2: Levels of distress

A	No distress
B	Mild
C	Moderate
D	Severe

Source: Kind, P., R. Rosser and A. Williams (1982)

Using this approach it is possible to assign any disease or condition a quality of life score by placing it within one of the 32 health states devised by Rosser. While the actual index assigned to any state of health has been criticised, Robinson (1993c) notes Gudex and Kind's finding that:

> a single training session on the approach was sufficient to obtain a high level of agreement between doctors on rating patients ... these descriptions could be used to categorise patients reliably, accurately and quickly.

Having established a method for expressing health status in a single score from 0-1, the next step was to continue it with a measure of the life years gained as a result of a particular treatment or intervention. One of the best known studies in this area is Williams' (1985) evaluation, using QALYs, of treatment options for angina patients. In it he asked three cardiologists to give their judgements about the life expectancy and relative states of health of angina patients, some of whom had received surgery for the condition (coronary artery bypass) and others of whom had not.

Williams was then able to estimate the number of quality-adjusted life years (QALYs) for patients with mild to severe angina, distinguishing between different types of the disease (e.g. left main vessel, triple vessel, etc). Comparisons of the quality and expected length of life could then be made between those undergoing surgery and those receiving medical management alone, i.e. without surgery.

Having calculated the QALYs gained from treatments, it is then possible to attach costs to them so that the cost per QALY of alternative treatments (or other health care interventions) can be estimated. A series of 'league tables' has been calculated in the UK, which draw attention to large variations in the cost per QALY of different interventions. An extract from one such league table is shown in Table 11.3. It demonstrates, for example, that the cost per QALY of cholesterol testing and treatment by diet was £220, compared with £1,180 for a hip replacement and £17,260 for home haemodialysis.

At the extreme, a neurosurgical intervention for malignant intracranial tumours was estimated to cost over £100,000 per QALY.

The results from league tables of the type shown in Table 11.3 are not intended to suggest that resources should automatically be transferred to interventions with a lower cost per QALY. Instead they are meant to make decisions about allocating resources between alternative interventions more explicit. If however the intention is to achieve as much health gain and social gain as possible from health care programmes, then the cost per QALY of competing priorities cannot be ignored. The ultimate decision may be to channel resources towards interventions that produce the highest net benefits, but equally it may be that certain procedures with a relatively high cost per QALY should still be accorded a high priority. The advantage of this approach is that decision-makers have been made more fully aware of the resource implications of the priorities that they have established.

Table 11.3: Sample QALY league table
(costs as in August 1990)

Treatment	Cost (£) per QALY
Cholesterol testing and treatment by diet (age 40-69)	220
Neurosurgical intervention for head injury	240
Pacemaker implantation	1,100
Hip replacement	1,180
Kidney transplantation	4,710
Breast cancer screening	5,780
Home haemodialysis	17,260
Neurosurgical intervention for malignant intracranial tumours	107,780

Source: Extracted from Mason J., M. Drummond and G. Torrance (1993)

Criticisms of the QALY approach

It is not surprising that the QALY approach, and its use in CUA, has been the subject of strong criticism. At a methodological level, the complaints centre on the means of assigning values to different states of health, through the use of interviews. McGuire, Henderson and Mooney (1988) note a number of these as follows:

- A person may respond in a markedly different way to a hypothetical question than to a real one. Preferences may alter as more information is acquired, or as the choice assumes greater practical significance.
- Most of the surveys for estimation of health status have assessed movements from a position of good health to poorer health than, for example, from a previously chronic condition to a better one. The law of diminishing marginal utility, if applied to health, would suggest that the results of movements from good to poor instead of poor to good health states may be significantly different.

Added to the methodological criticisms of QALYs and their calculation are several practical charges. These include the argument that, by focusing on the benefits that health care can bring and the cost of those benefits, they discriminate against the elderly. QALYs are also criticised for paying insufficient attention to equity; once again the focus on the cost of achieving a particular health gain, and the length of time for which it may be of practical value, is cited as an attack on fairness in decision-making.

Some of the critics of QALYs, such as Gafni et al (1993), argue in favour of alternative measures such as healthy year equivalents which estimate the number of years of good health that is equivalent to a longer lifetime of poor health, claiming that they are more in accordance with the principles of economics and therefore superior to QALYs for economic evaluation of health care interventions. However, other studies, such as Culyer and Wagstaff (1993), suggest that both measures produce identical rankings under most assumptions.

Appropriate use of CUA

Many of the criticisms of the QALY approach, and the use of CUA generally, can best be addressed by bearing in mind the early stage of development of CUA, and the qualifications attached to it by its advocates. The key elements to take into account are that it must be used appropriately, bearing in mind its limitations, and that its results should be judged in that light. Robinson (1993c) points out that CUA:

> is probably the most sophisticated form of economic evaluation available at present. However, sensible use of the technique and interpretation of research findings based on the approach should recognise that cost-utility analysis is at a fairly early development stage and treat it accordingly.

Drummond, Stoddart and Torrance (1987) provide guidelines on the appropriate use of CUA. They suggest it might be used in the following circumstances:

- when quality of life is *the* important outcome (as in the case of alternative programmes for treating arthritis)
- when quality of life is *an* important outcome (such as a life-saving treatment, where quality as well as survival is important)
- when a programme effects both morbidity and mortality and a common unit of outcome is required for combining both effects. (Drummond et al quote the example of oestrogen therapy for menopausal symptoms which improves quality of life by reducing discomfort, and which reduces mortality from hip fractures, but which increases mortality from certain complications such as uterine bleeding and gall bladder disease)
- when the programmes being compared have a wide range of different outcomes and a common unit of output is needed (the advantage of CUA over CEA in this regard was noted earlier)
- when a programme is being compared with others that have already been the subject of CUA.

Drummond et al argue that CUA should not be used in the following circumstances:

- when only intermediate indicators of effectiveness can be obtained. (This means that final measures of outcome are not available, leaving no scope for conversion to QALYs for application to CUA)

- when other forms of analysis are sufficient. (If for example, it is clear that the options are equally effective, a CMA may be all that is required)

- when indicators relating to quality of life can be captured in natural units. (Drummond et al quote the example of alternative treatments for leg fractures being compared to a single variable – reduction in days of restricted activity)

- when the extra cost involved in obtaining and applying measures of utility is itself not cost effective. (This might arise, for example, where CEA shows one alternative to be so superior to all others as to make a CUA unlikely to change the result).

These guidelines suggested by Drummond et al underline the importance of the appropriate use of CUA, and of avoiding CUA where the results would be misleading or more easily obtained by less complex methods.

Cost benefit analysis (CBA)

A critical disadvantage of the three methods of economic evaluation in health care discussed to date is that they have no means of judging whether the options under review offer a net benefit to society. CMA, CEA and CUA can all offer important insights into the relative costliness of alternative options, and into their differing outcomes. However, they cannot in themselves measure whether the benefits of any option exceed the costs involved, i.e. whether there is a net gain for society. This is because they usually measure costs and benefits in different units.

By contrast, cost benefit analysis (CBA) attempts to place a value (usually in monetary terms) on both the costs and benefits of health care. It is the most comprehensive form of economic appraisal, but is technically difficult to carry out. Attaching monetary values to costs and benefits that are often intangible raises practical and methodological problems. Because of these difficulties, CBA has had a relatively limited application in the health care market to date.

Since valuation of the more intangible benefits and costs present a particular challenge in health care, it is important to set criteria at the outset for determining how far these valuations should be taken. Drummond et al suggest that the following questions should be asked in the valuation of health care programmes:

- Are the results of the study likely to be altered by gathering additional information on intangible items?
- Can the costs of gathering the information be afforded?
- Will the valuation of intangible outcomes lead to more informed decision-making? Drummond et al argue that this may depend on how decision-makers interpret and use the valuations offered.

Two of the most popular approaches to valuing benefits and costs are based on human capital and willingness-to-pay.

Human capital approach

In health care the early applications of CBA placed valuations on intangible benefits and costs using the human capital approach. This equated an individual's rate of pay, or other estimates of productive activity, with benefits achieved or costs incurred. Estimates were made on the basis that human beings, like capital equipment, could be regarded as having a flow of productive activity which could be discounted over time. Benefits of health status could therefore be measured by reference to the flow of income (or other monetary value) foregone as a result of ill health.

In an example of a possible CBA, Drummond et al (1987) deal with the case of a breast screening programme for cancer, in which the valuation of women's time taken up in mammographic screening tests is estimated using the human capital principle. Lost earnings for women in employment and imputed earnings for those not in paid employment are taken into account. However, the authors point to problems in using lost wages as an estimate of the true value of lost production. These include factors such as restrictive market practices and distortions in the labour market which may result in a gap between the value of production and the actual wage rates paid.

Another criticism of the human capital approach in health care is that is does not place a valuation on pain or discomfort of patients or on the distress of relatives. A further difficulty arises in wider economic terms because the human capital approach depends on external valuations of benefits (such as pay rates and wages foregone) rather than on individuals' judgements of cost and benefits to themselves. The approach thus runs contrary to the standard economic assumption that the consumer is best placed to judge his or her own welfare.

Willingness-to-pay approach

This approach uses observed behaviour or stated preferences (as measured by individuals' actions) to estimate the value of intangible costs and benefits. Observing behaviour is, according to Robinson (1993d), useful only in limited circumstances; acceptance of 'danger-money' for high-risk jobs or payments of premium prices for extra safety features in consumer goods are examples.

However, the willingness-to-pay approach can survey individuals directly to establish their readiness to meet the cost of avoiding illness, curing disease or reducing pain or discomfort. In the Drummond et al (1987) breast screening example quoted above, the valuations placed on reassurance of those being screened and on the life-years saved is put forward, in part, on the basis of willingness-to-pay.

A difficulty of this approach is its dependence on an individual's income; Robinson (1993d) points out that people's answers to questions of this type 'may reflect the value people attached to money itself as well as to their valuation of the benefits of health care'.

Various other methodological problems arise, including the need to cross-check for consistency of answers with related questions about willingness-to-pay and the need to take account of the fact that the questions, by their nature, are hypothetical.

However, some of the difficulties associated with willingness-to-pay valuation in health care can, according to Morrison and Gyldmark (1992), be addressed if the following criteria are observed:

- Questions regarding willingness-to-pay should be expressed in terms of how much an individual would pay in the form of an insurance premium. This would take account of the fact that a person's demand for health care is uncertain both in timing and volume.
- The likelihood of needing a treatment or service should be stated in terms of probability so that is can be expressed as a mathematical prospect.
- Care must be taken to survey representative samples of the population so as to establish the willingness-to-pay of the relevant population being studied.

Use of CBA

It is clear that the problems of valuation of costs, and particularly of benefits, lessen the applicability of CBA to the health sector. The difficulty of expressing those costs and benefits in terms of a single unit is especially significant in health care, as noted for example by Tolley and Rowland (1995) in relation to counselling services. However, there are some useful examples in which CBA has been applied to health care, including Weisbrod et al's (1980) study of hospital-based versus community-based treatment in mental health. Robinson (1993d) notes that a number of studies of willingness-to-pay have also been made, including the cases of mobile coronary care units, treatment for rheumatoid arthritis, provision of pacemakers in the context of freedom from certain symptoms associated with heart disease, and continuing care accommodation for the elderly.

Strength of CBA

Despite its apparently limited application to health care, CBA offers a valuable tool of analysis. Its principal strength is in offering scope for comparison between a wide range of alternative programmes, both within and outside the health sector. The fact that it establishes the net benefit to society makes it superior to all other forms of economic evaluation since it examines not only the relative performance of options but whether their benefits actually exceed their costs. When it is possible to express costs and benefits in a common unit, CBA helps clarify greatly the implications of alternatives.

While it may not be possible to carry out a complete CBA for practical or methodological reasons, even an application of its main principles will be of considerable use in the health care studies. At the very least, it can help decision-makers to formulate the most relevant questions, and it is likely to do much more than that.

Treatment of costs and benefits in health care evaluation

Finally, two issues relating to the conduct of economic appraisals in health care may be noted. The first is of relevance to all forms of economic evaluation – the inclusion and exclusion of certain costs. The second is of particular concern to health projects because of disagreement regarding the correct approach, namely whether benefits as well as costs of health care projects should be discounted.

Costs

Identification and correct valuation of appropriate costs are critical to the validation of all forms of economic evaluation. So too is the exclusion of costs which would represent double-counting or which arise irrespective of whether or not the programme under review was to proceed.

In health care three main elements of cost arise: those relating to the health service itself (including treatment, staff time, drugs, medical supplies and 'hotel'-related items); costs incurred by patients and their relatives (including travel time and hours spent taking care of the patient, as well as indirect costs such as stress and loss of income); and costs incurred by society as a whole (including losses to the economy from absenteeism due to illness).

In each case we must ask, Who bears the cost (the health services, patients and their relatives or society in general)? It is also important to take account of marginal as opposed to total costs where appropriate. This arises particularly where the question being examined is concerned with how much of the programme of service should be provided, rather than whether it should be provided at all.

A distinction must also be drawn between marginal and average cost. There are numerous examples of where the marginal cost of additional production in health care has been shown to be substantially greater than the average cost involved. These include Oster and Epstein's (1987) study of the cost-effectiveness of antihyperlipaemic treatment in the prevention of heart disease, where the marginal cost per life saved greatly exceeded average costs as patients grew older. Another example is Neuhauser and Lewicki's (1975) study of sequential guaiac stool tests, where the sixth successive test was shown to have a marginal cost of $47.1 million compared with an average cost of just $2,451.

Discounting costs and benefits in health care

The same considerations in relation to discounting of costs apply to health care projects as to appraisals in other areas. Discounting relies on the principle that account must be taken of how soon the costs will arise. The later the cost is incurred, the more attractive, irrespective of inflation or interest charges.

Similar considerations normally arise in the case of benefits and it would at first seem logical to discount benefits over time in the same way as costs. However, in the health area, it is sometimes argued that benefits should not be subject to discounting. Typically, as in Drummond et al (1987) it is argued that

- individuals cannot 'trade' their health in the same way as other resources

- individuals do not 'invest' in health status, unlike other goods

- there is no evidence that individuals necessarily place a higher value on future health states than present ones, making a discounting approach inadvisable

- it makes little sense to discount 'future' years of life gained at a higher rate than 'present' ones.

However, there are some practical reasons why discounting cost but not benefits would produce unrealistic results. The most obvious is that undiscounted benefits flowing over very long time periods (as perhaps, in the case of health promotion programmes) would eventually exceed time-discounted costs almost irrespective of the initial cost. Moreover, there may be some justification, as in Michael Grossman's (1972) model of demand for health care, to assume that people invest in their health in a similar way as in a capital good.

A common conclusion is that, while there may be strong theoretical arguments for using a zero discount rate for benefits in economic appraisals in health care, the present state of development in evaluations will not make this approach likely for some time to come.

Use of casemix measurement in economic evaluation

Casemix measurement techniques offer a valuable additional tool of analysis for the evaluation of health care projects.

Casemix measurement involves classifying hospital patients into defined categories, usually by reference to their clinical and economic characteristics. The most commonly used casemix measure for in-patients is the diagnosis related group (DRG). Other classification methods are used for day cases, such as day patient groups (DPGs) and ambulatory patient groups (APGs). DRGs classify in-patients in terms of the patient's diagnosis and the treatment provided (clinical characteristics) and the amount of hospital resources used (economic characteristics). DPGs and APGs classify day cases using similar principles, although the focus is on medical or surgical procedures provided rather than on diagnosis.

It is possible to classify the vast majority of in-patients into one of about 500 DRGs. Similarly day cases can be categorised into one of 60 DPGs or into a combination reflected from over 200 APGs. When classified in this way, the scope for meaningful comparison between groups of cases and between hospitals is substantial. For example, economic evaluations using CEA can use DRG or DPG data when studying the most cost effective treatment for a particular condition. Similarly, CUA can draw upon casemix data when reviewing changes in the quality of life of a defined set of patients following a particular surgical procedure.

Casemix data has been used since 1993 to influence the level of funding allocated to acute general hospitals in Ireland, but the role of casemix in assisting economic evaluations has yet to be developed. Casemix measurement is not a tool of evaluation in itself. Its value lies in classifying cases into comparable groups which can be analysed using a technique such as CEA or CUA in the knowledge that the data is accurate and has been categorised in a meaningful way. A fuller treatment of casemix measurement and its application in Ireland can be found in Fitzgerald and Lynch (1998).

Conclusion

Economic evaluation in health care is of growing importance. The use of cost minimisation analysis, cost effectiveness analysis and increasingly, cost utility analysis, can greatly assist decision-makers in clarifying options and in making the implications of alternative approaches all the more explicit.

While all approaches, including the more sophisticated cost benefit analysis, encounter some disadvantages, their use in health care offers significant potential if properly applied. There is a growing emphasis on ensuring that health care evaluation studies meet certain minimum criteria in design and analysis and that the results between studies are comparable. For example, the Panel on Cost Effectiveness in Health and Medicine, an independent multidisciplinary expert group established by the US public health service, has published a report edited by Gold et al (1996) aimed at providing guidance on the conduct of economic evaluations in health care, with particular reference to cost effectiveness analysis. Guidance of this sort helps promote the validity and reliability of economic evaluation in health care.

NOTES

1 Productive efficiency may be defined in terms of minimising inputs per unit of output, or of maximising output per unit of input. Allocative efficiency can be expressed in terms of an optimal mix of products, having regard to consumer preferences. Productive and allocative efficiency are more fully explained in chapter 1 of this volume.

2 Health gain is defined in the Irish strategy for health as being 'concerned with health status, both in terms of increase in life expectancy and in terms of improvements in the quality of life through the cure or alleviation of an illness or disability or through any other general improvement in the health of the individual or the population at whom the service is directed'. Social gain is defined in the strategy as being 'concerned with broader aspects of the quality of life. It includes, for example, the quality added to the lives of dependent elderly people and their carers as a result of the provision of support services, or the benefits to a child of living in an environment free of physical and psychological abuse' Department of Health (1994).

REFERENCES

Acton, J. P. (1973). *Evaluating Public Programmes to Save Lives: the Case of Heart Attacks*, Santa Monica: Rand

Boyle, M. H., G. W. Torrance, J. C. Sinclair, A. Sargent, P. Horwood (1983). 'Economic Evaluation of Neonatal Intensive Care of Very-Low-Birth-Weight Infants', *New England Journal of Medicine*, Vol. 308, pp. 1330-7

Culyer, A. J. and A. Wagstaff, (1993). 'QALYs versus HYEs', *Journal of Health Economics*, Vol. 11, pp. 311-323

Department of Health (1994). *Shaping a Healthier Future*, Dublin: Stationery Office

Drummond, M. F., G. L. Stoddart and G. W. Torrance (1987). *Methods for the Economic Evaluation of Health Care Programmes*, Oxford: Oxford University Press

Fitzgerald, A and F. Lynch, (1988). 'Casemix Measurement: Assessing the Impact in Irish Acute Hospitals', *Administration*, Vol. 46, No 1, pp. 29-54

Gafni, A., S. Birch, and A. Mehrez, (1993). 'Economics, Health and Health Economics: HYEs versus QALYs', *Journal of Health Economics*, Vol. 11, pp. 325-39

Gold M. R., J. E. Siegel, L. B. Russell and M. C. Weinstein (eds) (1996). *Cost-Effectiveness in Health and Medicine*, New York: Oxford University Press

Grossman, M. (1972). *The Demand for Health*, New York: National Bureau of Economics Research

Gudex, C. P. and P. Kind (1988). The QALY Toolkit, York: University of York, Discussion Paper No. 38

Hunt S., S. P. McKenna and J. McEwan (1986). *Measuring Health Status*, London: Croom Helm

Kind, P., R. Rosser, and A. Williams (1982). 'Valuation of Quality of Life: some Psychometric Evidence', in Jones-Lee, M. W. (ed) *The Value of Life and Safety*, Amsterdam: North Holland

McGuire A., J. Henderson and G. Mooney (1988). 'The Economics of Health Care', *International Library of Economics*, London: Routledge and Kegan Paul

Mason, J., M. Drummond, and G. Torrance (1993) 'Some Guidelines on the Use of Cost-Effectiveness League Tables', *British Medical Journal*, Vol. 306, pp. 570-2

Mendelblatt, J., and M. Fahs, M (1988). 'Cost Effectiveness of Cervical Screening for Low Income Elderly Women', *Journal of the American Medical Association*, Vol. 259, pp. 2409-13

Morrison, G. C. and M. Gyldmark (1992). *Appraising the Use of Contingent Valuation in Health Economics*, Vol. 1, pp. 233-43

Neuhauser, D., and A. M. Lewicki (1975). 'What do we Gain from the Sixth Stool Guaiac?', *New England Journal of Medicine*, Vol. 293, pp. 226-8

Oster, G. and A. M. Epstein (1987). 'Cost-Effectiveness of Antihyperlipaemic Therapy in the Prevention of Coronary Disease: the Cost of Cholesthramine', *Journal of the American Medical Association*, Vol. 258, pp. 2381-7

Percival S. P. B. and S. S. Setty (1992). 'Prospective Audit Comparing Ambulatory Day Surgery with In-Patients Surgery for Treating Cataracts', *Quality in Health Care*, Vol. 1, pp. 38-42

Robinson, R. (1993a). 'Economic Evaluation & Health Care: What does it mean?', *British Medical Journal*, Vol. 307, pp. 670-3

Robinson, R. (1993a), 'Economic Evaluation & Health Care: Cost-effectiveness analysis', *British Medical Journal*, Vol. 307, pp. 793-5

Robinson, R. (1993c). 'Economic Evaluation and Health Care: Cost utility Analysis', *British Medical Journal*, Vol. 307, pp. 859-62

Robinson, R. (1993d). 'Economic Evaluation and Health Care: Cost-benefit Analysis', *British Medical Journal*, Vol. 309, pp. 924-6

Thwaites, B, (1987). *The NHS: the End of the Rainbow*, Southampton: Institute for Health Policy Studies

Tolley, H. and N. Rowland (1995). *Evaluating the Cost Effectiveness of Counselling in Health Care*, London: Routledge

Weisbrod, B. A., M. A. Test and L. L. Stein (1980). 'Alternatives to Mental Hospital Treatment', *Archives of General Psychiatry*, Vol. 37, pp. 400-5

Williams, A. (1985). 'Economics of Coronary Artery By-Pass Grafting', *British Medical Journal*, Vol. 291, pp. 326-9

12

Performance Measurement and Irish Local Authorities

MARTINA MALONEY

Public service initiatives

The quest for improvement in public sector performance is not new. It is more than 100 years since Woodrow Wilson spoke of the need for civil service reform to identify 'first what governments can properly and successfully do and, secondly, how it can do these proper things with the utmost possible efficiency and with the least possible cost of either money or energy' (Quoted in Jackson 1995a).

In recent years there has been a trend to reform national and local institutions in Ireland to provide better services, accountability and freedom of information. 'An Action Programme for the Millennium', the policy document of the government elected in June 1997 notes among its key priorities for local government the introduction of comprehensive value for money audits, the improvement of efficiency and the enhancement of customer service (Government Information Service 1997).

Previous governments had also worked toward public sector reform. The Strategic Management Initiative whereby each government department was required to initiate a process of strategic management was launched in 1994. This approach to public service management has already been introduced in other countries such as New Zealand, Britain and Australia.

One of the strands running through the reforms is the emphasis on performance management. The reforms in Australia saw the enactment of the Financial Management Improvement Programme in 1984, which sought the introduction of techniques and systems to help departmental and agency managers focus on results. There was an emphasis on reporting of performance alongside programme costs. In Canada, a similar initiative in 1984 insisted that each department's operational plan framework should include a reasonable number of key performance indicators of efficiency and effectiveness along with the particular targets, results and issues on which the department will give account to the treasury board.

In Britain, the Financial Management Initiative (FMI) emphasised the need for departments to set clear objectives and performance measures. The introduction of the Citizen's Charter aimed to improve the quality of the public service through setting specific quality targets, monitoring these targets and offering redress to citizens when targets are not met. The role of the Audit Commission was enhanced and performance indicators were introduced in a number of areas.

Many attempts have been made to ensure that efficiency in local government is achieved. These include putting limits on budgets, the introduction of market disciplines like privatisation and contracting-out, manpower control policies and customer choice programmes. These measures have met with some degree of success but are not appropriate to all services provided by Irish local authorities. The measurement of performance in local government is another mechanism to help ensure efficiency. Performance measurement assists the management and delivery of services by prompting questions regarding the achievement of value for money and the meeting of objectives.

As Chapter 1 of this volume explains, the measurement of value for money is concerned with allocative and productive efficiency, involving inputs, outputs and outcomes. The economic, efficient and effective use of resources by the public sector should increase positive influences and reduce adverse effects on other sectors of the economy. The achievement of value for money, i.e. the three 'E's, involves the minimisation of the cost of resources required or used, the economically optimal relationship between inputs and outputs and between intended results and actual outcomes.

Local authorities do not operate in a vacuum. The environment in which they deliver services is very complex. It is a dynamic environment, with numerous stakeholders, limited resources and sometimes contradictory objectives. These issues differ from those prevailing in the private sector, which is largely governed by the profit motive. However, as Golden (1977) points out, 'The criteria used for measuring efficiency of operation and effectiveness of service in the local authority sector cannot, therefore, be the same as those applied in the case of commercial enterprises. But measurement there must be. It is always important to ensure that services being provided from scarce resources are maximal in benefit and quality, whilst at the same time being reasonable in cost.' In the context in the late 1990s of an annual revenue expenditure in excess of £1.2 billion by Irish local authorities, it is important that this expenditure is seen to be demonstrably well applied.

There is a continuing debate regarding the use of performance measurement systems as an effective mechanism for examining performance in the public sector. Jackson et al (1991) cite the following benefits:

- enhancement of accountability by making responsibilities explicit and providing evidence of success or failure
- assistance in the change towards active management by providing a basis for planning, monitoring, control and review
- assistance in staff motivation by providing for a staff appraisal system.

Opponents of measurement point to the difficulties of defining what constitutes 'good performance', the potential for bias in performance measurement systems, the degree to which value judgements are inherent in the measures used and the difficulty in apportioning accountability. They also highlight the impossibility of measuring some outputs of local authority activity, for instance where intangible outputs arise.

Undoubtedly there are difficulties associated with designing an appropriate system for performance measurement to cover most eventualities. Initially, it is essential to define organisational objectives, identify system outputs and outcomes, and clarify responsibilities. While the measurement of intangible outputs is difficult, many local authority services have tangible outputs such as roads, houses and waste disposal for which the identification of performance measures is possible. Even where outputs are intangible some proxy measure may be used. For instance, it may not be possible to design a single measure of effectiveness for tenant participation programmes. However, a proxy measure could be used such as the level of vandalism of public property in the estate. Political accountability should be enhanced as performance measurement makes explicit the facts on which policy decisions are made, thus allowing these decisions to be judged. The problem of inherent bias in the system should be addressed by properly designed systems, with enough information to assess various aspects of the service. Ridley (1995) points out that 'the fact that manipulation (of indicators) may occur, as critics often note, does not invalidate the principle, however, any more than electoral corruption invalidates the principles of electoral democracy'. He maintains that 'comparative performance indicators stimulate efficiency where no real consumer choice exists and focus citizen control of the delivery of services better than elections'.

Appropriate measurement systems are needed for reasons which are both internal and external to organisations. Performance information can enhance the internal control process. It allows managers and staff to see how far objectives and targets are actually being met. It can be a key element in setting future priorities. It can be used to praise and reward high achievers as well as to support or motivate low achievers. Externally, the information produced can form part of a scrutiny process by audit, value for money studies, central government, outside bodies or consumer interests. Comparative information can act as a substitute for market competition, and can be used to reward good performance or as a basis for awards such as ISO 9000.

In recent times, much of the literature dealing with the reform of local government in Ireland mentions the issue of performance measurement. The Strategic Management Initiative for local government, *Better Local Government – A Programme for Change* (Department of the Environment 1996a) mentions a number of proposed areas where targets will be required and against which performance will be measured. It refers extensively to the need for improved quality services, demonstrating value for money through the use of performance indicators and service standards. It states that 'Local authorities will be required to publish details of their performance against the standards. This will greatly enhance transparency ... and taken with the preparation and publication of financial performance indicators ... will be a powerful stimulus to efficiency in the system.' In addition, it is proposed that 'a financial incentive scheme will be put in place under which awards will be made to local authorities which demonstrate innovations in reducing costs/increasing efficiencies'.

The emphasis on performance is reiterated in the Report of the Review Body on Higher Remuneration in the Public Sector which recommends a performance-related pay scheme for local authority managers (Stationery Office 1996).

With this emphasis on performance measurement, it is opportune to examine the systems developed in British local government which have been operating for several years, focusing in particular on the possible applicability to Ireland of some of the indicators and statistics produced by British local authorities. Although local government in Britain differs in several significant respects from that in Ireland there are many areas of similarity. Originally, the Irish system was based on the British. Subsequently they developed somewhat differently. For instance British local government has responsibility for the police service and this is not the case in Ireland. Notwithstanding the differences there are many important lessons to be learned from evaluation of local government services in Britain in areas such as housing and roads which also come under local government control in Ireland.

Performance measurement in local authorities in Britain

Performance measurement has been in existence for a number of years in British local authorities; indeed these bodies are statutorily obliged to produce and publish performance information. Performance indicators for British local authorities have been published each year since 1995. Between 1995 and 1997 some of the worst performing councils have shown significant improvement in performance (Local Government Chronicle 1997). The time taken to re-let dwellings has improved, 65 per cent of councils have improved processing of council tax benefit, half have cut the cost of collecting tax and 50 per cent have recycled more waste.

The Local Government Chronicle (1997) states, 'There is little doubt that the Audit Commission's performance indicator programme is working. It encourages, pressurises and occasionally shames local authorities into improving services.' In a new initiative a number of regional groups has been established within which local authority officers compare their performance indicators and draw on the experience of the best of the group. In addition, councillors are being encouraged to use the indicators to inform their review of service performance. Emphasis is being placed on the development of more indicators of quality, which include the consumers' view of services. The process is evolutionary and appears to be assisting in improving performance in service delivery.

What do the indicators measure?

The aim of the indicators is to measure the performance of the main local authority services. The Audit Commission (1995a) cautions that performance may be contingent on external forces over which the local authority has little or no control. However, this will not be clear from the indicator. Perhaps some other organisations have been the cause of the poor service, or perhaps lack of resources is a problem. Such issues should be highlighted by local authorities when publishing their indicators.

The Audit Commission (1995a, 1995b) divides its indicators into four broad groups as follows:

• Indicators of performance

These include indicators of efficiency (for example, the percentage of housing benefit claims dealt with within 14 days) and indicators of effectiveness (for example, the percentage of crimes solved by police). In some cases indicators and targets are set by the Audit Commission; in other cases local authorities have discretion.

- Indicators of cost

Cost indicators should help identify if the public is getting good value for money. Where possible cost indicators are based on unit costs, for example per capita spending on book stock in libraries. This facilitates comparisons. Of course, high cost may not mean lack of value for money. Local circumstances must be considered, such as ground conditions and road maintenance costs when looking at infrastructural services.

- Indicators of quality

Indicators of performance and cost may also indicate quality of service, but the Audit Commission goes beyond this to include a check-list to allow citizens to assess quality. Information must be provided on the content of the service, for example whether a refuse service provides for the disposal of garden waste, large household items such as fridges and so forth. To assist with quality measurement, the Audit Commission suggests that judgement should be based on looking at a group of indicators.

- Indicators providing background information

Some indicators provide a useful background against which to view performance information. Among these are the size of population served by the waste disposal operations of local authorities, mileage of road and the unemployment profile. This information helps to link performance to the amount of work involved in service provision. The Audit Commission cautions that in examining performance, the public should be aware of the targets set by the local authorities and whether these targets are suitable. Comparative information on targets set by different authorities should also be considered. For example, if one authority is successful in answering 90 per cent of its telephone calls within its target of 30 seconds, could performance be compared with another authority which sets its target at 10 seconds and achieves this target only 50 per cent of the time? Which authority provides the better service?

The Audit Commission highlights the use of performance measures as an aid to local accountability. Members of the public should, it feels, be given the opportunity to say whether or not they feel they are getting a good service. This feedback could be achieved through communication with local authority chief executives, local councillors or the ballot box. In addition, an opportunity for dialogue could be afforded through the establishment of local consultative groups and/or interest groups. Such participation should, according to the Audit Commission, be encouraged by local authorities. The local input should help measure the effectiveness of the service, from the consumer's point of view.

What indicators are used?

The Publication of Information (Standards of Performance) Direction 1994 (Audit Commission 1994) sets out the indicators which local authorities must use to measure their performance and also details the information which they must publish. A selection of these indicators is reviewed hereunder. They are: dealing with the public, housing, refuse collection and waste disposal, control over development, collection of council tax, library service, fire, highway maintenance and street lighting.

These indicators apply to services which are also provided by Irish local authorities and it is useful to examine the possibility of introducing such measures in Ireland.

• Dealing with the public

Indicators under this heading include answering telephones, replying to letters, handling complaints, equal opportunities and access to and use of buildings. Authorities are required to set targets for answering telephone calls. Targets are set and monitoring mechanisms decided locally. Similar arrangements apply to letters received. An example of how the system operates for telephone calls in Camden Borough Council is as follows: the authority aims to answer calls to its switchboard within 5 rings. Performance is checked by automatic monitoring throughout the year. Performance figures published by the Audit Commission indicate that 95 per cent of calls were answered within the target of 5 rings.

Complaints systems cover both complaints received by the Ombudsman and those dealt with locally. Indicators include the number of complaints received by the Ombudsman, and the number which are classified as settled locally, maladministration with no injustice and maladministration with injustice. Local complaints procedures should address the processes for following-up complaints, written policy on complaints and systems for reviewing the causes of complaint. Targets and time limits must be set for dealing with complaints, with publication of a report concerning the handling of complaints.

Access to buildings involves looking at the number of the authority's buildings which are open to the public and the number in which the public areas are suitable for and accessible by disabled people. The equal opportunities issue is addressed by examining whether authorities have a published policy to provide services fairly to all sections of the community, whether there is a suitable monitoring system and whether authorities follow the Commission for Racial Equality and the Equal Opportunities Commission codes of practice on employment.

These indicators should go some way to identifying how well an authority responds to contact with its clients. However, answering the telephone in five rings does not indicate how effective the organisation is in actually dealing with a query. Further measures are required for this purpose. If performance is inadequate and not meeting the required target, the need for improvement will be highlighted by the performance indicators. Revised arrangements may then be put in place. Of course, the actual target set must also be examined. If it is too low, 100 per cent achievement means little.

- Housing

Because various strands make up a housing service, a number of different indicators are used. These include details of the housing stock, allocations and lettings, vacant properties, repairs policies, rent collection and success in dealing with homeless clients.

Information on housing stock includes the number of houses managed by each authority, the percentage of these adapted for the elderly or disabled, the number of flats in blocks of three stories or over and the percentage of these with controlled entry.

Published details on allocations and lettings include the number of dwellings let to new tenants, broken down between allocations of the local authorities' own dwellings, and local authority nominations to dwellings provided and owned by housing associations.

In addition, the proportion of lettings to homeless households must be reported. An indicator must also be provided for the area of vacant properties showing the percentage of dwellings that are empty and available for letting or awaiting minor repairs and those that are empty for other reasons such as being scheduled for major improvements, demolition or sale.

A further indicator identifies the average time taken to re-let dwellings available for letting or awaiting minor repairs.

Local authorities usually identify different categories of repair such as emergency, urgent or non-urgent. Targets are set for response times and details of performance against targets are published. Information to be published, therefore, includes the number of repairs requested at each priority level, the target response time for each priority level and the percentage of jobs completed within target time.

The use of appointment systems for repairs is also examined through use of an indicator measuring the percentage of repair jobs for which appointments were made and kept by each authority.

Information required about rent collection includes the rent collected as a percentage of the rent due and the percentage of all tenants owing over 13 weeks rent at a given time, say the end of the first quarter of the year, excluding these owing a small amount, say less than £250.

Details on the average weekly costs per dwelling are required, itemised as follows: management, repairs, bad debts, empty properties, rent rebates, capital charges and other items. The amount spent on major repairs and refurbishment is also required.

Information on the homeless is conveyed by indicators detailing the number of homeless households at a given time, say the end of the first quarter of the year, in temporary accommodation classified as bed and breakfast, hostel and other. These are complemented by indicators detailing the average length of stay in bed and breakfast and hostel accommodation.

- Refuse collection and waste disposal

By law, British local authorities must collect household rubbish and 'trade waste', if required. However, the way the service is organised is a matter for local discretion. Information required in this area includes an explanation of the local policy on collection. This would clarify important questions such as: Is waste collected from the back door of domestic properties? Is garden waste or bulky waste collected free of charge? Is bulky waste collected by appointment? Are recyclable materials collected separately? Is there a telephone query facility available and are special arrangements made for disabled people?

Indicators of reliability of service are required which show the number of household waste collections which were missed per hundred thousand collections and the percentage of missed collections put right by the end of the next working day.

Information is also required on the percentage of household waste recycled, the number of households served and the net cost per household.

For waste disposal the information to be provided covers the amount of household waste received, the percentage recycled, the percentage incinerated with recovery of heat and power, incinerated without recovery of heat and power or disposed of in other ways such as landfill. The net cost per tonne of household waste received is also required.

The information and indicators selected will help consumers identify whether the service they are receiving is comparable to that provided by other authorities. The quality of service can be assessed by looking at the description of the service provided such as arrangements for collection of bulky items of refuse. With the increased interest in environmental matters, performance in the recycling area is growing in importance particularly in light of the target set by the British government to recycle 25 per cent of rubbish by the year 2000. Cost is significant but local circumstances must be considered, such as the availability of suitable landfill sites, population density and so forth.

- Control over development

For control over development the information required includes the number of applications for planning permission decided, categorised into householder or other. The indicator used for dealing with applications includes a target set by the authority for dealing with householder applications and the performance against target. The Audit Commission sets a target of eight weeks for householder applications. For instance, the target used by Kensington and Chelsea Borough Council is to process 60 per cent within 8 weeks – in 1994/1995 the achievement level was 59 per cent.

Another measure used relates to the percentage of the population served by a unitary or local development plan and the number of departures from the statutory plan. The cost of the planning operation per head of population is also sought.

Details are also required of the percentage of searches of the local land register carried out within 10 working days and the standard search fee. Again, of course, when using comparative indicators in this area it is important to take account of local circumstances. For instance, in historic conservation areas like old city centres, applications are often more complicated and may take longer than in areas where the rules are not as strict.

Statistics are also required on the number of planning appeals taken and the number of successful appeals. Statistics on appeals may be useful in identifying whether applicants are satisfied with the planning process. If a large proportion of appeals are successful it may indicate problems in the planning process. The number of departures from the plan may indicate a need to review and change the plan, perhaps because of changes in local conditions and circumstances.

- Collection of council tax

In Britain, local authorities have to collect council tax from all homes, with a few exceptions, in their areas. Information required includes the net amount for collection and the percentage collected. In addition the net cost of collecting council tax per chargeable dwelling is required. Again, local circumstances may impinge on collection. Rates of collection may be lower due to high levels of poverty. Cost of collection may be higher due to local circumstances and the mechanisms used. For instance, direct debit is cheaper than office collection but is ineffective if the clients do not have bank accounts.

- Library service

By law each local authority must run a 'comprehensive and efficient' library service. In order to measure performance, the following areas are examined:

- Items issued, categorised into books and other
- The opening hours:
  - number open 45 hours per week or more
  - number open 10-44 hours per week
  - mobile libraries
- Usage, i.e. the number of visits by members of the public
- Costs:
  - per capita spending on books and other materials
  - net expenditure per head of population.

The London Borough of Westminster, for example, issued 2.2 million books and 399,000 other items in the year ended March 1994. It had 12 libraries open more than 45 hours per week, one open for between 10 and 29 hours per week, and one mobile library. It had 2.4 million visits and spent £6.05 per head on books etc. and £38.41 per head on the library service in total. This level of spending was the highest of any of the authorities. However, the number of visits was not the highest. Croydon, which spent just £15.17 per capita on the library service had 2.7 million visits, with its libraries open for fewer hours.

This information provides some food for thought. For example, is there a need to review opening hours policies in Westminster? Of course, the cost of the service will be determined by local policies and other factors. Perhaps the library infrastructure is old, with high maintenance costs. Library usage often varies with social class. Consequently, usage in areas with a high level of unemployment may be low in comparison with areas which have considerable employment in the professional and managerial sectors. Demographic and other factors must, therefore, be considered when making comparisons.

- The fire service

Information on the fire service is broken down into responding to calls, rescues and costs. The number of calls including details of false fire alarms and other incidents must be given. In addition, the percentage of fire calls at which attendance standards have been met is required. Details of the number of rescues must also be provided, together with per capita cost of the fire service. Such information allows comparison between authorities. Local discretion in the provision of fire services is quite small since national guidelines issued by the UK Home Office set out the minimum number of fire engines and fire fighters that should go to a fire in an area with a particular fire risk. High risk areas require higher levels of cover and consequently are more expensive to run.

Of course, the indicators of performance against attendance targets are useful but they fail to identify how effectively brigades deal with fire when crews arrive. Measurement of this area is much more difficult.

• Highway maintenance and street lighting

The following information is required for street lighting: the percentage of streetlights not working as planned, the percentage of non-working street-lights awaiting action by the local authority, and the method of inspection used for monitoring.

For road and pavement maintenance the information required is the authority's definition of damage to roads/pavements which should be repaired or made safe within 24 hours and the percentage achievement.

Information is also required on the cost of highway maintenance per 100 miles travelled by a vehicle and the percentage of pedestrian crossings with facilities for disabled people.

Again, local conditions will have an impact on cost comparisons. The current state of the infrastructure is significant. In addition the geology and climatic conditions will affect costs; for example some authorities will require snow ploughs and other equipment to deal with blizzard conditions whereas others will have no such demands.

In addition to the items mentioned above, authorities also provide information in accordance with the Publication of Information (Standards of Performance) Direction produced by the Audit Commission (1994) on a vast range of other activities including leisure and recreation, litter control, education, policing, social services and general details of per capita spending for the various services and financing sources.

Review of operation

Any review of the operation of the system of performance indicators must point out that the system is relatively new: authorities published the indicators in local newspapers for the first time in the period April to December, 1994.

The Audit Commission cautions about the use of the information and indicators. It mentions a number of issues which may affect local authority performance, and which may be unclear from the published information.

These include resourcing issues, demographic factors, levels of social deprivation, geographic differences and so forth. Bearing this in mind, any comparative information must be viewed in a balanced manner, taking account of disparities between authorities.

Reaction to the publication of the information and the use of performance measurement has been mixed. On the one hand, the Audit Commission

(1995a) has stated that 'The extent to which local authorities fulfilled the spirit of the initiative rather than just the letter of the law is a testament to their commitment to the principles of open and accountable government'.

The Audit Commission (1995a) looked at the experiences of a sample of local authorities and found that more than one in three of the people who received the performance indicators read at least some of them; and that people find the information interesting if it is presented attractively.

On the other hand, other commentators mention a poor response rate from the general public. One authority published a two-page advertisement in a paper with a readership of 455,000 and received one totally irrelevant enquiry. The average response rate for English counties was five. Swarbrick (1995) comments, 'If the objective was to arouse public interest, then, the publication of performance indicators can only be classified as one of the great advertising disasters of the century.'

Jackson (1995b) points out that different organisational stakeholders, e.g. politicians, customers, suppliers, employees etc., require different measures. He goes on to point out that performance measures do not provide information unless they are compared with something such as a pre-determined target, the previous year's performance or a benchmark. Benchmarking involves comparing specific activities and outcomes of one organisation or department with those of another, usually the best in the class. Jackson considers that the Audit Commission requirements are a weak form of benchmarking where 'best in class' is not specifically identified. They are more correctly described as 'league tables' which Jackson (1995b) states 'are very crude indicators of performance and, at best, signal the need to carry out detailed investigative studies to explain why there is a range of performance outcomes. League tables illustrate the importance of understanding the complex set of environmental factors that influence performance'.

The value of the information provided by performance indicators is in the signals they provide about relative performance or the trend in performance. Absolute measures give little information. They simply signal issues and suggest supplementary questions. However, while inter-authority comparison may pose problems, other options for comparison exist including comparison against standards and over time. The Audit Commission (1987) suggests five types of comparisons for use in local government. These are:

- Temporal – e.g. comparing this year's performance with last year's
- Standards – comparing performance with some standard which may be locally or nationally derived
- Intra-service – comparing performance of a number of units which provide the same service or services within a department

- Private sector – comparison with provision in the private sector such as legal or architectural services
- Inter-authority – comparison can be made with all other authorities, with all authorities of the same type, with specially selected authorities which have similar characteristics, or with neighbouring authorities.

Jackson (1995b) also highlights the costs associated with the production and use of indicators and the danger of 'information overload' or 'analysis paralysis'. Too much information may result in indicators being ignored, relegated to the waste bin, or treated with cynicism. He also points out that 'the incentive for managers in the public sector seemed to be to produce and publish performance indicators rather than incorporate them into active strategic and operational management of public services'. Production and publication as required of local authorities by the Audit Commission does not of itself mean any improvements in efficiency or effectiveness. The indicators must be seen as a means to improve management.

Likierman (1995) carried out a three year survey of public sector managers using performance indicators and concluded that 'Performance indicators are a valuable managerial tool if properly used; if not, managerial time and cash resources could be wasted, and, more seriously, managerial action could be distorted.' He cites twenty lessons which have been highlighted by early use of indicators and quotes a number of public sector managers. One such lesson is that 'performance indicators should not spawn their own cottage industry of forms and monitoring returns.'

Likierman notes the need to avoid having too many indicators in case they lose their impact and value. The UK Central Statistics Office noted that some indicators had improved staff motivation. A local authority is quoted as saying, 'We have made significant changes in the light of our experience and that of others, particularly other local authorities.'

The importance of realistic targets is mentioned by Torbridge and Malling Borough Council. It was noted that implementation of performance measurement systems takes time and, to be effective, must be integrated into existing management systems. Likierman comments that 'early experience of performance indicators in the health service was blighted by their apparent irrelevance to many managers'. By contrast, one local authority had linked the City Council Charter to annual service plans and also intended to tie it into the Citizen's Charter. In another, performance service contracts had become the norm for managers and in some areas were used for all staff. This enables performance indicators to be built into the fabric of the organisations.

The need for simplicity and clarity is also essential. One authority, in reviewing its annual service plan, noted that 'some lessons are clear –

terminology needs to be clearly understood'. The need for organisational change was also highlighted. The chief executive of Hertfordshire County Council observed that 'without other management changes, for example financial devolution, the performance indicator culture will not flourish ... PIs would merely bob along the top of the organisation making the occasional appearance on the agenda of management teams.'

The reliability of available data is seen to be of paramount importance for system credibility. Results provide guidance, not answers. The chief executive of Arun District Council advised that 'it is the dialogue that arises from review that is the important message'. Follow-up also gives credibility to the system. No feedback means atrophy; negative-only feedback encourages 'gaming'. Information should be as easy as possible to understand and should result in action.

There is evidence that action has resulted from the use of the indicators. But, in the case of schools, the ability of league tables of indicators to capture sufficiently finely the 'educational experience' was questioned. A number of local authorities including Newcastle, Sheffield, Birmingham and Southwark established independent educational commissions to examine the conditions of schooling locally. In a similar vein comparative information on responses by staff to the public prompted Surrey County Council to reduce its target for answering telephones from 60 seconds, which was out of line with other authorities, to 20 seconds. So, performance indicators can result in positive action in the public service, contributing to improved efficiency and effectiveness.

An empirical survey of performance measurement in local government carried out by Palmer (1993) found that quantitative indicators such as cost, productivity, utilisation rates, time targets and volume of service are most frequently used and 'indicators of quality of service, customer satisfaction and the achievement of goals appear less often, if at all'.

Authorities tend to measure what is measurable and to over-emphasise costs. Approximately two-thirds of respondents indicated that performance measurement was introduced as part of an internal management proposal, with only one-third citing external pressure from the Audit Commission as the main stimulus.

Suggestions for improvement in performance measurement systems focused on the need for improved information systems and increased computerisation, increased staff training to raise knowledge and awareness of performance measurement, and improved systems of accountability to ensure that managers are accountable for their performance.

Based on her research work, Palmer concludes that 'the commitment of managers in local authorities to performance measurement will ensure its development, improvement and continuation'. Her survey found that the overwhelming majority of respondents (85 per cent) thought performance indicators should be used more often. Results also indicated that managers were satisfied that performance indicators had improved their ability to evaluate final outcomes, thereby justifying the use of resources and indicating that, although the existing systems may have some shortcomings, continued development should yield improvements.

To conclude, the use of performance measurement in British local government, in its existing format, is relatively new. As Jackson (1993) states, 'At this moment in time it is impossible to know the value of performance indicators ... The article of faith is that overall performance is better with the availability of the information than without.' He continues: 'if the introduction of performance measures/indicators is to give the expected pay-off then it is necessary for public service organisations to have the capacity to learn from information signals that indicators provide, as well as the organisational capabilities to act upon that learning. Only then will additional value be created which justifies the costs of measuring performance.' Palmer (1993) indicates that, if properly used, benefits can accrue in terms of improved service management.

In the light of the foregoing review of performance measures in local authorities in Britain we can proceed to ask if there are lessons for the development of such systems in Ireland.

Performance measurement in Irish local government

Irish local government, as currently established, is derived from the British system. Some structural differences exist. For example, the British system does not have a 'county manager' as exists in the Irish system. In addition, the range of functions performed by British local authorities is much broader than the range carried out by Irish authorities; for instance, British local authorities provide police and education services. However, many of the services such as housing, roads, and fire are similar. It would appear possible, therefore, to transpose some of the arrangements for performance measurement and information gathering carried out by British local authorities into the Irish system.

Areas which could benefit from performance measurement

Many of the indicators used by British local authorities could be carried out in Irish local authorities providing a similar range of services. I will focus on a limited selection of the many policy and service areas which could benefit from the use of performance measurement. The sections which follow examine these areas and suggest measures of performance in each case. The appendix to this chapter contains a number of tables most of which are

presented as models on a 'pro-forma' basis. Some stylised data is introduced
to these tables for illustrative purposes.

• Dealing with the public

Irish local authorities deal with the public. Consequently some mechanism
for measuring response times would be useful. Improved information
technology may be required in some authorities before a monitoring system
could be implemented. A computerised telephone system, recording the time
taken to answer each call, would be useful for the measurement of actual
performance against any pre-determined target. Accurate logging of mail by
means of a computerised input system incorporating document imaging
would facilitate improved mail management. Improved response times to
mail would most likely reduce volumes, as repeat queries, for instance, would
be eliminated. Obviously, improvements in information technology would
require a substantial financial investment which may not be possible in all
cases.

Table 12.1 in the appendix sets out a sample of the type of indicator which
could be used, along with sample targets and monitoring mechanisms. The
information produced could facilitate in-house management or inter-authority
comparison.

• Housing

There were over 98,000 rented local authority housing units in Ireland at 31
December, 1996. The management of these units is the responsibility of local
authorities and management and maintenance costs amounted to £105.34m
(Department of the Environment 1998). The indicators and informational
requirements in use in British local authorities such as housing stock
statistics, allocations and lettings, repairs, rent collection costs, level of rent
arrears and homelessness, as discussed earlier in this chapter, are also
relevant to Ireland. In fact, many of these items were covered in the
*Memorandum on the Preparation of a Statement of Policy on Housing
Management* issued by the Department of the Environment (1993) to housing
authorities requiring them to analyse and assess existing systems and identify
proposals for improved standards and cost effectiveness. Specific timescales
were sought for the implementation of proposals. The memorandum also
covered allocations and lettings, including the issue of minimising vacancy
periods. This ties in with the indicator of the 'average time taken to re-let
dwellings' used in Britain. The control and monitoring of rent arrears was
also treated.

According to the memorandum the housing maintenance function should
be examined by looking at response to maintenance requests, planned

maintenance, organisation and methods of assessing and monitoring performance of direct labour units and contractors to ensure effectiveness and value for money. In order to establish an adequate performance measurement system for housing maintenance it is essential that clear standards of service are established for emergencies, urgent and non-urgent work. Quality, efficiency and cost issues must be examined. Surveys of tenant satisfaction with maintenance performance, including a 'sign-off' system, would be useful. This sign-off system would allow the tenant to indicate satisfaction with the quality of service received.

Many of these requirements, such as repairs response times targeted and achieved at each priority level, are in line with the information and indicators in use in British authorities. The suggested 'sign-off' system would facilitate measurement of performance by the tenant, i.e. the customer of the service. Clear service standards would clarify objectives against which the service could be measured. Comparative information about the costs of using private contractors compared to the costs of the local authorities' own direct labour resources is useful in assessing productivity. Of course, adequate accurate information is essential.

Since the preparation of the original statements of policy, further developments have taken place including the establishment of a housing management group comprised of senior officials of local authorities and the Department of the Environment and Local Government. Among its terms of reference this group is required to identify appropriate key housing performance indicators for use by local authorities. The indicators in use in British authorities could form a useful framework for the design of indicators for use in Ireland. Further indicators could be developed for individual circumstances such as time taken to assess housing applications.

The focus of these indicators is on local authority housing. However, the housing function extends to a much broader range of areas including the processing of house loan applications, shared ownership transactions, traveller accommodation, voluntary housing scheme administration and private rented dwelling registration. Indicators would also be required for these areas. Some statistical information is already available from the Department of the Environment and Local Government in the annual and quarterly housing statistics bulletins. Information is provided, for example, on the number of loans under each of the categories of housing aid included in the *Plan for Social Housing* (Department of the Environment 1991) as amended by *Social Housing – The Way Ahead* (Department of the Environment 1995a). This comparative information may identify areas for further examination by raising questions such as why one authority might have completed significantly more shared ownership transactions than another.

Much valuable comparative information is already in place and may be used for analytical purposes. Of course, local demographic and social issues, such as the level of unemployment, house prices and so forth, must be taken into account, as must the level of local commitment.

It is useful to set target periods for elements of service such as the assessment and processing of applications for housing loans. For instance, Galway County Council in its strategic plan (1996) includes a standard of issuing all applicants for housing loan assistance with a decision within two weeks of receipt of the completed application. Of course, the quality of the housing service in not necessarily reflected in these statistics. The quality of service would also require some form of assessment arrived at by taking on board the views of the service users. As Nicholson (1993) pointed out, performance indicators should cover 'the public's experience of using or receiving the service'. A simple questionnaire concerning issues such as quality of information, staff attitude, premises, waiting periods for attention, the effectiveness of any appointment system, the way in which complaints are dealt with, would be useful in this regard.

While the adoption of indicators in use in British authorities should be useful in Ireland also, a more comprehensive approach would be required to cover all areas of housing activity. This more comprehensive approach would, of course, face some difficulties. One such would be the intangible elements of the housing service such as the effectiveness of the housing advice service. Another would be the conflicting goals as when the need to collect rent through the eviction process conflicts with the housing authority's responsibility to the homeless. Adequate information systems and adequate finance are also essential. If measurement identifies weaknesses in the system, it serves no useful purpose unless there are resources to address these weaknesses. A more efficient housing maintenance service may improve the condition of houses, but if the housing stock is in a poor state of repair additional resources will also be required.

Given the varied nature of the housing service, additional indicators to those used in Britain would also be required. The involvement of tenant groups in housing management could be measured by statistics on the number of tenants represented in such initiatives. However, such statistics would give no indication of effectiveness. Similarly, questionnaires to be completed by both housing managers and tenants might be useful. The views of the recipients of the service should be built into the process, in order to judge the effectiveness of the housing service. The use to which the information is put is of paramount importance. It should be built into the management process and be considered in any resourcing decisions.

Tables 12.2, 12.3, 12.4, and 12.5 in the appendix provide some suggestions for useful information and measures, both for local authority housing and for other schemes in the *Plan for Social Housing*. The performance information which could be provided by such measures would be useful in assessing the efficiency and effectiveness of the delivery of the housing service. Of course, this list is not exhaustive and many other suitable measures also exist.

• The roads programme

Expenditure by local authorities on the roads programme, including both capital and revenue items, is estimated at approximately £700m for 1998 (Department of the Environment 1998) and represents the major expenditure area for the majority of Irish local authorities. The Publication of Information (Standards of Performance) Direction produced by the Audit Commission (1994) requires the publication of information regarding highway lighting, road and pavement maintenance and the provision of pedestrian crossing by British local authorities.

The indicators to be used in respect of lighting are the percentage of lights not working, the percentage awaiting action from the authority, and the monitoring mechanism. Such indicators could be used also by Irish authorities. However, other indicators would also be useful, particularly in relation to costing and level of coverage of the lighting system.

The issue of value for money in the area of public lighting in Ireland has been the subject of a report by the Value for Money Unit of the Audit Service (Department of the Environment 1995b). It identified costs and economies associated with various types of lighting. The use of an indicator measuring the proportion of the different types of lighting used by local authorities may identify the potential for greater economy by substituting one type of lighting for another. The level of public satisfaction with existing lighting as indicated in correspondence and other communications may also help identify whether the lighting meets the customers' needs. Are there requests for extensions to the network? Does the network satisfy any recognised standards for the provision of lighting? Such indicators may help promote action on more economical lighting, good maintenance performance and customer satisfaction.

Table 12.6 in the appendix sets out some suggested measures which would indicate the efficiency and effectiveness of the public lighting service and perhaps identify areas for improvement such as the percentage of lights requiring modernisation.

Indicators on road and pavement maintenance used by British authorities measure the percentage of repairs to roads and pavements achieved within a 24 hour target. The cost of maintenance per 100 miles travelled by a vehicle is another such indicator.

The identification of targets for emergency maintenance may be useful for

Irish local authorities also. However, the cost of maintenance per 100 miles is an indicator which would be likely to vary significantly between areas. Geographic factors such as soil quality would have an impact as would the existing state of repair of roads. An authority which had not maintained the roads adequately for some time, whether due to lack of resources or prioritisation of improvement works in preference to maintenance works, would most likely require increased spending on maintenance. Cost per 100 miles gives no indication of the quality of the service. One cannot judge what the level of maintenance was. Maintenance costs per mile, without taking other factors into consideration, would seem to be a weak performance measure.

In Irish local authorities, much of the emphasis in the road maintenance area is on the inputs into the system such as the estimated provision for maintenance work. Some statistics are available on output measures but their use is limited. For example, details of expenditure incurred by local authorities must be returned to the Department of the Environment and Local Government in order to claim the road grants. The Departmental guidance notes (Department of the Environment 1995c) associated with these grant claims highlight the intended use of the returns 'as a tool to measure outputs against proposed ... work programmes'. Variations between output returns and original proposals must be fully explained in an accompanying statement. The actual forms require information on total cost, length and area of schemes. This information is returned to the Department by each local authority and could form the basis of an evaluation system. Of course, the information would have to be taken in conjunction with other factors including topography and state of repair but varying costs would at least prompt questions. Inter-county comparisons may be difficult due to varying environmental conditions and cost structures, as occur for instance when the levels of direct labour employed differ between counties. Notwithstanding such difficulties, inter-authority variations in statistics provide useful signals. In addition, comparison with standard costs or private sector costs and year-on-year comparisons are useful.

Because roads and pavements use such a large proportion of local authority, exchequer and European Union resources, the identification of a suitable and adequate set of indicators to evaluate outputs is essential. Table 12.7 in the appendix sets out some suggestions for statistical information and performance measures which may assist in assessing performance in the area of road maintenance.

- Fire service

In 1996, the total cost of the fire service in Ireland was £71.46m compared to £8.12m in 1976. In the same period the number of full time fire personnel increased from 870 to 1,218 and the total number of fires attended grew from 24,806 to 33,352 (Department of the Environment 1997). The cost of running the fire service places a considerable demand on local authority resources, representing 5.6 per cent of the annual revenue expenditure in 1996. This demand has increased significantly over the years. It is important, therefore, that value for money be pursued.

The information published by British authorities on the fire service shows the number of call-outs categorised by type, the percentage where attendance standards were met, the number of rescues and the net expenditure per head of population on the fire service.

The situation in Ireland is similar to Britain. In fact, statistics about call-outs are published annually by the Department of the Environment and Local Government. Information is provided on expenditure, employees, number of fires and other incidents, level of fatalities and the causes of fires attended. The statistics provide a breakdown by fire authority.

I have extracted some of the statistical information in relation to county fire authorities (excluding county boroughs and the Dublin authorities) from the Department of the Environment's 1995 publication. The information is contained in Tables 12.8, 12.9 and 12.10 in the appendix.

The British figures give details of number of fires, level of achievement of standards, expenditure per head and so forth. Per capita expenditure varies from £16.30 in Leicestershire to £34.08 in London. The results of my analysis, as shown on the attached tables indicate that in Ireland, per capita expenditure varied from £6.92 to £22.98 in county areas in 1995. The information on expenditure per head of population is a useful indicator which begs the question why the figure varies to such an extent between authorities. Of course local circumstances may account for variations in some cases. These include higher fire risk, lower population density and different types of incidents, for example hay-barn fires which tend to take longer to deal with than domestic chimney fires. However, the expenditure comparison may at least prompt basic questions for the service manager. Do local work practices maximise efficiency? Is the number of employees appropriate? Is rostering an option? Are there too many fire stations? Is the time spent on incidents the minimum necessary? Are there unnecessary responses to call-outs? What can be done to reduce call-out expenditure?

Once the existence of local variations is accepted, inter-authority comparison may facilitate some form of benchmarking. Perhaps better practices apply in some authorities from which others may learn. Alternatively, the statistics may indicate variations within authorities over time, such as an increase in the incidence of chimney fires, which could encourage action in the area of fire prevention education.

The British Fire Service operates a system of risk categorisation and nationally established service standards. Details of the success rate in achieving the attendance standards are published. No such national standards have been established in Ireland. Some service standards may be useful for assessing performance in Ireland, although care should be taken in setting these standards. The Audit Commission (1995c) found that there is a need to update the method of assessing fire risk and that more discretion should be allowed for brigades to set standards locally. A monitoring system to identify achievement of standards could probably be built into the computerised central call-out systems which are being established in a number of centres around the country. This information would facilitate monitoring of response rates against pre-set targets. Of course, response rates alone are inadequate. They give no information on the quality of service once the brigade arrives on site.

The fire brigade indicators in use in Britain may be useful if introduced in Ireland. However, other areas should also be measured. Fire prevention is an important aspect of the work of fire authorities. The Audit Commission (*op. cit.*) has stated, 'There is ample evidence that fire prevention initiatives are a cost-effective way of tackling the problems of deaths, injuries and losses from fire.' Fire prevention helps minimise the risk to life. The time taken to discover a fire is a major factor in fire deaths. Therefore, the promotion of smoke alarms and fire safety in buildings can assist in risk reduction. In addition, fire prevention and fire safety promotion can have the added benefit of reducing fire call-outs and expenditure on the fire service.

Some fires such as chimney fires are avoidable. If households get their chimneys cleaned, the likelihood of chimney fires is reduced and therefore, the cost of running the fire service. Consequently, some indicator of the level of chimney fires may be useful in highlighting a need for education. Table 12.10 in the appendix indicates that the number of chimney fires in 1995 per 1,000 population varied from 1.13 in Meath to 9.10 in Laois. In some counties less than one quarter of fire call-outs are chimney fires whereas in others the percentage exceeds 60 per cent. Attention to this indicator may help managers to decide on a response, for example, through a publicity campaign to improve public awareness or a charging system which would encourage householders to clean their chimneys. Progress in this area could lead to reduced costs, resulting in a more cost-effective fire service.

The use of information and performance indicators highlights some issues which may be worth examining further in the fire service. Of course, all issues are not within the power of the service managers and historical and political considerations may have an impact. Regardless of the statistical evidence, the political feasibility of closing uneconomic fire stations may be questionable. However, the indicators help to highlight the values inherent in the system.

Table 12.11 in the appendix sets out some suggestions for performance indicators and statistics which could assist in identifying the quality of the fire service. These include response times and other features which could prompt management action in improving the efficiency of the service. Tables 12.8, 12.9 and 12.10 in the appendix compare performance in Ireland and give rise to important questions. For instance, why is per capita expenditure on the fire service in County Meath only 30 per cent of the level in Louth? Why are people in Laois almost eight times more likely to have a chimney fire that those in Meath? The answers to these questions, prompted by performance information, could assist in improving efficiency in the fire service.

- Litter control

Litter control is part of the remit of the Irish local authorities. The question of performance measures is relevant in the context of local authority litter action plans.

For keeping land and highways clear of litter and refuse British local authorities use the following measures:

- the percentage that are of a high standard of cleanliness and of an acceptable standard of cleanliness
- the method of inspection used to monitor the standard of cleanliness
- the average time taken to remove 'fly-tips'.

These measures may also be appropriate in the Irish context, provided adequate resources are made available. There is little point in measuring the standards of cleanliness if discovery of poor standards does not lead to necessary action.

Statistics on current levels of cleanliness are not readily available in most authorities. Some measuring mechanism is required. It may be useful to follow the methodology used by the consultants in the national litter survey undertaken by the Department of the Environment (1996b). This involved the selection of locations for the survey including urban, rural, tourist areas and beaches. Survey sites were randomly chosen to give a representative sample and locations were graded on the following basis:

- grade A   complete absence of litter
- grade B   scattered small amounts of litter
- grade C   small accumulations of litter
- grade D   significant accumulations of litter.

A cleanliness rating was calculated for each location. Composition of the litter was analysed and other 'environment quality indicators' such as dog fouling and fly-posting were noted. The results were computerised for ease of retrieval, analysis and reporting.

If performance measurement is to be introduced in the litter area an adequate data collection system is an essential prerequisite. The adoption of the indicators in use in Britain in the area of litter control therefore, would be appropriate in Ireland, provided an adequate system of data collection was introduced. Such indicators should facilitate decision-making about the use of resources.

Table 12.12 in the appendix suggests some statistics and indicators which could assist in identifying local authority performance in the area of litter control. These include target times for removal of 'fly-tips', the standard of street cleanliness and the number of prosecutions taken. The information gathered would be useful for inter-authority comparison and could assist in decisions about such issues as the employment of litter wardens. Moreover, it helps identify potential areas for improvement.

Conclusion

The above mentioned selection of services provided by Irish local authorities indicates that there is scope for the use of performance indicators in the measurement of performance. The areas chosen, namely dealing with the public, housing, roads, fire and litter control represent only a portion of the services within the remit of Irish authorities. The use of performance indicators would also facilitate informed decision-making about service provision in many other areas such as planning, sanitary services, environmental protection, libraries, parks, recreation centres, motor taxation and driver licensing. Information is a key ingredient for good management which should, if properly used, result in the more effective use of limited resources.

The issues which must be addressed for an effective performance measurement system in Irish local government include management commitment to the process, the availability of adequate, accurate and timely information, the amendment, if appropriate, of organisational structure and culture and finally the incorporation of the measurement system into the decision-making process so that action is taken where necessary. The design of an appropriate system will take time. The existing indicators in use in British authorities may provide a useful framework around which to build indicators which are appropriate to the Irish context. Some of the British indicators could be adopted, with little adjustment. However, the design of additional indicators would also be required.

Of course, any performance measurement system is evolutionary. Indicators need to be changed over time in light of experience of their use and because of the dynamic environment in which Irish authorities operate.

Any system which would assist management to better utilise scarce resources in the delivery of public services must receive serious consideration. As Boyle (1993) points out 'performance measurement is central to the current agenda of public service management improvements'.

The following are some recommendations for the implementation of a performance measurement system in Irish local authorities:

- The performance measurement process must be incorporated into the management system of local authorities. The strategic management process which local authorities are currently undertaking presents an opportunity to introduce such an initiative. The process of strategic management should facilitate the definition of objectives and targets, the clarification of accountability structures and the issues of structural and cultural change which are essential for a successful performance measurement system. It also presents an ideal opportunity to involve staff in system and indicator design, thereby improving motivation and ownership. As Jackson (1993) states: 'Performance indicators are the end of a story which should begin with strategic thinking'.

- Managers must only be held accountable for areas over which they have control.

- If valid, functional, reliable and legitimate indicators are to be identified, then adequate resources must be provided for system design. It takes time to design indicators which will overcome dysfunctional difficulties.

- Indicators should be designed for policy making and implementation in order to address the issue of effectiveness of services.

- Qualitative and quantitative measures should be introduced.

- Long-term, as well as short-term issues should be considered, and indicators should be designed accordingly.

- Indicators should focus on key functions and provide management with enough information to identify problem areas.

- The availability of an adequate information system is essential. Some statistical information is already available. However, new data requirements will arise and must be met, perhaps through enhanced information technology systems. Information must be reliable, accurate and timely.

- The performance measures used by the Audit Commission in Britain may be taken as a guide to the design of Irish service indicators. However, they do not cover all the areas necessary. The indicators selected for Irish local government must reflect the circumstances in which Irish authorities operate. These may differ from British authorities in some instances. The people best placed to design indicators for the Irish local government service are those involved in delivering the service and its customers.

- Targets against which performance is to be judged should as far as possible be set locally, in line with the objectives of local government and local identification of priorities.

- The use of inter-authority 'league tables' should be approached with caution. If information is used without due regard to the pit-falls associated with such comparison the credibility of the system will be affected. However, benchmarking may be useful to improve performance, particularly among weaker authorities.

- Comparisons may be made over time, against target, inter-service, with the private sector or with a control group.

- Management commitment to the process, including a commitment to respond to the issues brought to light by the indicators, is vital for success. This may entail structural change or additional resources.

- Publication of indicators should be incorporated into existing local authority literature such as annual reports, budget documents or final accounts.

- Performance measurement is not static and the process must allow regular review in the light of experience and changing circumstances.

The design and use of performance measures should help focus attention on objectives, outputs and outcomes. Measures are not ends in themselves but instead provide an insight for local authority managers, politicians and citizens. They are a management tool which, if designed and used properly, can lead to a more efficient and effective use of the scarce resources on which local authorities depend. Improvements in economy, efficiency and effective-ness are undoubtedly the substance of accountable management. In this vein, Jackson (1993) points out: 'Performance indicators are a means of assisting responsible management to make efficient and effective decisions. They are not, however, a mechanical substitute for good judgement, political wisdom or leadership.' Measurement systems provide an opportunity to identify performance against objectives, to reflect on this performance, learn from the best and enhance service to the public. Boyle (1993) states: 'Performance management is as much about creating an appropriate culture as it is a technical process.'

The implementation of well-constructed systems has the potential to benefit all interested parties. Workers will benefit from clearer direction, better informed decisions, equitable distribution of workloads and perhaps even improved incentives such as performance-related pay. Managers will benefit as they improve control. Politicians will benefit from efficiently and effectively operated services which the electors will appreciate. Customers will benefit from improved services, reduced waiting times and fewer frustrations in dealing with local authorities. Finally, as Holzer (1995) states: 'as the "bottom line", the general public and the economy will benefit from more efficient and effective public services and goods, which translate into higher standards of living'.

REFERENCES

A Government of Renewal, a Policy Agreement between Fine Gael, the Labour Party and Democratic Left, (1994). Dublin: The Stationery Office

An Action Programme for the Millenium (1997). Dublin: Government Information Service

Audit Commission, (1987). *A Handbook for Auditors and Local Authorities,* London: HMSO

Audit Commission, (1994). *Publication of Information (Standards of Performance) Direction,* London: HMSO

Audit Commission, (1995a). *Have We Got News for You: A guide to good practice in publishing the local authority performance indicators,* London: HMSO

Audit Commission (1995b). *Local Authority Performance Indicators: Appendix to Volumes 1 & 2,* London: HMSO

Audit Commission (1995c). *In the Line of Fire: Value for Money in the Fire Service,* London: HMSO

Boyle, R. (1993). *Developing Management Skills,* Dublin: IPA

Department of the Environment (1991) *A Plan for Social Housing,* Dublin: Department of the Environment.

Department of the Environment (1993). *Memorandum on the Preparation of a Statement of Policy on Housing Management,* Dublin: Department of the Environment

Department of the Environment (1995a). *Social Housing – The Way Ahead,* Dublin: Department of the Environment

Department of the Environment (1995b). *Value for Money: Study No. 10 Public Lighting,* Dublin: The Stationery Office

Department of the Environment, (1995c). *Memorandum on 1995 Grants for Non-national Roads,* Dublin: Department of the Environment

Department of the Environment (1996a). *Better Local Government: A Programme for Change,* Dublin: The Stationery Office

Department of the Environment (1996b). *National Litter Survey,* Dublin: Department of The Environment

Department of the Environment (1996c). *Strategic Management and the Local Authority,* Dublin: Department of the Environment

Department of the Environment (1997). *Fire Statistics,* Dublin: Department of the Environment

Department of the Environment (1998). *Local Authority Estimates 1998,* Dublin: The Stationery Office

Department of the Environment, annually. *Annual Housing Statistics*, Dublin: The Stationery Office

Galway County Council (1996). *Strategic Plan 1996-2000*, Galway: Galway County Council

Golden, T. P. (1997). *Local Authority Accounting in Ireland*, Dublin: IPA.

Holzer, M. (1995). 'The Public Productivity Challenge', in A. Halachmi and G. Bouckaert, *Enduring Challenges in Public Management: Surviving and Excelling in a Changing World*, San Francisco: Jossey-Bass

Jackson, P. M, D. Beeton, A. G. J. Haselbekke and A. P. Ros (1991). *Developments in Performance Measurement and Financial Management: Ideas for use in the Public Service*, London: CIPFA & FEE

Jackson, P. M. (1993). *Public Service Performance Evaluation: A Strategic Perspective, Public Money & Management*, Volume 13, Number 4 (October–December

Jackson, P. M. (ed) (1995a). *Measures for Success in the Public Sector*, London: CIPFA

Jackson, P. M. (1995b). *Introduction: Reflections on Performance Measurement in Public Service Organisations*, London: CIPFA

Likierman, A. (1995). 'Performance Indicators: 20 Early Lessons from Managerial Use', in P.M. Jackson (ed), *Measures for Success in the Public Sector*, London: CIPFA

Local Government Chronicle (1997). Pl's Supplement, London.

Nicholson, N. (1993). *Performance Indicators: An Introductory Guide*, Luton: Local Government Management Board.

Palmer, A. J. (1993). *Performance Measurement in Local Government: An Empirical Survey, Public Money & Management*, Volume 13, Number 4 (October–December).

Review Body on Higher Remuneration in the Public Sector – Report No. 37 (1996), Dublin: The Stationery Office

Ridley F. F. (1995). *Competition for Quality, Performance Indicators and Re-inventing Government*, London: CIPFA

Swarbrick, P. (1995). Supplement, *Local Government Chronicle*, March

APPENDIX

Table 12.1: Pro forma comparative table of performance indicators on dealing with the public

County	Target for answering phones	Monitoring mechanism	% achievement	Target for answering letters	Monitoring mechanism	% achievement
A						
B						
C				3 Days	Manual log	70%
D						
E						
F	10 seconds	External survey	93%			
G						
H	95% Within 10 rings	Electronic and manual	72%	1 Week	Electronic log	85%
I						
J						
K						
L				10 Days	Internal survey	76%
M						
N	5 Seconds	Call logging	91.50%			
O						
P				5 Days	Random sample	93%
Q						
R	6 Rings	Computerised call logging	64.50%			
S						
T						
U				8 Days	External survey	87%
V						
W						
X	80% Within 10 rings	Random sampling	73%			
Y						
Z						

NB – Information is purely for illustration purposes

Table 12.2: Pro forma comparative table of performance indicators for the housing service

County	Activity under plan for social housing schemes								
	Shared ownership			Mortgage allowance			Improvement works in lieu of Local Authority housing		
	Transactions completed	Approvals issued	Applications received	Transactions completed	Approvals issued	Applications received	Transactions completed	Approvals issued	Applications received
A									
B									
C							45		50
D	7	19	50			18			
E									
F				4					
G								14	
H									
I							10		
J		10	35						
K					7				
L	23					16			
M									
N				13				9	
O							7		
P									
Q									
R		35							
S					3				
T									
U	141		200						
V						35			
W									
X									17
Y				7					
Z					15		16		

NB – Information is purely for illustration purposes

Table 12.3: Pro forma comparative table of performance indicators for the housing service

County	Rental subsidy schemes			Capital assistance scheme			Housing loans and grants administration	
	Number of Dwellings			Number of Dwellings			Target for issue of decision	% Achievement
	Completed	In progress	In planning	Completed	In progress	In planning		
A								
B								
C								
D	=15	0	5				2 Weeks	50%
E								
F				14	5			
G						25		
H								
I								
J		3						
K							10 Days	70%
L								
M								
N			17					
O								
P				13				
Q					6	41	1 Month	60%
R			10					
S	34	0						
T								
U								
V								
W				19	5		5 Weeks	80%
X								
Y						17		
Z								

NB – Information is purely for illustration purposes

Table 12.4: Pro forma comparative table of performance indicators for the housing service

County	% of tenants represented on tenant involvement initiatives	Average time to re-let dwelling	Housing Repairs							
			Response–target emergency repairs	% achievement	Response target – urgent repairs	% achievement	Response target – non-urgent repairs	% achievement	Appointments system	Sign-off system
A										
B										
C	10%									Yes
D		7 Days	24 Hours	50	5 Days	50	5 Weeks	90		
E										
F					10 Days	75				
G									Yes	
H	15%									
I										
J			48 Hours	35						No
K										
L		3 Weeks								
M	20%				7 Days	80	3 Weeks	55		
N									No	
O										
P										
Q			8 Hours	60						
R										
S										
T		6 Months					6 Weeks	80	No	Yes
U										
V										
W										
X										
Y										
Z										

NB – Information is purely for illustration purposes

Table 12.5: Pro forma comparative table of performance indicators for the housing service

County	% of tenants 13 weeks + in arrears	Rent collection percentage	Average weekly rent	Minimum weekly rent	Number of repossessions	Average weekly management costs	Tenancy turnover rate
A							
B	10%						
C		93	11	7		2500	3%
D							
E							
F					5	7500	
G							
H	15%						
I							
J			13.5	5			
K							
L		97					5%
M	20%				10	1500	
N							
O							
P							
Q							
R			9	4			
S		89					
T							
U							
V							10%
W							
X							
Y							
Z							

NB – Information is purely for illustration purposes

Table 12.6: Pro forma comparative table of performance indicators and statistics for public lighting service

County	% Lights not working	% Awaiting repair	Monitoring mechanism	% of network requiring modernisation	Public lighting extensions	
					Outstanding requests	Completions
A						
B						
C					10	5
D	10%		Internal survey	30%		
E						
F		5%				
G						
H						
I	2%					
J						
K					30	
L						7
M		10%	ESB survey	35%		
N						
O	15%					
P						
Q						
R		6%	Random survey			
S					120	
T	5%			20%		2
U						
V						
W		30%				
X						
Y	8%			5%		0
Z						

NB – Information is purely for illustration purposes

Table 12.7: *Pro forma comparative table of performance indicators and statistics for non-national road maintenance service*

County	Miles of road	% Seriously deficient	Target for emergency response	% achievement	Cost of maintenance per 100 kms	Expenditure	Surface dressing Length (m)	Area (sq. m)
A								
B								
C				90				
D			8 Hours					
E								
F		5						
G			5 Hours					
H								
I								
J				85				
K								
L			24 Hours					
M								
N		10						
O								
P								
Q								
R		6						
S				95				
T								
U								
V								
W								
X		30						
Y								
Z								

NB – Information is purely for illustration purposes

Table 12.8: Analysis of fire service expenditure by county for 1995

County	Population	Expenditure £	Per capita expenditure £
Meath	105,370	728,690	6.92
Kildare	122,656	1,082,209	8.82
Monaghan	51,293	494,985	9.65
Donegal	128,117	1,251,985	9.77
Clare	90,918	963,058	10.59
Wicklow	97,265	1,033,869	10.63
Wexford	102,069	1,094,924	10.73
Cavan	52,796	575,969	10.91
Cork	283,116	3,272,443	11.56
Kerry	121,894	1,459,955	11.98
Carlow	40,942	502,566	12.28
Limerick	109,873	1,354,287	12.33
Roscommon	51,897	643,011	12.39
Tipperary SR	74,918	957,866	12.79
Sligo	54,756	751,510	13.72
Leitrim	25,301	348,558	13.78
Mayo	110,713	1,569,870	14.18
Laois	52,314	756,740	14.47
Galway	129,511	1,893,470	14.62
Westmeath*	61,880	929,445	15.02
Tipperary NR	57,854	876,345	15.15
Kilkenny	73,635	1,127,834	15.32
Offaly	58,494	911,087	15.58
Longford	30,296	506,149	16.71
Waterford	51,296	939,827	18.32
Louth*	90,724	2,085,075	22.98
Total Expenditure		28,111,727	

*Note: Louth includes urban areas
        Westmeath includes Athlone

Table 12.9: Analysis of fire service statistics by county for 1995

County	Domestic Fires		Other incidents	Total	Chimney fires as % of total activities
	Chimney	Other			
Louth*	114	104	922	1,140	10.00%
Wicklow	188	64	585	837	22.46%
Meath	119	86	314	519	22.93%
Waterford	153	54	272	479	31.94%
Cork	552	164	913	1,629	33.89%
Monaghan	137	35	227	399	34.34%
Donegal	289	80	433	802	36.03%
Wexford	403	66	605	1,074	37.52%
Cavan	83	31	100	214	38.79%
Tipperary SR	215	52	283	550	39.09%
Kerry	364	80	401	845	43.08%
Kildare	505	80	577	1,162	43.46%
Galway	538	106	560	1,204	44.68%
Carlow	175	27	178	380	46.05%
Sligo	186	57	156	399	46.62%
Kilkenny	300	49	274	623	48.15%
Longford	209	37	171	417	50.12%
Clare	327	49	251	627	52.15%
Leitrim	88	12	65	165	53.33%
Roscommon	227	0	194	421	53.92%
Mayo	580	110	374	1,064	54.51%
Westmeath*	426	47	303	776	54.90%
Limerick	274	62	159	495	55.35%
Offaly	424	36	251	711	59.63%
Laois	476	49	250	775	61.42%
Tipperary NR	373	49	160	582	64.09%
	7,725	1,586	8,978	18,289	

*Note: Louth includes urban areas
          Westmeath includes Athlone

Table 12.10: Analysis of fire service statistics by county for 1995

County	Population	Domestic fires		Other call outs	Total call outs	Chimney fires as % of total call outs	Chimney fire per 1000 population	Call outs per 1000 population
		Chimney	Other					
Meath	105,370	119	86	314	519	22.93%	1.13	4.93
Louth*	90,724	114	104	922	1,140	10.00%	1.26	12.57
Cavan	52,796	83	31	100	214	38.79%	1.57	4.05
Wicklow	97,265	188	64	585	837	22.46%	1.93	8.61
Cork	283,116	552	164	913	1,629	33.89%	1.95	5.75
Donegal	128,117	289	80	433	802	36.03%	2.26	6.26
Limerick	109,873	274	62	159	495	55.35%	2.49	4.51
Monaghan	51,293	137	35	227	399	34.34%	2.67	7.78
Tipperary SR	74,918	215	52	283	550	39.09%	2.87	7.34
Waterford	51,296	153	54	272	479	31.94%	2.98	9.34
Kerry	121,894	364	80	401	845	43.08%	2.99	6.93
Sligo	54,756	186	57	156	399	46.62%	3.40	7.29
Leitrim	25,301	88	12	65	165	53.33%	3.48	6.52
Clare	90,918	327	49	251	627	52.15%	3.60	6.90
Wexford	102,069	403	66	605	1,074	37.52%	3.95	10.52
Kilkenny	73,635	300	49	274	623	48.15%	4.07	8.46
Kildare	122,656	505	80	577	1,162	43.46%	4.12	9.47
Galway	129,511	538	106	560	1,204	44.68%	4.15	9.30
Carlow	40,942	175	27	178	380	46.05%	4.27	9.28
Roscommon	51,897	227	0	194	421	53.92%	4.37	8.11
Mayo	110,713	580	110	374	1,064	54.51%	5.24	9.61
Tipperary NR	57,854	373	49	160	582	64.09%	6.45	10.06
Westmeath*	61,880	426	47	303	776	54.90%	6.88	12.54
Longford	30,296	209	37	171	417	50.12%	6.90	13.76
Offaly	58,494	424	36	251	711	59.63%	7.25	12.16
Laois	52,314	476	49	250	775	61.42%	9.10	14.81
Total		7,725	1,586	8,978	18,289			

*Note – Louth includes urban areas

Table 12.11: Pro forma comparative table of performance indicators and statistics for fire service

County	% Calls where attendance standard met	Number of fires (not false alarms)	False alarms	Other incidents	Per capita expenditure	Chimney fires as % of total fires	Call outs per 1000 population	Per capita expenditure on fire prevention	Number of inspections carried out
A									
B	92%	685							
C									
D	68%		45		10		5.66	1	260
E									
F									
G				31					
H						24%			
I			69				9.91		
J									
K	79%	579			13				45
L									
M				120			17.91		
N									
O									
P						37%		1.75	
Q									
R		1,209			20		10.42		75
S	95%		35						
T									
U									
V				75					
W						47%		2	
X									
Y	80%		80		13	60%			
Z		620							

NB – Information is purely for illustration purposes

Table 12.12: Pro forma comparative table of performance indicators and statistics for litter monitoring and control

| County | Target time for removal of fly-tips | % achievement | Expenditure on litter removal | Percentage of streets | | Monitoring mechanism | Is Litter Warden employed? | Number of prosecutions |
				Of a high standard of cleanliness	Of an acceptable standard of cleanliness			
A								
B								
C								
D	3 Days	60%	10000	50%	70%	Internal survey	Yes	15
E								
F								
G								
H								
I								
J								
K	1 Week	50%	50000	45%	60%	Weekly recording	No	0
L								
M								
N								
O								
P	1 Month	55%	75000	60%	65%	Sample survey	No	0
Q								
R								
S								
T								
U								
V								
W								
X								
Y								
Z								

NB – Information is purely for illustration purposes

13

Evaluating Police Performance

PATRICK CLAVIN

Introduction

In recent years there has been much discussion on the topic of evaluation in the public sector in Ireland. This has occurred in the context of the heightened interest in efficiency and effectiveness in the OECD. Evaluation is seen as a necessary condition for the monitoring of improvements in efficiency and effectiveness.

In the United Kingdom, Margaret Thatcher was determined to introduce private sector ideals into the public sector in an effort to improve efficiency and effectiveness. Two key tools of evaluation have been employed there, namely, setting targets and monitoring the results. The Audit Commission in Britain has drawn up a list of performance indicators in an effort to make worthwhile comparisons between public sector service providers across various regions. Under the Local Government Act, 1992 the Audit Commission has a duty to specify information about performance which local authorities, including the police service (which for the most part in England and Wales is an element of local government), must collect and publish. The Audit Commission also has a duty to facilitate comparisons between authorities.

Performance indicators have been drawn up in the United Kingdom for education services, social services, fire services and police services. In the context of the police service the Audit Commission chose the following indicators: police 999 calls and emergencies, crime and detection, and police resources. In the Republic of Ireland the Garda Síochána is responsible for policing throughout the state. The Garda Síochána is an agency of central government, whereas in England and Wales policing is carried out by 41 separate police forces, which are run by police authorities. The existence of separate police forces facilitates comparisons between the performance of the various forces in terms of their achievement of the Audit Commission performance indicators. Each year, league tables are published by the Audit

Commission, setting out how all the police forces have performed during the previous year. The public are encouraged to examine these tables in an effort to find out how their own local forces have performed. In Ireland, the publication of such league tables is not possible given that we have only one police force.

According to the OECD:

> Performance measurement is not an exact science. It has to be undertaken with recognition of its conceptual and practical limitations. In the general government sector it is used to get a better feel for performance in order to assist in decision-making, rather than to arrive at some precise bottom line. In particular, a performance measure does not speak for itself: it must be evaluated with reference to some base. Compiling a time series of indicators and making comparisons with other similar organisations are seen as useful ways to develop benchmarks. Appropriate benchmarking is a key aspect of performance evaluation. (OECD, 1995).

In the context of police service evaluation, Boyle (1989) tells us that 'Performance indicators are often used to assist monitoring. Indicators are more tentative than measures.' When performance is not directly measurable then indicators are clearly useful. For example, Boyle states that 'the number of complaints received is an indicator of quality of service, but it does not represent the whole picture.' Evaluating performance in a police service, e.g. the Garda Síochána, is most difficult. The inputs, such as financial expenditure, can easily be measured. The financial expenditure is known with certainty because the houses of the Oireachtas vote on it each year. The real difficulty lies in the area of measuring the output or the outcome of the Garda service.

Garda Chief Superintendent Patrick A. Culhane, when addressing colleagues on the subject of performance evaluation, uses the following example of the difficulty of measuring police output. Members of a Garda investigation team were seeking the whereabouts of a man in connection with a serious crime. They received information that the man was to be found in an area in rural Ireland. When the investigators arrived in the rural area they met the local Sergeant and asked him for information about the suspect. The Sergeant assured them that he would locate the suspect within one hour if he were in his area. Within the hour the Sergeant returned and informed the members of the investigation team that the suspect was not in his area but was in a neighbouring one. In fact the Sergeant was able to tell the investigators exactly where to find the suspect. The output of a member of the Garda Síochána in instances such as this saves valuable Garda time in attempting to locate suspects; however, the output based on detailed local knowledge is difficult to measure.

Policing and the market

In economic terms the market system is a means of allocating goods and services. Problems of supply and demand are resolved through the mechanism of price. Under perfect market conditions there is no rationale for government intervention. According to Stiglitz (1988), there are six conditions or market failures which provide a rationale for government intervention, namely: failure of competition, for example monopoly, public goods, which refers to goods or services which the market will not supply or will under-supply; externalities such as pollution; incomplete or missing markets, for example where the insurance industry refuses to insure certain categories of risk; information failure, such as might be the case in relation to a health hazard where the public would not be informed about the danger were it not for government intervention; and finally unemployment and inflation.

The rationale for the provision of policing by government is that policing and national defence are 'public goods'. Public goods have two properties, namely, they are 'non-rival' and 'non-excludable'. 'Non-rival' means that it does not cost any more for an additional consumer to enjoy the good or service; the more utility one person derives does not mean a reduction of utility for others. 'Non-excludable' means that it is not possible to exclude anyone from consuming the output being produced. Foot patrols, which are provided by the Gardaí for the purpose of crime prevention and public reassurance, are an example of public goods. Some services that are provided by the Gardaí are not public goods. For example the provision of cash escorts to the private sector is a service which the market might otherwise provide.

Ideally it should be possible to have true performance measures of outcomes. Many aspects of the police service are not measurable by conventional means. It is very difficult to imagine how one might measure a crime prevention patrol. One can never be sure if a Garda on foot patrol has prevented any crimes, or if so how many. The problem of crime prevention is further compounded by the fact that foot patrols may serve only to displace criminals from one location to another and, if this were to happen, the effectiveness of the patrol for society in general may be negligible.

One of the main outcomes arising from police foot patrols is public reassurance. The public benefits in terms of a better feeling of security in the belief that owing to police patrols it is safer to walk about. An output such as public reassurance is impossible to measure accurately. It is, however, possible to devise 'proxy' measures of reassurance, e.g. opinion surveys and analyses of complaints made by members of the public.

There may be conflicts caused by the introduction of methods of evaluation into the police service. In the Dublin Metropolitan Area, following the introduction of a computerised 'command and control' system, the Garda Síochána adopted a policy of withdrawing service from premises which were the cause of an excessive number of false burglar alarm calls. The policy was effective in that the number of false alarm calls reduced dramatically. This resulted in reductions in terms of opportunity cost: there were more resources available for crime prevention patrolling as a result. Garda management has to consider policies that would yield greater efficiency and effectiveness, while at the same time being mindful of the need to maintain public confidence in the organisation.

Measuring crime

Traditionally one of the most frequently used methods of evaluating police performance has been to measure the level of recorded crime and the 'clear-up' rate or the detection rate. Since 1947 a *Report on Crime* has been published annually by the Garda Commissioner. The report is nowadays called *Garda Síochána Annual Report*. This report provides a breakdown of the incidence, detection rate and court disposal of cases for around one hundred and twenty five offence categories. Public attention normally focuses upon one statistic, namely, the total number of indictable crimes recorded and the number detected.

Officially recorded crime statistics do not claim to be a real measure of the actual level of crime. Instead they reflect the number of crimes which are reported to the Gardaí and the number of reported crimes which are subsequently recorded as crimes in accordance with the Garda classification scheme. The problem associated with officially recorded statistics is twofold: firstly not all crime is reported and secondly the police in the official statistics do not subsequently record some incidents that are reported as crime. An ESRI report (1985), gave the results of a survey carried out between October 1982 and October 1983 on a national sample of 8,902 persons in the Republic of Ireland. It concluded that the officially recorded statistics under-recorded the true levels of crime in Ireland. The report was based on a sample that was open to the possibility of errors, whereas the Garda statistics are based on consistent national recording of actual crimes reported and recorded.

The problem with official crime statistics is not confined to Ireland and indeed the situation here is favourable by international standards. A continuous series of crimes recorded by the Gardaí since 1927 is available. The crime statistics in Ireland were a useful indicator that the level of crime increased dramatically since the 1960s. In 1966, 19,029 crimes were recorded and in 1983 the level of crime reached 102,387. For the remainder of the 1980s the level of recorded crime in Ireland was less than the 1983 figure. From 1990 to 1995 the level of recorded crime began to increase again and in 1995 the number of recorded crimes in Ireland reached a figure of 102,484 which is marginally greater than the figure for 1983. For 1996 the number of recorded crimes was 100,785; this represents a reduction of 2 per cent over the previous year. In 1997 the Garda Síochána recorded 90,888 crimes in Ireland. The 1997 figure represents a reduction of approximately 10 per cent over 1996.

The alternative methods used to measure crime are: firstly, 'victimisation studies' as used by the ESRI where surveys are carried out among the population to determine the level of crime victimisation and, secondly, 'self-report' studies whereby, for the purpose of the study, a sample of the population would be surveyed and asked to report crimes which they had committed. These alternatives may well turn out to be less reliable than the officially recorded statistics. In the case of 'victimisation studies' it is possible that a number of respondents would regard themselves as having been the victim of a single crime. In addition 'victimisation studies' would be incapable of measuring the level of serious crimes such as murder and manslaughter where the victims have been killed. The problem associated with 'self-report' studies is that respondents may either exaggerate the amount of crime which they have committed, or they may choose not to report the true level of crime which they have committed.

One area of difficulty for officially recorded crimes is the scenario that some crimes are 'victimless' and therefore can only be recorded if detected by the Gardaí. Drug trafficking offences may be described as being 'victimless' crimes in the sense that no one person can be identified as being the victim of the drug dealer's crime. Another example of a 'victimless' crime is the offence of handling stolen goods. The extent of handling offences can never be measured because these offences only come to light when detected by the Gardaí since there is no specific victim who can report the offence of handling stolen goods. The official crime statistics can never fully measure the incidence of these types of crimes. The extent of the drug problem can only be estimated by reference to a number of indicators, including, the number of seizures, the quantity of drugs seized, the number of persons charged with drug offences, the increase in crime which is committed by drug abusers, the number of addicts, etc. The Garda Annual Report has been useful in showing that the drug problem has increased in Ireland since the start of the 1980s. The number and quantity of seizures as well as the number of persons charged are useful 'proxy' measures of the trend in the drug problem in Ireland. Another 'proxy' measure of police performance in relation to drug dealing is the increase in the price of drugs as the supply falls.

The rationale for police service evaluation

The main rationale for police service evaluation has been the existence of budgetary stress in the public sector. Given that additional financial resources were not available, the focus of attention moved towards concerns about 'economy', 'efficiency' and 'effectiveness'. There has been a move towards ensuring that the police are achieving value for money and even more importantly that they are achieving the best value possible. This involves making the correct choice from a number of options aimed at achieving the best value. Guy (1992) tells us that 'standards for outputs are rare in the police service. Officers are allocated to general patrol duties, but few forces conduct regular analyses to find out what they are actually doing.' Guy questions the effectiveness of the police officer on foot patrol. 'The PC (police constable) on the average urban foot-beat passes within 100 yards of a burglary in progress once every eight years and is even then unlikely to be able to detect that it is occurring.' This does not suggest that the police should not employ any resources on the beat. On the contrary, research has shown that the public can often place a higher value on the police officer showing a genuine concern for the victim when taking a crime report, than on whether the crime is solved.

Leishman and Savage (1993) have challenged two main objections to police service evaluation. Those objections are 'that much police work is symbolic and thus non-measurable, and that those indicators traditionally available through officially recorded figures of offences and clear-ups are unreliable'. As regards the symbolic nature of police work, Leishman and Savage feel that there is no reason why the effects of it cannot in some way be measured. The 'feeling that something is being done' which crime victims may appreciate can be measured as an outcome through the use of customer satisfaction forms. The concept of evaluating all kinds of outcomes arising from police activity has resulted in Her Majesty's Inspectorate Branch developing a matrix of indicators, including force establishment and personnel information, incidents recorded, crimes recorded and detected, arrests and traffic accidents.

One very strong argument in the area of police performance evaluation is the view that only that which is measured gets done. If one goes along with that view then it is important to ensure that evaluation is focused upon all of the important areas of activity. Otherwise resources will be concentrated in areas of activity which are subject to performance evaluation, to the possible detriment of areas of equal importance which are not monitored. Performance evaluation is an effective tool to develop control and accountability and to promote transparency in the police service. Behaviour will be modified when members of the police service are aware that their activity is subject to scrutiny and to publication in reports.

There are many public servants who are firmly of the view that evaluation is not appropriate at all in the context of the caring services which are provided in health, education and policing. There is also a view that it may negatively affect quality of service. It would be undesirable if police officers were perceived, by members of the public, to be in a hurry to respond to the next call rather than spending time to reassure the victim.

It can be argued that it is not possible ever to get over the technical behavioural difficulties involved in measuring non-tangible outputs such as are produced by the police. For example, the temptation may present itself to massage the figures in order to reach the required targets. Another problem area may occur when an emphasis on evaluation may lead to a concentration on solving large numbers of less serious crimes to the detriment of solving the major crimes such as homicide and sexual offences.

The cost of evaluation is a factor which must be considered. It would be undesirable to have a situation whereby the measurement function within the organisation grew at the expense of the core service. To counteract this it is important to ensure that as much as possible of the measurement required for evaluation is generated automatically by computer.

Despite the problems which exist in relation to police service evaluation, the case in favour is strong provided that the difficulties mentioned above can be overcome. Evaluation will lead to a better awareness of opportunity costs, i.e. the next best alternative use of police resources. Good management will result in the allocation of resources in a way that will lead to a reduction in the level of crime recorded or to an increase in the number of offenders who are apprehended. Evaluation of police performance will be most effective when related to the organisational goals of the police force.

Evaluation in the police service in practice

One of the classic examples of a survey-based quasi-experimental design is the Kansas City patrol experiment conducted in the early 1970s by the Police Foundation, a non-profit organisation established by the Ford Foundation to study law enforcement practices. The purpose of the Kansas City experiment was to determine whether or not police patrols made a difference in the reduction of crime rates, police response times to crime, and citizen perceptions of the police.

The basic design of the experiment was structured around the division of city-wide levels of police protection. One area of the city was assigned two to three times the normal number of patrol cars, another area had no patrol cars, and a third area was assigned the regular number of patrol cars; the third area represented the control group. The central hypothesis behind the experiment was the contention that crime would increase in an area with fewer patrols, decrease in an area with more patrols, and remain the same in an area where the patrol levels remained unchanged. Similarly, researchers hypothesised that an area with greater police presence would demonstrate a better police response time to the report of crimes and show more positive attitudes among the citizens towards the police generally. A team of investigators conducted the research over a one-year period.

One of the most interesting survey outcomes was the revelation that the number of police patrols had little or no relationship with the level of crime. There was no change at all in the time it took the police to respond to the report of a crime.

Many commentators felt that there were flaws in the design of the research because the experiment was not conducted under properly controlled experimental conditions and for that reason the results could not be generalised to apply to other locations. Others felt that the scheme lacked external validity. It was also considered to lack internal validity. For instance people moving from one location to another may have come to believe that the police were present in areas where this was not the case. Also police cars pursued criminals through areas which were supposed to have no police cars. The experiment came to an end for ethical reasons. Many people felt that it was outrageous that the police should take it upon themselves to decide to deploy resources in one location and at the same time to leave others unprotected. The evaluators were criticised for not considering this aspect of the matter and eventually the project was abandoned.

Such an attempt at creating laboratory conditions to carry on an experiment in the real world has not been tried elsewhere and it is not likely to be repeated. Although this is an extreme example of evaluating police performance, it nevertheless points to one of the major unresolved issues, namely, the question of whether policing patrols are effective in preventing crime or if they only serve to reassure the public. The Audit Commission in the United Kingdom has introduced more conventional forms of evaluation in order to improve efficiency and effectiveness in the police and fire services.

For example, the Audit Commission (1990) has drawn up a system whereby the police are in a position to charge for services in certain circumstances. Under this system the cost of providing the service is greater than the wage costs of the officers concerned. The total cost is made up of: (a) a basic hourly rate multiplied by the number of hours, (b) a charge for administration, (c) a charge for extra hours (including travel, briefing and planning), and (d) transport costs. Charging for services in the UK can apply not only to outside agencies but also between police forces. Training courses are regularly purchased by one police force from another.

In the context of the Garda Síochána, a topical example is the 'Value for money examination' which was carried out, by the Comptroller and Auditor General (1995), on the management of Garda transport. The report concluded that a labour chargeout rate of £74 an hour would be required to absorb all costs from the hours scheduled for repair work. This figure compared very unfavourably with the industry norm of £20 to £30 an hour in commercial garages. The report also found that the cost of maintenance of vehicles at the Garda garage, for each completed mile, was over three times that of vehicles maintained at commercial garages. In addition the time used for a sample of jobs at the Garda garage was found to be almost twice that recommended by manufacturers for those jobs.

Following the report of the Comptroller and Auditor General a Transport Working Group was established in 1995. This group produced a report which is called 'Management of the Garda Transport Services (A Review)'. This report made a number of recommendations aimed at improving efficiency. It included: setting targets for productivity in the workshop, agreeing an objective measurement for productivity, developing a fleet allocation model, and setting minimum utilisation levels for all vehicle categories. The report of the Comptroller and Auditor General and the report of the Transport Working Group were meaningful because there is a commercial alternative to the Garda garage where market forces are in operation. In other areas of policing no such alternatives exist and therefore real evaluation would be more indeterminate.

The foregoing examples of costing systems and independent evaluation illustrate in a practical way efforts to identify cost anomalies and to devise rational methods of costing the police resources used in services. These are useful in helping to ensure efficiency in the police service. The issue of effectiveness, as noted in this and other chapters in this volume, is much more difficult to address. It requires assessing public satisfaction, which is estimated through surveys, etc.

Applying UK performance indicators: 999 calls

In the United Kingdom each force sets its own target for answering 999 calls but there is a high level of consistency between forces. Most forces aim to answer 999 telephone calls within 10 to 15 seconds. The second indicator chosen in the area of emergency calls is the time it takes for the first mobile police resource to arrive at the scene. In general, the target time set is between 10 and 15 minutes in urban areas and 20 minutes in rural areas. Experience has shown that it is possible to achieve a 90 per cent performance in the target of 10 minutes in urban areas and 20 minutes in rural areas. Figure 13.1 below shows a sample of the performance of some forces in England and Wales in 1994.

The Garda Síochána in Ireland, particularly in Dublin, could set targets similar to those used by the Audit Commission in England and Wales. Figure 13.2 shows the percentage of 999 calls answered per 5-second interval in the Dublin Metropolitan Area in 1993.

Of course, caution is necessary when looking at the performance of police forces in different countries because in a strict sense 'like' is not being compared with 'like'. However, in a broad sense it is useful to look at different police forces to gain a general picture.

Figure 13.1: UK 999 call and immediate response incident target times and performance in 1994

	Local target for answering 999 calls	Performance	Target time for response to incidents requiring immediate response	Performance
English shire Police forces				
Avon & Somerset	90% in 10 seconds (96.8% within target times)	86%	15 minutes, urban areas 20 seconds rural areas	95%
Bedfordshire	10 seconds	84%	Urban = 10 minutes Rural = 20 minutes	70%
Cleveland	90% of 999 calls within 20 seconds	97%	90% of calls within 10 minutes in urban areas and 20 minutes in rural areas	66%

Figure 13.2: Garda 999 response times for the Dublin Metropolitan Area in 1993

Time in seconds	0-5	5-10	10-15	15-20	20-25	25-30	30-60
Percentage of calls	47.00%	15.00%	9.00%	13.00%	7.00%	7.00%	2.00%
Cumulative percentage		47.00%	62.00%	71.00%	84.00%	91.00%	98.00%	100.00%

The technology is available to monitor the call 'pick-up' time at the Garda Communications Centre at Harcourt Square. In the Dublin Metropolitan Area the Gardaí already monitor the time it takes for mobile resources to arrive at the scene of emergency calls.

For the purpose of applying the Audit Commission indicators, 'Emergency' and 'Priority 1' calls are re-grouped into a single group which is referred to as incidents which require an immediate response. Figure 13.3 shows a sample of 'Emergency', Priority 1, Priority 2 and Priority 3 calls as classified by the Garda Síochána.

Figure 13.3: Garda classification of incidents by order of priority

Call Code	Description	Priority
ARMD	ARMED PERSON	EMERGENCY
BOMB	BOMB ON PREMISES	EMERGENCY
PLANE	AIR CRASH	EMERGENCY
ROBB	ROBBERY	EMERGENCY
ACCS	SERIOUS ACCIDENT	PRIORITY 1
GDASS	GARDA REQUIRES ASSISTANCE	PRIORITY 1
PALM	PANIC ALARM	PRIORITY 1
PUBORD	BREACH OF PUBLIC ORDER	PRIORITY 1
ALRM	BURGLAR ALARM	PRIORITY 2
ASLT	ASSAULT	PRIORITY 2
CTHF	CRIME RELATING TO THEFT	PRIORITY 2
DDRIVE	DANGEROUS DRIVING	PRIORITY 2
ACC	MINOR TRAFFIC ACCIDENT	PRIORITY 3
COMP	COMPLAINT FROM MEMBER OF PUBLIC	PRIORITY 3
LCAR	THEFT FROM CAR	PRIORITY 3
SOC	SCENE OF CRIME TO BE EXAMINED	PRIORITY 3

For comparative purposes Figure 13.4 applies the Audit Commission response times to the Garda Síochána performance in the Dublin Metropolitan Area in 1996. The figure indicates that the Garda Síochána performs relatively well. Of course, the need to pursue improvement in performance is ever present.

Figure 13.4: Comparison between UK and Garda response times

	Local target for answering 999 calls	Performance	Target time for response to incidents requiring immediate response	Performance
English shire Police forces				
Avon & Somerset	90% in 10 seconds 100% in 20 seconds	86%	15 minutes, urban areas 20 minutes, rural areas	95%
Bedfordshire	10 seconds	84%	Urban = 10 minutes Rural = 20 minutes	70% 70%
Warwickshire	15 seconds	89%	Urban = 10 minutes Rural = 20 minutes	73%
West Mercia	10 seconds	95%	Urban 85% in 10 minutes Rural 85% in 20 minutes	87%
Ireland	*An Garda Síochána*			
Dublin Metropolitan Area	No target but 88% of calls answered within 20 seconds and 98% answered within 30 seconds		Target of 15 minutes in the Dublin Metropolitan Area for Emergency and Priority 1 Calls	81%

Applying UK performance indicators: crime and detection

Crime and detection rates are reasonable performance indicators for any police service to choose in order to evaluate its performance. It should be realised that there may be variations in the definition of what constitutes a recorded crime in various jurisdictions. The three Audit Commission indicators for crime are:

- Number of recorded crimes per 1,000 of population
- Percentage of crimes detected by primary means
- Number of crimes detected by primary means per officer.

Number of recorded crimes per 1,000 of population

At the time of writing the 1996 figures are the most recently published figures for recorded and detected crime in Ireland. Therefore these figures are used here when applying the Audit Commission indicators. The 1996 census of population found that there were 3,621,035 people in the Republic of Ireland compared with 3,525,719 in 1991, an increase of 95,316. The total number of recorded crimes in Ireland in 1996 was 100,785. There were 27.8 indictable crimes recorded in the Republic of Ireland per 1,000 of population in 1996. This figure is lower than the figure for any police force in England and Wales where it ranges from a high of 148 crimes per 1,000 people to a low of 65 crimes per 1,000 people.

In 1996, the population of the Dublin Metropolitan Area (DMA) was 1,082,048. The recorded level of crime in the DMA in 1996 was 58,759, which amounts to 54.3 crimes per 1,000 of population in Dublin. Compared with England and Wales this figure is well below the low range of 65 crimes per 1,000 of population. One must always be careful about comparisons in relation to crime figures. The crime classifications may vary somewhat between the UK and Ireland.

Percentage of crimes detected by primary means

The Audit Commission (1995) defines the term 'primary means' to denote cases where the police need to carry out an investigation to solve the crime. Figure 13.5 shows a summary table for England and Wales for crime and detection. 'Secondary means' covers cases where crimes are solved without the need for direct investigation, e.g. as a result of a tip-off or as a result of a culprit asking a court to take other undetected crimes into consideration before sentence is passed.

Figure 13.5: Crime and detection for England and Wales

	High range	Average	Low range
Crimes per 1,000 population	148	96	65
% of crimes detected by primary means	35%	23%	16%
Detections per officer per annum	14	10	7

In Ireland no distinction is drawn between crimes which are solved by 'primary' or 'secondary' means. Because of this it is not possible to have a true comparison between the Irish and UK figures for crimes detected by 'primary means'. In 1996 in Ireland 41,056 crimes were solved, out of a total recorded figure of 100,785, to give a detection rate of 41per cent.

Detections per officer

In the United Kingdom detections per officer range from a high of fourteen to a low of seven detections per officer. In 1996 in Ireland the number of detections per Garda was approximately four. It may seem as if the number of detections per Garda is low by comparison with the UK but it should be pointed out that the level of recorded crime in Ireland per 1,000 of population is considerably lower than in the UK. If the number of crimes committed per 1,000 of population is lower then, other things being equal, the number of detections per Garda may also be lower.

Applying United Kingdom performance indicators: police resources

In the United Kingdom the Audit Commission has chosen two indicators in the area of evaluating resources. These are the number of officers per 1,000 of population and the expenditure on policing per head of population. Figure 13.6 shows a summary for England and Wales.

Figure 13.6: Police resources in England and Wales compared with those of the Garda Síochána

	England and Wales			Garda Síochána
	High Range	Average	Low Range	
Officers per 1,000 population	3.3	2.2	1.8	2.99
Expenditure on policing per head	£140	£97	£81	£116

In 1996 the Garda Síochána had a strength of 10,817 and in the same year, according to the census of population, there were 3,621,035 people living in the Republic of Ireland. The cost of running the Garda Síochána in 1996 is estimated to have been approximately £425,672,000. Therefore, the number of Gardaí per 1,000 of population in Ireland in 1996 was 2.99 and policing in Ireland cost £116 per head of population. The cost of policing per head of population in Ireland in 1996 is well within the range of UK costs as set out in the Audit Commission report (1995). The range for the UK varies from a lower figure of £81 per head of population to an upper figure of £140 per head. The number of Gardaí per 1,000 of population, at 2.99 Gardaí per 1,000, is approaching the higher figure for the UK, which is 3.3 officers for every 1,000 people.

Recent developments in Ireland

On 2 July 1996 the Steering Group on the Review of the Garda Síochána was established. The review was conducted within the framework of the Strategic Management Initiative and the Delivering Better Government Programme. Its terms of reference were as follows:

- to examine the operation of the Garda Síochána, against the background of the challenges it now faces and is likely to face
- to consider the relationship between the Garda Síochána and other state agencies in the broad crime area
- to recommend changes that would enhance the efficiency and effectiveness of the Garda Síochána, particularly relating to:
  - the role and function of the Force
  - its management structures and systems
  - policing practices
  - manpower and other resource issues
  - training and development
  - deployment of resources, including manpower.

The terms of reference were extended on 4 of September 1996 by a government decision as follows:

> The future arrangements for promotion to the Assistant Commissioner ranks, and the interview process for promotion to all ranks under the Garda Promotion Regulations, should be considered within the context of the Strategic Management Initiative Review of the Garda Síochána.

The government had asked the Steering Group to report by the end of December 1996. In fact the Steering Group found that it was unable to report within that time. The Steering Group submitted its report to government in June 1997 and it was published in November 1997. To assist the Steering Group in addressing its terms of reference, it commissioned Deloitte and Touche, Management Consultants, to undertake an operations and organisation review of the Garda Síochána. The study was carried out from September to December 1996.

Garda deployment, inter-departmental group report, executive summary

The government decided that there should be a joint review by the Departments of Justice and Finance in consultation with the Garda Síochána, of the use and distribution of staffing and resources in the Gardaí. The study established that 58 per cent of Gardaí are deployed on regular uniformed duties, 16 per cent are engaged on detective duties and the remaining 26 per cent are in other posts such as protection posts, clerical/administrative posts, the Traffic Corps and the Transport Unit.

Changes proposed

Greater flexibility in rostering
The Steering Committee is of the view that there should be a more rational rostering system, which would mean that the supply of Garda service would be linked to the demand. The current roster system divides the number of available Gardaí evenly over the 24-hour period while there are considerable variations in the demand for Garda service.

Rationalisation of station opening hours
In the Dublin Metropolitan Area there are 42 stations which are manned on a 24-hour basis. More Gardaí would be available for patrol duty if the opening hours of some of the stations were adjusted to more realistic levels commensurate with actual public usage and demand.

Civilianisation
The Steering Committee is of the view that civilianisation of clerical/administrative and specialised positions is a cost-effective way of increasing the operational strength of the Force without actually increasing Garda numbers.

Transfer of non-operational duties
A number of duties which have been traditionally carried out by the Garda Síochána are due to be transferred to other bodies. These include weights and measures, fines on the spot/tow away services and car pound.

Legal/administrative changes
The following are among the areas identified for change:
• More stringent procedures with regard to false alarms
• Delivery of summonses by non-Garda personnel
• Replacement of court officers by civilian personnel
• Reduction of Garda time spent in Court by:
   – Having evidence of arrest, charge and caution given by certificate in Court
   – The use of prosecuting inspectors in Dublin courts
   – The introduction of alternatives to prosecution, particularly with regard to road traffic offences.

Some of the recommendations for change are already being implemented. The Criminal Justice (Miscellaneous Provisions) Act, 1997 has allowed for the admission of evidence of arrest, charge and caution to be given by way of certificate in court. The Weights and Measures function has been transferred to another statutory agency. The recommendations in relation to civilianisation, changes in rosters and rationalisation of station opening hours have for a long time been both recognised and supported by Garda management.

Conclusion

Many aspects of policing are not quantifiable. The evaluating of police outputs and outcomes such as crime prevention and public reassurance is most difficult. Nevertheless, there has been a growing belief in recent years that attempts should be made to introduce some form of evaluation of non-tangible outputs. The way forward is to make comparisons between different forces within a country or between countries and to continue to compare the performance of individual forces over time. It would be necessary to be satisfied that one was comparing like with like in order to ensure consistency. It would really bring confidence to the whole process of police evaluation if an international organisation, e.g. the EU or the OECD, were to draw up definitions and standards which could be applied across police forces and indeed in regions and divisions in particular police forces.

Actual measures of performance are best for evaluating the service provided by the police. In the absence of actual measures of performance, some form of 'proxy' measures or 'indicators' are a second best alternative. Actual or proxy measures, when properly conducted, help to ensure that the police service is yielding value for money and assist managers in deciding upon resource allocation. Measures are just part of the story; the results need to be acted upon and action requires a programme for implementation.

REFERENCES

Audit Commission (1995). *Local Authority Performance Indicators,* Vol. 3: Police and Fire Services, London: HMSO

Audit Commission (1990). Police Papers, *Effective Policing: Performance Review in Police Forces,* Number 8, London: HMSO

Audit Commission (1990). Police Papers, *Taking Care of the Coppers: Income Generation by Provincial Forces.* No. 7, London: HMSO

Begg D., S. Fisher, R. Dornbusch (1995). *Economics,* British Edition, McGraw Hill

Boyle R. (1989). *Managing Public Sector Performance, A comparative study of performance monitoring systems in the public and private sectors,* Dublin: Institute of Public Administration

Comptroller and Auditor General (1995). *Report on Value for Money Examination, Department of Justice, Garda Transport,* Dublin: Stationery Office, August PN. 1858

Dáil Éireann (1995). Committee of Public Accounts, *Report on Value for Money Examinations*, PN.2643

Economist, The (1994). *Measuring Crime: A Shadow on Society*, October 15

Edmonds D., and D. McCready (1994). 'Costing and Pricing of Police Services', *International Journal of Public Sector Management*, Vol. 7 No. 5, MCB University Press

ESRI (1985). *Crime Victimisation in the Republic of Ireland*, Dublin: ESRI

Dept of Finance (1997). *Estimates for Public Services (Abridged Version) and Summary Capital Programme*, Dublin: Stationery Office

Garda Síochána (1997). *Annual Report, 1996,* Government of Ireland

Guy, B. (1992). 'Value-for-Money in the Police Service', *Public Money and Management*, January-March

Keogh E. (1994). MSc. Thesis, University of Dublin (Trinity College)

Leishman F., and S. P. Savage (1993). *Managing the New Public Services*, London: The MacMillan Press Ltd

An Garda Síochána, (1996). *Management of the Garda Transport Services (A Review)*, Dublin: Stationery Office

Mulreany M. (1991). *Efficiency and Effectiveness in the Public Domain*, Dublin: Institute of Public Administration

OECD (1995). *Governance in Transition, Public Management Reforms in OECD Countries*, Paris: OECD

Report of the Steering Group on the Efficiency and Effectiveness of the Garda Síochána, Dublin: Stationery Office, 1997

Sheehy Sir P. (Chairman) (1993). *Inquiry into Police Responsibilities and Rewards*, London: HMSO

Stiglitz J. E. (1988) *Economics of the Public Sector*, Second Edition, New York: W. W. Norton

I

Glossary

Appraisal: A process of defining objectives, assessing options and evaluating costs and benefits undertaken before making a decision.

Audit: An investigation into whether an activity meets the standards set out in an auditing document. An audit can be conducted by either external or internal auditors. An external auditor, whether a major firm of accountants or the Comptroller and Auditor General will, where possible, use externally agreed audit standards. Internal audit is an appraisal of the effectiveness of internal controls used to improve the efficient use of resources within an organisation.

Benchmarking: A systematic analysis of an organisation's performance against that of another. It may measure products, services, practices or the processes by which output is delivered.

Consumer surplus: A measure of the difference between the value consumers place on their consumption of a commodity and the amount they actually pay for it.

Contingent valuation: A method of evaluation which allows economic values to be estimated for commodities not traded in markets. It works by directly finding out from a sample of people in carefully designed hypothetical markets their willingness to pay or willingness to accept compensation for a change brought about by a project, programme or policy.

Cost-benefit analysis: An analysis which attempts to quantify costs and benefits in money terms. It includes the evaluation of costs and benefits where there are no market values as, for example, where lives are saved by improved road systems. A project is worth undertaking if social costs exceed social benefits. Cost benefit analysis can be carried out either 'ex ante' or 'ex post', i.e. before or after an intervention.

Cost effectiveness analysis: An analysis which examines alternative ways, with their associated costs, of achieving the same result. It assesses the relative costs of the options for achieving a set objective with the aim of selecting the option which minimises net present cost.

Cost utility analysis: An analysis which attempts to assess how much 'well being' is produced by different interventions in relation to their cost. It is used in health economics to value states of health. Cost utility evaluations often use the 'quality adjusted life year' measure which allows comparisons across healthcare programmes as varied as heart surgery, health education and ante-natal screening.

Deadweight: Deadweight occurs when part of a public expenditure programme confers benefits on recipients other than those at whom the expenditure was aimed.

Discounting: The process of finding the present value of a future amount. In essence, discounting reverses the process of compound interest.

Discount rate: The interest rate used to find the present value of a future amount by discounting.

Displacement: Displacement occurs when the creation of a positive programme output in one area leads to a loss of output in another area.

Economy: Minimising the cost of inputs or reducing waste. To achieve economy the quality should be specified and the cost of acquiring inputs of this quality should be the lowest obtainable.

Effectiveness: The extent to which objectives are achieved. Effectiveness involves the assessment of how well actual results met the intended results. Effectiveness does not refer to costs.

Efficiency: The relationship between inputs and outputs. An improvement in efficiency occurs where the level of output increases from a given level of input or where the level of input declines for a given level of output.

Evaluation: The 'ex post' assessment of the extent to which project, programme or policy objectives have been achieved and how economically and efficiently. An evaluation may use pre-set criteria and systematically collected and analysed data.

Externalities: Costs or benefits of a transaction that are incurred or received by members of society but are not taken into account through the market mechanism by the parties to the transaction.

Indicator: A less precise or proxy measure used when it is not possible directly to measure output or performance.

Internal rate of return: A discounted measure of project value. The maximum interest that a project can pay for the resources used if the project is to recover its investment and operating expenses and still just break even.

Investment appraisal: A systematic process of clarifying objectives, assessing alternative ways of meeting them and valuing the cost and benefit of each alternative.

Measure: A quantification of output (e.g. miles of pipeline laid or number of cases processed) or performance (e.g. cost per mile of pipeline or cases processed per person).

Net present value: A discounted measure of project value. The present value of the benefits less the present value of the costs of a project.

Opportunity cost: The benefit foregone by using a scarce resource for one purpose instead of its next best alternative use.

Outcomes: What has been achieved in relation to objectives. In the case of resource-use, for example, an outcome might be the use of fewer resources than planned. In the case of a health publicity campaign it might be a 10 per cent increase in awareness among those targeted. Outcomes are different than outputs which measure what is actually produced or done.

Outputs: The goods or services produced by an organisation. Outputs may be poor indicators of outcomes. For example, the number of training programmes delivered is an output but the effect of the gain in skills on long-term employment is an outcome. An intermediate output is one which contributes to the final output.

Performance budgeting: A form of budgeting organised around programmes and activities and linked to measurable performance goals. Performance budgeting focuses on the level of output and what it costs.

Performance management: A systematic approach to performance involving the setting of performance objectives, the managerial freedom to achieve these objectives, the measurement of actual performance and the use of the information gained in decision-making.

Performance measurement: The assessment of outcomes, outputs or inputs. For example, performance measurement will include ratios for economy and efficiency. Performance measures can be used for comparisons over time or at a given time between units doing comparable work.

Performance indicators: Measures used as proxies when output or performance is not directly measurable.

Police car effect: An effect of greater compliance with regulations by people when they think they are being evaluated than when they think they are not.

Productivity: An efficiency measure which usually relates a physical output to an input. For example, labour productivity may be stated in such terms as cases processed per 'man-day.'

Programme: Expenditure or activity covering a group of related projects or policy objectives.

Project: Expenditure or activity which is once-off and discrete in nature, for example a drainage project.

Randomised controlled trial: An experiment in which people are assigned in a random way to two groups one of which gets an intervention and the other of which does not. The group which does not get the intervention is the control group; instead it may be given a placebo. The control group is the basis against which to compare the effect of the intervention on the other group.

Reliability: The extent to which an evaluation outcome is predictable in the sense that the outcome would be the same if carried out more than once by the same or different assessors having access to the same evidence. An evaluation is reliable if the same results are obtained over time or if different evaluators make comparable judgement based on the same evidence.

Shadow price: A price attributed to a good or factor of production in preference to the market price. Market prices might not be appropriate in certain circumstances; for example because of minimum wage and other labour market regulations the wages actually paid may not be an accurate measure of the real cost of labour.

Target: A quantified objective with a defined timescale. Targets are often associated with cost or efficiency levels. A target may take the form of a 'milestone', i.e. an indicator agreed at the outset of what objectives should be achieved, by when.

Unit cost: The cost of producing an output divided by the number of units in the output; for example the cost of administration per welfare benefit paid or the cost per mile of road. Unit cost can also refer to input, for example, the cost per unit of manpower.

Validity: The extent to which an evaluation matches what is being evaluated. For example, a driving test is a valid test of driving ability whereas a written test is not. External validity refers to the likelihood that the outcome of an evaluation would be the same if the evaluation was replicated in a different setting.

Value for money: The economic and social benefit of a project, programme or policy in relation to the cost. Value for money is often used as a term to describe the optimum combination of economy, efficiency and effectiveness.

Variable: Variables are classified as dependent and independent. The dependent variable is associated with or perhaps caused by the independent variable. For example, when we say that consumption depends on income the dependent variable is consumption and the independent variable is income.

II

Discount Tables

Table 1: Present value of €1

Years	1%	2%	3%	4%	5%	6%	7%	8%	9%	10%
1	0.9901	0.9804	0.9709	0.9615	0.9524	0.9434	0.9346	0.9259	0.9174	0.9091
2	0.9803	0.9612	0.9426	0.9426	0.9070	0.8900	0.8734	0.8573	0.8417	0.8264
3	0.9706	0.9423	0.9151	0.8890	0.8638	0.8396	0.8163	0.7938	0.7722	0.7513
4	0.9610	0.9238	0.8885	0.8548	0.8227	0.7921	0.7629	0.7350	0.7084	0.6830
5	0.9515	0.9057	0.8626	0.8219	0.7835	0.7473	0.7130	0.6806	0.6499	0.6209
6	0.9420	0.8880	0.8375	0.7903	0.7462	0.7050	0.6663	0.6302	0.5963	0.5645
7	0.9327	0.8706	0.8131	0.7599	0.7107	0.6651	0.6227	0.5835	0.5470	0.5132
8	0.9235	0.8535	0.7894	0.7307	0.6768	0.6274	0.5820	0.5403	0.5019	0.4665
9	0.9143	0.8368	0.7664	0.7026	0.6446	0.5919	0.5439	0.5002	0.4604	0.4241
10	0.9053	0.8203	0.7441	0.6756	0.6139	0.5584	0.5083	0.4632	0.4224	0.3855
11	0.8963	0.8043	0.7224	0.6496	0.5847	0.5268	0.4751	0.4289	0.3875	0.3505
12	0.8874	0.7885	0.7014	0.6246	0.5568	0.4970	0.4440	0.3971	0.3555	0.3186
13	0.8787	0.7730	0.6810	0.6006	0.5303	0.4688	0.4150	0.3677	0.3262	0.2897
14	0.8700	0.7579	0.6611	0.5775	0.5051	0.4423	0.3878	0.3405	0.2992	0.2633
15	0.8613	0.7430	0.6419	0.5553	0.4810	0.4173	0.3624	0.3152	0.2745	0.2394
16	0.8528	0.7284	0.6232	0.5339	0.4581	0.3936	0.3387	0.2919	0.2519	0.2176
17	0.8444	0.7142	0.6050	0.5134	0.4363	0.3714	0.3166	0.2703	0.2311	0.1978
18	0.8360	0.7002	0.5874	0.4936	0.4155	0.3503	0.2959	0.2502	0.2120	0.1799
19	0.8277	0.6864	0.5703	0.4746	0.3957	0.3305	0.2765	0.2317	0.1945	0.1635
20	0.8195	0.6730	0.5537	0.4564	0.3769	0.3118	0.2584	0.2145	0.1784	0.1486
21	0.8114	0.6598	0.5375	0.4388	0.3589	0.2942	0.2415	0.1987	0.1637	0.1351
22	0.8034	0.6468	0.5219	0.4220	0.3418	0.2775	0.2257	0.1839	0.1502	0.1228
23	0.7954	0.6342	0.5067	0.4057	0.3256	0.2618	0.2109	0.1703	0.1378	0.1117
24	0.7876	0.6217	0.4919	0.3901	0.3101	0.2470	0.1971	0.1577	0.1264	0.1015
25	0.7798	0.6095	0.4776	0.3751	0.2953	0.2330	0.1842	0.1460	0.1160	0.0923

Table 1: (continued)

Years	11%	12%	13%	14%	15%	16%	17%	18%	19%	20%
1	0.9009	0.8929	0.8850	0.8772	0.8696	0.8621	0.8547	0.8475	0.8403	0.8333
2	0.8116	0.7972	0.7831	0.7695	0.7561	0.7432	0.7305	0.7182	0.7062	0.6944
3	0.7312	0.7118	0.6931	0.6750	0.6575	0.6407	0.6244	0.6086	0.5934	0.5787
4	0.6587	0.6355	0.6133	0.5921	0.5718	0.5523	0.5337	0.5158	0.4987	0.4823
5	0.5935	0.5674	0.5428	0.5194	0.4972	0.4761	0.4561	0.4371	0.4190	0.4019
6	0.5346	0.5066	0.4803	0.4556	0.4323	0.4104	0.3898	0.3704	0.3521	0.3349
7	0.4817	0.4523	0.4251	0.3996	0.3759	0.3538	0.3332	0.3139	0.2959	0.2791
8	0.4339	0.4039	0.3762	0.3506	0.3269	0.3050	0.2848	0.2660	0.2487	0.2326
9	0.3909	0.3606	0.3329	0.3075	0.2843	0.2630	0.2434	0.2255	0.2090	0.1938
10	0.3522	0.3220	0.2946	0.2697	0.2472	0.2267	02080	0.1911	0.1756	0.1615
11	0.3173	0.2875	0.2607	0.2366	0.2149	0.1954	0.1778	0.1619	0.1476	0.1346
12	0.2858	0.2567	0.2307	0.2076	0.1869	0.1685	0.1520	0.1372	0.1240	0.1122
13	0.2575	0.2292	0.2042	0.1821	0.1625	0.1452	0.1299	0.1163	0.1042	0.0935
14	0.2320	0.2046	0.1807	0.1597	0.1413	0.1252	0.1110	0.0985	0.0876	0.0779
15	0.2090	0.1827	0.1599	0.1401	0.1229	0.1079	0.0949	0.0835	0.0736	0.0649
16	0.1883	0.1631	0.1415	0.1229	0.1069	0.0930	0.0811	0.0708	0.0618	0.0541
17	0.1696	0.1456	0.1252	0.1078	0.0929	0.0802	0.0693	0.0600	0.0520	0.0451
18	0.1528	0.1300	0.1108	0.0946	0.0808	0.0691	0.0592	0.0508	0.0437	0.0376
19	0.1377	0.1161	0.0981	0.0829	0.0703	0.0596	0.0506	0.0431	0.0367	0.0313
20	0.1240	0.1037	0.0868	0.0728	0.0611	0.0514	0.0433	0.0365	0.0308	0.0261
21	0.1117	0.0926	0.0768	0.0638	0.0531	0.0443	0.0370	0.0309	0.0259	0.0217
22	0.1007	0.0826	0.0680	0.0560	0.0462	0.0382	0.0316	0.0262	0.0218	0.0181
23	0.0907	0.0738	0.0601	0.0491	0.0402	0.0329	0.0270	0.0222	0.0183	0.0151
24	0.0817	0.0659	0.0532	0.0431	0.0349	0.0284	0.0231	0.0188	0.0154	0.0126
25	0.0736	0.0588	0.0471	0.0378	0.0304	0.0245	0.0197	0.0160	0.0129	0.0105

Table 1: (continued)

Years	21%	22%	23%	24%	25%	26%	27%	28%	29%	30%
1	0.8264	0.8197	0.8130	0.8065	0.8000	0.7937	0.7874	0.7813	0.7752	0.7692
2	0.6830	0.6719	0.6610	0.6504	0.6400	0.6299	0.6200	0.6104	0.6009	0.5917
3	0.5645	0.5507	0.5374	0.5245	0.5120	0.4999	0.4882	0.4768	0.4658	0.4552
4	0.4665	0.4514	0.4369	0.4230	0.4096	0.3968	0.3844	0.3725	0.3611	0.3501
5	0.3855	0.3700	0.3552	0.3411	0.3277	0.3149	0.3027	0.2910	0.2799	0.2693
6	0.3186	0.3033	0.2888	0.2751	0.2621	0.2499	0.2383	0.2274	0.2170	0.2072
7	0.2633	0.2486	0.2348	0.2218	0.2097	0.1983	0.1877	0.1776	0.1682	0.1594
8	0.2176	0.2038	0.1909	0.1789	0.1678	0.1574	0.1478	0.1388	0.1304	0.1226
9	0.1799	0.1670	0.1552	0.1443	0.1342	0.1249	0.1164	0.1084	0.1011	0.0943
10	0.1486	0.1369	0.1262	0.1164	0.1074	0.0992	0.0916	0.0847	0.0784	0.0725
11	0.1228	0.1122	0.1026	0.0938	0.0859	0.0787	0.0721	0.0662	0.0607	0.0558
12	0.1015	0.0920	0.0834	0.0757	0.0687	0.0625	0.0568	0.0517	0.0471	0.0429
13	0.0839	0.0754	0.0678	0.0610	0.0550	0.0496	0.0447	0.0404	0.0365	0.0330
14	0.0693	0.0618	0.0551	0.0492	0.0440	0.0393	0.0352	0.0316	0.0283	0.0254
15	0.0573	0.0507	0.0448	0.0397	0.0352	0.0312	0.0277	0.0247	0.0219	0.0195
16	0.0474	0.0415	0.0364	0.0320	0.0281	0.0248	0.0218	0.0193	0.0170	0.0150
17	0.0391	0.0340	0.0296	0.0258	0.0225	0.0197	0.0172	0.0150	0.0132	0.0116
18	0.0323	0.0279	0.0241	0.0208	0.0180	0.0156	0.0135	0.0118	0.0102	0.0089
19	0.0267	0.0229	0.0196	0.0168	0.0144	0.0124	0.0107	0.0092	0.0079	0.0068
20	0.0221	0.0187	0.0159	0.0135	0.0115	0.0098	0.0084	0.0072	0.0061	0.0053
21	0.0183	0.0154	0.0129	0.0109	0.0092	0.0078	0.0066	0.0056	0.0048	0.0040
22	0.0151	0.0126	0.0105	0.0088	0.0074	0.0062	0.0052	0.0044	0.0037	0.0031
23	0.0125	0.0103	0.0086	0.0071	0.0059	0.0049	0.0041	0.0034	0.0029	0.0024
24	0.0103	0.0085	0.0070	0.0057	0.0047	0.0039	0.0032	0.0027	0.0022	0.0018
25	0.0085	0.0069	0.0057	0.0046	0.0038	0.0031	0.0025	0.0021	0.0017	0.0014

Table 1: (continued)

Years	31%	32%	33%	34%	35%	36%	37%	38%	39%	40%
1	0.7634	0.7576	0.7519	0.7463	0.7407	0.7353	0.7299	0.7246	0.7194	0.7143
2	0.5827	0.5739	0.5653	0.5569	0.5487	0.5407	0.5328	0.5251	0.5176	0.5102
3	0.4448	0.4348	0.4251	0.4156	0.4064	0.3975	0.3889	0.3805	0.3724	0.3644
4	0.3396	0.3294	0.3196	0.3102	0.3011	0.2923	0.2839	0.2757	0.2679	0.2603
5	0.2592	0.2495	0.2403	0.2315	0.2230	0.2149	0.2072	0.1998	0.1927	0.1859
6	0.1979	0.1890	0.1807	0.1727	0.1652	0.1580	0.1512	0.1448	0.1386	0.1328
7	0.1510	0.1432	0.1358	0.1289	0.1224	0.1162	0.1104	0.1049	0.0997	0.0949
8	0.1153	0.1085	0.1021	0.0962	0.0906	0.0854	0.0806	0.0760	0.0718	0.0678
9	0.0880	0.0822	0.0768	0.0718	0.0671	0.0628	0.0588	0.0551	0.0516	0.0484
10	0.0672	0.0623	0.0577	0.0536	0.0497	0.0462	0.0429	0.0399	0.0371	0.0346
11	0.0513	0.0472	0.0434	0.0400	0.0368	0.0340	0.0313	0.0289	0.0267	0.0247
12	0.0392	0.0357	0.0326	0.0298	0.0273	0.0250	0.0229	0.0210	0.0192	0.0176
13	0.0299	0.0271	0.0245	0.0223	0.0202	0.0184	0.0167	0.0152	0.0138	0.0126
14	0.0228	0.0205	0.0185	0.0166	0.0150	0.0135	0.0122	0.0110	0.0099	0.0090
15	0.0174	0.0155	0.0139	0.0124	0.0111	0.0099	0.0089	0.0080	0.0072	0.0064
16	0.0133	0.0118	0.0104	0.0093	0.0082	0.0073	0.0065	0.0058	0.0051	0.0046
17	0.0101	0.0089	0.0078	0.0069	0.0061	0.0054	0.0047	0.0042	0.0037	0.0033
18	0.0077	0.0068	0.0059	0.0052	0.0045	0.0039	0.0035	0.0030	0.0027	0.0023
19	0.0059	0.0051	0.0044	0.0038	0.0033	0.0029	0.0025	0.0022	0.0019	0.0017
20	0.0045	0.0039	0.0033	0.0029	0.0025	0.0021	0.0018	0.0016	0.0014	0.0012
21	0.0034	0.0029	0.0025	0.0021	0.0018	0.0016	0.0013	0.0012	0.0010	0.0009
22	0.0026	0.0022	0.0019	0.0016	0.0014	0.0012	0.0010	0.0008	0.0007	0.0006
23	0.0020	0.0017	0.0014	0.0012	0.0010	0.0008	0.0007	0.0006	0.0005	0.0004
24	0.0015	0.0013	0.0011	0.0009	0.0007	0.0006	0.0005	0.0004	0.0004	0.0003
25	0.0012	0.0010	0.0008	0.0007	0.0006	0.0005	0.0004	0.0003	0.0003	0.0002

Table 2: Present value of €1 received annually

Years	1%	2%	3%	4%	5%	6%	7%	8%	9%	10%
1	0.990	0.980	0.971	0.962	0.952	0.943	0.935	0.926	0.917	0.909
2	1.970	1.942	1.913	1.886	1.859	1.833	1.808	1.783	1.759	1.736
3	2.941	2.884	2.829	2.775	2.723	2.673	2.624	2.577	2.531	2.487
4	3.902	3.808	3.717	3.630	3.546	3.465	3.387	3.312	3.240	3.170
5	4.853	4.713	4.580	4.452	4.329	4.212	4.100	3.993	3.890	3.791
6	5.795	5.601	5.417	5.242	5.076	4.917	4.767	4.623	4.486	4.355
7	6.728	6.472	6.230	6.002	5.786	5.582	5.389	5.206	5.033	4.868
8	7.652	7.325	7.020	6.733	6.463	6.210	5.971	5.747	5.535	5.335
9	8.566	8.162	7.786	7.435	7.108	6.802	6.515	6.247	5.995	5.759
10	9.471	8.983	8.530	8.111	7.722	7.360	7.024	6.710	6.418	6.145
11	10.368	9.787	9.253	8.760	8.306	7.887	7.499	7.139	6.805	6.495
12	11.255	10.575	9.954	9.385	8.863	8.384	7.943	7.536	7.161	6.814
13	12.134	11.348	10.635	9.986	9.394	8.853	8.358	7.904	7.487	7.103
14	13.004	12.106	11.296	10.563	9.899	9.295	8.745	8.244	7.786	7.367
15	13.865	12.849	11.938	11.118	10.380	9.712	9.108	8.559	8.061	7.606
16	14.718	13.578	12.561	11.652	10.838	10.106	9.447	8.851	8.313	7.824
17	15.562	14.292	13.166	12.166	11.274	10.477	9.763	9.122	8.544	8.022
18	16.398	14.992	13.754	12.659	11.690	10.828	10.059	9.372	8.756	8.201
19	17.226	15.678	14.324	13.134	12.085	11.185	10.336	9.604	8.950	8.365
20	18.046	16.351	14.877	13.590	12.462	11.470	10.594	9.818	9.129	8.514
21	18.857	17.011	15.415	14.029	12.821	11.764	10.836	10.017	9.292	8.649
22	19.660	17.658	15.937	14.451	13.163	12.042	11.061	10.201	9.442	8.772
23	20.456	18.292	16.444	14.857	13.489	12.303	11.272	10.371	9.580	8.883
24	21.243	18.914	16.939	15.247	13.799	12.550	11.469	10.529	9.707	8.985
25	22.023	19.523	17.413	15.622	14.094	12.783	11.654	10.675	9.823	9.077

Table 2: (continued)

Years	11%	12%	13%	14%	15%	16%	17%	18%	19%	20%
1	0.901	0.893	0.885	0.877	0.870	0.862	0.855	0.847	0.840	0.833
2	1.713	1.690	1.668	1.647	1.626	1.605	1.585	1.566	1.547	1.528
3	2.444	2.402	2.361	2.322	2.283	2.246	2.210	2.174	2.140	2.106
4	3.102	3.037	2.974	2.914	2.855	2.798	2.743	2.690	2.639	2.589
5	3.696	3.605	3.517	3.433	3.352	3.274	3.199	3.127	3.058	2.991
6	4.231	4.111	3.998	3.889	3.784	3.685	3.589	3.498	3.410	3.326
7	4.712	4.564	4.423	4.288	4.160	4.039	3.922	3.812	3.706	3.605
8	5.146	4.968	4.799	4.639	4.487	4.344	4.207	4.078	3.954	3.837
9	5.537	5.328	5.132	4.946	4.772	4.607	4.451	4.303	4.163	4.031
10	5.889	5.650	5.426	5.216	5.019	4.833	4.659	4.494	4.339	4.192
11	6.207	5.938	5.687	5.453	5.234	5.029	4.836	4.656	4.486	4.327
12	6.492	6.194	5.918	5.660	5.421	5.197	4.988	4.793	4.611	4.439
13	6.750	6.424	6.122	5.842	5.583	5.342	5.118	4.910	4.715	4.533
14	6.982	6.628	6.302	6.002	5.724	5.468	5.229	5.008	4.802	4.611
15	7.191	6.811	6.462	6.142	5.847	5.575	5.324	5.092	4.876	4.675
16	7.379	6.974	6.604	6.265	5.954	5.668	5.405	5.162	4.938	4.730
17	7.549	7.120	6.729	6.373	6.047	5.749	5.475	5.222	4.990	4.775
18	7.702	7.250	6.840	6.467	6.128	5.818	5.534	5.273	5.033	4.812
19	7.839	7.366	6.938	6.550	6.198	5.877	5.584	5.316	5.070	4.843
20	7.963	7.469	7.025	6.623	6.259	5.929	5.628	5.353	5.101	4.870
21	8.075	7.562	7.102	6.687	6.312	5.973	5.665	5.384	5.127	4.891
22	8.176	7.645	7.170	6.743	6.359	6.011	5.696	5.410	5.149	4.909
23	8.266	7.718	7.230	6.792	6.399	6.044	5.723	5.432	5.167	4.925
24	8.348	7.784	7.283	6.835	6.434	6.073	5.746	5.451	5.182	4.937
25	8.422	7.843	7.330	6.873	6.464	6.097	5.766	5.467	5.195	4.948

Table 2: (continued)

Years	21%	22%	23%	24%	25%	26%	27%	28%	29%	30%
1	0.826	0.820	0.813	0.806	0.800	0.794	0.787	0.781	0.775	0.769
2	1.509	1.492	1.474	1.457	1.440	1.424	1.407	1.392	1.376	1.361
3	2.074	2.042	2.011	1.981	1.952	1.923	1.896	1.868	1.842	1.816
4	2.540	2.494	2.448	2.404	2.362	2.320	2.280	2.241	2.203	2.166
5	2.926	2.864	2.803	2.745	2.689	2.635	2.583	2.532	2.483	2.436
6	3.245	3.167	3.092	3.020	2.951	2.885	2.821	2.759	2.700	2.643
7	3.508	3.416	3.327	3.242	3.161	3.083	3.009	2.937	2.868	2.802
8	3.726	3.619	3.518	3.421	3.329	3.241	3.156	3.076	2.999	2.925
9	3.905	3.786	3.673	3.566	3.463	3.366	3.273	3.184	3.100	3.019
10	4.054	3.923	3.799	3.682	3.571	3.465	3.364	3.269	3.178	3.092
11	4.177	4.035	3.902	3.776	3.656	3.543	3.437	3.335	3.239	3.147
12	5.278	4.127	3.985	3.851	3.725	3.606	3.493	3.387	3.286	3.190
13	4.362	4.203	4.053	3.912	3.780	3.656	3.538	3.427	3.322	3.223
14	4.432	4.265	4.108	3.962	3.824	3.695	3.573	3.459	3.351	3.249
15	4.489	4.315	4.153	4.001	3.859	3.726	3.601	3.483	3.373	3.268
16	4.536	4.357	4.189	4.033	3.887	3.751	3.623	3.503	3.390	3.283
17	4.576	4.391	4.219	4.059	3.910	3.771	3.640	3.518	3.403	3.295
18	4.608	4.419	4.243	4.080	3.928	3.786	3.654	3.529	3.413	3.304
19	4.635	4.442	4.263	4.097	3.942	3.799	3.664	3.539	3.421	3.311
20	4.657	4.460	4.279	4.110	3.954	3.808	'3.673	3.546	3.427	3.316
21	4.675	4.476	3.292	4.121	3.963	3.816	3.679	3.551	3.432	3.320
22	4.690	4.488	4.302	4.130	3.970	3.822	3.684	3.556	3.436	3.323
23	4.703	4.499	4.311	4.137	3.976	3.827	3.689	3.559	3.438	3.325
24	4.713	4.507	4.318	4.143	3.981	3.831.	3.692	3.562	3.441	3.327
25	4.721	4.514	4.323	4.147	3.985	3.834	3.694	3.564	3.442	3.329

Table 2: (continued)

Years	31%	32%	33%	34%	35%	36%	37%	38%	39%	40%
1	0.763	0.758	0.752	0.746	0.741	0.735	0.730	0.725	0.719	0.714
2	1.346	1.331	1.317	1.303	1.289	1.276	1.263	1.250	1.237	1.224
3	1.791	1.766	1.742	1.719	1.696	1.673	1.652	1.630	1.609	1.589
4	2.130	2.096	2.062	2.029	1.997	1.966	1.935	1.906	1.877	.1849
5	2.390	2.345	2.302	2.260	2.220	2.181	2.143	2.106	2.070	2.035
6	2.588	2.534	2.483	2.433	2.385	2.339	2.294	2.251	2.209	2.168
7	2.739	2.677	2.619	2.562	2.508	2.455	2.404	2.355	2.308	2.263
8	2.854	2.786	2.721	2.658	2.598	2.540	2.485	2.432	2.380	2.331
9	2.942	2.868	2.798	2.730	2.665	2.603	2.544	2.487	2.432	2.379
10	3.009	2.930	2.855	2.784	2.715	2.649	2.587	2.527	2.469	2.414
11	3.060	2.978	2.899	2.824	2.752	2.683	2.618	2.555	2.496	2.438
12	3.100	3.013	2.931	2.853	2.779	2.708	2.641	2.576	2.515	2.456
13	3.129	3.040	2.956	2.876	2.799	2.727	2.658	2.592	2.529	2.469
14	3.152	3.061	2.974	2.982	2.814	2.740	2.670	2.603	2.539	2.478
15	3.170	3.076	2.988	2.905	2.825	2.750	2.679	2.611	2.546	2.484
16	3.183	3.088	2.999	2.914	2.834	2.757	2.685	2.616	2.551	2.489
17	3.193	3.097	3.007	2.921	2.840	2.763	2.690	2.621	2.555	2.492
18	3.201	3.104	3.012	2.926	2.844	2.767	2.693	2.624	2.557	2.494
19	3.207	3.109	3.017	2.930	2.848	2.770	2.696	2.626	2.559	2.496
20	3.211	3.113	3.020	2.933	2.850	2.772	2.698	2.627	2.561	2.497
21	3.215	3.116	3.023	2.935	2.852	2.773	2.699	2.629	2.562	2.498
22	3.217	3.118	3.025	2.936	2.853	2.775	2.700	2.629	2.562	2.438
23	3.219	3.120	3.026	2.938	2.854	2.775	2.701	2.630	2.563	2.499
24	3.221	3.121	3.027	2.939	2.855	2.776	2.701	2.630	2.563	2.499
25	3.222	3.122	3.028	2.939	2.856	2.777	2.702	2.631	2.563	2.499

III

Aspects of Project Appraisal

FERGAL SOMERVILLE

Projects are governed by objectives and success is measured in attaining set objectives. Projects are initiated to bring about benefits (e.g. growth) from costs (resources) and projects can be analysed from both financial and economic perspectives. In what follows we will distinguish between the two perspectives and outline the methodology for applying economic analysis to projects. The aim of this appendix is to outline a systematic approach to analysing the impact of projects.

Financial analysis

Financial analysis generally precedes economic analysis. It is predominantly concerned with assessing projects from an accounting perspective. Financial analysis assists in assessing potential returns by means of cash flow, profitability and so forth. It also highlights the funding requirements of projects over their useful lives. It takes a full-term view, outlining the costs and revenues directly attributable to a project.

Financial analysis identifies all financial flows associated with a project. Each resource used is recorded. Financial analysis is used extensively in private sector funded commercial projects where success may be defined in terms of indicators of commercial return such as payback, net present value and internal rate of return. In the private sector, projects must be capable of self-financing through income generation.

Annual financial statements are prepared in accordance with the matching principle which requires that costs are allocated to the period to which they relate, i.e. the period in which costs/resources generate economic benefits or revenues. As a result certain assets are stated at their unconsumed or unallocated costs amounts. This is most notable in the case of fixed assets which are generally stated at their historic cost values or at revalued amounts less accumulated depreciation.

The amounts shown in financial statements for certain assets, for example fixed assets which are shown at their net book value at a point in time, may well differ from the economic value of the assets to the organisation.

This divergence is important in interpreting financial statements. From an economic analysis point of view the values in financial statements will generally need to be adjusted.

Economic analysis

Economic analysis assesses the impact of a project on the economy as a whole. This is particularly necessary in publicly funded projects. Economic analysis complements financial analysis. Differences exist between both approaches; for example financial analysis treats wages as costs whereas economic analysis, taking the perspective of society, may treat wages as benefits. Similarly transfers, such as indirect taxes and subsidies, are taken into account in the financial analysis; economic analysis ignores transfers as there is no direct output associated with them. Economic analysis looks beyond financial analysis to include macroeconomic variables such as growth, public finance, foreign exchange and income distribution.

Financial analysis adopts market prices to represent the costs incurred. Full economic analysis applies 'shadow prices' to transactions where markets are distorted. Distortions occur in markets which are not fully competitive. Shadow prices represent an attempt to use prices that would be set by competitive markets and to reflect more truly the opportunity costs of factors of production.

Externalities are project outputs for which no market exists. Negative externalities include pollution, congestion, noise and disturbance. Positive externalities include security and aesthetic appeal conferred by projects. They are ignored in the financial analysis if their value cannot be directly attributed to the project.

Another important distinction between financial and economic appraisal is the recognition of costs attributed to a project's use of land, labour and capital. Economic analysis takes account of the 'opportunity cost' of resources – that is the value of their alternative use. Financial analysis takes into account market costs.

Economic analysis involves assembling data and restating the financial analysis so that the impact on society can be gauged. It determines a project's economic viability and examines the likely outputs in the light of the project's objectives.

Where aims include non-monetary goals, quantification of costs and benefits is difficult. Such projects are prevalent in the public sector. Assigning monetary values to social aims is a difficult exercise requiring unbiased subjective analysis.

Costs and benefits are assessed over the lifetime of the project. Economic analysis selects from competing alternatives, including the option of doing nothing, the project with the highest net present value (NPV). The incremental contribution offered by a project is the aggregate of benefits over costs through proceeding with a project, as against not proceeding with it. Project management involves cash flow analysis and projection and requires that finance be available to meet liabilities as they arise.

Project evaluation – an illustrative procedure

The procedure for conducting a full cost benefit analysis of a project can be illustrated in a series of steps. Cost benefit analysis of a project will involve the use of some or all of the steps. These include:

- data collection and analysis
- financial flows
- externalities
- labour
- national goods
- international tradable goods
- foreign exchange
- capital
- income distribution
- sociopolitical considerations

Direct effects associated with projects can be calculated as the resources used and the value-added created through the production process. For example, a direct effects analysis of a rail development project concentrates on construction and maintenance costs and profit and wage income directly attributable to the project.

Indirect effects can be assessed from economic activity associated with the project; they refer to extra profit and wage income created by the purchase of materials for use in the project. Indirect effects are difficult to quantify and harder to identify the further they occur from the main activity of the project. As such, indirect effects are sometimes omitted from cost benefit analysis of projects. More difficult to quantify and therefore often omitted from analysis are induced effects; these occur when the extra income arising out of the direct and indirect effects is spent thereby generating value added.

Data collection and analysis

The quality and quantity of data is an important factor in project analysis. A reliable set of microeconomic, macroeconomic and sociopolitical data enhances the ability to plan, forecast and review projects.

In a full cost benefit analysis capital items are recorded at their opportunity cost. Labour and other variables are represented by shadow prices where market distortions exist.

In projects there are two main categories of expenditure which help to illustrate periodic flows: inputs and value-added items. Inputs are made up of imports (net of tariffs), raw materials and 'intermediate goods and services'. Value-added items are comprised of wages, taxes, financial charges and operating profits.

Expenditure on inputs creates additional demand for suppliers of inputs and related goods. Value-added items of a project generate increased expenditure and savings in an economy.

Financial flows

Economic analysis categorises financial flows from the project as costs or benefits. Readily identifiable flows, taken at their relevant economic values, include expenditure on inputs and value-added components. Economic analysis also acknowledges values attributable to other economic activity. For example, where industrial production takes over from agricultural activity a cost benefit analysis study will take into account the value of ceased economic activity.

Transfer payments, indirect taxes and indirect subsidies are excluded from the assessment of costs and benefits as there is no direct output associated with them. Direct taxes and subsidies are included as benefits and costs respectively, directly associated with the project.

Externalities

Significant costs and benefits which are external to the project can accrue to individuals and groups. Externalities can be expressed in terms of 'income equivalence': the premium or penalty that would be attributed if a market mechanism existed. The upgrading of a rail network will convey benefits on its users. External benefits will accrue to road users if traffic congestion is eased and journey times reduced. External costs will be borne by those affected by the construction that accompanies any such development. In a full cost benefit analysis the economic analyst must impute values for these externalities. This is done by breaking activities down into their component parts and estimating market priced values. No market exists to charge beneficiaries or compensate losers and actual externalities may be difficult to identify and subsequently quantify.

Labour

The financial and economic costs of labour can differ significantly. A full cost benefit analysis records the shadow price of labour (and other variables) where market distortions exist. Consider the cost of labour on building projects where there is 20 per cent unemployment in the sector. In such cases economic analysis will impute the shadow price of labour, reducing the accounting cost of labour to a rate estimated to be attained in a fully competitive market.

National goods

National goods are domestically provided goods which are not traded internationally. They predominate where public policy imposes tariffs on goods and services or where transport costs are prohibitive. National goods are of greatest relevance in developing countries.

Economic analysis requires that the shadow price for national goods should reflect the opportunity cost associated with the resources in question. In the case of a monopoly the shadow price will be below the actual price set, as monopoly sets price in excess of the equilibrium of marginal revenue and marginal cost. Alternatively, for the purposes of economic analysis, it may be possible to split the national good into its individual components and determine internationally set prices.

Computing prices in this fashion is necessary, particularly where national goods represent a significant element of project costs. The most common national goods, in this respect, are utilities such as energy.

Internationally tradable goods

An assessment of internationally tradable goods involves an evaluation of the impact on the project of imports, exports and foreign capital. Shadow prices for raw materials are generally taken as the open (world) market price.

Adjustments to the shadow price must be made where the commodities are made scarce through foreign government action or cartel arrangements. Other adjustments are required where differences in the quality of commodities exist.

The purchase of foreign goods from outside free-trade agreement areas involves extra charges. Tariffs and import fees are transfers redirected to the public finances and are therefore ignored for the purposes of economic analysis.

Foreign exchange

Where market distortions exist, i.e. when the exchange rate is determined by non-market forces, the shadow price of foreign exchange has to be estimated. Indicators of shadow rates are unofficial market rates, purchasing power parities and trade balances between the country and its international traders.

Capital

Economies with freely floating exchange rates and no foreign exchange controls equate market and shadow price of capital. In the absence of competitive conditions a shadow price of capital is used. Generally, the price of money approximates to the prevailing interest rate. Borrowing for projects is related to the perceived risks and likely returns; the greater the risk associated with a project the higher the interest rate on loans used to fund it.

The shadow price of capital can be imputed from the average rate of return on similar projects or international financial benchmarks. The productivity of capital (k) employed in a project can be calculated as the excess of national income (Y) over the total wage bill (W) deflated by the aggregate of capital (K), land (L) and stocks (U).

By differentiating we can determine the rate of change in the productivity of capital with respect to the other variables.

$$k = \frac{Y - W}{(K + L + U)}$$

Income distribution

Identification of the participants in a project is the first step in identifying winners and losers. In its simplest form the wider the distribution of income in volume and value terms arising from a project, the greater the impact on subsequent consumption and investment.

In general it can be assumed that each extra unit of consumption confers greater benefit to lower income earners than to higher income earners and that policy makers will favour projects which disperse income distribution.

The benefit of a project is calculated by estimating the distribution of the increase in income across the project's 'participants' and the amount of the increase which is saved and thereby made available for further investment. Individuals and groups affected by a project include investors, workers, government, displaced land owners, banks, financial institutions and so forth.

If the benefit of a project accrues to a small amount of international investors the financial returns may subsequently be invested abroad, thereby exporting the value accruing to the project.

Sociopolitical considerations

Public policy identifies sectors to be targeted for development projects and strategies to be pursued. Cost benefit analysis aids decision-making about project selection. Invariably, the ultimate decision on selection of publicly funded projects rests with politicians.

The selection of a particular project may owe as much to compromise and negotiation as to economic analysis. Political horizons may not extend beyond the productive phase of project development. Hence, projects which take up current funding and offer few immediate benefits may be rejected in favour of shorter term projects.

Economic analysis selects from competing alternatives the project with the highest NPV. Political considerations can override economic ones and favour projects with lower NPVs. The implications of the political decisions can be estimated as the difference between the NPVs of the selected project and the project with the highest NPV.

Project effects analysis

The preceding steps briefly outline how to assess the economic impact of the different components of a project. We now examine the calculation of various project effects.

For each period covered by the project, flows are categorised as inflows (benefit) or outflows (cost). Net flows are calculated and discounted to their present value. The calculation of present value is treated in detail in Chapter 5 of this volume.

Direct and indirect effects analysis

Direct and indirect effects are assessed by means of the net flows associated with the project. The values for these can be taken from the financial analysis and adjusted for economic analysis purposes. A project is evaluated by assessing the inputs it uses and the value added to those resources. This can be represented as:

Inputs	INPs
Value Added	VA
Production/Output	Q

The main inputs of production include raw materials (RM), primary goods (PG), imports (M) and intermediate goods and services (IGS).

$$INPs = RM + PG + M + IGS$$

The value added items include wages (W), taxes (T), financial charges (FC) and operating profit (OP).

$$VA = W + T + FC + OP$$

Direct effect analysis considers the overall impact of a project. It is relatively easy to quantify from the economic and financial flows directly associated with a project.

Indirect effect analysis accounts for ancillary economic activity generated by a project. It looks at new activity indirectly associated with a project. For example, infrastructure projects will use a large amount of locally produced inputs and indirect effect analysis aims to identify the consequences for suppliers of the increased activity. Backward linkages which trace the source of inputs to suppliers are investigated when they are substantial in the overall context of the project.

The distinction between direct and indirect effects analysis can be seen in the case of the construction of a bridge. Direct effects analysis accounts for all the flows directly associated with the bridge's construction and associated externalities. Indirect effects analysis looks back through the supply chain to companies which provide the raw materials and intermediate goods for the construction project and assesses the additional economic activity that would not otherwise have been generated. The process of estimating indirect effects is similar to the process for identifying direct effects. The further back through the supply chain the analysis goes the lesser the impact.

Incremental effects

Incremental effects analysis examines the changes in production and consumption in 'with project' and 'without project' scenarios.

Consumer benefit from a project can be stated as:

$$P_{pjt} = p_{pjt} \times Q$$

where the 'with project' value of production (P_{PJT}) is equal to the unit price multiplied by the level of output (Q) and can be distinguished from the 'without project' production value, which can be represented as:

$$P_{orig} = p_{orig} \times Q$$

The incremental benefit of a project is the difference between the two. This assumes that there will always be consumer benefit uniquely identifiable through the pricing mechanism. The extent to which a project benefits consumers is dependent on how the project passes on or retains benefits. Total benefits (B) can be written as

$$\Sigma B = (p_{pjt} - p_{orig}) \times Q$$

Macroeconomic perspective

Macroeconomic analysis looks beyond the immediate impact of a project to evaluate how the project generated income is distributed throughout the economy. New income creates demand for goods and services which in turn creates income for other groups. The analysis therefore requires data on the incomes arising from the project, the recipients of the incomes and their propensities to save and spend.

Macroeconomic analysis is based on the variables growth, foreign exchange, public finance and income distribution.

Growth

Values for determining growth can be taken from national accounts statistics and the accounts of companies associated with the project. However, using these market prices may not reflect the economic impact of a project. Increasing third level education opportunities cannot be measured by the costs of providing buildings and books. Similarly the eradication of a disease is not measured by the cost of the treatment. The incremental value added of a project highlights its net contribution to overall economic development.

Foreign exchange

A stable foreign exchange rate is an important consideration for many projects. A project contributes to an economy's balance of payments position through its interaction with foreign economies. The impact is assessed through foreign currency earnings of exports and leakages due to imports and capital transfers.

Public finance

The commitment of public finances is an important element of projects, particularly noncommercial projects funded from a public capital programme and supported on a continuing basis by current government expenditure. Investigation of costs and benefits for noncommercial projects is a subjective exercise. Where there is no market for certain goods and services economic analysis will categorise goods and services into identifiable components and apply 'prices' so that in aggregate, returns on the public investment can be estimated. An important measure for the public sector is the return from the investment; a positive NPV will entail a positive return from the project and produce a positive impact on the public finances.

The conduits of public sector involvement in a project include taxation, subsidisation, capital expenditure, current expenditure and revenue receipts. Current public account inflows are represented by taxes and operating revenues. Exchequer funding is recorded through operating subsidies and capital flows, including the payment by government of both interest and capital component of loans linked to the overall project.

Income distribution

Economic analysis investigates the incomes created by a project and how these are distributed. Incomes can take the form of wages or profits. Production subsidies represent a cost reduction to producers and serve to reduce the final cost of output. To individuals subsidies represent increased disposable income.

The income distribution associated with a project involves the consideration of value-added components. As before, these components can be broken down into domestic and foreign parts. This facilitates analysis of changes in domestic income levels and distribution.

A project will contain forecasts for employment creation. The value attaching to the increase in employment will indicate how income from the project is distributed throughout different social groups.

Apart from direct costs, the analysis must account for indirect costs such as costs for those displaced by the development. Knowledge of the distribution of incomes across groups and propensities to consume and save will help to identify how the income will permeate through the economy.

Computation of externalities

Externalities must be taken into account in project evaluation. A capital development programme to build a bridge will have a significant economic effect. Figure 1 illustrates both the internal and external costs and benefits and the externalities associated with a bridge construction project.

By applying the methodology in Figure 1, the economist can identify the costs and benefits associated with the project. It is not difficult to identify the externalities that will be associated with the project; the difficulties arise in attempting to quantify them.

In the example of the bridge a recurring factor is infrastructure. The costs and benefits of the infrastructure are factored into the project. Positive externalities may result from the upgrading of the transport network to improve the quality of travel and safety for road-users. Negative externalities may stem from the bridge's construction adversely affecting individuals, firms and farms.

In transport projects a positive externality can take the form of reduced wear and tear on vehicles and reduced journey times. Maintenance costs are related to road quality and distance. Vehicles require less servicing per mile on better quality roads, thereby producing a positive impact on household income and reducing firms' transportation costs. If the provision of infrastructure substantially cuts commuting time then economic analysis will determine the income equivalence of that time as a multiple of the numbers availing of the saving. Income equivalence is a concept used in economic analysis to identify a cost that reflects the value people attach to their own time. The income equivalence can be calculated as the average hourly rate or shadow rate of labour. For example, if an individual benefits through a three hour reduction per week in travel time then the income equivalence may be estimated at the individual's opportunity cost of three hours.

Infrastructure can also create negative externalities. Improved infrastructure can induce extra traffic thereby generating increased pollution and disturbance.

There is a danger of overplaying positive externalities. Indeed, the omission of positive externalities from project analysis often produces negative NPVs. Overvaluation of positive externalities can transform negative net present values to positive and lead to the implementation of projects which will have a detrimental effect on the economy.

Figure 1: Bridge costs and benefits

Bridge – cost benefit analysis	
Internal	
Costs	*Benefits*
Infrastructure	Increased economic activity
Land, labour, capital	Infrastructure
Technology	Agricultural productivity
Plant & machinery	Industrial productivity
Externalities	
Negative	*Positive*
Adverse effects on lifestyles	Reduced traveling time
Displacement & relocation	Increased economic activity
Pollution	Leisure and amenities
Infrastructure	Infrastructure
Ecological damage	

Sensitivity analysis

It is important for project planners to be able to anticipate the effects of changes to variables within the project. Sensitivity analysis allows planners to gauge the effects of such changes on the overall outcome of the project. For example, if there is an unanticipated change in wage rates then the overall NPV of the project will change. The change in the NPV will be correlated with the relative importance of a particular variable to the overall project.

Sensitivity analysis can monitor the effect of simultaneous changes in one or more variables. The effect of an increase in the cost of imports, reduction in tax rate and appreciation of domestic currency on foreign exchange markets can be assessed through formulae within the template in Figure 2.

Sensitivity analysis is important in the analysis of competing projects. Alternative projects can have different labour and technology cost/benefit profiles. When evaluating projects with similar NPVs, sensitivity analysis may serve to promote the project with the lowest potential risk.

A framework for assessing costs and benefits

Figure 2 is a template which presents subheads under which costs and benefits can be quantified. Each input and value added subhead may be expanded as required to include more components. The template assists in capturing values for the categories in all periods and discounting these values to find the net present value for the project.

Figure 2: Cost benefit analysis – template

	Period 1..n							
	'With Project'				'Without Project'			
	Direct		Indirect		Direct		Indirect	
	Domestic	Foreign	Domestic	Foreign	Domestic	Foreign	Domestic	Foreign
Imports **Raw Materials** **Primary Goods** **IGS** **Other** **INPs** **W** **T** **FC** **OP** **VA**			N/A		N/A		N/A	N/A
Total								

NPV

Inputs

Inputs represent all of the components purchased for and used in the project. The major inputs as outlined in Figure 2 are imports, raw materials, primary goods, intermediate goods and services and 'other' inputs such as machinery and maintenance.

Value added

The major components of value added as outlined in Figure 2 are: wages, taxes, financial charges and operating profit. Wages comprise incomes of all employed in the project. The subhead can be itemised as:

	£
Management	
Administration	
Executive	
Operators	
Casual	
Travel & Subsistence	
Training	
Other	————
W	£

Financial charges represent the flows financing the project. Expenditure on financial charges can be calculated from analysis of accounts of the project companies. The overall effect of the project involves assessment of 'with project' against 'without project' scenarios.

Case study: Economic analysis of the construction of a bridge

This case study is adapted from a World Bank study (Adler, 1987) concerning a proposal to build a 500 metre long, two lane bridge to replace existing ferry services. This project can be investigated using the techniques outlined above. The project is situated in India and all values are in Rupees. Construction costs for the bridge are estimated at Rs54.000m over the four years in which the bridge will be built. Thereafter the bridge will have maintenance costs of Rs0.120m rising to Rs0.150m from year 24. These costs are set out in columns [1], [2] and [3] of Figure 5.

The existing ferry caters for 100 vehicles per day. Planners anticipate that a bridge, with associated time saving and reduced traffic congestion, will cater for a far greater amount of vehicles. Estimates are that, on opening (in year five), traffic will increase to 900 vehicles per day using the bridge; thereafter increasing at an average of ten per cent per annum and stabilising after 24 years. The increase is accounted for by historic trend plus additional traffic generated by the bridge. The bridge will be linked to the local highway. Figure 3 highlights the anticipated traffic increases.

Figure 3: Forecast of selected daily traffic for selected years

	Trucks		Buses		Cars		
Year	Normal Traffic	Generated Traffic	Normal Traffic	Generated Traffic	Normal Traffic	Generated Traffic	Total
0	35	0	15	0	50	0	100
5	70	180	30	90	100	430	900
10	170	430	50	150	200	800	1,800
15	280	720	70	210	340	1,360	2,980
24	640	1,660	130	400	800	3,200	6,830

The bridge and ferry alternatives differ in capital and continuing costs. Figure 4 shows the costs of the ferry service for the 25 years after the bridge opens. This can be extrapolated further. The ferry service has capital costs including increases in the number of ferries at a cost of some Rs5.400m per ferry. This is an economic cost derived from the actual cost of Rs3.450m with a 75 per cent foreign exchange component and a shadow rate of foreign exchange at a multiple of 1.755 the official rate. The construction costs attributable to terminals is Rs1.500m. Due to growth extra terminals will be required. Operating costs are Rs1.050m per ferry and Rs0.075m per terminal. Both ferries and terminals have an anticipated useful life of 20 years. The savings on the elimination of ferry services are itemised in Figure 4 and displayed in column [4] of Figure 5. The ferries in service at the end of the project period are deemed to have a residual value of Rs15.000m representing approximately 50 per cent of cost.

The cost of driving across the bridge is estimated to equal the cost of using the ferry; thereby producing no economic saving. The bridge will produce a significant reduction in delays; approximately 20 minutes per journey. By Year 5 this will produce a total saving of 24,000 hours for the vehicles using the bridge. The value of total time savings available to trucks, buses and cars amounts to Rs1.060m in the first year after the bridge opens and this increases in line with traffic growth, stabilising at a value of Rs7.950m in Year 24. The figures for the value of time saved are given in column [5] of Figure 5.

Figure 4: Annual economic costs of ferry service

Economic costs of ferry service (millions of Rupees)					
	Capital Costs		Operating Costs		
Years	Ferry	Terminal	Ferry	Terminal	Total
5	10.80	1.50	2.10	0.15	14.55
6-9	0.00	0.00	2.10	0.15	2.25
10	5.40	0.00	3.15	0.15	8.70
11-13	0.00	0.00	3.15	0.15	3.30
14	5.40	1.50	4.20	0.30	11.40
15-16	0.00	0.00	4.20	0.30	4.50
17	5.40	0.00	5.25	0.30	10.95
18-19	0.00	0.00	5.25	0.30	5.55
20	5.40	0.00	6.30	0.30	12.00
21-24	0.00	0.00	6.30	0.30	6.60
25	10.80	1.50	6.30	0.30	18.90
26-29	0.00	0.00	6.30	0.30	6.60
30	5.40	0.00	6.30	0.30	12.00

Columns [3] and [6] of Figure 5 show the total costs and benefits of the project. Columns [7] and [8] discount the values for each year at a rate of 12 per cent. The benefits of constructing the bridge amount to Rs55.496m compared to costs of Rs45.757m yielding an NPV for the project of Rs9.739m. It is therefore economically beneficial to build the bridge. Much of the benefit of the project comes from the estimate of increased traffic and the attendant saving in delays. An overestimation here exaggerates the benefits of the bridge.

The choice of 12 per cent for the discount rate plays an important role. Figure 6 sets out the discounted values for a selection of discount rates, demonstrating clearly that the choice of discount rate is important. Figure 6 also shows that the project's internal rate of return is approximately 14 per cent.

The bulk of the costs attributable to the construction of the bridge occur in the first four years. Thereafter, there is comparatively low maintenance. The benefits accrue from the reduction in costs from the discontinued ferry service and the time savings. The benefits accrue over the lifetime of the project. The values for the benefits are susceptible to changes in the discount rate.

Figure 5: Comparison of costs and benefits of construction of a bridge (Millions of Rupees)

Year	Costs			Benefits			PV Discount 12%	
	Capital Costs [1]	Maint'ce Costs [2]	Total Costs [3]	Eliminated Ferry Costs [4]	Time Saving [5]	Total Benefits [6]	Costs [7]	Benefits [8]
1	9.000	0.000	9.000	0.000	0.000	0.000	9.000	0.000
2	15.000	0.000	15.000	0.000	0.000	0.000	13.393	0.000
3	15.000	0.000	15.000	0.000	0.000	0.000	11.958	0.000
4	15.000	0.000	15.000	0.000	0.000	0.000	10.677	0.000
5	0.000	0.120	0.120	14.550	1.060	15.610	0.076	9.920
6	0.000	0.120	0.120	2.250	1.250	3.500	0.068	1.986
7	0.000	0.120	0.120	2.250	1.500	3.750	0.061	1.900
8	0.000	0.120	0.120	2.250	1.750	4.000	0.054	1.809
9	0.000	0.120	0.120	2.250	2.000	4.250	0.048	1.717
10	0.000	0.120	0.120	8.700	2.160	10.860	0.043	3.916
11	0.000	0.120	0.120	3.300	2.450	5.750	0.039	1.851
12	0.000	0.120	0.120	3.300	2.750	6.050	0.034	1.739
13	0.000	0.120	0.120	3.300	3.000	6.300	0.031	1.617
14	0.000	0.120	0.120	11.400	3.250	14.650	0.028	3.357
15	0.000	0.120	0.120	4.500	3.520	8.020	0.025	1.641
16	0.000	0.120	0.120	4.500	4.000	8.500	0.022	1.553
17	0.000	0.120	0.120	10.950	4.500	15.450	0.020	2.520
18	0.000	0.120	0.120	5.550	5.000	10.550	0.017	1.537
19	0.000	0.120	0.120	5.550	5.500	11.050	0.016	1.437
20	0.000	0.120	0.120	12.000	6.000	18.000	0.014	2.090
21	0.000	0.120	0.120	6.600	6.500	13.100	0.012	1.358
22	0.000	0.120	0.120	6.600	7.000	13.600	0.011	1.259
23	0.000	0.120	0.120	6.600	7.500	14.100	0.010	1.165
24	0.000	0.150	0.150	6.600	7.950	14.550	0.011	1.074
25	0.000	0.150	0.150	18.900	7.950	26.850	0.010	1.769
26	0.000	0.150	0.150	6.600	7.950	14.550	0.009	0.856
27	0.000	0.150	0.150	6.600	7.950	14.550	0.008	0.764
28	0.000	0.150	0.150	6.600	7.950	14.550	0.007	0.682
29	0.000	0.150	0.150	6.600	7.950	14.550	0.006	0.609
30	0.000	0.150	0.150	12.000	7.950	19.950	0.006	0.746
31	0.000	0.150	0.150	6.600	7.950	14.550	0.005	0.486
32	0.000	0.150	0.150	6.600	7.950	14.550	0.004	0.434
33	0.000	0.150	0.150	6.600	7.950	14.550	0.004	0.387
34	0.000	0.150	0.150	13.500	7.950	21.450	0.004	0.510
35	0.000	0.150	0.150	6.600	7.950	14.550	0.003	0.309
36	0.000	0.150	0.150	6.600	7.950	14.550	0.003	0.276
37	0.000	0.150	0.150	12.000	7.950	19.950	0.003	0.337
38	0.000	0.150	0.150	6.600	7.950	14.550	0.002	0.220
39	0.000	0.150	0.150	6.600	7.950	14.550	0.002	0.196
40	0.000	0.150	0.150	12.000	7.950	19.950	0.002	0.240
41	0.000	0.150	0.150	6.600	7.950	14.550	0.002	0.156
42	0.000	0.150	0.150	6.600	7.950	14.550	0.001	0.140
43	0.000	0.150	0.150	6.600	7.950	14.550	0.001	0.125
44	0.000	0.150	0.150	6.600	7.950	14.550	0.001	0.111
45	0.000	0.150	0.150	15.900	7.950	23.850	0.001	0.163
46	0.000	0.150	0.150	6.600	7.950	14.550	0.001	0.089
47	0.000	0.150	0.150	6.600	7.950	14.550	0.001	0.079
48	0.000	0.150	0.150	6.600	7.950	14.550	0.001	0.071
49	0.000	0.150	0.150	6.600	7.950	14.550	0.001	0.063
50	0.000	0.150	0.150	12.000	7.950	19.950	0.001	0.077
51	0.000	0.150	0.150	6.600	7.950	14.550	0.001	0.050
52	0.000	0.150	0.150	6.600	7.950	14.550	0.000	0.045
53	0.000	0.150	0.150	6.600	7.950	14.550	0.000	0.040
54	0.000	0.150	0.150	6.600	7.950	14.550	0.000	0.036
55	0.000	0.150	0.150	-15.000	7.950	-7.050	0.000	-0.016
							45.757	55.496

Figure 6: Effect of changes in discount rate (Millions of Rupees)

	Costs	Benefits	NPV
8%	48.890	101.620	52.730
9%	48.030	85.920	37.890
10%	47.230	73.510	26.280
11%	46.480	63.560	17.080
12%	45.757	55.496	9.739
13%	45.070	48.880	3.810
14%	44.410	43.380	−1.030
15%	43.780	38.780	−5.000
16%	43.180	34.890	−8.290

Conclusion

This appendix demonstrates some of the approaches which can be used in determining the value of projects. Differences exist between financial and economic analysis. Economic analysis aims to assign the true economic value to a project's component parts. This is achieved through the application of shadow pricing, a method of converting the recorded accounting transaction into an appropriate economic value. Such manipulation is necessary where markets are distorted. Economic analysis takes account of externalities, both positive and negative. In the absence of the time saving in the bridge case study the project would have produced a negative NPV, and might only have been undertaken if a toll could be introduced.

Sensitivity analysis plays an important role in project evaluation. For example, in the case study a relatively small change in the estimates of traffic growth and time savings could change the economic profile substantially.

Fundamental to project analysis is having a sufficient amount of information on which to base decisions. Planners must be able to identify flows and their timing and have sufficient information to adjust financial data for market distortions which may exist for labour and other products and services. Planners must also have adequate information to assign values to project components which are not normally traded.

Making decisions about projects is not just a technical exercise. There is a need for informed subjective evaluation. Also, sociopolitical considerations are important factors in determining the acceptance or rejection of a project.

Essentially it is the positive incremental contribution of a project which validates its implementation. Projects are accepted when they have a positive net present value. In the case study it is clearly of greater benefit to build a bridge rather than further develop the ferry service. However, caution must be exercised in any project analysis so that likely events are anticipated and quantified. The bridge construction would not be accepted if the benefits were overstated or the discount rate was 14 per cent or greater. Positive NPV projects abound and there is a finite source of capital from which they can be funded.

The success of project evaluation is dependent on analysis of the full range of variables. A structured approach to planning and evaluation of projects is essential. The outlines given in this appendix provide a framework for such structured analyses.

REFERENCES

Adler, H. A. (1987). *Economic Appraisal of Transport Projects: A Manual with Case Studies*, Baltimore: Johns Hopkins University Press

Sell, A. (1991). *Project Evaluation: An Integrated Financial and Economic Analysis*, Avebury: Academic Publishing Group

Index

accountability, 24, 25, 158, 174
acid-test ratio, 59
additionality, 181
allocative efficiency, 4, 5-10, 29, 258
alternatives, 179-180, 196-8, 227
ambulatory patient group, 276
appraisal, 1, 339
audit, 24, 157-8, 174, 339
average income on book value of
    investment, 192

avoided cost approach to valuation, 239

balanced scorecard, 89, 92-102
benchmarking, 66-7, 162, 292, 339
bequest value, 236
bias, 23, 35, 47, 244-7
bureaucracy, 8-10

casemix measurement, 276
cashflow analysis, 56-7
certainty equivalence, 135-7
coefficient of variation, 146-8
Comptroller and Auditor General, 154-5,
    168-71
consumer surplus, 185, 208, 238, 241,
    242, 243, 339
contestable markets, 6
contingent valuation, 186, 187, 223,
    242-9, 339
contracting out, 6, 28
control group, 23, 327
cost benefit analysis, 20, 177-204, 205-
    31, 232-57, 271-4, 339, 352-69
cost benefit ratio, 194
cost effectiveness, 29, 199-200, 262-5,
    340
cost minimisation analysis, 261-2
cost of capital, 106
cost utility analysis, 265-71, 340
credibility, 47, 48
creditors days ratio, 58-9
current ratio, 59

data envelopment analysis, 20-1
day patient group, 276
deadweight, 181, 340
debt-equity ratio, 60
debtors days ratio, 58-9
deciding between alternatives, 196-8
decision criteria, 191-4
decision tree, 139-142
deductive analysis, 43
diagnosis related groups, 15, 276
direct effects, 354, 358
discounting, 104-6, 188-9, 218-20, 249-
    50, 340
displacement, 181, 340
dissemination, 44-6
distribution of income, 195-6, 355, 361
dose-response functions, 240-1
double-counting, 16, 183-4, 228-9

economy, 1, 10-11, 155, 160, 164, 306,
    340
effectiveness, 1, 10-14, 155, 159-62,
    164, 165, 166, 281, 306, 340
efficiency, 1, 2-14, 155, 160, 164, 281,
    306, 340
efficiency ratios, 58-9, 66, 72
electability, 26
environment, 221-5, 232-79
environmental impact assessment, 235
equity, 26-7
equivalent annual cost, 127-30
evaluation, 1, 33-52, 340
evaluation parameters, 36
evaluation perspective, 37
evaluation sponsors, 34, 36, 44, 49-50
evaluation users, 36-37
evaluation techniques, 20-3
existence values, 237
expected value, 64-5, 74, 138-9
experimental evaluation 23-4, 327-8
experimental group, 23
external assessment, 37, 48

370